THE KNAPSACK

The Knapsack

A Pocket-book of Prose and Verse

Edited by

HERBERT READ

LONDON

GEORGE ROUTLEDGE & SONS, LTD.

BROADWAY HOUSE : CARTER LANE, E.C.

First published 1939
Second edition 1942
Third edition 1943
Fourth edition 1944
Fifth edition 1944
Sixth edition 1946
Seventh edition 1947

Printed in Great Britain by Butler & Tanner Ltd., Frome and London

Preface

DURING the last war, as a soldier on active service, I was very conscious of the need of a book which I could carry about with me as part of my kit, and which would suit the various moods and circumstances of my unsettled existence. Modern warfare is arduous enough ; but it does nevertheless involve, on sea and on land, in dugouts, billets and camps, many hours of inactivity in which the mind would willingly be engaged and distracted by reading. It is impracticable to carry about with one an adequate library—indeed, one book at a time is the most that the average soldier can conveniently accommodate. There are several famous classics—*Tristram Shandy* is the best in my own experience—which nearly supply this need ; but even the best of individual books lacks the necessary variety. An anthology of some kind is therefore indicated, and I remember, during the last war, with what pleasure I welcomed *The Spirit of Man*, the anthology by Robert Bridges which was published in 1916. The thin-paper edition of this book was thereafter my constant companion. But even that admirable anthology had, as time went on, noticeable defects. The very highness of its purpose, its sustained tone of moral

Preface

seriousness, a certain abstractness in its idealism, failed to satisfy completely the realistic standards of our daily life. I felt that I wanted, at any rate in a good part of my moods, something more objective, something more aware of material things, of flesh and blood, of action and experience. At least, I wanted the dialectic of life, the contradictions on which we have to meditate if we are to construct a workable philosophy. And in war, and in the daily struggle of everyday life, it is a workable philosophy that each man has to construct for himself if he is to preserve a serene mind.

The need for variety is, therefore, my excuse for the extreme contrasts which the reader will find in this anthology. I do deliberately affirm that the average lively mind can stretch over a range which includes, at one extreme, Plato and Spinoza, and, at the other, Edward Lear and the anonymous authors of " She was poor but she was honest "—can, and does, and should. At the same time I must admit that my anthology is not without its argument. I hope it is too objective to seem to have a " palpable design " on the reader. But in my choice I have been guided by certain convictions. One is that the love of glory, even in our materialistic age, is still the main source of virtue. The real good is not done by calculation nor defined by reason ; it is an act of courage or of grace. I have therefore given a certain prominence to great deeds and noble characters ; and here objectivity demands that we make no distinction of creeds—the persecuted anarchist like Nicola Sacco achieves absolutely the

Preface

same kind of nobility as the Christian saint. Another conviction I might mention, which is perhaps not so explicit though perfectly illustrated by the conduct of the Black Prince at Poitiers, is that even in action it is the virtue of humility that finally triumphs ; and that this same virtue is the secret of all human happiness.

The List of Contents is perhaps some guide to the free structure of the anthology, but few readers are likely to want such guidance—an anthology must justify itself from any haphazard approach. It will be seen that the prose extracts are in general longer than those usually given in such books, and this is again deliberate ; brevities in this looser harmony are too soon exhausted. In verse, however, I have not hesitated to include many poems that are well known, but whose purity is such that they never grow stale.

I am indebted to several authors and publishers for permission to include copyright material ; specific acknowledgements will be found in the Notes at the end of the book ; here I merely express my general sense of gratitude, a feeling which extends to those friends who have helped me with suggestions and criticism.

H. R.

October, 1939

Preface to the Second Edition

In this reprint I have taken the opportunity to correct a few misprints, but otherwise the text remains the same. I am grateful for many suggestions which have been made for pieces to be included in a new edition, and, indeed, have thought of several myself. But their insertion in their proper places would involve the re-setting of the whole book, and in the present circumstances this is unfortunately impossible.

H. R.

January, 1942.

Contents

Contents

PART ONE

PART ONE

FRAMINGHAM, MASS.

1 Hymn to Mars

MARS, most-strong, gold-helm'd, making chariots crack ;
Never without a shield cast on thy back ;
Mind-master, town-guard, with darts never driven ;
Strong-handed, all arms, fort, and fence of heaven ;
Father of victory with fair strokes given ;
Joint surrogate of justice, lest she fall
In unjust strifes a tyrant ; general
Only of just men justly ; that dost bear
Fortitude's sceptre ; to heaven's fiery sphere
Giver of circular motion, between
That and the Pleiads that still wand'ring been,
Where thy still-vehemently-flaming horse
About the third heaven make their fiery course ;
Helper of mortals ; hear !—As thy fires give
The fair and present boldnesses that strive
In youth for honour, being the sweet-beam'd light
That darts into their lives, from all their height,
The fortitudes and fortunes found in fight ;
So would I likewise wish to have the pow'r
To keep off from my head thy bitter hour,
And that false fire, cast from my soul's low kind,
Stoop to the fit rule of my highest mind,
Controlling that so eager sting of wrath
That stirs me on still to that horrid scathe
Of war, that God still sends to wreak his spleen
(Even by whole tribes) of proud injurious men.

3

The Knapsack

But O thou Ever-Blessed ! give me still
Presence of mind to put in act my will,
Varied, as fits, to all occasion ;
And to live free, unforc'd, unwrought upon,
Beneath those laws of peace that never are
Affected with pollutions popular
Of unjust hurt, or loss to any one ;
And to bear safe the burthen undergone
Of foes inflexive, and inhuman hates,
Secure from violent and harmful fates.

CHAPMAN'S HOMER

2 *Atrides Goes into Battle*

ATRIDES summoned all to arms, to arms himself disposed.
First on his legs he put bright greaves with silver buttons
   closed ;
Then with rich curace armed his breast, which Cinyras
   bestowed
To gratify his royal guest ; for even to Cyprus flowed
Th' unbounded fame of those designs the Greeks proposed
   for Troy,
And therefore gave he him those arms, and wished his
   purpose joy.
Ten rows of azure mixed with black, twelve golden like
   the sun,
Twice ten of tin, in beaten paths, did through this armour
   run.
Three serpents to the gorget crept, that like three rainbows
   shined
Such as by Jove are fixed in clouds when wonders are
   divined.
About his shoulders hung his sword, whereof the hollow hilt
Was fashioned all with shining bars, exceeding richly gilt ;

4

Atrides Goes into Battle

The scabbard was of silver plate, with golden hangers
    graced.
Then took he up his weighty shield, that round about him
    cast
Defensive shadows ; ten bright zones of gold-affecting brass
Were driven about it, and of tin, as full of gloss as glass,
Swelled twenty bosses out of it ; in centre of them all
One of black metal had engraven, full of extreme appall,
An ugly gorgon, compassed with terror and with fear.
At it a silver bawdrick hung, with which he used to bear,
Wound on his arm, his ample shield, and in it there was
    woven
An azure dragon, curled in folds, from whose one neck was
    cloven
Three heads contorted in an orb. Then placed he on his
    head
His four-plumed casque ; and in his hands two darts he
    managed,
Armed with bright steel that blazed to heaven. Then
    Juno, and the Maid
That conquers empires, trumpets served to summon out
    their aid
In honour of the General, and on a sable cloud,
To bring them furious to the field, sat thund'ring out aloud
    Then all enjoined their charioteers to rank their chariot
    horse
Close to the dike. Forth marched the foot, whose front
    they did r'enforce
With some horse troops. The battle then was all of
    charioteers,
Lined with light horse. But Jupiter disturbed this form
    with fears,
And from air's upper region did bloody vapours rain,
For sad ostent much noble life should ere their times be
    slain.

The Knapsack

The Trojan host at Ilus' tomb was in battalia led
By Hector and Polydamas, and old Anchises' seed
Who god-like was esteemed in Troy, by grave Antenor's
race
Divine Agenor, Polybus, unmarried Acamas
Proportioned like the States of heaven. In front of all the
field,
Troy's great Priamides did bear his all-ways-equal shield,
Still plying th' ordering of his power. And as amidst the
sky
We sometimes see an ominous star blaze clear and dread-
fully,
Then run his golden head in clouds, and straight appear
again ;
So Hector otherwhiles did grace the vaunt-guard, shining
plain,
Then in the rear-guard hid himself, and laboured every-
where
To order and encourage all ; his armour was so clear,
And he applied each place so fast, that, like a lightning
thrown
Out of the shield of Jupiter, in every eye he shone.
And as upon a rich man's crop of barley or of wheat,
Opposed for swiftness at their work, a sort of reapers sweat,
Bear down the furrows speedily, and thick their handfuls
fall ;
So at the joining of the hosts ran slaughter through them all,
None stooped to any fainting thought of foul inglorious
fight,
But equal bore they up their heads, and fared like wolves
in flight.
Stern Eris, with such weeping sights, rejoiced to feed her
eyes,
Who only showed herself in field of all the Deities ;
The other in Olympus' tops sat silent, and repined

Atrides Goes into Battle

That Jove to do the Trojans grace should bear so fixed a
    mind.
He cared not, but, enthroned apart, triumphant sat in sway
Of his free power, and from his seat took pleasure to display
The city so adorned with towers, the sea with vessels filled,
The splendour of refulgent arms, the killer and the killed.
As long as bright Aurora ruled, and sacred day increased,
So long their darts made mutual wounds, and neither had
    the best ;
But when in hill-environed vales the timber-feller takes
A sharp set stomach to his meat, and dinner ready makes,
His sinews fainting, and his spirits become surcharged and
    dull,
Time of accustomed ease arrived, his hands with labour full,
Then by their valours Greeks brake through the Trojan
    ranks, and cheered
Their general squadrons through the host, then first of all
    appeared
The person of the king himself, and then the Trojans lost
Bianor by his royal charge, a leader in the host.
Who being slain, his charioteer, Oïleus, did alight,
And stood in skirmish with the king ; the king did deadly
    smite
His forehead with his eager lance, and through his helm it
    ran,
Enforcing passage to his brain quite through the hard'ned
    pan,
His brain mixed with his clottered blood, his body strewed
    the ground.
There left he them, and presently he other objects found ;
Isus and Antiphus, two sons king Priam did beget,
One lawful, th' other wantonly.   Both in one chariot met
Their royal foe ; the baser born, Isus, was charioteer,
And famous Antiphus did fight ; both which king Peleus'
    heir,

7

The Knapsack

Whilome in Ida keeping flocks, did deprehend and bind
With pliant osiers, and, for price, them to their sire resigned.
Atrides with his well-aimed lance smote Isus on the breast
Above the nipple ; and his sword a mortal wound im-
    pressed
Beneath the ear of Antiphus ; down from their horse they
    fell.
The king had seen the youths before, and now did know
    them well,
Remembering them the prisoners of swift Æacides,
Who brought them to the sable fleet from Ida's foody leas.

CHAPMAN'S HOMER

3 Vulcan Forges the Shield of Achilles

THIS said, he left her there, and forth did to his bellows go,
Apposed them to the fire again, commanding them to blow.
Through twenty holes made to his hearth at once blew
    twenty pair,
That fired his coals, sometimes with soft, sometimes with
    vehement, air,
As he willed, and his work required. Amids the flame he
    cast
Tin, silver, precious gold, and brass ; and in the stock he
    placed
A mighty anvil ; his right hand a weighty hammer held,
His left his tongs. And first he forged a strong and spacious
    shield
Adorned with twenty several hues ; about whose verge he
    beat
A ring, threefold and radiant, and on the back he set
A silver handle ; fivefold were the equal lines he drew
About the whole circumference, in which his hand did shew

Vulcan Forges the Shield of Achilles

(Directed with a knowing mind) a rare variety ;
For in it he presented Earth ; in it the Sea and Sky ;
In it the never-wearied Sun, the Moon exactly round,
And all those Stars with which the brows of ample heaven
    are crowned,
Orion, all the Pleiades, and those seven Atlas got,
The close-beamed Hyades, the Bear, surnamed the Chariot,
That turns about heaven's axle-tree, holds ope a constant eye
Upon Orion, and of all the cressets in the sky
His golden forehead never bows to th' Ocean empery.

    Two cities in the spacious field he built, with goodly state
Of divers-languaged men.   The one did nuptials celebrate,
Observing at them solemn feasts, the brides from forth their
    bow'rs
With torches ushered through the streets, a world of
    paramours
Excited by them ; youths and maids in lovely circles
    danced,
To whom the merry pipe and harp their spritely sounds
    advanced,
The matrons standing in their doors admiring.   Other-
    where
A solemn court of law was kept, where throngs of people
    were . . .

    The other city other wars employed as busily,
Two armies glittering in arms, of one confederacy,
Besieged it, and a parlè had with those within the town.
Two ways they stood resolved ; to see the city overthrown,
Or that the citizens should heap in two parts all their
    wealth,
And give them half.   They neither liked, but armed them-
    selves by stealth,
Left all their old men, wives, and boys, behind to man
    their walls,

The Knapsack

And stole out to their enemy's town. The Queen of martials
And Mars himself conducted them ; both which, being forged of gold,
Must needs have golden furniture, and men might so behold
They were presented Deities. The people Vulcan forged
Of meaner metal. When they came where that was to be urged
For which they went, within a vale close to a flood, whose stream
Used to give all their cattle drink, they there enambushed them,
And sent two scouts out to descry when th' enemy's herds and sheep
Were setting out. They straight came forth, with two that used to keep
Their passage always ; both which piped, and went on merrily,
Nor dreamed of ambuscadoes there. The ambush then let fly,
Slew all their white-fleeced sheep, and neat, and by them laid their guard.
When those in siege before the town so strange an uproar heard,
Behind, amongst their flocks and herds (being then in counsel set)
They then start up, took horse, and soon their subtle enemy met,
Fought with them on the river's shore, where both gave mutual blows
With well-piled darts. Amongst them all perverse Contention rose,
Amongst them Tumult was enraged, amongst them ruinous Fate
Had her red-finger ; some they took in an unhurt estate,

Vulcan Forges the Shield of Achilles

Some hurt yet living, some quite slain, and those they tugged
    to them
By both the feet, stripped off and took their weeds, with all
    the stream
Of blood upon them that their steels had manfully let out.
They fared as men alive indeed drew dead indeed about.
  To these the fiery Artizan did add a new-eared field,
Large and thrice ploughed, the soil being soft, and of a
    wealthy yield ;
And many men at plough he made, that drave earth here
    and there,
And turned up stitches orderly, at whose end when they
    were,
A fellow ever gave their hands full cups of luscious wine ;
Which emptied, for another stitch, the earth they under-
    mine,
And long till th' utmost bound be reached of all the ample
    close.
The soil turned up behind the plough all black like earth
    arose,
Though forged of nothing else but gold, and lay in show as
    light
As if it had been ploughed indeed, miraculous to sight.
  There grew by this a field of corn, high, ripe, where
    reapers wrought,
And let thick handfuls fall to earth, for which some other
    brought
Bands, and made sheaves. Three binders stood, and took
    the handfuls reaped
From boys that gathered quickly up, and by them armfuls
    heaped.
Amongst these at a furrow's end the king stood pleased at
    heart,
Said no word, but his sceptre showed. And from him,
    much apart,

The Knapsack

His harvest-bailiffs underneath an oak a feast prepared,

And having killed a mighty ox, stood there to see him
shared,

Which women for their harvest folks (then come to sup) had
dressed,

And many white wheat-cakes bestowed, to make it up a
feast.

He set near this a vine of gold, that cracked beneath the
weight

Of bunches black with being ripe ; to keep which at the
height,

A silver rail ran all along, and round about it flowed

An azure moat, and to this guard a quickset was bestowed

Of tin, one only path to all, by which the pressmen came

In time of vintage. Youths and maids, that bore not yet
the flame

Of manly Hymen, baskets bore of grapes and mellow fruit.

A lad that sweetly touched a harp, to which his voice did
suit,

Centered the circles of that youth, all whose skill could not
do

The wanton's pleasure to their minds, that danced, sung,
whistled too.

A herd of oxen then he carved, with high raised heads,
forged all

Of gold and tin, for colour mixed, and bellowing from their
stall

Rushed to their pastures at a flood that echoed all their
throats,

Exceeding swift, and full of reeds ; and all in yellow coats

Four herdsmen followed ; after whom nine mastiffs went.
In head

Of all the herd, upon a bull, that deadly bellowed,

Two horrid lions rampt, and seized, and tugged off bellowing still ;

Vulcan Forges the Shield of Achilles

Both men and dogs came ; yet they tore the hide, and
    lapped their fill
Of black blood, and the entrails ate. In vain the men assayed
To set their dogs on ; none durst pinch, but cur-like stood
    and bayed
In both the faces of their kings, and all their onsets fled.
  Then in a passing pleasant vale the famous Artsman fed,
Upon a goodly pasture ground, rich flocks of white-fleeced
    sheep,
Built stables, cottages, and cotes that did the shepherds keep
From wind and weather. Next to these he cut a dancing
    place,
All full of turnings, that was like the admirable maze
For fair-haired Ariadne made by cunning Dædalus ;
And in it youths and virgins danced, all young and
    beauteous,
And glewed in another's palms. Weeds that the wind did
    toss
The virgins wore ; the youths woven coats, that cast a faint
    dim gloss
Like that of oil. Fresh garlands too the virgins' temples
    crowned ;
The youths gilt swords wore at their thighs, with silver
    bawdricks bound.
Sometimes all wound close in a ring, to which as fast they
    spun,
As any wheel a turner makes, being tried how it will run,
While he is set ; and out again as full of speed they wound,
Not one left fast, or breaking hands. A multitude stood
    round,
Delighted with their nimble sport ; to end which two begun,
Mids all, a song, and turning sung the sport's conclusion.
All this he circled in the shield, with pouring round about,
In all his rage, the Ocean, that it might never out.

CHAPMAN'S HOMER

The Knapsack

4 *The Seafarer*

MAY I for my own self song's truth reckon,
Journey's jargon, how I in harsh days
Hardship endured oft.
Bitter breast-cares have I abided,
Known on my keel many a care's hold,
And dire sea-surge, and there I oft spent
Narrow nightwatch nigh the ship's head
While she tossed close to cliffs.   Coldly afflicted,
My feet were by frost benumbed.
Chill its chains are ; chafing sighs
Hew my heart round and hunger begot
Mere-weary mood.   Lest man know not
That he on dry land loveliest liveth,
List how I, care-wretched, on ice-cold sea,
Weathered the winter, wretched outcast
Deprived of my kinsmen ;
Hung with hard ice-flakes, where hail-scur flew,
There I heard naught save the harsh sea
And ice-cold wave, at whiles the swan cries,
Did for my games the gannet's clamour,
Sea-fowls' loudness was for me laughter,
The mews' singing all my mead-drink.
Storms, on the stone-cliffs beaten, fell on the stern
In icy feathers ; full oft the eagle screamed
With spray on his pinion.

                       Not any protector
May make merry man faring needy.
This he little believes, who aye in winsome life
Abides 'mid burghers some heavy business,
Wealthy and wine-flushed, how I weary oft
Must bide above brine.
Neareth nightshade, snoweth from north,

The Seafarer

Frost froze the land, hail fell on earth then
Corn of the coldest.   Nathless there knocketh now
The heart's thought that I on high streams
The salt-wavy tumult traverse alone.
Moaneth alway my mind's lust
That I fare forth, that I afar hence
Seek out a foreign fastness.
For this there's no mood-lofty man over earth's midst,
Not though he be given his good, but will have in his youth
    greed ;
Nor his deed to the daring, nor his king to the faithful
But shall have his sorrow for sea-fare
Whatever his lord will.
He hath not heart for harping, nor in ring-having
Nor winsomeness to wife, nor world's delight
Nor any whit else save the wave's slash,
Yet longing comes upon him to fare forth on the water.
Bosque taketh blossom, cometh beauty of berries,
Fields to fairness, land fares brisker,
All this admonisheth man eager of mood,
The heart turns to travel so that he then thinks
On flood-ways to be far departing.
Cuckoo calleth with gloomy crying,
He singeth summerward, bodeth sorrow,
The bitter heart's blood.   Burgher knows not—
He the prosperous man—what some perform
Where wandering them widest draweth.
So that but now my heart burst from my breast-lock,
My mood 'mid the mere-flood,
Over the whale's acre, would wander wide.
On earth's shelter cometh oft to me,
Eager and ready, the crying lone-flyer,
Whets for the whale-path the heart irresistibly,
O'er tracks of ocean ; seeing that anyhow
My lord deems to me this dead life

The Knapsack

On loan and on land, I believe not
That any earth-weal eternal standeth
Save there be somewhat calamitous
That, ere a man's tide go, turn it to twain.
Disease or oldness or sword-hate
Beats out the breath from doom-gripped body.
And for this, every earl whatever, for those speaking after--
Laud of the living, boasteth some last word,
That he will work ere he pass onward,
Frame on the fair earth 'gainst foes his malice,
Daring ado, . . .
So that all men shall honour him after
And his laud beyond them remain 'mid the English,
Aye, for ever, a lasting life's-blast,
Delight mid the doughty.

                    Days little durable,
And all arrogance of earthen riches,
There come now no kings nor Cæsars
Nor gold-giving lords like those gone.
Howe'er in mirth most magnified,
Whoe'er lived in life most lordliest,
Drear all this excellence, delights undurable !
Waneth the watch, but the world holdeth.
Tomb hideth trouble.   The blade is laid low.
Earthly glory ageth and seareth.
No man at all going the earth's gait,
But age fares against him, his face paleth,
Grey-haired he groaneth, knows gone companions,
Lordly men are to earth o'ergiven,
Nor may he then the flesh-cover, whose life ceaseth,
Nor eat the sweet nor feel the sorry,
Nor stir hand nor think in mid heart,
And though he strew the grave with gold,
His born brothers, their buried bodies
Be an unlikely treasure hoard.

5 *Beowulf's Fight in the Enchanted Mere*

BEOWULF spake,/Ecgtheow's boy :
" Bethink thee now, mighty/man of Halfdane,
Duke most wise,/now that for the deed am I ready,
Gold-friend of thy lads,/of what lately we said
That if I should,/sharing thy need,
Of life be stripped,/thou wouldst stand to me ever,
When forth I have fared,/in a father's place.
Do thou be kind/to my kinsmen-thegns,
My boon-companions,/if me the battle take ;
Do thou also the treasures/that in tribute thou gavest me,
Hrothgar dearest,/to Higelac send.
May he learn then from that gold,/the Lord of the Geats,
May Hrethel's son see,/when on that hoard he stareth,
That I had found/a fine and good
Jewel-giver,/and had joy while I might.
And do thou let Unferth/the old heirloom,
The well-wrought wave-sword,/—a widely known man
Have that hard edge./For me, I with Hrunting
Glory will gain,/or death shall get me."
After those words/the Weder-Geats' Prince
Sped boldly on,/nor any answer
Would he abide ;/the brimming flood whelmed
That man of battle./'Twas the breadth of a day
Ere he might get/to the ground beneath.
Soon found she out/who the flood's extent
Had held, a sword-glutton,/an hundred seasons,
Grim and greedy,/that some groom there
That home of else-things/over head was scouting.
She groped then towards him ;/the warrior gripped
In an awful clutch ;/not at all might she scathe
His hale body ;/the rings without guarded him,
So that through his coat of mail/she might not come at him,

The Knapsack

Through the locken limb-sark/with loathly fingers.
Bare then the mer-wolf,/when to the bottom she came,
The ringed Prince/to her own place,
So that he might not,/for all his proud mind,
Wield his weapons ;/for such wondrous things
Swinked him in the sound,/sea-deer many
With worrying tusks/his war-sark tare,
Chased him the creatures./Then the earl knew
That he was in some or other/enemy's hall,
Where no water/a whit might scathe him,
Nor, for the hall's roof,/might get hold upon him
The fierce grip of the flood ;/fire-light he saw,
A blinding gleam/that brightly shone.
The good one grew ware then/of the ground-lying wolf,
A mighty mer-wife ;/a main-stroke he gave her
With his sword of battle,/nor its swing did his hand withhold,
Till the ring-set sword/rang out on her head
A greedy war-lay./Then her guest found
That his battle-gleamer/would not bite,
Nor fetch to her heart,/but the edge of it failed
The lord in his need./It had lasted many
Hard-fought meetings,/helms oft had shorn,
Fated-men's war-coats ;/this was the first time
For the goodly weapon/that its glory waned.
Still was he purposeful,/of his prowess lost nothing ;
Of his honour mindful/was Higelac's mate.
Threw down then the banded sword/with jewels blended
That angry warrior,/so that on the earth it lay,
Stiff and steel-edged./In his strength he trusted,
Hand-muscles of might./So a man should do
Then when in war/he thinketh to win
Lasting praise/nor of his life recketh.
Caught then by the shoulder/(for the fight he cared not)
The War-Geats' Master/Grendel's mother ;
Flung he then, battle-hardy,/so furious was he,

18

Beowulf's Fight in the Enchanted Mere

The foe of his life,/till she lay on the floor.
She quickly again/requited his handiwork
With her grim grip,/and against him reached.
Stooped over then wearily/the strongest of warriors,
The foot-men's champion,/until that he fell.
Sate she then on the hall-guest/and her saxe she drew,
Broad and brown-edged ;/her bairn she'ld avenge,
Her only offspring./Over his arm there lay
A woven breast-net ;/that warded his life,
Withstood the entry/of point and of edge.
Then had sped/the son of Ecgtheow.
Beneath the wide ground,/the Geatish champion,
If his battle-byrny/had not brought him help,
A hard war-net ;/did not Holy God
Rule the winning of wars./The Wisest Lord,
The Justice of Heaven/judged it aright
Easily ;/so up he stood.

He saw then among the armour/a sword rich in victories.
An old Eotenish blade,/doughty of edge,
To warriors worshipful ;/'twas the choicest of weapons,
But it was mightier/than any man other
Into the play of battle/might have borne,
Good and glorious,/giants' work.
He seized then the belted hilt ;/that Wolf of the Shieldings,
Rough and war-rude,/the ringed blade drew ;
Hopeless of living,/with heat he struck
So that hard it gripped/her on the neck,
Her bone-rings brake ;/the bill went through all
Her fated flesh-cover ;/on the floor she crashed.
The sword was sweating ;/the soldier rejoiced in his work.
A flash was kindled,/light filled it within,
Even so as from the sky/brightly shineth
The Candle of Heaven./He looked through the house,
Turned then to the wall ;/the weapon heaved he,

The Knapsack

Hard, by the hilt,/Higelac's thegn,
Angry, one-minded./That edge was not worthless
To the man of war,/for at once he would
Settle with Grendel/the many assaults
That he had wrought/on the Wester-Danes,
Far more often/than one time only,
When he Hrothgar's hearth-companions
Slew in their slumber,/swallowed sleeping
Fifteen men/of the folk of Danes,
And others also/carried out,
A loathly loot./For that loss repaid him
The raging champion,/inas resting he saw
Grendel lie,/of war grown weary,
All unliving,/as erstwhile had left him
The battle in Heorot./His body sprang aside
When he after death/endured that stroke
The hardy sword-swing ;/then he carved off his head.
Soon they saw,/the subtle churls,
They who with Hrothgar/on the holm were gazing,
That the eddying waves/all were mingled,
The water blood-foul./White of hair
The elders about the good one/said together
That they expected not ever/of that atheling
That he, swelled with conquest,/would come to seek
Their mighty Prince,/for to many it seemed
That the wolf of the brine/had broken him up.
Then came nones of the day ;/from the ness departed
The haughty Shieldings./Went homewards from thence
The Gold-Friend of men./The guests were sitting
Sick in mind,/and staring on the mere ;
They feared, and they felt not/that their friend and lord
Himself they might see./Then that sword began
From the sweat of death/in icicle drops,
The war-bill, to wane ; that was something wondrous
That it all melted,/to ice most likened

Beowulf's Fight in the Enchanted Mere

When the bond of frost/the Father unlooseth,
Unwindeth the whirlpool-ropes,/He that wieldeth
Times and climes./That is a true Creator !
Nor took he in those places,/the Weder-Geats Prince,
More of rich treasures,/though many he saw there,
But that head/and the hilt therewith
Medalled and jewelled./The sword was now melted,
Burned up the patterned blade ;/the blood was so hot,
So deadly the strange spirit/that had swooned there in
    death.
Soon was he swimming,/he who was saved from the struggle,
The onslaught of his enemies ;/up he dived through the
    water.
The eddying waves/all were cleansed,
The spreading tracts/where the stranger-spirit
Finished his lifetime/and this fleeting state.
Came then to the shore/that Helm of Sailors,
Strong of heart, swimming,/in his sea-spoil rejoicing,
In the mighty burden/that he brought up with him.
Going then towards him,/God they thanked,
The gallant band of thegns/were glad of their Prince,
That they might see him/safe and sound.
Then from that bold one/byrny and helmet
Were hastily loosened./The lake grew smooth,
Water under the welkin,/weltering with blood.
Fared they forth thence/the foot-paths over,
Fain of mind/the field-way measured,
Streets well-known,/those kingly-bold men ;
From that holm-cliff/the head they bare,
No easy thing/for any among them,
The fiercest-minded ;/four of them must
Swinking carry/on a killing-shaft
Grendel's head/to the golden hall,
Until there quickly/came to that hall
Fierce, whetted to fight,/four and ten

Geats a-going ;/their Guardian with them,
Proud-minded among his troop,/the mead-plains trod.
Then came and entered/that elder among thegns,
A deed-keen man,/and duly cherished,
A hero, battle-hardy,/Hrothgar to greet.
Then into the house/by the hair was borne
Grendel's head,/where the host were drinking,
Awful before the earls/and that lady also ;
On a wondrous prospect/the warriors peered.

6 *The Death of Oliver*

ROLLANT ad mis l'olifan a sa buche,
Empeint le ben, par grant vertut le sunet.
Halt sunt li pui e la voiz est mult lunge,
Granz .xxx. liwes l'oirent il respundre.
Karles l'oit e ses cumpaignes tutes.
Co dit li reis, " Bataille funt nostre hume."
E Guenelun li respundit encuntre,
" S'altre le desist, ja semblast grant mencunge." A O I.

Roland has put the olifant to his mouth. He blows it
hard, he sounds it by his great force. The hills are high
and the voice goes very far, they heard it echo thirty great
leagues away. Charles heard it, and all his companions.
The king says, " Our men are making battle." And
Guenelun answered against him, " If another had said it,
it would have seemed a great lie." A O I.

Li quens Rollant, par peine e par ahans,
Par grant dulor sunet sun olifan.
Par mi la buche en salt fors li cler sancs,
De sun cervel le temple en est rumpant.
Del corn qu'il tient l'oie en est mult grant,

The Death of Oliver

Karles l'entent, ki est as porz passant.
Naimes li duc l'oid, si l'escultent li franc ;
Ce dist li reis, " Jo oi le corn Rollant.
Unc nel sunast, se ne fust cumbatant."
Guenes respunt, " De bataille est nient.
Ja estes veilz e fluriz e blancs,
Par tels paroles vus resemblez enfant.
Asez savez le grant orgoill Rollant,
Co est merveille que Deus le soefret tant.
Ja prist il Noples seinz le vostre comant,
Fors s'en eissirent li sarrazins dedenz,
Sis cumbatirent al bon vassal Rollant,
Puis od les ewes lavat les prez del sanc,
Pur cel le fist ne fust . . .[1] arissant.
Pur un sul levre vait tute jur cornant.
Devant ses pers vait il ore gabant.
Suz cel n'ad gent ki l'osast querre en champ.
Car chevalcez, pur qu'alez arestant ?
Tere major mult est loinz ca devant." A O I.

With pain and agony, with great sorrow count Roland
sounds his olifant. The clear blood leaps through his
mouth, the temple of his brain is bursting. The voice of
the horn which he holds is very loud. Charles hears it,
who is at the passage of the gates. Neimun the duke
heard it and the french listen. The king said, " I hear
Roland's horn. He would not have sounded it if he were
not fighting." Guenelun answers, " There is no battle.
You are old and flowered and white. By such words
you seem as a child. You well know Roland's great
pride ; it is wonder that God suffers him so far. He took
Noples without your word ; the saracens came out from
the town against him, and fought with the good soldier
Roland. Then he washed the blood from the field with

[1] The beginning of the word is illegible.

23

The Knapsack

waters. . . . He will be blowing his horn all day for a single hare, and now he is boasting before his peers. There is no people under heaven that would dare look for him in the field. Now ride, for what are you holding back? Terra Major is very far before us." A O I.

> Li quens Rollant ad la buche sanglente.
> De sun cervel rumput en est li temples.
> L'olifan sunet a dulor e a peine.
> Karles l'oit e ses franceis l'entendent.
> Co dist li reis, " Cel corn ad lunge aleine."
> Respont dux Neimes, " Baron i fait la peine.
> Bataille i ad, par le men escientre.
> Cil l'at trait ki vos en roevet feindre.
> Adubez vos, si criez vostre enseigne,
> Si sucurez vostre maisnee gente.
> Asez oez que Rollant se dementet."

Count Roland is bleeding from his mouth. The temple of his brain is burst. He blows the olifant in sorrow and in pain. Charles heard it and his french listen. The king said, " That horn has a long blast." Duke Neimun answers, " That is the agony of a brave man. There is a battle, and I know it. And he has betrayed Roland who tells you to fail him. Arm yourself and shout your cry and go to help the good men of your house. You can hear Roland's despair."

> Li empereres ad fait suner ses corns.
> Franceis descendent, si adubent lor cors
> D'osbercs e de helmes e d'espees a or.
> Escuz unt genz e espiez granz e forz,
> E gunfanuns blancs e vermeilz e blois.
> Es destrers muntent tuit li barun de l'ost,
> Brochent ad ait tant cum durent li port,

The Death of Oliver

N'i ad celoi a l'altre ne parolt,
" Se veissum Rollant einz qu'il fust mort,
Ensembl'od lui i durriums granz colps."
De co qui calt ? car demuret i unt trop.

The emperor has made them blow his horns. The french dismount and arm their bodies with mailed coats and helmets and golden swords. They have fine shields and spears that are big and strong, and white flags and red and blue. All the barons of the army mount on their horses and spur them hard down the length of the pass. There is not one who does not say to another, " Should we see Roland before he is dead, we would make great blows in his company." But what of their word ? for they have waited too long.

Esclargiz est li vespres e li jurz.
Cuntre le soleil reluisent cil adub,
Osbercs e helmes i getent grant flambur,
E cil escuz, ki ben sunt peinz a flurs,
E cil espiez, cil oret gunfanun.
Li empereres cevalchet par irur
E li franceis dolenz e curucus.
N'i ad celoi ki durement ne plurt,
E de Rollant sunt en grant pour.
Li reis fait prendre le cunte Guenelun,
Sil cumandat as cous de sa maisun.
Tut li plus maistre en apelet, Besgun,
" Ben le me guarde, si cume tel felon.
De ma maisnee ad faite traisun."
Cil le receit, si met .c. cumpaignons
De la quisine des mielz e des peiurs.
Icil li peilent la barbe e les gernuns,
Cascun le fiert .iiii. colps de sun puign,
Ben le batirent a fuz e a bastuns

The Knapsack

E si li metent el col un caeignun,
Si l'encaeinent altresi cum un urs.
Sur un sumer l'unt mis a deshonor.
Tant le guardent quel rendent a Charlun.

The evening and the day grows clear. The arms shine against the sun; mailed coats and helmets throw a great flame, and their shields which are painted fine with flowers, and their spears and their golden flags. The emperor rides in anger, and the french sorrowing and furious. There is not one of them that does not weep heavily, and they are in a great fear for Roland. The king has count Guenelun taken up, and charged the cooks of his house with him. He calls Besgun the master of the cooks to him. "Guard him well for me as you would a felon. He has made a betrayal of my house." He takes him and sets around him a hundred of his companions, from the better and the worse in the kitchen. They pluck his beard and moustache, and each one strikes him four blows with his fist. They beat him hard with sticks and cudgels, and put a chain on his neck and chain him like a bear. They have put him in dishonour on a baggage horse, and guard him till they may give him back to Charles.

Halt sunt li pui e tenebrus e grant, A O I.
Li val parfunt e les ewes curant.
Sunent cil graisle e derere e devant
E tuit rachatent encuntre l'olifant.
Li empereres chevalchet ireement
E li franceis curucus e dolent.
N'i ad celoi n'i plurt e se dement,
E prient Deu qu'il guarisset Rollant
Josque il vengent el camp cumunement.
Ensembl'od lui i ferrunt veirement.
De co qui calt? car ne lur valt nient.
Demurent trop, n'i poedent estre a tens. A O I.

26

The Death of Oliver

The hills are high and full of shadow and great. A O I.
The valleys are deep and the waters running. The trumpets sound in front and behind, and all make answer to the olifant. The emperor rides angrily and the french furious and sorrowing. There is not one who does not weep and despair, and they pray to God that he will save Roland until they come together in the field. With him they will give real blows. But what of their words? for they are worth nothing; they have stayed too long, they cannot be in time. A O I.

> Par grant irur chevalchet li reis Charles,
> Desur sa brunie li gist sa blanche barbe.
> Puignent ad ait tuit li barun de France.
> N'i ad icel ne demeint irance
> Que il ne sunt a Rollant le cataigne,
> Ki se cumbat as sarrazins d'Espaigne,
> Si est blecet, ne quit qu'anme i remaigne.
> Deus, quels seisante humes i ad en sa cumpaigne.
> Unches meillurs n'en out reis ne cataignes. A O I.

King Charles rides in great anger. His white beard lies on his breastplate. All the barons of France are spurring hard, there is not one that has not strong despair because they are not with Roland the captain who is fighting with the saracens of Spain. He is so pressed that I do not think that his soul can be left in him. God, what sixty he has in his company. No king nor captain ever had better. A O I.

> Rollant reguardet es munz e es lariz,
> De cels de France i veit tanz morz gesir,
> E il les pluret cum chevaler gentill :
> " Seignors barons, de vos ait Deus mercit,
> Tutes voz anmes otreit il pareis,

27

The Knapsack

En seintes flurs il les facet gesir.
Meillors vassals de vos unkes ne vi.
Si lungement tuz tens m'avez servit,
A oes Carlon si granz pais cunquis.
Li empereres tant mare vos nurrit.
Tere de France, mult estes dulz pais,
Oi desertet a tant rubostl exill.
Barons franceis, pur mei vos vei murir,
Jo ne vos pois tenser ne guarantir,
Ait vos Deus, ki unkes ne mentit.
Oliver, frere, vos ne dei jo faillir.
De doel murrai, s'altre ne m'i ocit.
Sire cumpainz, alum i referir."

Roland looks at the mountains and the bare slopes. He sees so many of France lying there dead, and he weeps for them as a gentle knight. "Lord barons, God have mercy for you ; may he give paradise to all your souls, make you lie in blessed flowers. I have never seen better soldiers than you. You have at all times served me for so long, you have won such great countries for Charles's work. The emperor nursed you to sorrow. Land of France, you are a very sweet country, wasted to-day by a hard loss. French barons, I see you die through me, and I cannot hold you up or save you. May God help you, who never lied. Oliver, brother, I shall not fail you. I shall die of grief, if no other thing kills me. My lord companion, let us go back there and fight."

Li quens Rollant el champ est repairet.
Tient Durendal, cume vassal i fiert.
Faldrun de Pui i ad par mi trenchet,
E .xxiiii. de tuz les melz preisez.
Jamais n'iert home plus se voeillet venger.
Si cum li cerfs s'en vait devant les chiens,

The Death of Oliver

Devant Rollant si s'en fuient paiens.
Dist l'arcevesque, " Asez le faites ben.
Itel valor deit aveir chevaler
Ki armes portet e en bon cheval set,
En bataille deit estre forz e fiers,
U altrement ne valt .iiii. deners,
Einz deit monie estre en un de cez mustiers,
Si prierat tuz jurz por noz peccez."
Respunt Rollant, " Ferez, nes esparignez."
A icest mot l'unt francs recumencet.
Mult grant damage i out de chrestiens.

Count Roland has come back to the field. He holds
Durendal and is striking as a soldier. He has cut through
Faldrun de Pui and twenty-four others of those whom
they thought their best. There will never be a man who
had so great a will to avenge himself. As the deer runs
before the hounds, so the pagans fly before Roland. The
archbishop said, "You fight well. Such should be the
worth of a knight who wears arms and sits on a good
horse. He should be strong and fierce in battle, or else
he is not worth four pence ; he should be a monk in one
of these monasteries and pray every day for our sins."
Roland answers, " Strike and do not spare them." When
he speaks the french have begun again. There was great
loss of the christians.

Home ki co set que ja n'avrat prisun
En tel bataill fait grant defension.
Pur co sunt francs si fiers cume leuns.
As vus Marsille en guise de barun.
Siet el cheval qu'il apelet Gaignun,
Brochet le ben, si vait ferir Bevon,
Icil ert sire de Belne e de Digun.
L'escut li freint e l'osberc li derumpt,

The Knapsack

Que mort l'abat seinz altre descunfisun,
Puis ad ocis Yvoeries e Ivon,
Ensembl'od els Gerard de Russillun.
Li quens Rollant ne li est guaires loign.
Dist al paien, " Damnesdeus mal te duinst.
A si grant tort m'ociz mes cumpaignuns.
Colp en avras einz que nos departum,
E de m'espee enquoi savras le nom."
Vait le ferir en guise de baron.
Trenchet li ad li quens le destre poign,
Puis prent la teste de Jurfaleu le blund,
Icil ert filz al rei Marsilliun.
Paien escrient, " Aie nos, Mahum.
Li nostre Deu, vengez nos de Carlun.
En ceste tere nus ad mis tels feluns.
Ja pur murir le camp ne guerpirunt."
Dist l'un a l'altre, " E ! car nos en fuiums."
A icest mot tels .c. milie s'en vunt,
Ki ques rapelt, ja n'en returnerunt. A O I.

A man who knows that there will be no taking of
prisoners makes great defence in such a battle, and for
this the french are as fierce as lions. You may see Marsiliun coming with the bearing of a baron. He sits on his
horse which he calls Gaignun ; he spurs it hard and
goes to strike Bevun, he was lord of Belne and Digun.
He breaks his shield and bursts his mailed coat and throws
him down dead without another wound. Then he has
killed Yvoerie and Ivun, and with them Gerard of
Russillun. Count Roland is not far from him. He said
to the pagan, " May God give you every bad thing. You
have done such wrong and killed my companions. Before
we part you shall have a blow for this, and today you
shall know the name of my sword." He goes to strike
him as a baron. The count has struck off his right fist,

The Death of Oliver

and then he has taken the head of Jurfaleu the blond, he was king Marsiliun's son. The pagans shout, " Help us Mahumet. Give us vengeance, our Gods, on Charles. He has sent such terrible men against us into this country. They will not leave the field, not for death." One said to the other, " E ! let us fly." And when the word is said a hundred thousand are in flight. Let who wills call them, they will not turn back. A O I.

> De co qui calt ? Se fuit s'en est Marsilies,
> Remes i est sis uncles, Marganices,
> Ki tint Kartagene al frere Garmalie
> E Ethiope, une tere maldite.
> La neire gent en ad en sa baillie.
> Granz unt les nes e lees les oreilles,
> E sunt ensemble plus de cinquante milie.
> Icil chevalchent fierement e a ire,
> Puis escrient l'enseigne paenime.
> Co dist Rollant, " Ci recevrums matyrie,
> E or sai ben n'avons guaires a vivre.
> Mais tut seit fel cher ne se vende primes.
> Ferez, seignurs, des espees furbies,
> Si calengez e vos mors e voz vies,
> Que dulce France par nus ne seit hunie,
> Quant en cest camp vendrat Carles mi sire,
> De sarrazins verrat tel discipline
> Cuntre un des noz en truverat morz .xv.,
> Ne lesserat que nos ne beneisse." A O I.

But what of their flight ? If Marsiliun has fled, his uncle, Marganice, has stayed, who held Cartagene . . . and Ethiopia, a cursed country. He has the black people in his rule. Their noses are big and their ears broad, and they are together more than fifty thousand. They ride fiercely and furiously, and they shout the cry of the pagans.

The Knapsack

Roland said, "Now we shall have martyrdom, and I know well that we have short time to live. But damnation to him who does not first sell himself dear. Strike, lords, with your burnished swords and make challenge for your deaths and your lives, that sweet France may not be shamed by us. When Charles my lord comes to this field, he will see such discipline on the saracens, that for one of us he will find fifteen dead of them. He will not grudge us his blessing for this." A O I.

> Quan Rollant veit la contredite gent
> Ki plus sunt neirs que nen est arrement
> Ne n'unt de blanc ne mais que sul les denz,
> Co dist li quens, " Or sai jo veirement
> Que hoi murrum par le mien escient.
> Ferez, franceis, car jol vos recumenz."
> Dist Oliver, " Dehet ait li plus lenz."
> A icest mot franceis se fierent enz.

When Roland sees the unbelieving people, who are blacker than ink and have no white about their bodies except their teeth, the count said, " Now I know truly that we shall die today, and this is my knowledge. Strike, french men, for I fight again with you." Oliver said, " The curse of God be on the slowest." When they speak, the french charge to the fight.

> Quant paien virent que franceis i out poi,
> Entr'els en unt e orgoil e cunfort.
> Dist l'un a l'altre, " L'empereor ad tort."
> Li Marganices sist sur un ceval sor,
> Brochet le ben des esperuns a or :
> Fiert Oliver derere en mie le dos.
> Le blanc osberc li ad descust el cors,
> Par mi le piz sun espiet li mist fors,
> E dit apres, " Un col avez pris fort.

32

The Death of Oliver

Carles li Magnes mar vos laissat as porz.
Tort nos ad fait, nen est dreiz qu'il s'en lot,
Kar de vos sul ai ben venget les noz."

When the pagans see that the french are few, they are proud and comforted, and one said to another, "The emperor is false." Marganice sat on a sorrel horse, he spurs it hard with his gilded spurs and strikes Oliver from behind in the middle of his back. He has broken the white mail on his body and has thrust his spear through his chest; and afterwards he says, "You have taken a fine blow. Charles the great left you at the pass for your death. He has done us wrong, and he will have no cause to give himself praise for this. For with you alone I have paid well for our men."

Oliver sent que a mort est ferut.
Tient Halteclere, dunt li acer fut bruns,
Fiert Marganices sur l'elme a or, agut,
E flurs e cristaus en acraventet jus.
Trenchet la teste d'ici qu'as denz menuz,
Brandist sun colp, si l'ad mort abatut,
E dist apres, " Paien, mal aies tu.
Ico ne di que Karles n'i ait perdut.
Ne a muiler ne a dame qu'aies veud
N'en vanteras el regne dunt tu fus
Vaillant a un dener que m'i aies tolut,
Ne fait damage ne de mei ne d'altrui."
Apres escriet Rollant qu'il li aiut. A O I.

Oliver feels that he is struck to death. He holds Halt-clere whose steel was polished, and strikes Marganice on the point of his gilded helmet, and he beats down the flowers and the crystals of it. He cuts through his head from the top to the small teeth in front. He shook his sword and has thrown him down dead; and afterwards

he said, " Pagan, may curses come to you. I do not say
that Charles has lost nothing here, but you shall not boast
to any wife, to any lady that you see in the kingdom
from which you came, that you brought away the worth
of a penny from me, nor that you did harm to me or any
other." Then he shouts to Roland to help him. A O I.

Oliver sent qu'il est a mort nasfret.
De lui venger jamais ne li ert sez.
En la grant presse or i fiert cume ber,
Trenchet cez hanstes e cez escuz buclers
E piez e poinz e seles e costez.
Ki lui veist sarrazins desmembrer
Un mort sur altre geter,
De bon vassal li poust remembrer.
L'enseigne Carle n'i volt mie ublier.
" Munjoie ! " escriet e haltement e cler.
Rollant apelet, sun ami e sun per,
" Sire cumpaign, a mei car vus justez.
A grant dulor ermes hoi desevrez." A O I.

Oliver feels that he is wounded to death. He will never
avenge himself to his fill. He strikes like a baron in the
thick fight, he cuts through the shafts of spears and the
spiked shields, through feet and fists and saddles and
sides. Had you seen him tearing the saracens, throwing
one dead on another, you would hold the memory of a
good soldier. He will not forget the cry of Charles. He
shouts Munjoie high and clear. He calls Roland, his friend
and his peer, " My lord companion, come close by me.
Today we shall be parted in great sorrow." A O I.

Rollant reguardet Oliver al visage.
Teint fut e pers, desculuret e pale.
Li sancs tuz clers par mi le cors li raiet.
Encuntre tere en cheent les esclaces.

The Death of Oliver

" Deus," dist li quens, " or ne sai jo que face.
Sire cumpainz, mar fut vostre barnage.
Jamais n'iert hume ki tun cors cuntrevaillet.
E ! France dulce, cun hoi remendras guaste
De bons vassals, cunfundue e chaiete.
Li emperere en avrat grant damage."
A icest mot sur sun cheval se pasmet. A O I.

Roland looks at Oliver in the face. He was wan and blue, pale and without colour. The bright blood runs down his body and the drops fall to the ground. " God," said the count, " I do not know what I shall do. My lord companion, your courage was made for death. There will never be a man who has worth against your body. E ! sweet France, how you will be left wasted today of good soldiers, brought down and fallen. The emperor's damage will be great in their loss." When he speaks he faints on his horse. A O I.

As vus Rollant sur sun cheval pasmet
E Oliver ki est a mort naffret.
Tant ad seinet li oil li sunt trublet.
Ne loinz ne pres ne poet vedeir si cler
Que reconoistre poisset nuls hom mortel.
Sun cumpaignun, cum il l'at encuntret,
Sil fiert amunt sur l'elme a or gemet,
Tut li detrenchet d'ici qu'al nasel,
Mais en la teste ne l'ad mie adeset.
A icel colp l'ad Rollant reguardet,
Si li demandet dulcement e suef,
" Sire cumpain, faites le vos de gred ?
Ja est co Rollant, ki tant vos soelt amer.
Par nule guise ne m'aviez desfiet."
Dist Oliver, " Or vos oi jo parler.
Jo ne vos vei, veied vus Damnedeu.

Ferut vos ai, car le me pardunez."
Rollant respunt, " Jo n'ai nient de mel.
Jol vos parduins ici e devant Deu."
A icel mot l'un a l'altre ad clinet.
Par tel amur as les vos desevred.

You see Roland fainted on his horse, and Oliver who is wounded to death. He has bled so much that his eyes are darkened. Far or close, he cannot see clearly enough to know any mortal man. When he has met his companion he strikes him on his golden jewelled helmet. He cuts it through from the top to the nose-piece, but he did not touch his head at all. Roland has looked at him when he strikes him, and asks him sweetly and softly, " Lord companion, is it of your will that you do this? This is Roland who is used to love you. You gave me no defiance." Oliver said, " Now I hear you speak. I do not see you, may God my lord see you. I have struck you, give me your pardon." Roland answers, " I have no hurt. I pardon you here and before God." At that word they have leant one to the other. You see them parted in their great love.

Oliver sent que la mort mult l'angoisset.
Ansdous les oilz en la teste li turnent,
L'oie pert e la veue tute.
Descent a piet, a la tere se culchet,
Durement en halt si recleimet sa culpe,
Cuntre le ciel ambesdous ses mains juintes,
Si priet Deu que pareis li dunget
E beneist Karlun e France dulce,
Sun cumpaignun Rollant sur tuz humes.
Falt li le coer, le helme li embrunchet,
Trestut le cors a la tere li justet.
Morz est li quens, que plus ne se demurct.

The Death of Oliver

Rollant li ber le pluret, sil duluset.
Jamais en tere n'orrez plus dolent hume.

Oliver feels the great pain of death. Both his eyes roll
in his head, he loses his hearing and all his sight. He
dismounts on foot and lies on the ground. He makes
aloud a great confession of his sin, he lifts his joined
hands to heaven and prays to God that he may give
him paradise and bless Charles and sweet France, and
his companion Roland above all men. His heart fails
him, his helmet falls forward, all his body is one with the
ground. The count is dead, he stays no more. Roland
the baron weeps for him and laments him. You will
never hear a more sorrowful man on the earth.

Or veit Rollant que mort est sun ami,
Gesir adenz, a la tere sun vis.
Mult dulcement a regreter le prist,
" Sire cumpaign, tant mar fustes hardiz.
Ensemble avum estet e anz e dis,
Nem fesis mal ne jo nel te forsfis.
Quant tu es mor, dulur est que jo vif."
A icest mot se pasmet li marchis
Sur sun ceval que cleimet Veillantif.
Afermet est a ses estreus d'or fin :
Quel part qu'il alt, ne poet mie chair.

Roland sees that his friend lies dead, his face against the
ground. He began to call his name very sweetly, " My
lord companion, your strength was made for death. We
have been together through years and days. You never
did me wrong and I was not untrue to you. Now you are
dead and it is my grief that I live." When he has spoken
the marquis faints on his horse which he calls Veillantif.
He is held up by the stirrups of fine gold. Whichever side
he leans, he cannot fall.

The Knapsack

7 *The Ancient Ballad of Chevy-Chase*

> I never heard the old song of Percie and Douglas, that I
> found not my heart moved more than with a trumpet : and
> yet " it " is sung but by some blinde crowder, with no
> rougher voice, than rude style ; which beeing so evill
> apparelled in the dust and cobweb of that uncivill age,
> what would it work, trimmed in the gorgeous eloquence
> of Pindare !
>
> SIR PHILIP SIDNEY'S DEFENCE OF POETRY

THE fine heroic song of Chevy-Chase has ever been admired
by competent judges. Those genuine strokes of nature and
artless passion which have endeared it to the most simple
readers, have recommended it to the most refined ; and it
has equally been the amusement of our childhood, and the
favourite of our riper years.

Mr. Addison has given an excellent critique [1] on this
very popular ballad, but is mistaken with regard to the
antiquity of the common-received copy ; for this, if one
may judge from the style, cannot be older than the time of
Elizabeth, and was probably written after the elogium of
Sir Philip Sidney : perhaps in consequence of it. I flatter
myself I have here recovered the genuine antique poem ;
the true original song, which appeared rude even in the
time of Sir Philip, and caused him to lament that it was
so evil-apparelled in the rugged garb of antiquity.

This curiosity is printed, from an old manuscript, at the
end of Hearne's preface to Gul. Newbrigiensis Hist., 1719,
8vo, vol. i. To the MS. copy is subjoined the name of the
author, Rychard Sheale [2] ; whom Hearne had so little
judgment as to suppose to be the same with a R. Sheale,
who was living in 1588. But whoever examines the grada-
tion of language and idiom in the following volumes, will

---

[1] *Spectator*, Nos. 70, 74.

[2] Subscribed after the usual manner of our old poets, **explicet**
(explicit) **quoth Rychard Sheale.**

The Ancient Ballad of Chevy-Chase

be convinced that this is the production of an earlier poet. It is indeed expressly mentioned among some very ancient songs in an old book entituled, The Complaint of Scotland, under the title of the *Huntis of Chevet*, where the two following lines are also quoted :

> The Perssee and the Mongumrye mette,
> That day, that day, that gentil day :

which though not quite the same as they stand in the ballad yet differ not more than might be owing to the author's quoting from memory. Indeed, whoever considers the style and orthography of this old poem will not be inclined to place it lower than the time of Henry VI : as on the other hand the mention of James the Scottish king, with one or two anachronisms, forbids us to assign it an earlier date. King James I, who was prisoner in this kingdom at the death of his father,[1] did not wear the crown of Scotland till the second year of our Henry VI,[2] but before the end of that long reign a third James had mounted the throne.[3] A succession of two or three Jameses, and the long detention of one of them in England, would render the name familiar to the English, and dispose a poet in those rude times to give it to any Scottish king he happened to mention.

So much for the date of this old ballad : with regard to its subject, although it has no countenance from history there is room to think it had originally some foundation in fact. It was one of the Laws of the Marches frequently renewed between the two nations, that neither party should hunt in the other's borders, without leave from the proprietors or their deputies. There had long been a rivalship

[1] Who died Aug. 5, 1406, in the 7th year of our Hen. IV.

[2] James I was crowned May 22, 1424 ; murdered Feb. 21, 1436-7.

[3] In 1460—Hen. VI was deposed 1461 ; restored and slain, 1471.

The Knapsack

between the two martial families of Percy and Douglas, which, heightened by the national quarrel, must have produced frequent challenges and struggles for superiority, petty invasions of their respective domains and sharp contests for the point of honour ; which would not always be recorded in history. Something of this kind, we may suppose, gave rise to the ancient ballad of the *Hunting a' the Cheviat*. Percy earl of Northumberland had vowed to hunt for three days in the Scottish border without condescending to ask leave from earl Douglas, who was either lord of the soil, or lord warden of the marches. Douglas would not fail to resent the insult, and endeavour to repel the intruders by force : this would naturally produce a sharp conflict between the two parties ; something of which, it is probable, did really happen, though not attended with the tragical circumstances recorded in the ballad : for these are evidently borrowed from the *Battle of Otterbourn*, a very different event, but which aftertimes would easily confound with it. That battle might be owing to some such previous affront as this of *Chevy-Chase*, though it has escaped the notice of historians. Our poet has evidently jumbled the two subjects together : if indeed the lines in which this mistake is made, are not rather spurious, and the after-insertion of some person who did not distinguish between the two stories.

THE FIRST FIT

THE Persè owt of Northombarlande,
  And a vowe to God mayd he,
That he wolde hunte in the mountayns
  Off Chyviat within dayes thre,
In the mauger [1] of doughtè Dogles,
  And all that ever with him be.

[1] despite.

40

The Ancient Ballad of Chevy-Chase

The fattiste hartes in all Cheviat
　　He sayd he wold kill, and cary them away :
Be my feth, sayd the dougheti Doglas agayn,
　　I wyll let [1] that hontyng yf that I may.

Then the Persè owt of Banborowe cam,
　　With him a myghtye meany [2] ;
With fifteen hondrith archares bold ;
　　The wear chosen out of shyars thre. [3]

This begane on a monday at morn
　　In Cheviat the hillys so he ;
The chyld may rue that ys un-born,
　　It was the mor pitté.

The dryvars thorowe the woodes went
　　For to reas the dear ;
Bomen bickarte uppone the bent
　　With ther browd aras cleare.

Then the wyld thorowe the woodes went
　　On every syde shear ;
Grea-hondes thorowe the greves glent
　　For to kyll thear dear.

The begane in Chyviat the hyls above
　　Yerly on a monnyn day ;
Be that it drewe to the oware off none [4]
　　A hondrith fat hartes ded ther lay.

---

[1] prevent.　　　　　　　　　[2] company.
[3] By these " *shyars thre* " is probably meant three districts in Northumberland, which still go by the name of *shires*, and are all in the neighbourhood of *Cheviot*. These are *Islandshire*, being the district so named from Holy-Island ; *Norehamshire*, so called from the town and castle of Noreham, or Norham ; and *Bamboroughshire*, the ward or hundred belonging to Bamborough-castle and town.
[4] hour of noon.

The Knapsack

The blewe a mort [1] uppone the bent,
  The semblyd on sydis shear ;
To the quyrry then the Persè went
  To se the bryttlyng [2] off the deare.

He sayd, It was the Duglas promys
  This day to meet me hear ;
But I wyste he wold faylle verament :
  A gret oth the Persè swear.

At the laste a squyar of Northombelonde
  Lokyde at his hand full ny,
He was war ath the doughetie Doglas comynge :
  With him a mightè meany.

Both with spear, byll, and brande :
  Yt was a myghti sight to se.
Hardyar men both off hart nar hande
  Wear not in Christiantè.

The wear twenty hondrith spear-men good
  Withouten any fayle ;
The wear borne a-long be the watter a Twyde
  Yth bowndes of Tividale.

Leave off the brytlyng of the dear, he sayde,
  And to your bowys look ye tayk good heed
For never sithe ye wear on your mothars borne
  Had ye never so mickle need.

The dougheti Dogglas on a stede
  He rode att his men beforne ;
His armor glytteryde as dyd a glede ;
  A bolder barne was never born.

The Ancient Ballad of Chevy-Chase

Tell me ' what ' men ye ar, he says,
   Or whos men that ye be :
Who gave youe leave to hunte in this
   Chyviat chays in the spyt of me ?

The first mane that ever him an answear mayd,
   Yt was the good lord Persè :
We wyll not tell the what men we ar, he says,
   Nor whos men that we be ;
But we wyll hount hear in this chays
   In the spyte of thyne, and of the.

The fattiste hartes in all Chyviat
   We have kyld, and cast to carry them a-way.
Be my troth, sayd the doughtè Dogglas agayn,
   Ther-for the ton of us shall de [1] this day.

Then sayd the doughtè Doglas
   Unto the lord Persè :
To kyll all thes giltless men,
   A-las ! it wear great pittè.

But, Persè, thowe art a lord of lande,
   I am a yerle callyd within my countre ;
Let all our men uppone a parti stande ;
   And do the battell off the and of me.

Nowe Cristes cors on his crowne, sayd the lord Persè,
   Who-soever ther-to says nay.
Be my troth, doughtè Doglas, he says,
   Thow shalt never se that day ;

---

[1] the one of us shall die.

The Knapsack

Nethar in Ynglonde, Skottlonde, nar France,
  Nor for no man of a woman born,
But and fortune be my chance,
  I dar met him on man for on.[1]

Then bespayke a squyar off Northombarlonde,
  Ric. Wytharynton was his nam ;
It shall never be told in Sothe-Ynglonde, he says,
  To kyng Herry the fourth for sham.

I wat youe byn great lordes twaw,
  I am a poor squyar of lande ;
I wyll never see my captayne fyght on a fylde,
  And stande my-selffe, and looke on,
But whyll I may my weppone welde,
  I wyll not ' fayl ' both harte and hande.

That day, that day, that dredfull day :
  The first Fit here I fynde.
And youe wyll here any mor athe hountyng athe Chyviat,
  Yet ys ther mor behynde.

THE SECOND FIT

The Yngglishe men hade ther bowys yebent,
  Ther hartes were good yenoughe ;
The first [2] of arros that the shote off,
  Seven skore spear-men the sloughe.

Yet bydys the yerle Doglas uppon the bent,
  A captayne good yenoughe,
And that was sene verament,
  For he wrought hom both woo and wouche.[3]

---

[1] *i.e.* one.   [2] *i.e.* flight.   [3] evil.

44

The Ancient Ballad of Chevy-Chase

The Dogglas pertyd his ost in thre,
  Lyk a cheffe cheften off pryde,
With suar speares off myghttè tre
  The cum in on every syde.

Thrughe our Yngglishe archery
  Gave many a wounde full wyde ;
Many a doughete the garde to dy,
  Which ganyde them no pryde.

The Ynggylshe men let thear bowys be,
  And pulde owt brandes that wer bright ;
It was a hevy syght to se
  Bryght swordes on basnites [1] lyght.

Thorowe ryche male, and myne-ye-ple [2]
  Many sterne [3] the stroke downe streght :
Many a freyke [4], that was full free,
  Ther undar foot dyd lyght.

At last the Duglas and the Persè met,
  Lyke to [5] captayns of myght and mayne ;
The swapte togethar tyll the both swat
  With swordes, that were of fyn myllàn.

Thes worthè freckys for to fyght
  Ther-to the wear [6] full fayne,
Tyll the bloode owte off thear basnetes sprente,
  As ever dyd heal or rayne.

Holde the, Persè, sayd the Doglas,
  And i' feth I shall the brynge
Wher thowe shalte have a yerls wagis [7]
  Of Jamy our Scottish kynge.

[1] steel helmets.   [2] manoplie : long gauntlet.
[3] stern men.   [4] bold fellow.
[5] *i.e.* two.   [6] they were.   [7] wages.

The Knapsack

Thoue shalte have thy ransom fre,
    I hight [1] the hear this thinge,
For the manfullyste man yet art thowe,
    That ever I conqueryd in filde fightyng.

Nay then sayd the lord Persè,
    I tolde it the beforne,
That I wolde never yeldyde be
    To no man of a woman born.

With that ther cam an arrowe hastely
    Forthe off a mightie wane,[2]
Hit hathe strekene the yerle Duglas
    In at the brest bane.

Thoroue lyvar and lunges bathe
    The sharp arrowe ys gane,
That never after in all his lyffe days,
    He spake mo wordes but ane,
That was, Fyghte ye, my merry men, whyllys ye may,
    For my lyff days ben gan.

The Persè leanyde on his brande,
    And sawe the Duglas de ;
He tooke the dede man be the hande,
    And sayd, Wo ys me for the !

To have savyde thy lyffe I wold have pertyd with
    My landes for years thre,
For a better man of hart, nare of hande
    Was not in all the north countrè.

[1] promise.
[2] *i.e.* ane, one, sc. man, an arrow came from a mighty one :
from a mighty man.

The Ancient Ballad of Chevy-Chase

Off all that se a Skottishe knyght,
  Was callyd Sir Hewe the Mongon-byrry,
He sawe the Duglas to the deth was dyght ;
  He spendyd a spear a trusti tre :

He rod uppon a corsiare
  Throughe a hondrith archery ;
He never styntyde, nar never blane,[1]
  Tyll he cam to the good lord Persè.

He set uppone the lord Persè
  A dynte,[2] that was full soare ;
With a suar spear of a myghtè tre
  Clean thorow the body he the Persè bore,

Athe tothar syde, that a man myght se,
  A large cloth yard and mare :
Towe bettar captayns wear nat in Christiantè,
  Then that day slain wear ther.

An archer off Northomberlonde
  Say[3] slean was the lord Persè,
He bar a bende-bow in his hande,
  Was made off trusti tre :

An arow, that a cloth yarde was lang,
  To th' hard stele halyde[4] he ;
A dynt, that was both sad and soar,
  He sat on Sir Hewe the Mongon-byrry.

The dynt yt was both sad and soar,
  That he of Mongon-byrry sete ;
The swane-fethars, that his arrowe bar,
  With his hart blood the wear wete.

[1] stopped.   [2] stroke.
[3] *i.e.* saw.   [4] pulled.

47

The Knapsack

Ther was never a freake wone foot wold fle,
    But still in stour [1] dyd stand,
Heawing on yche othar, whyll the myght dre,
    With many a bal-ful brande.

This battell begane in Chyviat
    An owar befor the none,
And when even-song bell was rang
    The battell was nat half done.

The tooke on on ethar hand
    Be the lyght off the mone ;
Many hade no strength for to stande,
    In Chyviat the hyllys aboun.

Of fifteen hondrith archars of Ynglonde
    Went away but fifti and thre ;
Of twenty hondrith spear-men of Skotlonde,
    But even five and fifti :

But all wear slayne Cheviat within :
    The hade no strengthe to stand on hie ;
The chylde may rue that ys un-borne,
    It was the mor pittè.

Thear was slayne with the lord Persè
    Sir John of Agerstone,
Sir Roge the hinde [2] Hartly,
    Sir Wyllyam the bolde Hearone.

Sir Jorg the worthè Lovele
    A knyght of great renowen,
Sir Raff the ryche Rugbè
    With dyntes wear beaten dowene.

[1] press of battle.   [2] courteous.

The Ancient Ballad of Chevy-Chase

For Wetharryngton my harte was wo,
   That ever he slayne shulde be ;
For when both his leggis wear hewyne in two,
   Yet he knyled and fought on hys kne.

Ther was slayne with the dougheti Douglas
   Sir Hewe the Mongon-byrry,
Sir Davye Lwdale, that worthè was,
   His sistars son was he :

Sir Charles a Murrè, in that place,
   That never a foot wolde fle ;
Sir Hewe Maxwell, a lorde he was,
   With the Duglas dyd he dey.

So on the morrowe the mayde them byears
   Off byrch, and hasell so ' gray ' ;
Many wedous with wepyng tears
   Cam to fach ther makys [1] a-way.

Tivydale may carpe off care,
   Northombarlond may mayk grat mone,
For towe such captayns, as slayne wear thear,
   On the march perti shall never be none.

Word ys commen to Edden-burrowe,
   To Jamy the Skottishe kyng,
That dougheti Duglas, lyff-tenant of the Merches.
   He lay slean Chyviot with-in.

His handdes dyd he weal [2] and wryng,
   He sayd, Alas, and woe ys me !
Such another captayn Skotland within,
   He sayd, y-feth shuld never be.

       [1] mates.   [2] clench.

The Knapsack

Worde ys commyn to lovly Londone
   Till the fourth Harry our kyng,
That lord Persè, leyff-tennante of the Merchis,
   He lay slayne Chyviat within.

God have merci on his soll, sayd kyng Harry,
   Good lord, yf thy will it be !
I have a hondrith captayns in Ynglonde, he sayd,
   As good as ever was hee :
But Persè, and I brook [1] my lyffe,
   Thy deth well quyte shall be.

As our noble kyng made his a-vowe,
   Lyke a noble prince of renowen,
For the deth of the lord Persè,
   He dyd the battell of Hombyll-down [2] :

Wher syx and thritte Skottish knyghtes
   On a day wear beaten down :
Glendale glytteryde on ther armor bryght,
   Over castill, towar, and town.

This was the hontynge off the Cheviat ;
   That tear begane this spurn [3] :
Old men that knowen the grownde well yenoughe,
   Call it the Battell of Otterburn.

---

[1] retain.

[2] The battle of Hombyll-down, or Humbledon, was fought Sept. 14, 1402 (anno 3 Hen. IV), wherein the English, under the command of the earl of Northumberland, and his son Hotspur, gained a complete victory over the Scots. The village of Humbledon is one mile north-west from Wooler in Northumberland.

[3] This seems to be a proverb, " That tearing or pulling occasioned his spurn or kick."

The Ancient Ballad of Chevy-Chase

At Otterburn began this spurne
   Uppon a monnyn day :
Ther was the doughtè Doglas slean,
   The Persè never went away.

Ther was never a tym on the march partes
   Sen the Doglas and the Persè met,
But yt was marvele, and the redde blude ronne not,
   As the reane doys in the stret.

Jhesue Christ our balys bete,[1]
   And to the blys us brynge !
Thus was the hountynge of the Chevyat :
   God send us all good ending !

[1] our woes relieve.

PART TWO

PART TWO

8 *The Taking of Constantinople*

To return to the croisaders, who still lay before Constantinople, and were preparing their perrieres, and all the military
engines which are used in the assault of cities ; and were
planting their mangonels upon the ships and palanders ;
and were raising ladders against the yards of the vessels,
which were very lofty.   As soon as the Greeks beheld these
operations, they began to strengthen that side of the city,
though it was already guarded by high towers and walls.
On every tower they raised two or three platforms of wood,
the better to secure it, so that no city was ever more surely
fortified.   These labours occupied both parties a considerable part of Lent.

When all was prepared, a parliament was held for the
purpose of finally deciding upon their situation. After
long debate, it was agreed, that if God should grant them
the capture of the city, all the booty which they might
take, should be collected together, and shared equally
among the pilgrims.   And that when they were possessed
of the city, six French and six Venetians should be chosen,
who should swear upon the saints to elect for emperor
whomever they should deem most capable of governing
the country ; that the emperor so chosen, should receive
a fourth part of all that was conquered, both within and
without the city, with the palaces of Bucoleon and
Blachernæ ; that the remainder should be divided into

two parts, one of which should be given to the French, the other to the Venetians. That they should then choose twelve of the most experienced of the pilgrims, and the same number of the Venetians, who should allot the fiefs and honours among their companions, and appoint what service should be paid for them to the emperor. This treaty was made and sworn to both by French and Venetians, under pain of the excommunication of any who infringed it, with liberty for those who desired, to depart at the end of March twelvemonth; while those who chose to remain, were to be retained in the emperor's service.

In the mean time, the fleet was manned and prepared and furnished with provisions for the whole army; and on the Thursday after Midlent, the pilgrims embarked, and the horses were carried on board the palanders. Each division embarked in its proper vessels, and the whole fleet was drawn up in a line, the ships being distinct from the galleys and palanders. It was a noble prospect, for the line of battle extended more than half a French league. On Friday morning the ships and galleys and other vessels approached the city, and commenced a vigorous assault. In many places the pilgrims leaped ashore, and charged up to the very walls. In others the ladders on the ships were brought so near, that those who mounted them, and the soldiers who defended the walls and towers, fought hand to hand with their lances.

This hot assault continued in more than a hundred places until near noon, when, for their sins, the pilgrims were repulsed; and those who had advanced from the galleys and palanders were driven back to them by main force. On that day our loss was much greater than that of the Greeks, who were in consequence greatly elated.

The Taking of Constantinople

There were some of the pilgrims who kept themselves at a distance after the assault ; and others who cast anchor so near the city, that they were within range of the perrieres and mangonels.

In the evening a council was held by the barons and the duke of Venice in a church, beyond the place where they had encamped. A variety of opinions was offered, for the army was much dejected on account of its defeat. Some thought it advisable to make an attempt upon that side of the city which was less strongly fortified ; but the Venetians, who were most conversant with naval warfare, were of opinion, that the current would bear them so rapidly down the straight, that they should not be able to bring up their vessels. And truly there were many who in their hearts wished the winds and waves might carry away the fleet, they cared not whither, so that they might quit that country, and return to their homes. It was a natural desire, for the dangers were very great. After much debating, it was resolved, that they should employ that day, which was Saturday, and the following Sunday, in reorganizing their force ; and on Monday that they should return to the assault, with the ships, on which the ladders were mounted, linked in pairs together. This expedient would bring two ships to the attack of a single tower ; for it was evident that on the preceding day, when ship was opposed to tower, the force on the towers far exceeded the assailants in number, and the odds were in consequence too great. But as it appeared that the towers might be attacked more effectually by means of two ladders, than of one, the plan I have mentioned was projected. Thus Saturday and Sunday passed over.

The emperor Mourzuphles had come before the assault to encamp in a large square, where he had pitched his scarlet tents. Things remained in this state until Monday

The Knapsack

morning, when the pilgrims of the ships, the galleys, and the palanders, again put on their arms, inspiring the inhabitants of the city with greater terror than before. The pilgrims on their side were astounded at beholding the walls and towers covered with soldiers, but notwithstanding began a bold and terrible assault. Each ship attacked the place before it, and the earth trembled with the shouts. The battle had continued a long time, when the Lord raised a northerly wind, which drove the ships nearer to the shore. Two ships, the Pilgrim and the Paradise, linked together, approached a tower, one on one side, the other on the other, as God and the winds directed. The ladder of the Pilgrim touched the tower, and in an instant a Venetian, and a knight of France, called Andrew d'Urboise, sprang upon the tower, and were followed by other warriors. The warders of the tower were discomfited, and fled.

When the knights, who were on board the palanders, beheld this sight, they leaped upon the shore; and raising their ladders against the open wall, mounted them in spite of every obstacle, and possessed themselves of four towers more. The men of the ships, the galleys, and the palanders, drove on in strife who should be foremost; and forcing open three of the city gates, entered, and, mounting their horses, rode to the place where the emperor Mourzuphles was encamped. Mourzuphles had arrayed his troops in the front of his camp, but at the sight of the mounted knights, they dispersed in all directions. The emperor himself fled along the streets to the castle of Bucoleon. The Greeks were everywhere vanquished; horses, palfreys, mules, and other booty, were secured; and of the wounded and the dead there was neither end, nor measure. Most of the Greek lords had fled towards the gate of Blachernæ; and it was late in the evening, when

The Taking of Constantinople

the pilgrims, fatigued with battle and slaughter, began to assemble in the great square of Constantinople. There they resolved that it were safer to encamp near the walls and the towers they had stormed ; for they could not yet believe that in a brief month they had captured the city, with all the strong churches and palaces, and the multitudes which were within them.

So they encamped before the walls and towers, which lay contiguous to the fleet. The count of Flanders lodged in the scarlet tents, which the emperor Mourzuphles had left behind him ; and his brother Henry encamped before the palace of Blachernæ. The marquis of Montferrat encamped with his men on the verge of the city. Thus on Palm Monday were the pilgrims quartered, and Constantinople taken. Louis, count of Blois, who had languished all the winter of a quartan fever, and was unable to bear arms, lay at the same time in a palander, to the great loss of the croisaders, for he was a knight of undaunted valour. On that memorable night, while the wearied host reposed, the emperor Mourzuphles took no rest ; but assembling his servants, he gave out he was about to attack the Franks instead of which he hastened along streets, as far distant as possible from the neighbourhood of the pilgrims, to the golden gate, through which he fled, and finally abandoned the city. All who had the ability followed him ; nor were the pilgrims aware of what had taken place.

On the same night, in the vicinity of the quarters of the marquis of Montferrat, some unknown people, fearing the Greeks might attack the fleet, set fire to the buildings, which were betwixt the Greeks and themselves. The fire spread and blazed, and burned all that night and all the next day, until vespers. This was the third fire which had happened since the arrival of the Franks; and there were more houses consumed than are contained in three of the most populous cities of France. The night waned, and the day, which was Tuesday, dawned; and the whole host, knight and serjeant, being armed and assembled in their respective posts, marched from their quarters, in the anticipation of a more serious resistance than they had hitherto experienced, for they knew not of the flight of the emperor; but they found no enemy to oppose them.

The marquis of Montferrat, on the same morning, rode to the palace of Bucoleon, which was surrendered to him, saving the lives of those who were within. There he found the most high-born ladies in the world, who had fled for safety to the palace. Among them were the sister of the king of France, and the sister of the king of Hungary, each of whom had been empress of Constantinople, with many other dames of the highest quality. Of the treasures which were in this palace, I cannot speak; for their value was inestimable. At the same time that this palace was yielded to the marquis Boniface, the palace of Blachernæ was given up to Henry, the brother of the count of Flanders, saving the lives of the inhabitants; and there a treasure so immense was found, that it rivalled that in the palace of Bucoleon.

Each of them garrisoned with his soldiers, the palace which had been yielded, and placed the treasures under ward. The other pilgrims, who were scattered over the city, gained incalculable plunder; for there was no estimating the quantity of silver and gold, precious vessels, jewels, rich stuffs, silks, robes of vair, gris, and ermine, and other valuables, the productions of all the climates in the world. And it is the belief of me, Geoffry de Villehardouin, marshal of Champagne, that the plunder of this city exceeded all that had been witnessed since the creation of the world.

GEOFFRY DE VILLEHARDOUIN

9 *Greek Fire*

ONE night the Turks brought forward an engine, called by them *la perriere*, a terrible engine to do mischief, and placed it opposite to the chas-chateils, which Sir Walter de Curel and I were guarding by night. From this engine they flung such quantities of Greek fire,[1] that it was the most

---

[1] This fire was so called, because it was first invented among the Greeks by Callinicus the architect, a native of Heliopolis, a town in Syria, under Constantinus Barbatus ; and likewise because the Greeks were for a long time the only people who preserved the use of it, which they very rarely communicated to any of their allies. Anna Comnena says, that this fire was made with pitch and other gums from trees, mixed with sulphur, and the whole ground together. Abbon, in the first book of the *Wars of Paris*, has given the composition of it in these verses :

" Addit eis oleum, ceramque, picemque ministrans,
    Mixta simul liquefacta foco ferventia valde,
    Quæ Danis cervice comas uruntque trahuntque."

The author of the *History of Jerusalem*, p. 1167, makes oil a part of the composition : at least, he names it, " oleum incendarium, quod ignem Græcum vocant ". It may perhaps be naphtha, which Procopius, in the fourth book of the *War of the Goths*, ch. 11, says, the Greeks call $M\eta\delta\epsilon\iota\alpha\varsigma$ $\epsilon\lambda\alpha\iota\sigma\nu$, and the Medes *naphtha*, which Lambecius, in his observations on Codinus, thinks should be corrected to $M\eta\delta\iota\alpha\varsigma$ $\epsilon\lambda\alpha\iota\sigma\nu$, oil of Media, and that for this reason the same Greeks have given to this artificial fire the name of $M\eta\delta\iota\kappa\sigma\nu$ $\pi\sigma\rho$, which is met with in Cinnamus, p. 308, and in Codinus, p. 7 of the royal edition. There are others, however, who imagine naphtha was called $M\eta\delta\epsilon\iota\alpha\varsigma$ $\epsilon\lambda\alpha\iota\sigma\nu$, or $\pi\sigma\rho$, because Medea, according to Pliny (l. 2, ch. 105), burnt her husband Jason with this fire. Whatever may be thought of this, Procopius, in the part quoted, informs us, that in the composition of this artificial fire, there was a mixture of naphtha with sulphur and bitumen. Vanoccio Biringuccio, in the tenth

horrible sight ever witnessed. When my companion, the good Sir Walter, saw this shower of fire, he cried out, "Gentlemen, we are all lost without remedy; for should they set fire to our chas-chateils we must be burnt; and if we quit our post we are for ever dishonoured; from which I conclude, that no one can possibly save us from this peril but God, our benignant Creator; I therefore advise all of you, whenever they throw any of this Greek fire, to cast yourselves on your hands and knees, and cry for mercy to our Lord, in whom alone resides all power."

As soon, therefore, as the Turks threw their fires, we flung ourselves on our hands and knees, as the wise man had advised; and this time they fell between our two cats

---

book of his *Pyrotechny*, chap. 9, has described all the materials that form part of the artificial fireworks which the Greeks made use of to burn the vessels of their enemies. The Greeks made use of this fire when at sea, in two ways; first by fire-ships filled with this fire, that were floated among the enemies' fleet, and thus set them on fire. Fire-ships were used before the time of the emperor Constantinus Barbatus, for Theophanes informs us, p. 100, that under the empire of Leon le Grand, Genseric, king of Africa, burnt with vessels that were filled with dry wood and other combustibles, and which he floated down the stream, the whole of the Grecian fleet. Secondly, by artificial fires on the prows of these vessels, placed in large tubes of copper, through which they blew them into the enemy's ships. With regard to the use of the Greek fire in battles on land, it was different, for soldiers were then supplied with copper tubes, and blew it through them on their enemies.—See Anna Comnena, in the thirteenth book of her *Alexiade*. Sometimes they threw sharp bolts of iron, covered with tow, well oiled and pitched, with which they set fire to the engines. Joinville speaks of this fire, " and they opened a very quick fire upon us with balls made of the Greek fire ". Sometimes this fire was put into phials and pots, and it was also discharged from perrieres and cross-bows. Albert d'Aix, l. 7, ch. 5, remarks, that " hujus ignis genus aqua erat inextinguibile " ; but there were other materials by which it could be extinguished, namely, vinegar and sand. Jacques de Vitry, l. 3, ch. 84, adds urine as an extinguisher; and Cinnamus, in the place before quoted, says that ships were frequently covered with cloths dipped in vinegar, to prevent the bad effects of this fire.

into a hole in front, which our people had made to extinguish them ; and they were instantly put out by a man appointed for that purpose. This Greek fire, in appearance, was like a large tun, and its tail was of the length of a long spear ; the noise which it made was like to thunder ; and it seemed a great dragon of fire flying through the air, giving so great a light with its flame, that we saw in our camp as clearly as in broad day. Thrice this night did they throw the fire from la perriere, and four times from cross-bows.

Each time that our good king St. Louis heard them make these discharges of fire, he cast himself on the ground, and with extended arms and eyes turned to the heavens, cried with a loud voice to our Lord, and shedding heavy tears, said, " Good Lord God Jesus Christ, preserve thou me, and all my people " ; and believe me, his sincere prayers were of great service to us. At every time the fire fell near us, he sent one of his knights to know how we were, and if the fire had hurt us. One of the discharges from the Turks fell beside a chas-chateil, guarded by the men of the Lord Courtenay, struck the bank of the river in front, and ran on the ground towards them burning with flame. One of the knights of this guard instantly came to me, crying out,—" Help us, my lord, or we are burnt ; for there is a long train of Greek fire, which the Saracens have discharged, that is running straight for our castle."

We immediately hastened thither, and good need was there ; for as the knight had said, so it was. We extinguished the fire with much labour and difficulty ; for the Saracens, in the mean time, kept up so brisk a shooting from the opposite bank, that we were covered with arrows and bolts.

The count of Anjou, brother to the king, guarded these castles during the day, and annoyed the Saracen army with his cross-bows. It was ordered by the king, that after the count of Anjou should have finished his daily guard, we, and others of my company, should continue it during the night. We suffered much pain and uneasiness ; for the Turks had already broken and damaged our tandies and defences. Once these Turkish traitors advanced their perriere in the daytime, when the count d'Anjou had the guard, and had brought together all their machines, from which they threw Greek fires on our dams, over the river, opposite to our tandies and defences, which completely prevented any of the workmen from shewing themselves ; and our two chas-chateils were in a moment destroyed and burnt. The count d'Anjou was almost mad at seeing this ; for they were under his guard, and like one out of his senses, wanted to throw himself into the fire to extinguish it, whilst I and my knights returned thanks to God ; for if they had delayed this attack to the night, we must have all been burnt.

The king, on hearing what had happened, made a request to each of his barons, that they would give him as much of the largest timbers from their ships that were on the coast as they could spare, and have them transported to where the army lay ; for there was not any timber near fit to make use of. After the king had made this request, they all aided him to the utmost ; and before the new chas-chateils were finished, the timber employed was estimated to be worth upwards of 10,000 livres. You may guess from this that many boats were destroyed, and that we were then in the utmost distress.

When the chas-chateils were completed, the king would not have them fixed, or pointed, until the count of Anjou resumed the guard : he then ordered that they should be placed on the exact spot where the others had been burnt. This he did to recover the honour of his said brother, under whose guard the two others had been destroyed. As the king had ordered, so it was done ; which the Saracens observing, they brought thither all their machines, and,

Greek Fire

coupling them together, shot at our new chas-chateils vigorously. When they perceived that our men were afraid of going from one castle to the other, for fear of the showers of stones which they were casting, they advanced the perriere directly opposite to them, and again burnt them with their Greek fires. I and my knights returned thanks to God for this second escape. Had they waited until night to make the attack, when the guard would have devolved to us, we must all have been burnt with them.

The king, seeing this, was, as well as his army, much troubled, and he called his barons to council, to consider what should be done ; for they now perceived themselves that it would be impossible to throw a causeway over the river to cross to the Turks and Saracens, as our people could not make such advance on their side, but they were more speedily ruined by the Turks on the other.

Sir Humbert de Beaujeu, constable of France, then addressed the king, and said, that a Bedouin had lately come to him to say, that if we would give him 500 golden besants, he would shew a safe ford, which might easily be crossed on horseback. The king replied, that he most cheerfully granted this, provided he spoke the truth ; but the man would on no account shew the ford before the money demanded was paid.

It was determined by the king, that the duke of Burgundy, and the nobles beyond sea his allies, should guard the army from the alarms of the Saracens ; whilst he, with his three brothers, the counts of Poitiers, Artois, and Anjou, who was afterward king of Sicily, as I have said before, should with their attendants on horseback make trial of the ford the Bedouin was to shew them. The day appointed for this purpose was Shrove-Tuesday, which, when arrived, we all mounted our horses, and, armed at all points, followed the Bedouin to the ford.

On our way thither, some advanced too near the banks

of the river, which being soft and slippery, they and their horses fell in and were drowned. The king seeing it, pointed it out to the rest, that they might be more careful and avoid similar danger. Among those that were drowned was that valiant knight Sir John d'Orleans, who bore the banner of the army. When we came to the ford, we saw, on the opposite bank, full 300 Saracen cavalry ready to defend this passage. We entered the river, and our horses found a tolerable ford with firm footing, so that by ascending the stream we found an easy shore, and, through God's mercy, we all crossed over with safety. The Saracens, observing us thus cross, fled away with the utmost despatch.

Before we set out, the king had ordered that the Templars should form the van, and the count d'Artois, his brother, should command the second division of the army ; but the moment the count d'Artois had passed the ford with all his people, and saw the Saracens flying, they stuck spurs into their horses and galloped after them ; for which those who formed the van were much angered at the count d'Artois, who could not make any answer, on account of Sir Foucquault du Melle, who held the bridle of his horse ; and Sir Foucquault, being deaf, heard nothing the Templars were saying to the count d'Artois, but kept bawling out " Forward, forward ! "

When the Templars perceived this, they thought they should be dishonoured if they allowed the count d'Artois thus to take the lead, and with one accord they spurred their horses to their fastest speed, pursuing the Saracens through the town of Massoura, as far as the plains before Babylon ; but on their return the Turks shot at them plenty of arrows, and other artillery, as they repassed through the narrow streets of the town. The count d'Artois and the lord de Coucy, of the name of Raoul, were there slain, and as many as 300 other knights. The Templars lost, as their chief informed me, full fourteen score men-at-arms

Greek Fire

and horses. My knights, as well as myself, noticing on our left a large body of Turks who were arming, instantly charged them; and when we were advanced into the midst of them, I perceived a sturdy Saracen mounting his horse, which was held by one of his esquires by the bridle, and while he was putting his hand on the saddle to mount, I gave him such a thrust with my spear, which I pushed as far as I was able, that he fell down dead. The esquire, seeing his lord dead, abandoned master and horse; but, watching my motions, on my return struck me with his lance such a blow between the shoulders as drove me on my horse's neck, and held me there so tightly that I could not draw my sword, which was girthed round me. I was forced to draw another sword which was at the pommel of my saddle, and it was high time; but, when he saw I had my sword in my hand, he withdrew his lance, which I had seized, and ran from me.

It chanced that I and my knights had traversed the army of the Saracens, and saw here and there different parties of them, to the amount of about 6,000, who, abandoning their quarters, had advanced into the plain. On perceiving that we were separated from the main body, they boldly attacked us, and slew Sir Hugues de Trichatel, lord d'Escoflans, who bore the banner of our company. They also made prisoner Sir Raoul de Wanon, of our company, whom they had struck to the ground. As they were carrying him off, my knights and myself knew him, and instantly hastened, with great courage, to assist him, and deliver him from their hands. In returning from this engagement the Turks gave me such heavy blows, that my horse, not being able to withstand them, fell on his knees, and threw me to the ground over his head. I very shortly replaced my shield on my breast, and grasped my spear, during which time the Lord Errat d'Esmeray, whose soul may God pardon! advanced towards me, for he had also been struck down by the enemy; and we retreated together towards an old ruined house to wait for the king, who was coming, and I found means to recover my horse.

As we were going to this house, a large body of Turks came galloping towards us, but passed on to a party of ours whom they saw hard by: as they passed, they struck me to the ground, with my shield over my neck, and galloped over me, thinking I was dead; and indeed I was nearly so. When they were gone, my companion, Sir Errart, came and raised me up, and we went to the walls of the ruined house. Thither also had retired Sir Hugues d'Escosse, Sir Ferreys de Loppei, Sir Regnault de Menoncourt, and several others; and there also the Turks came to attack us, more bravely than ever, on all sides. Some of them entered within the walls, and were a long time fighting with us at spear's length, during which my knights gave me my horse, which they held, lest he should run away, and at the same time so vigorously defended us against the Turks, that they were greatly praised by several able persons who witnessed their prowess.

Sir Hugues d'Escosse was desperately hurt by three great wounds in the face and elsewhere. Sir Raoul and Sir Ferreys were also badly wounded in their shoulders, so that the blood spouted out just like to a tun of wine when tapped. Sir Errart d'Esmeray was so severely wounded in the face by a sword, the stroke of which cut off his nose, that it hung down over his mouth. In this severe distress, I called to my mind St. James, and said, "Good Lord St. James, succour me, I beseech thee; and come to my aid in this time of need." I had scarcely ended my prayer, when Sir Errart said to me, "Sir, if I did not think you might suppose it was done to abandon you, and save myself, I would go to my lord of Anjou, whom I see on the plain, and beg he would hasten to your help."—"Sir Errart," I replied, "you will do me great honour and

pleasure, if you will go and seek succour to safe our lives ;
for your own also is in great peril " ; and I said truly,
for he died of the wound he had received. All were of
my opinion that he should seek for assistance ; and I then
quitting hold of the rein of his bridle, he galloped towards
the count d'Anjou, to request he would support us in the
danger we were in.

There was a great lord with him who wished to detain
him, but the good prince would not attend to what he
urged, but, spurring his horse, galloped towards us followed
by his men. The Saracens, observing them coming, left
us ; but when on their arrival they saw the Saracens carrying away their prisoner, Sir Raould de Wanon, badly
wounded, they hastened to recover him, and brought him
back in a most pitiful state.

Shortly after, I saw the king arrive with all his attendants,
and with a terrible noise of trumpets, clarions, and horns.
He halted on an eminence, with his men-at-arms, for something he had to say ; and I assure you I never saw so
handsome a man under arms. He was taller than any of
his troop by the shoulders ; and his helmet, which was
gilded, was handsomely placed on his head ; and he bore
a German sword in his hand.

Soon after he had halted, many of his knights were
observed intermixed with the Turks : their companions
instantly rushed into the battle among them ; and you
must know, that in this engagement were performed, on
both sides, the most gallant deeds that were ever done in
this expedition to the Holy Land ; for none made use of
the bow, cross-bow, or other artillery. But the conflict
consisted of blows given to each other by battle-axes,
swords, butts of spears, all mixed together. From all I
saw, my knights and myself, all wounded as we were, were
very impatient to join the battle with the others.

JOHN LORD DE JOINVILLE

10 *A Priest in Arms*

In the evening of this severe engagement that I spoke of, and when we had taken up our quarters in those from whence we had driven the Saracens, my people brought me, from the main army, a tent, which the master of the Templars, who had the command of the van, had given me. I had it pitched on the right of those machines we had won from the enemy, as each of us was eager for repose : indeed we had need of it, from the wounds and fatigues we had suffered in the late battle.

Before daybreak, however, we were alarmed by the cries of " To arms, to arms ! " and I made my chamberlain rise, who lay by my side, to go and see what was the matter. He was not long in returning, much frightened, and crying out, " My lord, up instantly ; for the Saracens have entered the camp, both horse and foot, and have already defeated the guard which the king had appointed for our security, and to defend the engines we had won from them."

These engines were in front of the king's pavilions, and of us who were near to him. I immediately rose, threw a cuirass on my back, and put my iron skull-cap on my head ; and having roused our people, wounded as we were, we drove the Saracens from the engines which they were so anxious to recover.

The king, seeing that scarcely any of us had armour on, sent Sir Walter de Chastillon, who posted himself between us and the Turks, for the better guard of the engines. After Sir Walter had several times repulsed the enemy, who made frequent attempts during the night to carry off these engines, the Saracens, finding they could not succeed, retreated to a large body of their horse, that were drawn

A Priest in Arms

up opposite to our lines, to prevent us from surprising their camp, which was in their rear.

Six of the principal Turks dismounted, armed from head to foot, and made themselves a rampart of large stones, as a shelter from our cross-bows, and from thence shot volleys of arrows, which often wounded many of our men. When I and my men-at-arms who had the guard of that quarter saw their stone rampart, we took counsel together, and resolved that, during the ensuing night, we would destroy this rampart, and bring away the stones.

Now I had a priest called John de Waysy, who, having overheard our counsel and resolution, did not wait so long, but set out alone towards the Saracens, with his cuirass on, his cap of iron, and his sword under his arm. When he was near the enemy, who neither thought of nor suspected any one coming against them thus alone, he rushed furiously on, sword in hand, and gave such blows to these six captains, that they could not defend themselves, and took to flight, to the great astonishment of the other Turks and Saracens.

When the Turks saw their leaders fly, they stuck spurs into their horses, and charged the priest, who was returning to our army, whence had sallied fifty of our men to oppose them, as they were pursuing him on horseback : the Turks would not meet them, but wheeled off two or three times. It happened, however, that during these wheelings, one of our men threw his dagger at a Turk, and hit him between the ribs : he carried off the dagger, but it caused his death. The other Turks, seeing this, were more shy than before, and never dared to approach while our men were carrying away the stones of the rampart. My priest was well known ever after by the whole army, who said when they saw him, " That is the priest who, single-handed, defeated the Saracens."

JOHN LORD DE JOINVILLE

The Knapsack

11 *The Black Prince at Poitiers*

WHEN the prince saw that he should have battle and that the cardinal was gone without any peace or truce making, and saw that the French king did set but little store by him, he said then to his men : " Now, sirs, though we be but a small company as in regard to the puissance of our enemies, let us not be abashed therefor ; for the victory lieth not in the multitude of people, but whereas God will send it. If it fortune that the journey be ours, we shall be the most honoured people of all the world ; and if we die in our right quarrel, I have the king my father and brethren, and also ye have good friends and kinsmen ; these shall revenge us. Therefore, sirs, for God's sake I require you do your devoirs this day ; for if God be pleased and Saint George, this day ye shall see me a good knight." These words and such other that the prince spake comforted all his people. The lord sir John Chandos that day never went from the prince, nor also the lord James Audley of a great season ; but when he saw that they should needs fight, he said to the prince : " Sir, I have served always truly my lord your father and you also, and shall do as long as I live. I say this because I made once a vow that the first battle that other the king your father or any of his children should be at, how that I would be one of the first setters on, or else to die in the pain : therefore I require your grace, as in reward for any service that ever I did to the king your father or to you, that you will give me licence to depart from you and to set myself thereas I may accomplish my vow." The prince accorded to his desire and said, " Sir James, God give you this day that grace to be the best knight of all other," and so took him by the hand. Then the knight departed from the prince and went to the foremost front of all the battles, all only accompanied with four squires, who promised not to fail him. This lord James was a right sage and a valiant knight, and by him was much of the host ordained and governed the day before. Thus sir James was in the front of the battle ready to fight with the battle of the marshals of France. In like wise the lord Eustace d'Aubrecicourt did his pain to be one of the foremost to set on. When sir James Audley began to set forward to his enemies, it fortuned to sir Eustace d'Aubrecicourt as ye shall hear after. Ye have heard before how the Almains in the French host were appointed to be still a-horseback. Sir Eustace being a-horseback laid his spear in the rest and ran into the French battle, and then a knight of Almaine, called the lord Louis of Recombes, who bare a shield silver, five roses gules, and sir Eustace bare ermines, two hamedes of gules,—when this Almain saw the lord Eustace come from his company, he rode against him and they met so rudely, that both knights fell to the earth. The Almain was hurt in the shoulder, therefore he rose not so quickly as did sir Eustace, who when he was up and had taken his breath, he came to the other knight as he lay on the ground ; but then five other knights of Almaine came on him all at once and bare him to the earth, and so perforce there he was taken prisoner and brought to the earl of Nassau, who as then took no heed of him ; and I cannot say whether they sware him prisoner or no, but they tied him to a chare and there let him stand.

Then the battle began on all parts, and the battles of the marshals of France approached, and they set forth that were appointed to break the array of the archers. They entered a-horseback into the way where the great hedges were on both sides set full of archers. As soon as the men of arms entered, the archers began to shoot on both sides and did slay and hurt horses and knights, so that the horses when they felt the sharp arrows they would in no wise go forward, but drew aback and flang and took on so fiercely, that many of them fell on their masters, so that for press they could not rise again; insomuch that the marshals' battle could never come at the prince. Certain knights and squires that were well horsed passed through the archers and thought to approach to the prince, but they could not. The lord James Audley with his four squires was in the front of that battle and there did marvels in arms, and by great prowess he came and fought with sir Arnold d'Audrehem under his own banner, and there they fought long together and sir Arnold was there sore handled. The battle of the marshals began to disorder by reason of the shot of the archers with the aid of the men of arms, who came in among them and slew of them and did what they list, and there was the lord Arnold d'Audrehem taken prisoner by other men than by sir James Audley or by his four squires; for that day he never took prisoner, but always fought and went on his enemies.

Also on the French party the lord John Clermont fought under his own banner as long as he could endure: but there he was beaten down and could not be relieved nor ransomed, but was slain without mercy: some said it was because of the words that he had the day before to sir John Chandos. So within a short space the marshals' battles were discomfited, for they fell one upon another and could not go forth; and the Frenchmen that were behind and could not get forward reculed back and came on the battle of the duke of Normandy, the which was great and thick and were afoot, but anon they began to open behind; for when they knew that the marshals' battle was discomfited, they took their horses and departed, he that might best. Also they saw a rout of Englishmen coming down a little mountain a-horseback, and many archers with them, who brake in on the side of the duke's

The Black Prince at Poitiers

battle. True to say, the archers did their company that day great advantage; for they shot so thick that the Frenchmen wist not on what side to take heed, and little and little the Englishmen won ground on them.

And when the men of arms of England saw that the marshals' battle was discomfited and that the duke's battle began to disorder and open, they leapt then on their horses, the which they had ready by them: then they assembled together and cried, "Saint George! Guyenne!" and the lord Chandos said to the prince: "Sir, take your horse and ride forth; this journey is yours: God is this day in your hands: get us to the French king's battle, for their lieth all the sore of the matter. I think verily by his valiantness he will not fly: I trust we shall have him by the grace of God and Saint George, so he be well fought withal: and, sir, I heard you say that this day I should see you a good knight." The prince said, "Let us go forth; ye shall not see me this day return back," and said, "Advance, banner, in the name of God and of Saint George." The knight that bare it did his commandment: there was then a sore battle and a perilous, and many a man overthrown, and he that was once down could not be relieved again without great succour and aid. As the prince rode and entered in among his enemies, he saw on his right hand in a little bush lying dead the lord Robert of Duras and his banner by him, and a ten or twelve of his men about him. Then the prince said to two of his squires and to three archers: "Sirs, take the body of this knight on a targe and bear him to Poitiers, and present him from me to the cardinal of Perigord, and say how I salute him by that token." And this was done. The prince was informed that the cardinal's men were on the field against him, the which was not pertaining to the right order of arms, for men of the church that cometh and goeth for treaty of peace ought not by reason to bear harness nor to fight for neither of the parties ; they ought to be indifferent : and because these men had done so, the prince was displeased with the cardinal, and therefore he sent unto him his nephew the lord Robert of Duras dead : and the chatelain of Amposte was taken, and the prince would have had his head stricken off, because he was pertaining to the cardinal, but then the lord Chandos said : " Sir, suffer for a season : intend to a greater matter : and peradventure the cardinal will make such excuse that ye shall be content."

Then the prince and his company dressed them on the battle of the duke of Athens, constable of France. There was many a man slain and cast to the earth. As the Frenchmen fought in companies, they cried, " Mountjoy ! Saint Denis ! " and the Englishmen, " Saint George ! Guyenne ! " Anon the prince with his company met with the battle of Almains, whereof the earl of Sarrebruck, the earl Nassau and the earl Nidau were captains, but in a short space they were put to flight : the archers shot so wholly together that none durst come in their dangers : they slew many a man that could not come to no ransom : these three earls was there slain, and divers other knights and squires of their company, and there was the lord d'Aubrecicourt rescued by his own men and set on horseback, and after he did that day many feats of arms and took good prisoners. When the duke of Normandy's battle saw the prince approach, they thought to save themselves, and so the duke and the king's children, the earl of Poitiers and the earl of Touraine, who were right young, believed their governours and so departed from the field, and with them more than eight hundred spears, that strake no stroke that day. Howbeit the lord Guichard d'Angle and the lord John of Saintré, who were with the earl of Poitiers, would not fly, but entered into the thickest press of the battle. The king's three sons took the way to

The Black Prince at Poitiers

Chauvigny, and the lord John of Landas and the lord Thibauld of Vaudenay, who were set to await on the duke of Normandy, when they had brought the duke a long league from the battle, then they took leave of the duke and desired the lord of Saint-Venant that he should not leave the duke, but to bring him in safeguard, whereby he should win more thank of the king than to abide still in the field. Then they met also the duke of Orleans and a great company with him, who were also departed from the field with clear hands : there were many good knights and squires, though that their masters departed from the field, yet they had rather a died than to have had any reproach.

Oftentimes the adventures of amours and of war are more fortunate and marvellous than any man can think or wish. Truly this battle, the which was near to Poitiers in the fields of Beauvoir and Maupertuis, was right great and perilous, and many deeds of arms there was done the which all came not to knowledge. The fighters on both sides endured much pain : king John with his own hands did that day marvels in arms : he had an axe in his hands wherewith he defended himself and fought in the breaking of the press. Near to the king there was taken the earl of Tancarville, sir Jaques of Bourbon earl of Ponthieu, and the lord John of Artois earl of Eu, and a little above that under the banner of the captal of Buch was taken sir Charles of Artois and divers other knights and squires. The chase endured to the gates of Poitiers : there were many slain and beaten down, horse and man, for they of Poitiers closed their gates and would suffer none to enter ; wherefore in the street before the gate was horrible murder, men hurt and beaten down. The Frenchmen yielded themselves as far off as they might know an Englishman : there were divers English archers that had four, five or six prisoners : the lord of Pons, a great baron of Poitou, was there slain, and many other knights and squires; and there was taken the earl of Rochechouart, the lord of Dammartin, the lord of Partenay, and of Saintonge the lord of Montendre and the lord John of Saintré, but he was so sore hurt that he had never health after: he was reputed for one of the best knights in France. And there was left for dead among other dead men the lord Guichard d'Angle, who fought that day by the king right valiantly, and so did the lord of Charny, on whom was great press, because he bare the sovereign banner of the king's: his own banner was also in the field, the which was of gules, three scutcheons silver. So many Englishmen and Gascons came to that part, that perforce they opened the king's battle, so that the Frenchmen were so mingled among their enemies that sometime there was five men upon one gentleman. There was taken the lord of Pompadour and the lord Bartholomew de Burghersh, and there was slain sir Geoffrey of Charny with the king's banner in his hands: also the lord Raynold Cobham slew the earl of Dammartin. Then there was a great press to take the king, and such as knew him cried, "Sir, yield you, or else ye are but dead." There was a knight of Saint-Omer's, retained in wages with the king of England, called sir Denis Morbeke, who had served the Englishmen five year before, because in his youth he had forfeited the realm of France for a murder that he did at Saint-Omer's. It happened so well for him, that he was next to the king when they were about to take him: he stept forth into the press, and by strength of his body and arms he came to the French king and said in good French, "Sir, yield you." The king beheld the knight and said: "To whom shall I yield me? Where is my cousin the prince of Wales? If I might see him, I would speak with him." Denis answered and said: "Sir, he is not here; but yield you to me and I shall bring you to him." "Who be you?" quoth the king. " Sir," quoth he, " I am Denis of Morbeke, a knight of Artois ; but I serve the king of England because I am banished the realm of France and I have forfeited all that I had there." Then the king gave him his right gauntlet, saying, " I yield me to you." There was a great press about the king, for every man enforced him to say, " I have taken him," so that the king could not go forward with his young son the lord Philip with him because of the press.

The prince of Wales, who was courageous and cruel as a lion, took that day great pleasure to fight and to chase his enemies. The lord John Chandos, who was with him, of all that day never left him nor never took heed of taking of any prisoner : then at the end of the battle he said to the prince : " Sir, it were good that you rested here and set your banner a-high in this bush, that your people may draw hither, for they be sore spread abroad, nor I can see no more banners nor pennons of the French party ; wherefore, sir, rest and refresh you, for ye be sore chafed." Then the prince's banner was set up a-high on a bush, and trumpets and clarions began to sown. Then the prince did off his bassenet, and the knights for his body and they of his chamber were ready about him, and a red pavilion pight up, and then drink was brought forth to the prince and for such lords as were about him, the which still increased as they came from the chase : there they tarried and their prisoners with them. And when the two marshals were come to the prince, he demanded of them if they knew any tidings of the French king. They answered and said : " Sir, we hear none of certainty, but we think verily he is other dead or taken, for he is not gone out of the battles." Then the prince said to the earl of Warwick and to sir Raynold Cobham : " Sirs, I require you go forth and see what ye can know, that at your return ye may shew me the truth." These two lords took their

The Knapsack

horses and departed from the prince and rode up a little hill to look about them : then they perceived a flock of men of arms coming together right wearily : there was the French king afoot in great peril, for Englishmen and Gascons were his masters ; they had taken him from sir Denis Morbeke perforce, and such as were most of force said, " I have taken him " ; " Nay," quoth another, " I have taken him " : so they strave which should have him. Then the French king, to eschew that peril, said : " Sirs, strive not : lead me courteously, and my son, to my cousin the prince, and strive not for my taking, for I am so great a lord to make you all rich." The king's words somewhat appeased them ; howbeit ever as they went they made riot and brawled for the taking of the king. When the two foresaid lords saw and heard that noise and strife among them, they came to them and said : " Sirs, what is the matter that ye strive for ? " " Sirs," said one of them, " it is for the French king, who is here taken prisoner, and there be more than ten knights and squires that challengeth the taking of him and of his son." Then the two lords entered into the press and caused every man to draw aback, and commanded them in the prince's name on pain of their heads to make no more noise nor to approach the king no nearer, without they were commanded. Then every man gave room to the lords, and they alighted and did their reverence to the king, and so brought him and his son in peace and rest to the prince of Wales.

The same day of the battle at night the prince made a supper in his lodging to the French king and to the most part of the great lords that were prisoners. The prince made the king and his son, the lord James of Bourbon, the lord John d'Artois, the earl of Tancarville, the earl of Estampes, the earl Dammartin, the earl of Joinville and the lord of Partenay to sit all at one board, and other lords, knights and squires at other tables; and always the prince served before the king as humbly as he could, and would not sit at the king's board for any desire that the king could make, but he said he was not sufficient to sit at the table with so great a prince as the king was. But then he said to the king: "Sir, for God's sake make none evil nor heavy cheer, though God this day did not consent to follow your will; for, sir, surely the king my father shall bear you as much honour and amity as he may do, and shall accord with you so reasonably that ye shall ever be friends together after. And, sir, methink ye ought to rejoice, though the journey be not as ye would have had it, for this day ye have won the high renown of prowess and have passed this day in valiantness all other of your party. Sir, I say not this to mock you, for all that be on our party, that saw every man's deeds, are plainly accorded by true sentence to give you the prize and chaplet." Therewith the Frenchmen began to murmur and said among themselves how the prince had spoken nobly, and that by all estimation he should prove a noble man, if God send him life and to persevere in such good fortune.

SIR JOHN FROISSART

12 *A Poor Woman of Bruges*

WHEN the earl of Flanders and the company that was about him saw the evil order and rule of them of Bruges, and saw how they were discomfited by their own folly, and could see no recoverance, for they fled away before the Gauntois, the earl then was abashed and all they that were about him, and so discomfited that they fled away every man to save himself. Of a truth, if they of Bruges would have returned again and assailed the Gauntois with their help, they had been likely to have recovered all again; but they saw no remedy, for they fled toward Bruges as fast as they might, the father tarried not for the son nor the son for the father. So then the men of arms and all brake their array, but they had no list to take the way to Bruges: the press was so great in the way toward Bruges, that it was marvel to see, and to hear the clamour and cry of them that were slain and hurt, and the Gauntois following them of Bruges crying, "Gaunt, Gaunt!" still going forward and beating down of people. The most part of the men of arms would not put themselves in that peril: howbeit, the earl was counselled to draw to Bruges and to be one of the first that should enter, and then to close the gates, to the intent that the Gauntois should not be lords of Bruges. The earl seeing none other remedy, nor no recoverance by abiding in the field, for he saw well every man fled and also it was dark night, wherefore he believed the counsel that was given him and so took the way toward Bruges with his banner before him, and so came to the gate and entered with the first, and a forty with him: then he set men to keep the gate, and to close it if the Gauntois did follow. Then the earl rode to his own lodging and sent all about the town commanding every man on pain of death to draw to the market-place. The intention of the earl was to recover the town by that means; but he did not, as ye shall hear after.

In the mean time that the earl was at his lodging and sent forth the clerks of every ward from street to street, to have every man to draw to the market-place to recover the town, the Gauntois pursued so fiercely their enemies, that they entered into the town with them of Bruges; and as soon as they were within the town, the first thing they did they went straight to the market-place and there set themselves in array. The earl as then had sent a knight of his called sir Robert Marescal to the gate to see what the Gauntois did, and when he came to the gate, he found the gate beaten down and the Gauntois masters thereof; and some of them of Bruges met with him and said: "Sir Robert, return and save yourself if ye can, for the town is won by them of Gaunt." Then the knight returned to the earl as fast as he might, who was coming out of his lodging a-horseback with a great number of cressets and lights with him, and was going to the market-place. Then the knight shewed the earl all that he knew: howbeit, the earl, willing to recover the town, drew to the market-place; and as he was entering, such as were before him seeing the place all ranged with the Gauntois, said to the earl: "Sir, return again: if ye go any farther ye are but dead or taken with your enemies, for they are ranged on the market-place and do abide for you." They shewed him truth; and when the Gauntois saw the clearness of the lights coming down the street, they said: "Yonder cometh the earl: he shall come into our hands." And Philip d'Arteveld had commanded from street to street as he went, that if the earl came among them, that no man should do to him any bodily harm, but take him alive and then to have him to Gaunt, and so to make their peace as they list. The earl, who trusted to have recovered all, came right near to the place whereas the Gauntois were. Then divers of his men said: "Sir, go no farther, for the Gauntois are lords of the market-place and of the town: if ye enter into the market-place, ye are in danger to be slain or taken: a great number of the Gauntois are going from street to street seeking for their enemies: they have certain of them of the town with them to bring them from house to house, whereas they would be. And, sir, out at any of the gates ye cannot issue, for the Gauntois are lords thereof; nor to your own lodging ye cannot return, for a great number of the Gauntois are going thither."

And when the earl heard those tidings, which were right hard to him, as it was reason, he was greatly then abashed and imagined what peril he was in. Then he believed the counsel and would go no farther, but to save himself if he might, and so took his own counsel. He commanded to put out all the lights, and said to them that were about him : " I see well there is no recovery : let every man depart and save himself as well as he may " : and as he commanded it was done ; the lights were quenched and cast into the streets, and so every man departed. The earl then went into a back lane and made a varlet of his to unarm him, and did cast away his armour and put on an old cloak of his varlet's, and then said to him : " Go thy way from me and save thyself if thou canst ; and have a good tongue, an thou fall in the hands of thine enemies, and if they ask thee anything of me, be not beknown that I am in the town." He answered and said : " Sir, to die therefor I will speak no word of you." Thus abode there the earl of Flanders all alone : he might then well say that he was in great danger and hard adventure, for at that time, if he had fallen in the hands of his enemies, he had been in danger of death ; for the Gauntois went from house to house searching for the earl's friends, and ever as they found any they brought them into the market-place, and there without remedy before Philip d'Arteveld and the captains they were put to death. So God was friend to the earl, to save him out of that peril : he was never in such danger before in his life, nor never after, as ye shall hear after in this history.

Thus about the hour of midnight the earl went from street to street and by back lanes, so that at last he was fain to take a house, or else he had been found by them of Gaunt ; and so, as he went about the town, he entered into a poor woman's house, the which was not meet for such a lord : there was nother hall, palace nor chamber, it was but a poor smoky house, there was nothing but a poor hall, black with smoke, and above a small plancher and a

A Poor Woman of Bruges

ladder of seven steps to mount upon, and on the plancher there was a poor couch, whereas the poor woman's children lay. Then the earl, sore abashed and trembling, at his entering said : " O good woman, save me : I am thy lord the earl of Flanders ; but now I must hide me, for mine enemies chase me, and if ye do me good now, I shall reward you hereafter therefor." The poor woman knew him well, for she had been oftentimes at his gate to fetch alms, and had often seen him as he went in and out a-sporting ; and so incontinent, as hap was, she answered, for if she had made any delay, he had been taken talking with her by the fire. Then she said : " Sir, mount up this ladder and lay yourself under the bed that ye find, thereas my children sleep " : and so in the mean time the woman sate down by the fire with another child that she had in her arms. So the earl mounted up the plancher as well as he might, and crept in between the couch and the straw and lay as flat as he could : and even therewith some of the rutters of Gaunt entered into the same house, for some of them said how they had seen a man enter into the house before them ; and so they found the woman sitting by the fire with her child. Then they said : " Good woman, where is the man that we saw enter before us into this house, and did shut the door after him ? " " Sirs," quoth she, " I saw no man enter into this house this night. I went out right now and cast out a little water and did close my door again. If any were here, I could not tell how to hide him : ye see all the easement that I have in this house : here ye may see my bed, and here above this plancher lieth my poor children." Then one of them took a candle and mounted up the ladder and put up his head above the plancher, and saw there none other thing but the poor couch, where her children lay and slept, and so he looked all about and then said to his company : " Go we hence ; we lose the more for the less : the poor woman saith truth ;

here is no creature but she and her children " : and then they departed out of the house. After that there was none entered to do any hurt. All these words the earl heard right well, whereas he lay under the poor couch : ye may well imagine then that he was in great fear of his life : he might well say, " I am as now one of the poorest princes of the world," and might well say that the fortunes of the world are nothing stable. Yet it was a good hap that he scaped with his life : howbeit, this hard and perilous adventure might well be to him a spectacle all his life after and an ensample to all other.

SIR JOHN FROISSART

13 *The Death of Talbot*

WHEN therefore the men of Bordeaux were assembled in the presence of this Talbot, they showed him how King Charles and his army were already far entered, and had overrun the countries of Guienne and Bordeaux with great puissance of men-at-arms : then they reminded him how that they had given over the said town and city of Bordeaux on condition that he should fight against the King of France and his puissance if he came into the aforesaid country, and they submitted to him how he had said more than once, while they were making the aforesaid treaty of surrender, that he needed but ten thousand fighting men to make head against the French armies. " Wherefore," said they, " If you will keep your promise given when this city made obeisance and subjection to you, now is the hour and time for the accomplishment thereof. We pray you go and raise the siege which the French have laid to the town of Châtillon in Périgord." Talbot, hearing these words, and recognising that they had reason, showed no

The Death of Talbot

change of countenance at this complaint, but answered them coolly enough, for he was full of natural good sense and valiant in battle as any knight that bore arms in those days ; thus then he said to them : " We may let them come nearer still ; yet be sure that, God willing, I will keep my promise when I see due time and opportunity." Upon which answer those of the town of Bordeaux showed a face of discontent, misdoubting that this Talbot had no great intention and will to do what he said ; nay, they even began to murmur sore one with the other, which was told to my lord Talbot ; whereof he was inwardly troubled, and resolved forthwith to send for all who were dispersed in the garrisons of towns and fortresses that obeyed the English around Bordeaux, and for the garrison of the town of Bordeaux itself. He made such haste that within a few days he had from eight to ten thousand fighting men gathered together. Then on St Mary Magdalene's Day, which fell on a Monday that year (1453), he set out from the good city of Bordeaux with his company, and lay that same night at a place called Libourne, five leagues distant from Bordeaux and three leagues from the aforesaid town of Châtillon. But to know and better discover the bearing of the French his enemies, who were lodged before this town of Châtillon, he sent his spies secretly around their quarters ; moreover he sent word to those who were within the said town that they should take courage, for he came with might and puissance, intending to succour them ; and he bade them prepare themselves on the morrow when they should see him approach, that each man might be under arms and ready to sally forth without their walls and fall upon the enemy, for he was purposed, as he told them, never to turn back until he had driven away the beleaguering army or were slain himself in the fight. At which news those of Châtillon were filled with joy, and took good heart again, for it seemed to them that the lord

The Knapsack

Talbot had great will to succour them, forasmuch as he came so hastily and that the French had as yet only lain two days about the town ; wherefore they sent back word that he should come when it pleased him, but they thought it fitting that he should first of all drive out those who were lodged in the abbey hard by their town, and that they, for their part, would come and help him with all their might, in this assault. Which news being thus brought back to him, he started without long delay from his lodging in Libourne and marched all night long until he came to a wood hard by the aforesaid abbey, wherein were lodged the free-archers of the duchies of Anjou and Périgord, who had with them Pierre de Bauval lieutenant to Charles of Anjou, count of Maine, who commanded this guard with the aforesaid Joachim Rohault. Since, therefore, this Talbot had purposed to carry out his enterprise, and the French that lay in the aforesaid abbey had no tidings of his coming, then the Tuesday following at daybreak he drew with all his company towards this abbey, raising a terrible shout, at the sound whereof the French, who were within, fell into rout, and issued forth with the purpose of gaining the park, whereof we have already spoken and wherein those of their party were lodged ; and in this disorder the aforesaid free-archers sallied forth, and Pierre de Bauval and Joachim Rohault stayed behind, bearing the burden of the fight for a long space, making head against the English and withdrawing step by step towards the park. Yet, albeit the French who were therein became aware of the great travail which their own folk must needs undergo that had fled forth from the abbey, nevertheless they advanced not, nor brought no help nor succour to their comrades, by reason whereof in the very first onset five or six nobles were killed on the French part. Moreover the said Joachim, through his own valour, was more than once stricken to the ground ; but by the help of the free-

The Death of Talbot

archers, who loved him well, he was raised up and remounted on his horse ; whereon afterwards he did deeds of great prowess, for he had sworn to his free-archers that he would live and die with them ; and, for all that the English might do, yet the French reached the park ; but, before they had reached it, there were done great deeds and fair feats of arms on either side, and of the two parties some four-score or hundred men were left on that field. After which the lord Talbot, seeing that the French had gained the park, turned back to the abbey where he lodged, to take refreshment with his men ; wherein he found much victual which the French had brought thither, with five or six pipes and barrels of wine, which were forthwith burst open and put at the mercy of all the soldiers, by reason whereof they lasted but a short while ; and, seeing that the aforesaid skirmish had been begun and ended so early and that Talbot had as yet heard no mass, his chaplain made ready to sing one, and the altar with its ornaments was ready prepared. In the meanwhile he was of too light credence, for he gave faith to a man who brought him nought but lies, saying as it were in these words : " My lord, the French leave their park and flee away ; now is the hour or never, if ye will accomplish your promise." Alas ! here is a fair example for all princes, lords, and captains, who have people subjected to their governance, that they should not set too light faith in such tidings ; for in so weighty a matter we must not build upon the tale of a jongleur, but of true and loyal officers-at-arms, as of a knight or gentleman, sure of his mouth. But my lord Talbot, for the great desire that he had to serve King Henry his sovereign lord, and also to keep his promise made to the aforesaid town and city of Bordeaux, did otherwise at this time ; for, believing too lightly that these tidings were true, he left to hear the mass against his first purpose, and, issuing forthwith from this abbey, he was heard to say these words following : " Never shall I hear the mass until this day I shall have put to rout the company of the French whom I see before me in this park." Notwithstanding therefore that the French in the park were sore moved and troubled by the pursuit which my lord Talbot had made upon those who had fled from the abbey, yet they disposed their artillery straight in the vanguard on that side whereon they saw my lord Talbot come with his company, which advanced in excellent fair array with many trumpets and clarions sounding. Then these English uttered a horrible and terrible cry, shouting with all their voices : " Talbot, Talbot, St George ! " but, as they drew near to the park, an ancient gentleman of England who had seen and experienced in his life many doughty deeds of war, perceived that the French within the park gave no ground, whereupon, seeing that they were posted in a strong and advantageous place and that the tidings of their pretended flight were false, he said to the lord Talbot : " My lord, my counsel would be that ye should return again, for ye may well see how the tidings brought unto you were untrue. Ye see their camp and their bearing ; ye will gain nought at this time." At which words my lord Talbot was sore displeased, and made him a rough answer with exceeding injurious words : nay even, (if it be true that I have heard,) after this speech he struck him with the sword across the visage, of which stroke he died afterwards ; but of this I have never learned the right truth. Certain it is, nevertheless, that my lord Talbot followed the counsel of his own great valiance and marched on towards the park, at the entry whereof he caused his standard to be planted upon one of the stakes wherewith the entrance-gate on that side was closed ; and the standard-bearer, whose name I could never learn, clasped the stake with the lance of the banner, at which point and in which posture he was slain, and the standard

The Death of Talbot

smitten down to the earth in the ditch of the park. Then the English, by reason of the great number of artillery which the French had within their park and which played upon them with all their might, began to fall into disorder ; for at the entrance there, and at the planting of the aforesaid standard, some five or six hundred English were slain, which caused them great fear and rout ; seeing which the French opened the gate of their park and sallied forth, not only there but by the other gates, and over the ditches. Then they came valiantly to fight the English hand to hand, where marvellous deeds of arms were done on either side. In this sally the aforesaid lord Talbot, who was armed with a brigantine covered with scarlet velvet, was slain by a dagger-thrust in the throat, for he had already received a stroke across his face, and was sore wounded with arrows through the thighs and the legs ; and I have been assured by heralds and officers-at-arms, and by many lords and gentlemen, that at this hour and in that fight 4000 men or more were slain with Talbot, among whom were the son and one of the nephews of the aforesaid lord Talbot, and another whom men called the Bastard of England. The rest, seeing this defeat, withdrew ; some within the town of Châtillon, and others fleeing through the woods and through the river, wherein great numbers were drowned. Moreover a good two hundred were taken prisoners. All that day the dead lay exposed on the earth, and the French had much ado to know the truth of the death of the lord Talbot, for some assured that he had been slain, while others said, " No." When therefore all had been somewhat appeased, many officers-at-arms and heralds were sent to seek for the lord Talbot among the dead ; in which search they found among the rest a dead man who seemed somewhat advanced in age, and whom they surmised to be this same lord. Wherefore they laid him on an archer's shield and brought him

The Knapsack

into their park ; in which place he lay all night. Meanwhile there was much question, with great difficulty and doubt in the company of the lords and others, who said they had known and seen him in his lifetime, concerning the truth of his death ; for, though such as affirmed themselves to have known and seen him well maintained that this was he, yet there were many others who said the contrary. But on the morrow there came upon the field many heralds and officers-at-arms of the English party, among whom was the herald of lord Talbot himself, who bare his coat-of-arms ; which heralds besought grace to have leave and permission to seek for their master. Then men asked this herald of the lord Talbot whether he would know him well by sight, whereunto he answered joyously (deeming that he was yet alive and captive) that he would fain see him ; whereupon he was brought to the place where Talbot lay dead upon the archer's shield, where the men said unto him : " Look and see if this be your master." Then forthwith his colour was changed ; yet at first he withheld his judgment, not saying what he thought, for he saw his master much changed and disfigured by the stroke which he had in his face ; moreover he had lain there since his death all that night through and all the morrow until that hour ; wherefore he was much changed. Yet the herald kneeled down beside him, saying that he would presently know the truth. Then he thrust one of the fingers of his right hand into his lord's mouth, to seek on the left-hand side the place of a great tooth which he knew him certainly to have lost, which place he found, as his purpose was ; and no sooner had he found it than, being on his knees as we have said, he kissed the dead man on the mouth, saying : " My lord and master, my lord and master, it is you ! I pray to God that He pardon your misdeeds. I have been your officer-at-arms these forty years or more, and it is time that I render you all

your loving-kindness!" making in the meanwhile piteous cries and lamentations, and raining piteously with salt tears from his eyes. Then he drew off his coat-of-arms and laid it on his master: by which recognition there was an end of the question and debate which had been made concerning the good lord's death.

MATHIEU DE COUSSY

14 *The Retreat to Coruña*

WHILST we lay exhausted in the road, the rear guard, which was now endeavouring to drive on the stragglers, approached, and a sergeant of the Rifles came up and stopped to look at us. He addressed himself to me, and ordered me to rise; but I told him it was useless for him to trouble himself about me, as I was unable to move a step further. Whilst he was urging me to endeavour to rise up, the officer in command of the rear guard also stepped up. The name of this officer was Lieutenant Cox; he was a brave and good man, and observing that the sergeant was rough in his language and manner towards me, he silenced him, and bade the guard proceed, and leave me. "Let him die quietly, Hicks," he said to the sergeant. "I know him well; he's not the man to lie here if he could get on. I am sorry, Harris," he said, "to see you reduced to this, for I fear there is no help to be had now." He then moved on after his men, and left me to my fate.

After lying still for awhile, I felt somewhat restored, and sat up to look about me. The sight was by no means cheering. On the road behind me I saw men, women, mules, and horses, lying at intervals, both dead and dying; whilst far away in front I could just discern the

D*

The Knapsack

enfeebled army crawling out of sight, the women [1] huddled together in its rear, trying their best to get forward amongst those of the sick soldiery, who were now unable to keep up with the main body. After awhile, I found that my companion, the sergeant, who lay beside me, had also recovered a little, and I tried to cheer him up. I told him that opposite to where we were lying there was a lane down which we might possibly find some place of shelter, if we could muster strength to explore it. The sergeant consented to make the effort, but after two or three attempts to rise, gave it up. I myself was more fortunate : with the aid of my rifle I got upon my legs, and seeing death in my companion's face, I resolved to try and save myself, since it was quite evident to me that I could render him no assistance.

After hobbling some distance down the lane, to my great joy I espied a small hut or cabin, with a little garden in its front ; I therefore opened the small door of the hovel, and was about to enter, when I considered that most likely I should be immediately knocked on the head by the inmates if I did so. The rain, I remember, was coming down in torrents at this time, and, reflecting that to remain outside was but to die, I resolved at all events to try my luck within. I had not much strength left ; but I resolved to sell myself as dearly as I could. I therefore brought up my rifle, and stepped across the threshold. As soon as I had done so, I observed an old woman seated beside a small fire upon the hearth. She turned her head as I entered, and immediately upon seeing a strange soldier, she arose, and filled the hovel with her screams. As I drew back within the doorway, an elderly man, followed

---

[1] Some of these poor wretches cut a ludicrous figure, having the men's great-coats buttoned over their heads, whilst their clothing being extremely ragged and scanty, their naked legs were very conspicuous. They looked a tribe of travelling beggars.

by two, who were apparently his sons, rushed from a room in the interior. They immediately approached me ; but I brought up my rifle again, and cocked it, bidding them keep their distance.

After I had thus brought them to a parley, I got together what little Spanish I was master of, and begged for shelter for the night and a morsel of food, at the same time lifting my feet and displaying them a mass of bleeding sores. It was not, however, till they had held a tolerably long conversation among themselves that they consented to afford me shelter ; and then only upon the condition that I left by daylight on the following morning. I accepted the conditions with joy. Had they refused me, I should indeed not have been here to tell the tale. Knowing the treachery of the Spanish character, I however refused to relinquish possession of my rifle, and my right hand was ready in an instant to unsheath my bayonet as they sat and stared at me whilst I devoured the food they offered.

All they gave me was some coarse black bread, and a pitcher of sour wine. It was, however, acceptable to a half-famished man ; and I felt greatly revived by it. Whilst I supped, the old hag, who sat close beside the hearth, stirred up the embers that they might have a better view of their guest, and the party meanwhile overwhelmed me with questions, which I could neither comprehend nor had strength to answer. I soon made signs to them that I was unable to maintain the conversation, and begged of them, as well as I could, to show me some place where I might lay my wearied limbs till dawn.

Notwithstanding the weariness which pervaded my whole body, I was unable for some time to sleep except by fitful snatches, such was the fear I entertained of having my throat cut by the savage-looking wretches still seated before the fire. Besides which, the place they had permitted me to crawl into was more like an oven than anything else, and being merely a sort of berth scooped out of the wall was so filled with fleas and other vermin that I was stung and tormented most miserably all night long.

Bad as they had been, however, I felt somewhat restored by my lodging and supper, and with the dawn I crawled out of my lair, left the hut, retraced my steps along the lane, and once more emerged upon the high-road, where I found my companion, the sergeant, dead, and lying where I had left him the night before.

I now made the best of my way along the road in the direction in which I had last seen our army retreating the night before. A solitary individual, I seemed left behind amongst those who had perished. It was still raining, I remember, on this morning, and the very dead looked comfortless in their last sleep, as I passed them occasionally lying on the line of march.

It had pleased Heaven to give me an iron constitution, or I must have failed, I think, on this day, for the solitary journey and the miserable spectacles I beheld rather damped my spirits.

After progressing some miles, I came up with a cluster of poor devils who were still alive, but apparently, both men and women, unable to proceed. They were sitting huddled together in the road, their heads drooping forward, and apparently patiently awaiting their end.

Soon after passing these unfortunates, I overtook a party who were being urged forward under charge of an officer of the 42nd Highlanders. He was pushing them along pretty much as a drover would keep together a tired flock of sheep. They presented a curious example of a retreating force. Many of them had thrown away their weapons, and were linked together arm in arm, in order to support each other, like a party of drunkards. They were, I saw, composed of various regiments ; many were bare-headed, and without shoes ; and some with their heads tied up in old rags and fragments of handkerchiefs.

I marched in company with this party for some time, but as I felt after my night's lodging and refreshment in better condition I ventured to push forwards, in the hope of rejoining the main body, and which I once more came up with in the street of a village.

On falling in with the Rifles I again found Brooks, who was surprised at seeing me still alive ; and we both entered a house, and begged for something to drink. I remember that I had a shirt upon my back at this time, which I had purchased of a drummer of the 9th regiment before the commencement of the retreat. It was the only good one I had ; I stripped, with the assistance of Brooks, and took it off, and exchanged it with a Spanish woman for a loaf of bread, which Brooks, myself, and two other men shared amongst us.

I remember to have again remarked Craufurd at this period of the retreat. He was no whit altered in his desire to keep the force together I thought ; but still active and vigilant as ever he seemed to keep his eye upon those who were now most likely to hold out. I myself marched during many hours close beside him this day. He looked stern and pale ; but the very picture of a warrior. I shall never forget Craufurd if I live to a hundred years, I think. He was in everything a soldier.

Slowly and dejectedly crawled our army along. Their spirit of endurance was now considerably worn out, and judging from my own sensations, I felt confident that if the sea was much further from us, we must be content to come to a halt at last without gaining it. I felt something like the approach of death as I proceeded—a sort of horror, mixed up with my sense of illness—a feeling I have never experienced before or since. Still I held on ;

The Knapsack

but with all my efforts, the main body again left me behind. Had the enemy's cavalry come up at this time I think they would have had little else to do but ride us down without striking a blow.

It is, however, indeed astonishing how man clings to life. I am certain that had I lain down at this period, I should have found my last billet on the spot I sank upon. Suddenly I heard a shout in front, which was prolonged in a sort of hubbub. Even the stragglers whom I saw dotting the road in front of me seemed to have caught at something like hope ; and as the poor fellows now reached the top of a hill we were ascending, I heard an occasional exclamation of joy—the first note of the sort I had heard for many days. When I reached the top of the hill the thing spoke for itself. There, far away in our front, the English shipping lay in sight.

Its view had indeed acted like a restorative to our force, and the men, at the prospect of a termination to the march, had plucked up spirit for a last effort. Fellows who, like myself, seemed to have hardly strength in their legs to creep up the ascent seemed now to have picked up a fresh pair to get down with. Such is hope to us poor mortals !

There was, I recollect, a man of the name of Bell, of the Rifles, who had been during this day holding a sort of creeping race with me—we had passed and repassed each other, as our strength served. Bell was rather a discontented fellow at the best of times ; but during this retreat he had given full scope to his ill-temper, cursing the hour he was born, and wishing his mother had strangled him when he came into the world, in order to have saved him from his present toil. He had not now spoken for some time, and the sight of the English shipping had apparently a very beneficial effect upon him. He burst into tears as he stood and looked at it.

The Retreat to Coruña

"Harris," he said, "if it pleases God to let me reach those ships, I swear never to utter a bad or discontented word again."

As we proceeded down the hill we now met with the first symptoms of good feeling from the inhabitants it was our fortune to experience during our retreat. A number of old women stood on either side the road, and occasionally handed us fragments of bread as we passed them. It was on this day, and whilst I looked anxiously upon the English shipping in the distance, that I first began to find my eyesight failing, and it appeared to me that I was fast growing blind. The thought was alarming ; and I made desperate efforts to get on. Bell, however, won the race this time. He was a very athletic and strong-built fellow, and left me far behind, so that I believe at that time I was the very last of the retreating force that reached the beach, though doubtless many stragglers came dropping up after the ships had sailed, and were left behind.

As it was, when I did manage to gain the sea-shore, it was only by the aid of my rifle that I could stand, and my eyes were now so dim and heavy that with difficulty I made out a boat which seemed the last that had put off.

Fearful of being left half blind in the lurch, I took off my cap, and placed it on the muzzle of my rifle as a signal, for I was totally unable to call out. Luckily, Lieutenant Cox, who was aboard the boat, saw me, and ordered the men to return, and, making one more effort, I walked into the water, and a sailor stretching his body over the gunwale, seized me as if I had been an infant, and hauled me on board. His words were characteristic of the English sailor, I thought.

"Hollo there, you lazy lubber ! " he said, as he grasped hold of me, " who the h—ll do you think is to stay humbugging all day for such a fellow as you ? "

The Knapsack

The boat, I found, was crowded with our exhausted men, who lay helplessly at the bottom, the heavy sea every moment drenching them to the skin. As soon as we reached the vessel's side, the sailors immediately aided us to get on board, which in our exhausted state was not a very easy matter, as they were obliged to place ropes in our hands, and heave us up by setting their shoulders under us, and hoisting away as if they had been pushing bales of goods on board.

"Heave away!" cried one of the boat's crew, as I clung to a rope, quite unable to pull myself up, "heave away, you lubber!"

The tar placed his shoulder beneath me as he spoke, and hoisted me up against the ship's side; I lost my grasp of the rope and should have fallen into the sea had it not been for two of the crew. These men grasped me as I was falling, and drew me into the port-hole like a bundle of foul clothes, tearing away my belt and bayonet in the effort, which fell into the sea.

It was not very many minutes after I was on board, for I lay where the sailors had first placed me after dragging me through the port-hole, ere I was sound asleep. I slept long and heavily, and it was only the terrible noise and bustle on board consequent upon a gale having sprung up, that at length awoke me. The wind increased as the night came on, and soon we had to experience all the horrors of a storm at sea. The pumps were set to work; the sails were torn to shreds; the coppers were overset; and we appeared in a fair way, I thought, of going to the bottom. Meanwhile, the pumps were kept at work night and day incessantly till they were choked; and the gale growing worse and worse, all the soldiery were ordered below, and the hatches closed; soon after which the vessel turned over on one side, and lay a helpless log upon the water. In this situation an officer was placed over us, with his sword drawn in one hand, and a lantern in the other, in order to keep us on the side which was uppermost, so as to give the vessel a chance of righting herself in the roaring tide. The officer's task was not an easy one as the heaving waves frequently sent us sprawling from the part we clung to, over to the lowermost part of the hold where he stood, and he was obliged every minute to drive us back.

We remained in this painful situation for, I should think, five or six hours, expecting every instant to be our last, when, to our great joy, the sea suddenly grew calm, the wind abated, the vessel righted herself, and we were once more released from our prison, having tasted nothing in the shape of food for at least forty-eight hours. Soon after this we arrived in sight of Spithead, where we saw nine of our convoy, laden with troops, which had been driven on shore in the gale. After remaining off Spithead for about five or six days, one fine morning we received orders to disembark, and our poor bare feet once more touched English ground. The inhabitants flocked down to the beach to see us as we did so, and they must have been a good deal surprised at the spectacle we presented. Our beards were long and ragged ; almost all were without shoes and stockings ; many had their clothes and accoutrements in fragments, with their heads swathed in old rags, and our weapons were covered with rust ; whilst not a few had now, from toil and fatigue, become quite blind.

Let not the reader, however, think that even now we were to be despised as soldiers. Long marches, inclement weather, and want of food, had done their work upon us ; but we were perhaps better than we appeared, as the sequel showed. Under the gallant Craufurd we had made some tremendous marches, and even galled our enemies severely making good our retreat by the way of

Vigo. But our comrades in adversity, and who had retired by the other road to Coruña, under General Moore, turned to bay there, and showed the enemy that the English soldier is not to be beaten even under the most adverse circumstances.

The field of death and slaughter, the march, the bivouac, and the retreat, are no bad places in which to judge of men. I have had some opportunities of judging them in all these situations, and I should say that the British are amongst the most splendid soldiers in the world. Give them fair play, and they are unconquerable. For my own part I can only say that I enjoyed life more whilst on active service than I have ever done since ; and as I sit at work in my shop in Richmond Street, Soho, I look back upon that portion of my time spent in the fields of the Peninsula as the only part worthy of remembrance. It is at such times that scenes long passed come back upon my mind as if they had taken place but yesterday. I remember even the very appearance of some of the regiments engaged ; and comrades, long mouldered to dust, I see again performing the acts of heroes.

RIFLEMAN HARRIS

15 *Hunger*

THIS day's march was not so long as the preceding one ; it was still daylight when we stopped. A village had been burnt down, and only a few rafters here and there remained. The officers encamped against these for the night, getting a little shelter this way. Besides the fearful pains we felt all over through our great fatigue, we were by this time quite famishing. Those of us who still had a little rice or oatmeal hid themselves to eat it in secret.

Hunger

We had no friends left ; we looked suspiciously at each other, and even turned against our best comrade. I will not keep back a base act of ingratitude I committed against my truest friends. Like everyone else that day, I was devoured by hunger ; but besides that, I was also devoured by vermin I had got the previous day. We had not even a bit of horseflesh to eat, and we were waiting for some men of our company to come up who had stayed behind to cut up the fallen horses. I was standing near one of my friends, Poumot, a sergeant, close to a fire we had made, in quite indescribable torment, and looking round continually to see if no one was coming. Suddenly I seized his hand convulsively, and said :

" Look here : if I met anyone in the wood with a loaf of bread, I should force him to give me half ! " And then, correcting myself, " No," I said, " I would kill him to have it all ! "

Almost before I had finished I strode off towards the wood, just as if I expected to meet the man and the loaf. When I got there, I roamed about for a quarter of an hour, and then, turning in the opposite direction from our bivouac, close by the borders of the wood, I saw a man seated near a fire. On the fire was a pot in which something was evidently cooking, as the man took a knife and, plunging it into the pot, drew out a potato, which he pinched, and then put back again, as if it were not boiled enough.

I ran towards him as hard as I could, but fearing that he might escape me, I made a little circuit, so as to come up behind him without his seeing me. The brushwood crackled, however, as I came through, and he turned round ; but before he had time to speak, I said :

" Look here, comrade : you must either sell or give me your potatoes, or I shall carry away the pot by force ! "

He seemed quite taken by surprise, and as I put out my

sword to fish with it in the pot, he said it did not belong to him, but to his master, a Polish General, who was camping close by, and that he had been ordered to hide himself here to cook the potatoes ready for the next day.

Without answering him, I offered him money, and began to take the potatoes. He told me they were not boiled enough yet, and as I seemed not to believe him, he took one out for me to feel. I tore it from him, and devoured it just as it was.

" They are not fit to eat—you can see that for yourself," he said ; " hide yourself for a little while, try to be patient, and don't let anyone see you till the potatoes are boiled, and then I will give you some."

I did as he bade me, hiding behind a bush, but not losing sight of him. After about five or six minutes, thinking no doubt that I was some distance off, he looked stealthily to right and left, and taking the pot, he ran off with it. Not far, however, as I soon stopped him, and threatened to take the whole if he did not give me half. He said again that the potatoes belonged to his General.

" I must have them if they are the Emperor's," I cried. " I am dying of hunger."

Seeing he could not get rid of me, he gave me seven. I paid him fifteen francs, and left him. He then called me back, and gave me two more. They were hardly cooked at all, but that did not matter much to me. I ate one, and put the rest in my bag. I reckoned that, with a little horseflesh, they would last me for three days, allowing two each day.

As I walked on, thinking of my potatoes, I lost my way. I was made aware of this by hearing cries and curses from five men, who were fighting like dogs ; the leg of a horse on the ground was the cause of the disturbance. One of them, on seeing me, told me that he and his companion, both artillery soldiers, had killed a horse behind the wood,

Hunger

and that, on returning with their portion, they had been attacked by three men of another regiment. If I would help them they would give me a share. I feared the same sort of fate for my potatoes, so I replied that I could not wait, but that if they could hold on for a little I would send some people to help them. A little further on I met two men in our regiment to whom I told the story. The next day I heard that when they got to the place they only saw a man lying dead, covered with blood, killed by a great pine cudgel at his side. Probably the three aggressors had taken advantage of the absence of one of their enemies to fall on the other.

When at length I got back to my regiment, several of the men asked me if I had found anything. I answered " No," and, taking my place near the fire, I hollowed out a bed in the snow, stretched my bearskin coat to lie on, a cape lined with ermine for my head. Before going to sleep, I had my potato to eat. Hiding it by my cape, I was as quiet as possible, terrified lest anyone should observe that I was eating. I had a little snow for drink, and then went to sleep, holding my bag containing the rest of my provisions fast in my arms. Several times in the night, as I woke, I put in my hand, carefully counting my potatoes ; so I passed the night without sharing with my starving companions the bit of luck I had had. I shall never forgive myself for this selfishness. I was awake and sitting on my knapsack before the reveille sounded in the morning. I saw that a terrible day was in store for us, on account of the high wind. I made a hole in my bearskin coat, and put my head through it. The bear's head fell over my chest, and the rest over my back, but it was so long that it dragged on the ground. Before dawn we set out. We left behind us an enormous number of dead and dying. Further on it was worse still, as we had to stride over the dead bodies left on the road by the regiments going before

The Knapsack

113. It was worst of all for the rear-guard, as these were witnesses of all the horrors left by the whole army. The last corps were those commanded by Marshal Ney and Davoust, and the army of Italy under Prince Eugène. Daylight appeared when we had been marching for about an hour, and, as we had come up with the corps in front of us, we halted. Our *cantinière*, Mother Dubois, took advantage of the halt to feed her baby, when suddenly we heard a cry of anguish. The infant was dead, and as stiff as a piece of wood. Those nearest to her tried to comfort her by saying that it was the best thing for the baby and herself, and, in spite of her cries and tears, they took the infant from her breast. They gave it to a sapper, who, with the child's father, went a short distance from the road. The sapper dug a hole in the snow, the father on his knees holding the child in his arms. When the grave was made, he kissed the baby, and placed it in its tomb. It was covered with snow, and all was at an end.

We stopped an hour later for a long halt at the edge of a wood. Here a large party of artillery and cavalry had encamped, for we found a great many dead horses, some of them cut in pieces. There were many more still living, though numbed, standing still to be killed ; those that had died during the night were frozen so hard that it was impossible to cut the flesh. During this disastrous march I noticed that we were always placed as much as possible behind the cavalry and artillery ; so that when we halted where they had passed the night, the horses they had left behind were ready for us.

While we were all resting, and each busy in arranging some fearful meal for himself, I retired furtively into the thickest part of the wood to eat the potatoes I had hidden so carefully. But a fearful disappointment was in store for me. When I tried to bite, I felt nothing but ice ; my teeth slipped, and I could not get hold of a bit. I was

Hunger

sorry then that I had not shared the potatoes with the others, and I went back to them, holding in my hand the frozen one, covered with blood from my lips. They asked me what I had got, and I silently showed them the potato I held, and the others in my bag. They were snatched instantly from me ; but the result, when they tried to bite, was no better than mine. They tried to thaw them at the fire, but they melted away like ice. While this was going on, other men came up to ask me where I had found the potatoes, and when I pointed to the wood they ran there, returning to say they had found nothing. They were very good to me, as they invited me to share a potful of horse's blood which they had cooked. I did not need two invitations. I have always felt very sorry for behaving as I did. The men believed that I found the potatoes in the wood, and I did not undeceive them. But all this is only a hundredth part of what came afterwards.

After an hour's rest we set out again, crossing a wood, where every now and then we came on open spaces, with houses in them occupied by Jews. Some of them are large, and built very much like our barns, only of wood. At each end is a large door. These houses take the place of posting houses. A carriage is taken in at one end, and, after changing horses, goes out at the other. The houses are built about three leagues apart ; but most of them had disappeared, having been burnt at the army's first passage.

SERGEANT BOURGOGNE

PART THREE

16 *Invocation*

GIVE me a spirit that on this life's rough sea
Love's t' have his sails fill'd with a lusty wind,
Even till his sail-yards tremble, his masts crack,
And his rapt ship run on her side so low
That she drinks water, and her keel plows air.
There is no danger to a man that knows
What life and death is ; there's not any law
Exceeds his knowledge ; neither is it lawful
That he should stoop to any other law.
He goes before them, and commands them all,
That to himself is a law rational.

GEORGE CHAPMAN

17 *Rudiments of War*

Tamburlaine. But now, my boys, leave off, and list to me,
That mean to teach you rudiments of war.
I'll have you learn to sleep upon the ground,
March in your armour thorough watery fens,
Sustain the scorching heat and freezing cold,
Hunger and thirst, right adjuncts of the war ;
And, after this, to scale a castle-wall,
Besiege a fort, to undermine a town,
And make whole cities caper in the air :
Then next, the way to fortify your men ;

The Knapsack

In champion grounds what figure serves you best,
For which the quinque-angle form is meet,
Because the corners there may fall more flat
Whereas the fort may fittest be assail'd,
And sharpest where th' assault is desperate :
The ditches must be deep ; the counterscarps
Narrow and steep ; the walls made high and broad ;
The bulwarks and the rampires large and strong,
With cavalieros and thick counterforts,
And room within to lodge six thousand men,
It must have privy ditches, countermines,
And secret issuings to defend the ditch ;
It must have high argins and cover'd ways
To keep the bulwark-fronts from battery,
And parapets to hide the musketeers,
Casemates to place the great artillery,
And store of ordnance, that from every flank
May scour the outward curtains of the fort,
Dismount the cannon of the adverse part,
Murder the foe, and save the walls from breach.
When this is learn'd for service on the land,
By plain and easy demonstration
I'll teach you how to make the water mount,
That you may dry-foot march through lakes and pools,
Deep rivers, havens, creeks, and little seas,
And make a fortress in the raging waves,
Fenc'd with the concave of a monstrous rock,
Invincible by nature of the place.
When this is done, then are ye soldiers,
And worthy sons of Tamburlaine the Great.

Calyphas. My lord, but this is dangerous to be done ;
We may be slain or wounded ere we learn.

Tamb. Villain, art thou the son of Tamburlaine,
And fear'st to die, or with a curtle-axe
To hew thy flesh, and make a gaping wound ?

Rudiments of War

Hast thou beheld a peal of ordnance strike
A ring of pikes, mingled with shot and horse,
Whose shatter'd limbs, being toss'd as high as heaven,
Hang in the air as thick as sunny motes,
And canst thou, coward, stand in fear of death?
Hast thou not seen my horsemen charge the foe,
Shot through the arms, cut overthwart the hands,
Dying their lances with their streaming blood,
And yet at night carouse within my tent,
Filling their empty veins with airy wine,
That, being concocted, turns to crimson blood,
And wilt thou shun the field for fear of wounds?
View me, thy father, that hath conquer'd kings,
And, with his host, march'd round about the earth,
Quite void of scars and clear from any wound,
That by the wars lost not a drop of blood,
And see him lance his flesh to teach you all.

[He cuts his arm.

A wound is nothing, be it ne'er so deep;
Blood is the god of war's rich livery.
Now look I like a soldier, and this wound
As great a grace and majesty to me,
As if a chair of gold enamelled,
Enchas'd with diamonds, sapphires, rubies,
And fairest pearl of wealthy India,
Were mounted here under a canopy,
And I sat down, cloth'd with a massy robe
That late adorn'd the Afric potentate,
Whom I brought bound unto Damascus' walls.
Come, boys, and with your fingers search my wound,
And in my blood wash all your hands at once,
While I sit smiling to behold the sight.

CHRISTOPHER MARLOWE

18 *A Ballad of Agincourt*

FAIR stood the wind for France
When we our sails advance.
Nor now to prove our chance
   Longer will tarry ;
But putting to the main,
At Caux, the mouth of Seine,
With all his martial train,
   Landed King Harry.

And taking many a fort,
Furnish'd in warlike sort,
Coming toward Agincourt
   In happy hour,
Skirmishing day by day
With those that stopp'd his way,
Where the French gen'ral lay
   With all his power :

Which, in his height of pride,
King Henry to deride,
His ransom to provide
   Unto him sending ;
Which he neglects the while,
As from a nation vile,
Yet with an angry smile,
   Their fall portending ;

And turning to his men,
Quoth our brave Henry then,
' Though they to one be ten,
   Be not amazèd :

A Ballad of Agincourt

Yet have we well begun;
Battles so bravely won
Have ever to the sun
    By fame been raisèd.

' And for myself (quoth he)
This my full rest shall be :
England ne'er mourn for me
    Nor more esteem me :
Victor I will remain
Or on this earth lie slain,
Never shall she sustain
    Loss to redeem me.

' Poitiers and Cressy tell,
When most their pride did swell,
Under our swords they fell :
    No less our skill is
Than when our grandsire great,
Claiming the regal seat,
By many a warlike feat
    Lopp'd the French lilies.'

The Duke of York so dread
The eager vaward led ;
With the main Henry sped
    Among his henchmen.
Excester had the rear,
A braver man not there ;
O Lord, how hot they were
    On the false Frenchmen !

The Knapsack

They now to fight are gone,
Armour on armour shone,
Drum unto drum did groan,
    To hear was wonder ;
That with the cries they make
The very earth did shake ;
Trumpet to trumpet spake,
    Thunder to thunder.

Well it thine age became,
O noble Erpingham,
Which didst the signal aim
    To our hid forces !
When from a meadow by,
Like a storm suddenly
The English archery
    Struck the French horses.

With Spanish yew so strong,
Arrows a cloth-yard long,
That like to serpents stung,
    Piercing the weather ;
None from his fellow starts,
But playing manly parts,
And like true English hearts
    Stuck close together.

When down their bows they threw,
And forth their bilboes drew,
And on the French they flew,
    No man was tardy ;
Arms were from shoulders sent,
Scalps to the teeth were rent,
Down the French peasants went—
    Our men were hardy.

A Ballad of Agincourt

This while our noble king,
His broadsword brandishing,
Down the French host did ding,
    As to o'erwhelm it ;
And many a deep wound lent,
His arms with blood besprent,
And many a cruel dent
    Bruisèd his helmet.

Gloster, that duke so good,
Next of the royal blood,
For famous England stood,
    With his brave brother ;
Clarence, in steel most bright,
Though but a maiden knight,
Yet in that furious fight
    Scarce such another.

Warwick in blood did wade,
Oxford the foe invade,
And cruel slaughter made
    Still as they ran up ;
Suffolk his axe did ply,
Beaumont and Willoughby
Bare them right doughtily,
    Ferrers and Fanhope.

Upon Saint Crispin's Day
Fought was this noble fray,
Which fame did not delay
    To England to carry.
O when shall English men
With such acts fill a pen ?
Or England breed again
    Such a King Harry ?

MICHAEL DRAYTON

The Knapsack

19 *On the Late Massacher in Piemont*

AVENGE O Lord thy slaughter'd Saints, whose bones
    Lie scatter'd on the Alpine mountains cold,
    Ev'n them who kept thy truth so pure of old
When all our Fathers worship't Stocks and Stones,
Forget not : in thy book record their groans
    Who were thy Sheep and in their antient Fold,
    Slayn by the bloody Piemontese that roll'd
Mother with Infant down the Rocks.   Their moan
The Vales redoubl'd to the Hills, and they
    To Heav'n.   Their martyr'd blood and ashes sow
O'er all th' Italian fields where still doth sway
    The triple Tyrant : that from these may grow
    A hunder'd-fold, who having learnt thy way
Early may fly the Babylonian woe.

JOHN MILTON

20 *Into Battle*

THE naked earth is warm with Spring,
    And with green grass and bursting trees
Leans to the sun's gaze glorying,
    And quivers in the sunny breeze ;

And life is Colour and Warmth and Light,
    And a striving evermore for these ;
And he is dead who will not fight,
    And who dies fighting has increase.

The fighting man shall from the sun
    Take warmth, and life from the glowing earth
Speed with the light-foot winds to run,

118

Into Battle

And with the trees to newer birth ;
And find, when fighting shall be done,
  Great rest, and fullness after dearth.

All the bright company of Heaven
  Hold him in their high comradeship,
The Dog-star, and the Sisters Seven,
  Orion's Belt and sworded hip.

The woodland trees that stand together,
  They stand to him each one a friend ;
They gently speak in the windy weather ;
  They guide to valley and ridge's end.

The kestrel hovering by day,
  And the little owls that call by night,
Bid him be swift and keen as they,
  As keen of ear, as swift of sight.

The blackbird sings to him, ' Brother, brother,
  If this be the last song you shall sing
Sing well, for you may not sing another ;
  Brother, sing.'

In dreary doubtful waiting hours,
  Before the brazen frenzy starts,
The horses show him nobler powers ;—
  O patient eyes, courageous hearts !

And when the burning moment breaks,
  And all things else are out of mind,
And only Joy of Battle takes
  Him by the throat and makes him blind,

The Knapsack

Through joy and blindness he shall know,
　　Not caring much to know, that still
Nor lead nor steel shall reach him, so
　　That it be not the Destined Will.

The thundering line of battle stands,
　　And in the air Death moans and sings ;
But Day shall clasp him with strong hands,
　　And Night shall fold him in soft wings.

JULIAN GRENFELL

21　*Strange Meeting*

IT seemed that out of battle I escaped
Down some profound dull tunnel, long since scooped
Through granites which titanic wars had groined.
Yet also there encumbered sleepers groaned,
Too fast in thought or death to be bestirred.
Then, as I probed them, one sprang up, and stared
With piteous recognition in fixed eyes,
Lifting distressful hands as if to bless.
And by his smile, I knew that sullen hall,
By his dead smile I knew we stood in Hell.
With a thousand pains that vision's face was grained ;
Yet no blood reached there from the upper ground,
And no guns thumped, or down the flues made moan.
" Strange friend," I said, " here is no cause to mourn."
" None," said the other, " save the undone years,
The hopelessness.　Whatever hope is yours,
Was my life also ; I went hunting wild
After the wildest beauty in the world,
Which lies not calm in eyes, or braided hair,
But mocks the steady running of the hour,
And if it grieves, grieves richlier than here.
For by my glee might many men have laughed,
And of my weeping something had been left,

Strange Meeting

Which must die now. I mean the truth untold,
The pity of war, the pity war distilled.
Now men will go content with what we spoiled.
Or, discontent, boil bloody, and be spilled.
They will be swift with swiftness of the tigress,
None will break ranks, though nations trek from progress.
Courage was mine, and I had mystery,
Wisdom was mine, and I had mastery ;
To miss the march of this retreating world
Into vain citadels that are not walled.
Then, when much blood had clogged their chariot-wheels
I would go up and wash them from sweet wells,
Even with truths that lie too deep for taint.
I would have poured my spirit without stint
But not through wounds ; not on the cess of war.
Foreheads of men have bled where no wounds were.
I am the enemy you killed, my friend.
I knew you in this dark ; for so you frowned
Yesterday through me as you jabbed and killed.
I parried ; but my hands were loath and cold.
Let us sleep now. . . ."

WILFRED OWEN

22 *Vigil Strange*

VIGIL strange I kept on the field one night ;
When you, my son and my comrade, dropt at my side that
    day,
One look I but gave which your dear eyes return'd with a
    look I shall never forget,
One touch of your hand to mine, O boy, reach'd up as you
    lay on the ground,
Then onward I sped in the battle, the even-contested battle,
Till late in the night reliev'd to the place at last again I
    made my way,

The Knapsack

Found you in death so cold, dear comrade, found your body, son of responding kisses (never again on earth responding),

Bared your face in the starlight, curious the scene, cool blew the moderate night-wind,

Long there and then in vigil I stood, dimly around me the battle-field spreading,

Vigil wondrous and vigil sweet there in the fragrant silent night,

But not a tear fell, not even a long-drawn sigh, long, long I gazed,

Then on the earth partially reclining sat by your side leaning my chin in my hands,

Passing sweet hours, immortal and mystic hours with you, dearest comrade—not a tear, not a word,

Vigil of silence, love and death, vigil for you, my son and my soldier,

As onward silently stars aloft, eastward new ones upward stole,

Vigil final for you, brave boy (I could not save you, swift was your death,

I faithfully loved you and cared for you living, I think we shall surely meet again),

Till at latest lingering of the night, indeed just as the dawn appear'd,

My comrade I wrapt in his blanket, envelop'd well his form,

Folded the blanket well, tucking it carefully over head and carefully under feet,

And there and then and bathed by the rising sun, my son in his grave, in his rude-dug grave I deposited,

Ending my vigil strange with that, vigil of night and battle-field dim,

Vigil for boy of responding kisses (never again on earth responding),

Vigil Strange

gil for comrade swiftly slain, vigil I never forget, how as
    day brighten'd,
rose from the chill ground and folded my soldier well in
    his blanket,
nd buried him where he fell.

WALT WHITMAN

23 *Bermudas*

WHERE the remote Bermudas ride,
In the ocean's bosom unespied,
From a small boat, that rowed along,
The listening winds received this song :

  " What should we do but sing His praise,
That led us through the watery maze,
Unto an isle so long unknown,
And yet far kinder than our own ?
Where He the huge sea-monsters wracks,
That lift the deep upon their backs ;
He lands us on a grassy stage,
Safe from the storms, and prelate's rage.
He gave us this eternal spring,
Which here enamels every thing,
And sends the fowls to us in care,
On daily visits through the air ;
He hangs in shades the orange bright,
Like golden lamps in a green night,
And does in the pomegranates close
Jewels more rich than Ormus shows ;
He makes the figs our mouths to meet,
And throws the melons at our feet ;
But apples plants of such a price,
No tree could ever bear them twice ;

The Knapsack

With cedars chosen by His hand,
From Lebanon, He stores the land,
And makes the hollow seas, that roar,
Proclaim the ambergris on shore ;
He cast (of which we rather boast)
The Gospel's pearl upon our coast,
And in these rocks for us did frame
A temple where to sound His name.
Oh ! let our voice His praise exalt,
Till it arrive at Heaven's vault,
Which, thence (perhaps) rebounding, may
Echo beyond the Mexique Bay."

Thus sung they, in the English boat,
An holy and a cheerful note ;
And all the way, to guide their chime,
With falling oars they kept the time.

ANDREW MARVELL

24 *His Pilgrimage*

GIVE me my scallop-shell of quiet,
    My staff of faith to walk upon,
My scrip of joy, immortal diet,
    My bottle of salvation,
My gown of glory, hope's true gage ;
And thus I'll take my pilgrimage.

Blood must be my body's balmer ;
    No other balm will there be given ;
Whilst my soul, like quiet palmer,
    Travelleth towards the land of heaven ;
Over the silver mountains,
Where spring the nectar fountains.

His Pilgrimage

There will I kiss
The bowl of bliss ;
And drink mine everlasting fill
Upon every milken hill.
My soul will be a-dry before ;
But after it will thirst no more.

Then by that happy, blissful day,
    More peaceful pilgrims I shall see,
That have cast off their rags of clay,
    And walk apparelled fresh like me.
    I'll take them first
    To quench their thirst
And taste of nectar suckets,
    At those clear wells
    Where sweetness dwells,
    Drawn up by saints in crystal buckets.

And when our bottles and all we
Are filled with immortality,
Then the blessèd paths we'll travel,
Strowed with rubies thick as gravel ;
Ceilings of diamonds, sapphire floors,
High walls of coral and pearly bowers,
From thence to heaven's bribeless hall,
Where no corrupted voices brawl ;
No conscience molten into gold,
No forged accuser bought or sold,
No cause deferred, no vain-spent journey,
For there Christ is the king's Attorney,
Who pleads for all without degrees,
And he hath angels, but no fees.
And when the grand twelve-million jury
Of our sins, with direful fury,
Against our souls black verdicts give,
Christ pleads his death, and then we live.

The Knapsack

Be thou my speaker, taintless pleader,
Unblotted lawyer, true proceeder !
Thou givest salvation even for alms ;
Not with a bribèd lawyer's palms.
And this is mine eternal plea
To him that made heaven, earth, and sea,
That, since my flesh must die so soon,
And want a head to dine next noon,
Just at the stroke, when my veins start and spread,
Set on my soul an everlasting head !
Then am I ready, like a palmer fit,
To tread those blest paths which before I writ.

Of death and judgment, heaven and hell,
Who oft doth think, must needs die well.

SIR WALTER RALEIGH

25 *Like as a Ship*

LIKE as a ship, that through the Ocean wide
  by conduct of some star doth make her way,
  whenas a storm hath dim'd her trusty guide,
  out of her course doth wander far astray.
So I whose star, that wont with her bright ray
  me to direct, with clouds is overcast,
  do wander now in darkness and dismay
  through hidden perils round about me placed.
Yet hope I well, that when this storm is past
  my *Helice* the lodestar of my life
  will shine again, and look on me at last,
  with lovely light to clear my cloudy grief.
Till then I wander, carefull, comfortless,
  in secret sorrow and sad pensiveness.

EDMUND SPENSER

26 *To Lucasta, Going to the Wars*

TELL me not, Sweet, I am unkind,
  That from the nunnery
Of thy chaste breast and quiet mind
  To war and arms I fly.

True, a new mistress now I chase,
  The first foe in the field ;
And with a stronger faith embrace
  A sword, a horse, a shield.

Yet this inconstancy is such
  As you too shall adore ;
I could not love thee, Dear, so much,
  Loved I not Honour more.

RICHARD LOVELACE

27 *As ye Came from the Holy Land*

As ye came from the holy land
  Of Walsinghame,
Met you not with my true love
  By the way as you came ?

How should I know your true love,
  That have met many a one,
As I came from the holy land,
  That have come, that have gone ?

She is neither white nor brown,
  But as the heavens fair ;
There is none hath her form divine
  In the earth or the air.

The Knapsack

Such a one did I meet, good sir,
    Such an angelic face,
Who like a nymph, like a queen, did appear
    In her gait, in her grace.

She hath left me here alone
    All alone, as unknown,
Who sometime did me lead with herself,
    And me loved as her own.

What's the cause that she leaves you alone
    And a new way doth take,
That sometime did love you as her own,
    And her joy did you make ?

I have loved her all my youth,
    But now am old, as you see :
Love likes not the falling fruit,
    Nor the witherèd tree.

Know that Love is a careless child,
    And forgets promise past :
He is blind, he is deaf when he list,
    And in faith never fast.

His desire is a dureless content,
    And a trustless joy ;
He is won with a world of despair,
    And is lost with a toy.

Of womankind such indeed is the love,
    Or the word love abusèd,
Under which many childish desires
    And conceits are excusèd.

To His Coy Mistress

But true love is a durable fire,
  In the mind ever burning,
Never sick, never dead, never cold,
  From itself never turning.

SIR WALTER RALEIGH

28 *To His Coy Mistress*

HAD we but world enough, and time,
This coyness, lady, were no crime.
We would sit down, and think which way
To walk, and pass our long love's day.
Thou by the Indian Ganges' side
Shouldst rubies find : I by the tide
Of Humber would complain.   I would
Love you ten years before the flood,
And you should, if you please, refuse
Till the conversion of the Jews ;
My vegetable love should grow
Vaster than empires and more slow ;
An hundred years should go to praise
Thine eyes, and on thy forehead gaze ;
Two hundred to adore each breast,
But thirty thousand to the rest ;
An age at least to every part,
And the last age should show your heart.
For, lady, you deserve this state,
Nor would I love at lower rate.
  But at my back I always hear
Time's wingèd chariot hurrying near,
And yonder all before us lie
Deserts of vast eternity.
Thy beauty shall no more be found,
Nor, in thy marble vault, shall sound

My echoing song ; then worms shall try
That long-preserved virginity,
And your quaint honour turn to dust,
And into ashes all my lust :
The grave's a fine and private place,
But none, I think, do there embrace.
  Now therefore, while the youthful hue
Sits on thy skin like morning dew,
And while thy willing soul transpires
At every pore with instant fires,
Now let us sport us while we may,
And now, like amorous birds of prey,
Rather at once our time devour,
Than languish in his slow-chapt power.
Let us roll all our strength and all
Our sweetness up into one ball,
And tear our pleasures with rough strife,
Thorough the iron gates of life ;
Thus, though we cannot make our sun
Stand still, yet we will make him run.

ANDREW MARVELL

29 *Cleopatra*

THE barge she sat in, like a burnish'd throne,
Burn'd on the water ; the poop was beaten gold,
Purple the sails, and so perfumed that
The winds were love-sick with them, the oars were silver,
Which to the tune of flutes kept stroke, and made
The water which they beat to follow faster,
As amorous of their strokes.   For her own person,
It beggar'd all description ; she did lie
In her pavilion, cloth-of-gold of tissue,
O'er-picturing that Venus where we see

Cleopatra

The fancy outwork nature ; on each side her
stood pretty dimpled boys, like smiling Cupids,
With divers-colour'd fans, whose wind did seem
To glow the delicate cheeks which they did cool,
And what they undid did.

Agrippa.   O ! rare for Antony.

Enobarbus.   Her gentlewomen, like the Nereides,
So many mermaids, tended her i' the eyes,
And made their bends adornings ; at the helm
A seeming mermaid steers ; the silken tackle
Swell with the touches of those flower-soft hands,
That yarely frame the office.   From the barge
A strange invisible perfume hits the sense
Of the adjacent wharfs.   The city cast
Her people out upon her, and Antony,
Enthron'd i' the market-place, did sit alone,
Whistling to the air ; which, but for vacancy,
Had gone to gaze on Cleopatra too
And made a gap in nature.

Agr.   Rare Egyptian !

Eno.   Upon her landing Antony sent to her,
Invited her to supper ; she replied
It should be better he became her guest,
Which she entreated.   Our courteous Antony,
Whom ne'er the word of ' No ' woman heard speak,
Being barber'd ten times o'er, goes to the feast,
And for his ordinary pays his heart
For what his eyes eat only.

Agr.   Royal wench !
She made great Cæsar lay his sword to bed ;
He plough'd her, and she cropp'd.

Eno.   I saw her once
Hop forty paces through the public street ;
And having lost her breath, she spoke, and panted,
That she did make defect perfection,

The Knapsack

And, breathless, power breathe forth.

   Mec. Now Antony must leave her utterly.

   Eno. Never ; he will not.

Age cannot wither her, nor custom stale

Her infinite variety ; other women cloy

The appetites they feed, but she makes hungry

Where most she satisfies ; for vilest things

Become themselves in her, that the holy priests

Bless her when she is riggish.

W. Shakespeare

30 *From Epipsychidion*

Thy wisdom speaks in me, and bids me dare
Beacon the rocks on which high hearts are wrecked.
I never was attached to that great sect,
Whose doctrine is, that each one should select
Out of the crowd a mistress or a friend,
And all the rest, though fair and wise, commend
To cold oblivion, though it is in the code
Of modern morals, and the beaten road
Which those poor slaves with weary footsteps tread,
Who travel to their home among the dead
By the broad highway of the world, and so
With one chained friend, perhaps a jealous foe,
The dreariest and the longest journey go.

True Love in this differs from gold and clay,
That to divide is not to take away.
Love is like understanding, that grows bright,
Gazing on many truths ; 'tis like thy light,
Imagination ! which from earth and sky,
And from the depths of human fantasy,
As from a thousand prisms and mirrors, fills

Epipsychidion

The Universe with glorious beams, and kills
Error, the worm, with many a sun-like arrow
Of its reverberated lightning.   Narrow
The heart that loves, the brain that contemplates,
The life that wears, the spirit that creates
One object, and one form, and builds thereby
A sepulchre for its eternity.

   Mind from its object differs most in this :
Evil from good ; misery from happiness ;
The baser from the nobler ; the impure
And frail, from what is clear and must endure.
If you divide suffering and dross, you may
Diminish till it is consumed away ;
If you divide pleasure and love and thought,
Each part exceeds the whole ; and we know not
How much, while any yet remains unshared,
Of pleasure may be gained, of sorrow spared :
This truth is that deep well, whence sages draw
The unenvied light of hope ; the eternal law
By which those live, to whom this world of life
Is as a garden ravaged, and whose strife
Tills for the promise of a later birth
The wilderness of this Elysian earth.

PERCY BYSSHE SHELLEY

31 *Five Sonnets*

WHEN to the sessions of sweet silent thought,
I summon up remembrance of things past,
I sigh the lack of many a thing I sought,
And with old woes new wail my dear times' waste :
Then can I drown an eye (unus'd to flow)
For precious friends hid in death's dateless night,
And weep afresh love's long-since cancell'd woe,
And moan th' expense of many a vanish'd sight.

The Knapsack

Then can I grieve at grievances foregone,
And heavily from woe to woe tell o'er
The sad account of fore-bemoaned moan,
Which I new pay, as if not paid before.
  But if the while I think on thee (dear friend)
  All losses are restor'd, and sorrows end.

FULL many a glorious morning have I seen,
Flatter the mountain-tops with sovereign eye,
Kissing with golden face the meadows green,
Gilding pale streams with heavenly alchymy :
Anon permit the basest clouds to ride,
With ugly rack on his celestial face,
And from the forlorn world his visage hide
Stealing unseen to west with this disgrace :
Even so my Sun one early morn did shine,
With all triumphant splendour on my brow,
But out alack, he was but one hour mine,
The region cloud hath mask'd him from me now.
  Yet him for this, my love no whit disdaineth,
  Suns of the world may stain, when heaven's sun staineth.

THAT time of year thou mayst in me behold,
When yellow leaves, or none, or few do hang
Upon those boughs which shake against the cold,
Bare ruin'd choirs, where late the sweet birds sang.
In me thou seest the twilight of such day,
As after sunset fadeth in the West,
Which by and by black night doth take away,
Death's second self that seals up all in rest.
In me thou seest the glowing of such fire,
That on the ashes of his youth doth lie,
As the death-bed, whereon it must expire,
Consum'd with that which it was nourish'd by.
  This thou perceiv'st, which makes thy love more strong,
  To love that well, which thou must leave ere long.

Five Sonnets

LET me not to the marriage of true minds
Admit impediments, love is not love
Which alters when it alteration finds,
Or bends with the remover to remove.
O no, it is an ever-fixed mark
That looks on tempest and is never shaken ;
It is the star to every wand'ring bark,
Whose worth's unknown, although his height be taken,
Love's not Time's fool, though rosy lips and cheeks
Within his bending sickle's compass come,
Love alters not with his brief hours and weeks,
But bears it out even to the edge of doom :
   If this be error and upon me proved,
   I never writ, nor no man ever loved.

TH' expense of Spirit in a waste of shame
Is lust in action, and till action, lust
Is perjur'd, murd'rous, bloody full of blame,
Savage, extreme, rude, cruel, not to trust,
Enjoy'd no sooner but despised straight,
Past reason hunted, and no sooner had
Past reason hated as a swallowed bait,
On purpose laid to make the taker mad.
Mad in pursuit and in possession so,
Had, having, and in quest to have, extreme,
A bliss in proof and proud and very woe,
Before a joy propos'd behind a dream,
   All this the world well knows yet none knows well,
   To shun the heaven that leads men to this hell.

WILLIAM SHAKESPEARE

The Knapsack

32 *Porphyria's Lover*

THE rain set early in to-night,
  The sullen wind was soon awake,
It tore the elm-tops down for spite,
  And did its worst to vex the lake :
  I listened with heart fit to break.
When glided in Porphyria ; straight
  She shut the cold out and the storm,
And kneeled and made the cheerless grate
  Blaze up, and all the cottage warm ;
  Which done, she rose, and from her form
Withdrew the dripping cloak and shawl,
  And laid her soiled gloves by, untied
Her hat and let the damp hair fall,
  And, last, she sat down by my side
  And called me.   When no voice replied,
She put my arm about her waist,
  And made her smooth white shoulder bare,
And all her yellow hair displaced,
  And, stooping, made my cheek lie there,
  And spread, o'er all, her yellow hair,
Murmuring how she loved me—she
  Too weak, for all her heart's endeavour,
To set its struggling passion free
  From pride, and vainer ties dissever,
  And give herself to me for ever.
But passion sometimes would prevail,
  Nor could to-night's gay feast restrain
A sudden thought of one so pale
  For love of her, and all in vain :
  So, she was come through wind and rain.
Be sure I looked up at her eyes
  Happy and proud ; at last I knew
Porphyria worshipped me ; surprise

Porphyria's Lover

Made my heart swell, and still it grew
While I debated what to do.
That moment she was mine, mine, fair,
Perfectly pure and good : I found
A thing to do, and all her hair
In one long yellow string I wound
Three times her little throat around,
And strangled her. No pain felt she ;
I am quite sure she felt no pain.
As a shut bud that holds a bee,
I warily oped her lids : again
Laughed the blue eyes without a stain.
And I untightened next the tress
About her neck ; her cheek once more
Blushed bright beneath my burning kiss :
I propped her head up as before,
Only, this time my shoulder bore
Her head, which droops upon it still :
The smiling rosy little head,
So glad it has its utmost will,
That all it scorned at once is fled,
And I, its love, am gained instead !
Porphyria's love : she guessed not how
Her darling one wish would be heard.
And thus we sit together now,
And all night long we have not stirred,
And yet God has not said a word !

ROBERT BROWNING

33 *Song*

SWEETEST love, I do not go,
For weariness of thee,
Nor in hope the world can show
A fitter Love for me ;

The Knapsack

But since that I
Must die at last, 'tis best,
To use my self in jest
   Thus by fain'd deaths to die;

Yesternight the Sun went hence,
   And yet is here to day,
He hath no desire nor sense,
   Nor half so short a way:
     Then fear not me,
But believe that I shall make
Speedier journeys, since I take
   More wings and spurs than he.

O how feeble is man's power,
   That if good fortune fall,
Cannot add another hour,
   Nor a lost hour recall!
     But come bad chance,
And we join to'it our strength,
And we teach it art and length,
Itself o'r us to'advance.

When thou sigh'st, thou sigh'st not wind,
   But sigh'st my soul away,
When thou weep'st, unkindly kind,
   My life's blood doth decay.
     It cannot be
That thou lov'st me, as thou say'st,
If in thine my life thou waste,
   Thou art the best of me.

Let not thy divining heart
   Forethink me any ill,
Destiny may take thy part,
   And may thy fears fulfill;

Love's Deity

> But think that we
> Are but turn'd aside to sleep ;
> They who one another keep
> Alive, ne'r parted be.

JOHN DONNE

34 *Love's Deity*

I LONG to talk with some old lover's ghost,
  Who died before the god of love was born :
I cannot think that he, who then loved most,
  Sunk so low as to love one which did scorn.
But since this god produced a destiny,
And that vice-nature, custom, lets it be,
I must love her that loves not me.

Sure they which made him god meant not so much,
  Nor he in his young godhead practised it ;
But when an even flame two hearts did touch,
  His office was indulgently to fit
Actives to passives.   Correspondency
Only his subject was ; it cannot be
Love, till I love her that loves me.

But every modern god will now extend
  His vast prerogative as far as Jove ;
To rage, to lust, to write to, to commend ;
  All is the purlieu of the god of love.
O were we wakened by his tyranny
To ungod this child again, it could not be
I should love her who loves not me.

The Knapsack

Rebel and atheist too, why murmur I,
    As though I felt the worst that love could do?
Love may make me leave loving, or might try
    A deeper plague, to make her love me too,
Which, since she loves before, I am loath to see;
Falsehood is worse than hate; and that must be,
If she whom I love, should love me.

JOHN DONNE

35 *Amantium Irae*

IN going to my naked bed as one that would have slept,
I heard a wife sing to her child, that long before had wept;
She sighèd sore and sang full sweet, to bring the babe to rest,
That would not cease but crièd still, in sucking at her breast.
She was full weary of her watch, and grievèd with her child,
She rockèd it and rated it, till that on her it smiled.
Then did she say, Now have I found this proverb true to
    prove,
The falling out of faithful friends renewing is of love.

Then took I paper, pen, and ink, this proverb for to write,
In register for to remain of such a worthy wight:
As she proceeded thus in song unto her little brat,
Much matter utter'd she of weight, in place whereas she sat:
And provèd plain there was no beast, nor creature bearing
    life,
Could well be known to live in love without discord and
    strife:
Then kissèd she her little babe, and sware by God above,
The falling out of faithful friends renewing is of love.

She said that neither king nor prince nor lord could live
    aright,
Until their puissance they did prove, their manhood and
    their might.

Amantium Irae

When manhood shall be matchèd so that fear can take no
    place,
Then weary works make warriors each other to embrace,
And left their force that failèd them, which did consume
    the rout.
That might before have lived their time, their strength and
    nature out :
Then did she sing as one that thought no man could her
    reprove,
The falling out of faithful friends renewing is of love.

She said she saw no fish nor fowl, nor beast within her
    haunt,
That met a stranger in their kind, but could give it a taunt.
Since flesh might not endure, but rest must wrath succeed,
And force the fight to fall to play in pasture where they feed,
So noble nature can well end the work she hath begun,
And bridle well that will not cease her tragedy in some :
Thus in song she oft rehearsed, as did her well behove,
The falling out of faithful friends renewing is of love.

I marvel much pardy (quoth she) for to behold the rout,
To see man, woman, boy and beast, to toss the world about :
Some kneel, some crouch, some beck, some check, and some
    can smoothly smile,
And some embrace others in arm, and there think many a
    wile,
Some stand aloof at cap and knee, some humble and some
    stout,
Yet are they never friends in deed until they once fall out :
Thus ended she her song and said, before she did remove,
The falling out of faithful friends renewing is of love.

RICHARD EDWARDES

36 *Frost at Midnight*

THE Frost performs its secret ministry,
Unhelped by any wind.   The owlet's cry
Came loud—and hark, again ! loud as before.
The inmates of my cottage, all at rest,
Have left me to that solitude, which suits
Abstruser musings : save that at my side
My cradled infant slumbers peacefully.
'Tis calm indeed ! so calm, that it disturbs
And vexes meditation with its strange
And extreme silentness.   Sea, hill, and wood,
This populous village !   Sea, and hill, and wood,
With all the numberless goings-on of life,
Inaudible as dreams ! the thin blue flame
Lies on my low-burnt fire, and quivers not ;
Only that film, which fluttered on the grate,
Still flutters there, the sole unquiet thing.
Methinks, its motion in this hush of nature
Gives it dim sympathies with me who live,
Making it a companionable form,
Whose puny flaps and freaks the idling Spirit
By its own moods interprets, every where
Echo or mirror seeking of itself,
And makes a toy of Thought.

               But O ! how oft,
How oft, at school, with most believing mind,
Presageful, have I gazed upon the bars,
To watch that fluttering *stranger* ! and as oft
With unclosed lids, already had I dreamt
Of my sweet birth-place, and the old church-tower,
Whose bells, the poor man's only music, rang
From morn to evening, all the hot Fair-day,
So sweetly, that they stirred and haunted me

Frost at Midnight

With a wild pleasure, falling on mine ear
Most like articulate sounds of things to come !
So gazed I, till the soothing things I dreamt
Lulled me to sleep, and sleep prolonged my dreams !
And so I brooded all the following morn,
Awed by the stern preceptor's face, mine eye
Fixed with mock study on my swimming book :
Save if the door half opened, and I snatched
A hasty glance, and still my heart leaped up,
For still I hoped to see the *stranger's* face.
Townsman, or aunt, or sister more beloved,
My play-mate when we both were clothed alike !

Dear Babe, that sleepest cradled by my side,
Whose gentle breathings, heard in this deep calm,
Fill up the interspersed vacancies
And momentary pauses of the thought !
My babe so beautiful ! it thrills my heart
With tender gladness, thus to look at thee,
And think that thou shalt learn far other lore,
And in far other scenes !   For I was reared
In the great city, pent 'mid cloisters dim,
And saw nought lovely but the sky and stars.
But *thou*, my babe ! shalt wander like a breeze
By lakes and sandy shores, beneath the crags
Of ancient mountain, and beneath the clouds,
Which image in their bulk both lakes and shores
And mountain crags : so shalt thou see and hear
The lovely shapes and sounds intelligible
Of that eternal language, which thy God
Utters, who from eternity doth teach
Himself in all, and all things in himself.
Great universal Teacher ! he shall mould
Thy spirit, and by giving make it ask.

The Knapsack

Therefore all seasons shall be sweet to thee,
Whether the summer clothe the general earth
With greenness, or the redbreast sit and sing
Betwixt the tufts on the bare branch
Of mossy apple-tree, while the nigh thatch
Smokes in the sun-thaw ; whether the eave-drops fall
Heard only in the trances of the blast,
Or if the secret ministry of frost
Shall hang them up in silent icicles,
Quietly shining to the quiet Moon.

Samuel Taylor Coleridge

37 *O Sweet Woods*

O sweet woods, the delight of solitariness,
  O, how much do I love your solitariness !
From fame's desire, from love's delight retired,
  In these sad groves an hermit's life I led ;
And those false pleasures which I once admired,
  With sad remembrance of my fall, I dread.
To birds, to trees, to earth, impart I this,
For she less secret and as senseless is.

Experience, which alone repentance brings,
  Doth bid me now my heart from love estrange :
Love is disdained when it doth look at kings,
  And love low placed is base and apt to change.
Their power doth take from him his liberty,
Her want of worth makes him in cradle die.

O sweet woods, the delight of solitariness,
O, how much do I love your solitariness !

Sir Philip Sidney

38 *Composed upon Westminster Bridge, September 3, 1802*

EARTH has not anything to show more fair :
Dull would he be of soul who could pass by
A sight so touching in its majesty :
This City now doth, like a garment, wear
The beauty of the morning ; silent, bare,
Ships, towers, domes, theatres, and temples lie
Open unto the fields, and to the sky ;
All bright and glittering in the smokeless air.
Never did sun more beautifully steep
In his first splendour, valley, rock, or hill ;
Ne'er saw I, never felt, a calm so deep !
The river glideth at his own sweet will :
Dear God ! the very houses seem asleep ;
And all that mighty heart is lying still !

WILLIAM WORDSWORTH

39 *On the Sea*

IT keeps eternal whisperings around
  Desolate shores, and with its mighty swell
  Gluts twice ten thousand caverns, till the spell
Of Hecate leaves them their old shadowy sound.
Often 'tis in such gentle temper found,
  That scarcely will the very smallest shell
  Be moved for days from where it sometime fell,
When last the winds of heaven were unbound.
Oh ye ! who have your eye-balls vexed and tired,
  Feast them upon the wideness of the Sea ;
    Oh ye ! whose ears are dinn'd with uproar rude,
  Or fed too much with cloying melody,—
    Sit ye near some old cavern's mouth, and brood
Until ye start, as if the sea-nymphs quired !

JOHN KEATS

145

The Knapsack

40 *On First Looking into Chapman's Homer*

MUCH have I travell'd in the realms of gold,
  And many goodly states and kingdoms seen;
  Round many western islands have I been
Which bards in fealty to Apollo hold.
Oft of one wide expanse had I been told
  That deep-brow'd Homer rules as his demesne;
  Yet did I never breathe its pure serene
Till I heard Chapman speak out loud and bold:
Then felt I like some watcher of the skies
  When a new planet swims into his ken;
Or like stout Cortez when with eagle eyes
  He star'd at the Pacific—and all his men
Look'd at each other with a wild surmise—
  Silent, upon a peak in Darien.

JOHN KEATS

41 *Dover Beach*

THE sea is calm to-night.
The tide is full, the moon lies fair
Upon the straits;—on the French coast the light
Gleams and is gone; the cliffs of England stand,
Glimmering and vast, out in the tranquil bay.
Come to the window, sweet is the night-air!
Only, from the long line of spray
Where the sea meets the moon-blanch'd land,
Listen! you hear the grating roar
Of pebbles which the waves draw back, and fling,
At their return, up the high strand,
Begin, and cease, and then again begin,
With tremulous cadence slow, and bring
The eternal note of sadness in.

Dover Beach

Sophocles long ago
Heard it on the Ægæan, and it brought
Into his mind the turbid ebb and flow
Of human misery ; we
Find also in the sound a thought,
Hearing it by this distant northern sea.
   The sea of faith
Was once, too, at the full, and round earth's shore
Lay like the folds of a bright girdle furl'd.
But now I only hear
Its melancholy, long, withdrawing roar,
Retreating to the breath
Of the night-wind down the vast edges drear
And naked shingles of the world.

Ah, love, let us be true
To one another ! for the world, which seems
To lie before us like a land of dreams,
So various, so beautiful, so new,
Hath really neither joy, nor love, nor light,
Nor certitude, nor peace, nor help for pain ;
And we are here as on a darkling plain
Swept with confused alarms of struggle and flight,
Where ignorant armies clash by night.

MATTHEW ARNOLD

42   Tithonus

THE woods decay, the woods decay and fall,
The vapours weep their burthen to the ground,
Man comes and tills the field and lies beneath,
And after many a summer dies the swan.
Me only cruel immortality
Consumes : I wither slowly in thine arms,
Here at the quiet limit of the world,

The Knapsack

A white-hair'd shadow roaming like a dream
The ever silent spaces of the East,
Far-folded mists, and gleaming halls of morn.

Alas ! for this grey shadow, once a man—
So glorious in his beauty and thy choice,
Who madest him thy chosen, that he seem'd
To his great heart none other than a God !
I ask'd thee, ' Give me immortality.'
Then didst thou grant mine asking with a smile,
Like wealthy men who care not how they give.
But thy strong Hours indignant work'd their wills,
And beat me down and marr'd and wasted me,
And tho' they could not end me, left me maim'd
To dwell in presence of immortal youth,
Immortal age beside immortal youth,
And all I was, in ashes.   Can thy love,
Thy beauty, make amends, tho' even now,
Close over us, the silver star, thy guide,
Shines in those tremulous eyes that fill with tears
To hear me ?   Let me go : take back thy gift :
Why should a man desire in any way
To vary from the kindly race of men,
Or pass beyond the goal of ordinance
Where all should pause, as is most meet for all ?

A soft air fans the cloud apart ; there comes
A glimpse of that dark world where I was born.
Once more the old mysterious glimmer steals
From thy pure brows, and from thy shoulders pure,
And bosom beating with a heart renew'd.
Thy cheek begins to redden thro' the gloom,
Thy sweet eyes brighten slowly close to mine,
Ere yet they blind the stars, and the wild team
Which love thee, yearning for thy yoke, arise,

Tithonus

And shake the darkness from their loosen'd manes,
And beat the twilight into flakes of fire.

Lo ! ever thus thou growest beautiful
In silence, then before thine answer given
Departest, and thy tears are on my cheek.

Why wilt thou ever scare me with thy tears,
And make me tremble lest a saying learnt,
In days far-off, on that dark earth, be true ?
' The Gods themselves cannot recall their gifts.'

Ay me ! ay me ! with what another heart
In days far-off, and with what other eyes
I used to watch—if I be he that watch'd—
The lucid outline forming round thee ; saw
The dim curls kindle into sunny rings ;
Changed with thy mystic change, and felt my blood
Glow with the glow that slowly crimson'd all
Thy presence and thy portals, while I lay,
Mouth, forehead, eyelids, growing dewy-warm
With kisses balmier than half-opening buds
Of April, and could hear the lips that kiss'd
Whispering I knew not what of wild and sweet,
Like that strange song I heard Apollo sing,
While Ilion like a mist rose into towers.

Yet hold me not for ever in thine East :
How can my nature longer mix with thine ?
Coldly thy rosy shadows bathe me, cold
Are all thy lights, and cold my wrinkled feet
Upon thy glimmering thresholds, when the steam
Floats up from those dim fields about the homes
Of happy men that have the power to die,

The Knapsack

And grassy barrows of the happier dead.
Release me, and restore me to the ground :
Thou seëst all things, thou wilt see my grave :
Thou wilt renew thy beauty morn by morn ;
I earth in earth forget these empty courts,
And thee returning on thy silver wheels.

ALFRED LORD TENNYSON

43 On Time

FLY, envious Time, till thou run out thy race :
Call on the lazy leaden-stepping hours,
Whose speed is but the heavy Plummet's pace ;
And glut thy self with what thy womb devours,
Which is no more than what is false and vain,
And merely mortal dross ;
So little is our loss,
So little is thy gain !
For, when as each thing bad thou hast entomb'd,
And, last of all, thy greedy self consum'd,
Then long Eternity shall greet our bliss
With an individual kiss ;
And Joy shall overtake us as a flood,
When every thing that is sincerely good
And perfectly divine,
With Truth, and Peace, and Love, shall ever shine
About the supreme Throne,
Of him, t' whose happy-making sight alone
When once our heav'nly-guided soul shall clime,
Then, all this earthly grossness quit,
Attir'd with stars, we shall for ever sit,
    Triumphing over Death, and Chance, and thee O Time

JOHN MILTON

The Darkling Thrush

44 *The Darkling Thrush*

I LEANT upon a coppice gate
　　When Frost was spectre-gray,
And Winter's dregs made desolate
　　The weakening eye of day.
The tangled bine-stems scored the sky
　　Like strings of broken lyres,
And all mankind that haunted nigh
　　Had sought their household fires.

The land's sharp features seemed to be
　　The Century's corpse outleant,
His crypt the cloudy canopy,
　　The wind his death-lament.
The ancient pulse of germ and birth
　　Was shrunken hard and dry,
And every spirit upon earth
　　Seemed fervourless as I.

At once a voice arose among
　　The bleak twigs overhead
In a full-hearted evensong
　　Of joy illimited ;
An aged thrush, frail, gaunt, and small,
　　In blast-beruffled plume,
Had chosen thus to fling his soul
　　Upon the growing gloom.

So little cause for carolings
　　Of such ecstatic sound
Was written on terrestrial things
　　Afar or nigh around,

The Knapsack

That I could think there trembled through
    His happy good-night air
Some blessed Hope, whereof he knew
    And I was unaware.

THOMAS HARDY

45   *Out of the Cradle Endlessly Rocking*

OUT of the cradle endlessly rocking,

Out of the mocking-bird's throat, the musical shuttle,

Out of the Ninth-month midnight,

Over the sterile sands, and the fields beyond, where the child leaving his bed wander'd alone, bareheaded, barefoot,

Down from the shower'd halo,

Up from the mystic play of shadows twining and twisting as if they were alive,

Out from the patches of briers and blackberries,

From the memories of the bird that chanted to me,

From your memories, sad brother, from the fitful risings and fallings I heard,

From under that yellow half-moon late-risen and swollen as if with tears,

From those beginning notes of yearning and love there in the mist,

From the thousand responses of my heart never to cease,

From the myriad thence-arous'd words,

From the word stronger and more delicious than any,

From such as now they start the scene revisiting,

As a flock, twittering, rising, or overhead passing,

Borne hither, ere all eludes me, hurriedly,

A man, yet by these tears a little boy again,

Throwing myself on the sand, confronting the waves,

Out of the Cradle Endlessly Rocking

, chanter of pains and joys, uniter of here and hereafter,
Taking all hints to use them, but swiftly leaping beyond
    them,
A reminiscence sing.

Once Paumanok,
When the lilac-scent was in the air and Fifth-month grass
    was growing,
Up this seashore in some briers,
Two feather'd guests from Alabama, two together,
And their nest, and four light-green eggs spotted with brown,
And every day the he-bird to and fro near at hand,
And every day the she-bird crouch'd on her nest, silent, with
    bright eyes,
And every day I, a curious boy, never too close, never
    disturbing them,
Cautiously peering, absorbing, translating.

Shine ! shine ! shine !
Pour down your warmth, great sun !
While we bask, we two together.

Two together !
Winds blow south, or winds blow north,
Day come white, or night come black,
Home, or rivers and mountains from home,
Singing all time, minding no time,
While we two keep together.

Till of a sudden,
May-be kill'd, unknown to her mate,
One forenoon the she-bird crouch'd not on the nest,
Nor return'd that afternoon, nor the next,
Nor ever appear'd again.

The Knapsack

And thenceforward all summer in the sound of the sea,
And at night under the full of the moon in calmer weather
Over the hoarse surging of the sea,
Or flitting from brier to brier by day,
I saw, I heard at intervals the remaining one, the he-bird
The solitary guest from Alabama.

Blow ! blow ! blow !
Blow up sea-winds along Paumanok's shore ;
I wait and I wait till you blow my mate to me.

Yes, when the stars glisten'd,
All night long on the prong of a moss-scallop'd stake,
Down almost amid the slapping waves,
Sat the lone singer wonderful causing tears.

He call'd on his mate,
He pour'd forth the meanings which I of all men know.
Yes, my brother, I know,
The rest might not, but I have treasur'd every note,
For more than once dimly down to the beach gliding,
Silent, avoiding the moonbeams, blending myself with the
    shadows,
Recalling now the obscure shapes, the echoes, the sounds
    and sights after their sorts,
The white arms out in the breakers tirelessly tossing,
I, with bare feet, a child, the wind wafting my hair,
Listen'd long and long.

Listen'd to keep, to sing, now translating the notes,
Following you, my brother.

Soothe ! soothe ! soothe !
Close on its waves soothes the wave behind,
And again another behind embracing and lapping, every one close,
But my love soothes not me, not me.

Out of the Cradle Endlessly Rocking

Low hangs the moon, it rose late,
It is lagging—O I think it is heavy with love, with love.

O madly the sea pushes upon the land,
With love, with love.

O night ! do I not see my love fluttering out among the breakers ?
What is that little black thing I see there in the white ?

Loud ! loud ! loud !
Loud I call to you, my love !
High and clear I shoot my voice over the waves,
Surely you must know who is here, is here,
You must know who I am, my love.

Low-hanging moon !
What is that dusky spot in your brown yellow ?
O it is the shape, the shape of my mate !
O moon, do not keep her from me any longer.

Land ! land ! O land !
Whichever way I turn, O I think you could give me my mate back
        again if you only would,
For I am almost sure I see her dimly whichever way I look.
O rising stars !
Perhaps the one I want so much will rise, will rise with some of you.

O throat ! O trembling throat !
Sound clearer through the atmosphere !
Pierce the woods, the earth,
Somewhere listening to catch you must be the one I want.

Shake out carols !
Solitary here, the night's carols !
Carols of lonesome love ! death's carols !

The Knapsack

Carols under that lagging, yellow, waning moon !
O under that moon where she droops almost down into the sea !
O reckless despairing carols.

But soft ! sink low !
Soft ! let me just murmur,
And do you wait a moment you husky-nois'd sea,
For somewhere I believe I heard my mate responding to me,
So faint, I must be still, be still to listen,
But not altogether still, for then she might not come immediately t
    me.

Hither my love !
Here I am ! here !
With this just-sustain'd note I announce myself to you,
This gentle call is for you, my love, for you.

Do not be decoy'd elsewhere,
That is the whistle of the wind, it is not my voice,
That is the fluttering, the fluttering of the spray,
Those are the shadows of leaves.

O darkness ! O in vain !
O I am very sick and sorrowful.

O brown halo in the sky near the moon, drooping upon the sea !
O troubled reflection in the sea !
O throat ! O throbbing heart !
And I singing uselessly, uselessly all the night.

O past ! O happy life ! O songs of joy !
In the air, in the woods, over fields,
Loved ! loved ! loved ! loved ! loved !
But my mate no more, no more with me !
We two together no more.

156

Out of the Cradle Endlessly Rocking

The aria sinking,
All else continuing, the stars shining,
The winds blowing, the notes of the bird continuous echo-
ing,
With angry moans the fierce old mother incessantly moan-
ing,
On the sand of Paumanok's shore grey and rustling,
The yellow half-moon enlarged, sagging down, drooping,
the face of the sea almost touching,
The boy ecstatic, with his bare feet the waves, with his hair
the atmosphere dallying,
The love in the heart long pent, now loose, now at last
tumultuously bursting,
The aria's meaning, the ears, the soul, swiftly depositing,
The strange tears down the cheeks coursing,
The colloquy there, the trio, each uttering,
The undertone, the savage old mother incessantly crying,
To the boy's soul's questions sullenly timing, some drown'd
secret hissing,
To the outsetting bard.

Demon or bird ! (said the boy's soul),
Is it indeed toward your mate you sing ? or is it really to
me ?
For I, that was a child, my tongue's use sleeping, now I have
heard you,
Now in a moment I know what I am for, I awake,
And already a thousand singers, a thousand songs, clearer,
louder, and more sorrowful than yours,
A thousand warbling echoes have started to life within me,
never to die.

O you singer solitary, singing by yourself, projecting me,
O solitary me listening, never more shall I cease perpetuat-
ing you,

The Knapsack

Never more shall I escape, never more the reverberations,
Never more the cries of unsatisfied love be absent from me,
Never again leave me to be the peaceful child I was before
    what there in the night,
By the sea under the yellow and sagging moon,
The messenger there arous'd, the fire, the sweet hell within,
The unknown want, the destiny of me.
O give me the clew ! (it lurks in the night here somewhere),
O if I am to have so much, let me have more !

A word then (for I will conquer it),
The word final, superior to all,
Subtle, sent up—what is it ?—I listen ;
Are you whispering it, and have been all the time, you
    sea-waves ?
Is that it from your liquid rims and wet sands ?

Whereto answering, the sea,
Delaying not, hurrying not,
Whisper'd me through the night, and very plainly before
    daybreak,
Lisp'd to me the low and delicious word death,
And again death, death, death, death,
Hissing melodious, neither like the bird not like my arous'd
    child's heart,
But edging near as privately for me rustling at my feet,
Creeping thence steadily up to my ears and laving me softly
    all over,
Death, death, death, death, death.

Which I do not forget,
But fuse the song of my dusky demon and brother,
That he sang to me in the moonlight on Paumanok's grey
    beach,
With the thousand responsive songs at random,

Out of the Cradle Endlessly Rocking

My own songs awaked from that hour,
And with them the key, the word up from the waves,
The word of the sweetest song and all songs,
That strong and delicious word which, creeping to my feet,
(Or like some old crone rocking the cradle, swathed in sweet
    garments, bending aside),
The sea whisper'd me.

WALT WHITMAN

46 *Ode to Walt Whitman*

ALONG the East River and the Bronx
the boys were singing showing their waists
with the wheel, the oil, the leather and the hammer.
Ninety thousand miners extracted silver from the rocks
and the children drew scales and perspectives.

But none slept,
none wanted to be a river,
none loved the great leaves,
none, the blue tongue of the beach.

Along the East River and the Queensborough
the boys were fighting with Industry,
and the Jews were selling the rose of the circumcision
to the faun of the river,
and the sky rushed through bridges and roofs
herds of bison pushed by the wind.

But none halted,
none wanted to be a cloud,
none searched for the ferns
nor the yellow wheel of the tambourine.

The Knapsack

When the moon rises,
the pulleys will turn to disturb the sky;
a boundary of needles will circle the memory
and the coffins will carry away those who do not work.

New York of slime,
New York of wires and death;
What angel do you carry hidden in your cheek?
What perfect voice will tell the truths of the wheat?
Who, the terrible dream of your stained anemones?

Not for one moment, beautiful aged Walt Whitman,
have I failed to see your beard full of butterflies,
nor your shoulders of corduroy worn out by the moon,
nor your thighs of virginal Apollo,
nor your voice like a pillar of ashes;
ancient and beautiful as the mist,
you moaned like a bird
with the sex pierced by a needle.

Enemy of the satyr,
Enemy of the vine,
and lover of bodies under the rough cloth.
Not for one moment; virile beauty
who in mountains of coal, advertisements and railways,
dreamed of being a river and sleeping like a river
with that comrade who would place in your breast
the small pain of an ignorant leopard.

. . . . .

You searched for a nude who was like a river.
Bull and dream that would join the wheel with the seaweed,
father of your agony, camelia of your death
and would moan in the flames of your hidden Equator.

Ode to Walt Whitman

Because it is just that man does not search for his delight
in the jungle of blood of the following morning.
The sky has shores where to avoid life,
and certain bodies must not repeat themselves in the dawn.

Agony, agony, dream, ferment and dream.
This is the world, my friend, agony, agony.
The corpses decompose under the clock of the cities.
War passes weeping with a million grey rats,
the rich give to their mistresses
small illuminated moribunds,
and Life is not noble, nor good, nor sacred.

Man can, if he wishes, lead his desire
through vein of coral or celestial nude ;
to-morrow love will be rocks, and Time
a breeze which comes sleeping through the branches.

.   .   .   .   .   .

And you, beautiful Walt Whitman, sleep on the Hudson's
    banks,
with your beard towards the Pole and open hands.
Bland clay or snow, your tongue is calling for
comrades that keep watch on your gazelle without a body.

Sleep : nothing remains.
A dance of walls agitates the meadows
and America drowns itself in machines and lament.

I want the strong air of the most profound night
to remove flowers and letters from the arch where you
    sleep,
and a black boy to announce to the gold-mined whites
the arrival of the reign of the ear of corn.

FEDERICO GARCIA LORCA

The Knapsack

47 *Ship of Death*

I sing of autumn and the falling fruit
and the long journey towards oblivion.

The apples falling like great drops of dew
to bruise themselves an exit from themselves.
Have you built your ship of death, oh, have you?
Build then your ship of death, for you will need it!

Can man his own quietus make
with a bare bodkin?

With daggers, bodkins, bullets, man can make
a bruise or break of exit for his life
but is that a quietus, oh tell me, is it quietus?

Quietus is the goal of the long journey
the longest journey towards oblivion.

Slips out the soul, invisible one, wrapped still
in the white shirt of the mind's experiences
and folded in the dark-red, unseen
mantle of the body's still mortal memories.

Frightened and alone, the soul slips out of the house
or is pushed out
to find himself on the crowded, arid margins of existence.

Oh, it is not so easy, I tell you it is not so easy
to set softly forth on the longest journey, the longest journey.

It is easy to be pushed out of the silvery city of the body
through any breach in the wall,
thrust out on to the grey grey beaches of shadow

162

Ship of Death

the long marginal stretches of existence, crowded with lost
    souls
that intervene between our tower and the shaking sea of
    the beyond.

Oh build your ship of death, oh build it in time
and build it lovingly, and put it between the hands of your
    soul.

Once outside the gate of the walled silvery life of days
once outside, upon the grey marsh beaches, where lost souls
    moan
in millions, unable to depart
having no boat to launch upon the shaken soundless
deepest and longest of seas,
once outside the gate
what will you do, if you have no ship of the soul?

Oh pity the dead that are dead, but cannot take
the journey, still they moan and beat
against the silvery adamant walls of this our exclusive
    existence.
They moan and beat, they gnash, they rage
they fall upon the new outcoming souls with rage
and they send arrows of anger, bullets and bombs of
    frustration
over the adamant walls of this, our by-no-means impreg-
    nable existence.

Pity, oh pity the poor dead that are only ousted from life
and crowd there on the grey mud beaches of the margins
    gaunt and horrible
waiting, waiting till at last the ancient boatman with the
    common barge
shall take them aboard, towards the great goal of oblivion.

The Knapsack

Pity the poor gaunt dead that cannot die
into the distance with receding oars
but must roam like outcast dogs on the margins of life,
and think of them, and with the soul's deep sigh
waft nearer to them the bark of delivery.

But for myself, but for my soul, dear soul
let me build a little ship with oars and food
and little dishes, and all accoutrements
dainty and ready for the departing soul.

And put it between the hands of the trembling soul.
So that when the hour comes, and the last door closes
    behind him
he shall slip down the shores invisible
between the half-visible hordes
to where the furthest and the longest sea
touches the margins of our life's existence
with wincing unwilling waves.

And launching there his little ship,
wrapped in the dark-red mantle of the body's memories
the little, slender soul sits swiftly down, and takes the oars
and draws away, away, away, towards the dark depths
fathomless deep ahead, far, far from the grey shores
that fringe with shadow all this world's existence.

Over the sea, over the farthest sea
on the longest journey
past the jutting rocks of shadow
past the lurking, octopus arms of agonised memory
past the strange whirlpools of remembered greed
through the dead weed of a life-time's falsity,
slow, slow, my soul, in his little ship
on the most soundless of all seas

Ship of Death

taking the longest journey.
Pulling the long oars of a life-time's courage
drinking the confident water from the little jug
and eating the brave bread of a wholesome knowledge
row, little soul, row on
on the longest journey, towards the greatest goal

Neither straight nor crooked, neither here nor there
but shadows folded on deeper shadows
and deeper, to a core of sheer oblivion
like the convolutions of shadow-shell
or deeper, like the foldings and involvings of a womb.

Drift on, drift on, my soul, towards the most pure
most dark oblivion.
And at the penultimate porches, the dark-red mantle
of the body's memories slips and is absorbed
into the shell-like, womb like convoluted shadow.

And round the great final bend of unbroken dark
the skirt of the spirit's experience has melted away
the oars have gone from the boat, and the little dishes
gone, gone, and the boat dissolves like pearl
as the soul at last slips perfect into the goal, the core
of sheer oblivion and of utter peace,
the womb of silence in the living night.

Ah peace, ah lovely peace, most lovely lapsing
of this my soul into the plasm of peace.

Oh lovely last, last lapse of death, into pure oblivion
at the end of the longest journey
peace, complete peace !
But can it be that also it is procreation ?
Oh build your ship of death
oh build it !
Oh, nothing matters but the longest journey.

D. H. Lawrence

The Knapsack

48 *Life and Death*

BE absolute for death ; either death or life
Shall thereby be the sweeter.   Reason thus with life :
If I do lose thee, I do lose a thing
That none but fools would keep : a breath thou art,
Servile to all the skyey influences,
That do this habitation, where thou keep'st,
Hourly afflict.   Merely, thou art death's fool ;
For him thou labour'st by thy flight to shun,
And yet runn'st toward him still.   Thou art not noble ;
For all the accommodations that thou bear'st
Are nurs'd by baseness.   Thou art by no means valiant ;
For thou dost fear the soft and tender fork
Of a poor worm.   Thy best of rest is sleep,
And that thou oft provok'st ; yet grossly fear'st
Thy death, which is no more.   Thou art not thyself ;
For thou exist'st on many a thousand grains
That issue out of dust.   Happy thou art not ;
For what thou hast not, still thou striv'st to get,
And what thou hast, forget'st.   Thou art not certain ;
For thy complexion shifts to strange effects,
After the moon.   If thou art rich, thou'rt poor ;
For, like an ass whose back with ingots bows,
Thou bear'st thy heavy riches but a journey,
And death unloads thee.   Friend hast thou none ;
For thine own bowels, which do call thee sire,
The mere effusion of thy proper loins,
Do curse the gout, serpigo, and the rheum,
For ending thee no sooner.   Thou hast nor youth nor age,
But, as it were, an after-dinner's sleep,
Dreaming on both ; for all thy blessed youth
Becomes as aged, and doth beg the alms
Of palsied eld ; and when thou art old and rich,

Life and Death

Thou hast neither heat, affection, limb, nor beauty,
To make thy riches pleasant. What's yet in this
That bears the name of life? Yet in this life
Lie hid more thousand deaths; yet death we fear,
That makes these odds all even.

WILLIAM SHAKESPEARE

49 *Exequy on his Wife*

ACCEPT, thou shrine of my dead saint,
Instead of dirges this complaint;
And for sweet flowers to crown thy herse
Receive a strew of weeping verse
From thy griev'd friend, whom thou might'st see
Quite melted into tears for thee.

  Dear loss! since thy untimely fate,
My task hath been to meditate
On thee, on thee! Thou art the book,
The library whereon I look,
Tho' almost blind. For thee, lov'd clay,
I languish out, not live, the day,
Using no other exercise
But what I practise with mine eyes:
By which wet glasses I find out
How lazily time creeps about
To one that mourns: this, onely this
My exercise and bus'ness is:
So I compute the weary hours
With sighs dissolved into showers.

  Nor wonder if my time go thus
Backward and most preposterous;
Thou hast benighted me; thy set
This eve of blackness did beget,
Who wast my day (tho' overcast

The Knapsack

Before thou hadst thy noontide past) :
And I remember must in tears
Thou scarce hadst seen so many years
As day tells hours. By thy clear sun
My love and fortune first did run ;
But thou wilt never more appear
Folded within my hemisphere,
Since both thy light and motion,
Like a fled star, is fall'n and gone,
And 'twixt me and my soul's dear wish
The earth now interposèd is,
Which such a strange eclipse doth make
As ne'er was read in almanack.

  I could allow thee for a time
To darken me and my sad clime ;
Were it a month, a year, or ten,
I would thy exile live till then ;
And all that space my mirth adjourn,
So thou wouldst promise to return ;
And putting off thy ashy shroud
At length disperse this sorrow's cloud.

  But woe is me ! the longest date
Too narrow is to calculate
These empty hopes : never shall I
Be so much blest as to descry
A glimpse of thee, till that day come
Which shall the earth to cinders doom,
And a fierce fever must calcine
The body of this world—like thine,
My little world ! That fit of fire
Once off, our bodies shall aspire
To our souls' bliss : then we shall rise
And view ourselves with clearer eyes
In that calm region where no night
Can hide us from each other's sight.

Exequy on his Wife

Meantime thou hast her, earth : much good
May my harm do thee ! Since it stood
With Heaven's will I might not call
Her longer mine, I give thee all
My short-lived right and interest
In her whom living I lov'd best.
Be kind to her, and prithee look
Thou write into thy Doomsday book
Each parcel of this rarity
Which in thy casket shrin'd doth lie ;
See that thou make thy reck'ning straight,
And yield her back again by weight ;
For thou must audit on thy trust
Each grain and atom of this dust,
As thou wilt answer Him that lent,
Not gave thee my dear monument.

So close the ground, and 'bout her shade
Black curtains draw : my bride is laid.

Sleep on, my Love, in thy cold bed
Never to be disquieted !
My last good-night ! Thou wilt not wake
Till I thy fate shall overtake ;
Till age, or grief, or sickness must
Marry my body to that dust
It so much loves ; and fill the room
My heart keeps empty in thy tomb.
Stay for me there : I will not fail
To meet thee in that hollow vale.
And think not much of my delay :
I am already on the way,
And follow thee with all the speed
Desire can make, or sorrows breed.
Each minute is a short degree
And every hour a step towards thee.
At night when I betake to rest,

The Knapsack

Next morn I rise nearer my West
Of life, almost by eight hours' sail,
Than when sleep breath'd his drowsy gale.
   Thus from the sun my bottom steers,
And my days' compass downward bears :
Nor labour I to stem the tide
Through which to thee I swiftly glide.
   'Tis true—with shame and grief I yield—
Thou, like the van first tookst the field ;
And gotten hast the victory
In thus adventuring to die
Before me, whose more years might crave
A just precedence in the grave.
But hark ! my pulse, like a soft drum,
Beats my approach, tells thee I come ;
And slow howe'er my marches be
I shall at last sit down by thee.
   The thought of this bids me go on
And wait my dissolution
With hope and comfort. Dear—forgive
The crime—I am content to live
Divided, with but half a heart,
Till we shall meet and never part.

HENRY KING

50   The Funeral

WHOEVER comes to shroud me, do not harm
    Nor question much
That subtle wreath of hair about mine arm ;
The mystery, the sign, you must not touch,
    For 'tis my outward soul,
Viceroy to that which, unto heaven being gone,
    Will leave this to control
And keep these limbs, her provinces, from dissolution.

The Funeral

For if the sinewy thread my brain lets fall
    Through every part,
Can tie those parts, and make me one of all ;
Those hairs, which upward grow, and strength and art
    Have from a better brain,
Can better do 't : except she meant that I
    By this should know my pain,
As prisoners then are manacled, when they're condemn'd
    to die.
Whate'er she meant by it, bury it with me,
    For since I am
Love's martyr, it might breed idolatry
If into other hands these reliques came.
    As 'twas humility
T' afford to it all that a soul can do,
    So 'tis some bravery
That, since you would have none of me, I bury some of you.

JOHN DONNE

51 *Afterwards*

WHEN the Present has latched its postern behind my
    tremulous stay,
  And the May month flaps its glad green leaves like wings,
Delicate-filmed as new-spun silk, will the neighbours say,
  " He was a man who used to notice such things " ?

If it be in the dusk when, like an eyelid's soundless blink,
  The dewfall-hawk comes crossing the shades to alight
Upon the wind-warped upland thorn, a gazer may think,
  " To him this must have been a familiar sight."

The Knapsack

If I pass during some nocturnal blackness, mothy and warm,
    When the hedgehog travels furtively over the lawn,
One may say, " He strove that such innocent creatures
    should come to no harm,
    But he could do little for them ; and now he is gone."

If, when hearing that I have been stilled at last, they stand
    at the door,
    Watching the full-starred heavens that winter sees,
Will this thought rise on those who will meet my face no
    more,
    " He was one who had an eye for such mysteries " ?

And will any say when my bell of quittance is heard in the
    gloom,
    And a crossing breeze cuts a pause in its outrollings,
Till they rise again, as they were a new bell's boom,
    " He hears it not now, but used to notice such things " ?

Thomas Hardy

52 *When I Have Fears*

When I have fears that I may cease to be
    Before my pen has glean'd my teeming brain,
Before high-piled books, in charact'ry,
    Hold like rich garners the full-ripen'd grain ;
When I behold, upon the night's starr'd face,
    Huge cloudy symbols of a high romance,
And think that I may never live to trace
    Their shadows, with the magic hand of chance ;
And when I feel, fair creature of an hour !

When I Have Fears

That I shall never look upon thee more,
Never have relish in the faery power
Of unreflecting love !—then on the shore
Of the wide world I stand alone, and think
Till love and fame to nothingness do sink.

JOHN KEATS

53   Guests

YET if His Majesty, our sovereign lord,
Should of his own accord
Friendly himself invite,
And say, ' I'll be your guest to-morrow night,'
How should we stir ourselves, call and command
All hands to work !   ' Let no man idle stand.

' Set me fine Spanish tables in the hall,
See they be fitted all ;
Let there be room to eat,
And order taken that there want no meat.
See every sconce and candlestick made bright,
That without tapers they may give a light.

' Look to the presence : are the carpets spread,
The dazie o'er the head,
The cushions in the chairs,
And all the candles lighted on the stairs ?
Perfume the chambers, and in any case
Let each man give attendance in his place ! '

Thus, if the king were coming, would we do,
And 'twere good reason too ;
For 'tis a duteous thing
To show all honour to an earthly king,
And after all our travail and our cost,
So he be pleased, to think no labour lost.

The Knapsack

But at the coming of the King of Heaven
    All's set at six and seven :
      We wallow in our sin,
Christ cannot find a chamber in the inn.
We entertain Him always like a stranger,
And, as at first, still lodge Him in a manger.

                Christ Church MS.

54 *The Collar*

I STRUCK the board and cried, No more ;
    I will abroad.
What, shall I ever sigh and pine ?
My lines and life are free ; free as the road,
Loose as the wind, as large as store.
      Shall I be still in suit ?
Have I no harvest but a thorn
To let me blood, and not restore
What I have lost with cordial fruit ?
      Sure there was wine
Before my sighs did dry it : there was corn
Before my tears did drown it.
Is the year only lost to me ?
Have I no bays to crown it ?
No flowers, no garlands gay ?   All blasted ?
      All wasted ?
Not so, my heart ; but there is fruit,
    And thou hast hands.
Recover all thy sigh-blown age
On double pleasures : leave thy cold dispute
Of what is fit, and not ; forsake thy cage,
    Thy rope of sands
Which petty thoughts have made, and made to thee

The Collar

Good cable, to enforce and draw,
      And be thy law,
While thou didst wink and wouldst not see.
      Away; take heed:
      I will abroad.
Call in thy death's-head there: tie up thy fears.
      He that forbears
      To suit and serve his need
      Deserves his load.
But as I raved and grew more fierce and wild
      At every word,
Methought I heard one calling, *Child*:
And I replied *My Lord*.

GEORGE HERBERT

55 *The Flaming Heart*

O HEART! the equal poise of Love's both parts,
Big alike with wound and darts,
Live in these conquering leaves: live all the same;
And walk through all tongues one triumphant flame;
Live here, great heart; and love, and die, and kill;
And bleed, and wound, and yield, and conquer still.
Let this immortal life where'er it comes
Walk in a crowd of loves and martyrdoms.
Let mystic deaths wait on't; and wise souls be
The love-slain witnesses of this life of thee.

  O sweet incendiary! show here thy art,
Upon this carcase of a hard cold heart;
Let all thy scatter'd shafts of light, that play
Among the leaves of thy large books of day,
Combin'd against this breast at once break in,
And take away from me myself and sin;

The Knapsack

This gracious robbery shall thy bounty be
And my best fortunes such fair spoils of me.
O thou undaunted daughter of desires !
By all thy dower of lights and fires ;
By all the eagle in thee, all the dove ;
By all thy lives and deaths of love
By thy large draughts of intellectual day,
And by thy thirsts of love more large than they ;
By all thy brim-filled bowls of fierce desire,
By thy last morning's draught of liquid fire ;
By the full kingdom of that final kiss
That seized thy parting soul, and sealed thee His ;
By all the Heav'n thou hast in Him
(Fair sister of the seraphim !)
By all of Him we have in thee ;
Leave nothing of myself in me.
Let me so read thy life, that I
Unto all life of mine may die !

RICHARD CRASHAW

56 *The Tyger*

TYGER ! Tyger ! burning bright
In the forests of the night,
What immortal hand or eye
Could frame thy fearful symmetry ?

In what distant deeps or skies
Burnt the fire of thine eyes ?
On what wings dare he aspire ?
What the hand dare seize the fire ?

And what shoulder, and what art,
Could twist the sinews of thy heart ?
And when thy heart began to beat,
What dread hand ? and what dread feet ?

The Tyger

What the hammer ? what the chain ?
In what furnace was thy brain ?
What the anvil ? what dread grasp
Dare its deadly terrors clasp ?

When the stars threw down their spears,
And water'd heaven with their tears,
Did he smile his work to see ?
Did he who made the Lamb make thee ?

Tyger ! Tyger ! burning bright
In the forests of the night,
What immortal hand or eye,
Dare frame thy fearful symmetry ?

WILLIAM BLAKE

57 *A Hymn to the Name and Honour of the Admirable Saint Teresa*

Love, thou art absolute sole Lord
Of life and death.   To prove the word,
We'll now appeal to none of all
Those thy old soldiers, great and tall,
Ripe men of martyrdom, that could reach down
With strong arms their triumphant crown ;
Such as could with lusty breath
Speak loud into the face of death
Their great Lord's glorious name ; to none
Of those whose spacious bosoms spread a throne
For love at large to fill.   Spare blood and sweat :
And see him take a private seat,
Making his mansion in the mild
And milky soul of a soft child.
Scarce has she learnt to lisp the name

The Knapsack

Of martyr, yet she thinks it shame
Life should so long play with that breath
Which spent can buy so brave a death.
She never undertook to know
What death with love should have to do.
Nor has she e'er yet understood
Why, to show love, she should shed blood ;
Yet, though she cannot tell you why,
She can love, and she can die.

Scarce has she blood enough to make
A guilty sword blush for her sake ;
Yet has a heart dares hope to prove
How much less strong is death than love. . . .

Since 'tis not to be had at home,
She'll travel to a martyrdom.
No home for her, confesses she,
But where she may a martyr be.

She'll to the Moors, and trade with them
For this unvalued diadem ;
She offers them her dearest breath,
With Christ's name in 't, in change for death :
She'll bargain with them, and will give
Them God, and teach them how to live
In him ; or, if they this deny,
For him she'll teach them how to die.
So shall she leave amongst them sown
Her Lord's blood, or at least her own.

Farewell then, all the world, adieu !
Teresa is no more for you.
Farewell all pleasures, sports, and joys,
Never till now esteemèd toys !
Farewell whatever dear may be—
Mother's arms, or father's knee !
Farewell house, and farewell home !

The Admirable Saint Teresa

She's for the Moors and Martyrdom.
    Sweet, not so fast ; lo ! thy fair spouse,
Whom thou seek'st with so swift vows,
Calls thee back, and bids thee come
T' embrace a milder martyrdom. . . .

O how oft shalt thou complain
Of a sweet and subtle pain !
Of intolerable joys !
Of a death, in which who dies
Loves his death, and dies again,
And would for ever so be slain ;
And lives and dies, and knows not why
To live, but that he still may die !
    How kindly will thy gentle heart
Kiss the sweetly-killing dart !
And close in his embraces keep
Those delicious wounds, that weep
Balsam, to heal themselves with. Thus
When these thy deaths, so numerous,
Shall all at once die into one,
And melt thy soul's sweet mansion ;
Like a soft lump of incense, hasted
By too hot a fire, and wasted
Into perfuming clouds, so fast
Shalt thou exhale to heaven at last
In a resolving sigh, and then
O what ? Ask not the tongues of men.
Angels cannot tell ; suffice,
Thyself shalt feel thine own full joys,
And hold them fast for ever. There
So soon as thou shalt first appear,
The moon of maiden stars, thy white
Mistress, attended by such bright
Souls as thy shining self, shall come,

The Knapsack

And in her first ranks make thee room ;
Where, 'mongst her snowy family,
Immortal welcomes wait for thee.

O what delight, when she shall stand
And teach thy lips heaven, with her hand,
On which thou now may'st to thy wishes
Heap up thy consecrated kisses !
What joy shall seize thy soul, when she,
Bending her blessèd eyes on thee
(Those second smiles of heaven) shall dart
Her mild rays through thy melting heart !

Angels, thy old friends, there shall greet thee,
Glad at their own home now to meet thee.

All thy good works which went before,
And waited for thee at the door,
Shall own thee there ; and all in one
Weave a constellation
Of crowns, with which the King thy spouse
Shall build up thy triumphant brows.

All thy old woes shall now smile on thee,
And thy pains sit bright upon thee :
All thy sorrows here shall shine,
And thy sufferings be divine.
Tears shall take comfort, and turn gems,
And wrongs repent to diadems.
Even thy deaths shall live, and new
Dress the soul which erst they slew.
Thy wounds shall blush to such bright scars
As keep account of the Lamb's wars.

Those rare works, where thou shalt leave writ
Love's noble history, with wit
Taught thee by none but Him, while here
They feed our souls, shall clothe thine there.
Each heavenly word by whose hid flame
Our hard hearts shall strike fire, the same

The Admirable Saint Teresa

Shall flourish on thy brows, and be
Both fire to us and flame to thee ;
Whose light shall live bright in thy face
By glory, in our hearts by grace.

   Thou shalt look round about, and see
Thousands of crown'd souls throng to be
Themselves thy crown, sons of thy vows,
The virgin-births with which thy spouse
Made fruitful thy fair soul ; go now,
And with them all about thee bow
To Him ; put on (he'll say) put on
(My rosy love) that thy rich zone,
Sparkling with the sacred flames
Of thousand souls, whose happy names
Heav'n keeps upon thy score : thy bright
Life brought them first to kiss the light
That kindled them to stars ; and so
Thou with the Lamb, thy lord, shalt go ;
And, wheresoe'er he sets his white
Steps, walk with him those ways of light,
Which who in death would live to see,
Must learn in life to die like thee.

RICHARD CRASHAW

58   *Regeneration*

A WARD, and still in bonds, one day
        I stole abroad,
It was high-spring, and all the way
       Primros'd, and hung with shade ;
     Yet, was it frost within,
         And surly winds
Blasted my infant buds, and sin
     Like Clouds eclips'd my mind.

The Knapsack

Storm'd thus ; I straight perceiv'd my spring
      Meere stage, and show,
My walk a monstrous, mountain'd thing
      Rough-cast with Rocks, and snow ;
      And as a Pilgrims Eye
          Far from relief,
Measures the melancholy sky
      Then drops, and rains for grief,

So sigh'd I upwards still, at last
      'Twixt steps, and falls
I reach'd the pinacle, where plac'd
      I found a pair of scales,
      I took them up and layd
          In th'one late pains,
The other smoak, and pleasures weigh'd
      But prov'd the heavier grains ;

With that, some cryed, *Away* ; straight I
      Obey'd, and led
Full East, a fair, fresh field could spy,
      Some call'd it, *Jacobs Bed* ;
      A Virgin-soil, which no
          Rude feet ere trod,
Where (since he stept there,) only go
      Prophets, and friends of God.

Here, I repos'd ; but scarse well set,
      A grove descryed
Of stately height, whose branches met
      And mixt on every side ;
      I entred, and once in
          (Amaz'd to see't,)
Found all was chang'd, and a new spring
      Did all my senses greet ;

Regeneration

The unthrift Sun shot vital gold
                    A thousand pieces,
And heaven its azure did unfold
                    Checqur'd with snowie fleeces,
          The air was all in spice
                    And every bush
A garland wore ; Thus fed my Eyes
                    But all the Ear lay hush.

Only a little Fountain lent
                    Some use for Ears,
And on the dumb shades language spent
                    The Musick of her tears ;
          I drew her near, and found
                    The Cistern full
Of divers stones, some bright, and round,
                    Others ill-shap'd, and dull.

The first (pray mark,) as quick as light
                    Danc'd through the flood,
But, th'last more heavy than the night
                    Nail'd to the Center stood ;
          I wonder'd much, but tyr'd
                    At last with thought,
My restless Eye that still desir'd
                    As strange an object brought ;

It was a bank of flowers, where I descried
                    (Though 'twas mid-day,)
Some fast asleep, others broad-eyed
                    And taking in the Ray,
          Here musing long, I heard
                    A rushing wind
Which still increas'd, but whence it stirr'd
                    No where I could not find ;

The Knapsack

I turn'd me round, and to each shade
        Dispatch'd an Eye,
To see, if any leaf had made
        Least motion, or Reply,
        But while I listning sought
                My mind to ease
By knowing, where 'twas, or where not,
        It whisper'd ; *Where I please.*

Lord, then said I, *On me one breath,*
    And let me die before my death !

HENRY VAUGHAN

59 *On the Morning of Christ's Nativity :*
The Hymn

IT was the Winter wilde,
While the Heav'n-born-childe,
  All meanly wrapt in the rude manger lies ;
Nature in aw to him
Had doff't her gawdy trim,
  With her great Master so to sympathize :
It was no season then for her
To wanton with the Sun her lusty Paramour.

Onely with speeches fair
She woo's the gentle Air
  To hide her guilty front with innocent Snow,
And on her naked shame,
Pollute with sinfull blame,
  The Saintly Vail of Maiden white to throw,
Confounded, that her Makers eyes
Should look so near upon her foul deformities.

On the Morning of Christ's Nativity

But he her fears to cease,
Sent down the meek-eyd Peace,
  She crown'd with Olive green, came softly sliding
Down through the turning sphear
His ready Harbinger,
  With Turtle wing the amorous clouds dividing,
And waving wide her mirtle wand,
She strikes a universall Peace through Sea and Land.

No War, or Battails sound
Was heard the World around :
  The idle spear and shield were high up hung ;
The hooked Chariot stood
Unstain'd with hostile blood,
  The Trumpet spake not to the armed throng,
And Kings sate still with awfull eye,
As if they surely knew their sovran Lord was by.

But peacefull was the night
Wherein the Prince of light
  His raign of peace upon the earth began :
The Windes with wonder whist,
Smoothly the waters kist,
  Whispering new joyes to the milde Ocean,
Who now hath quite forgot to rave,
While Birds of Calm sit brooding on the charmed wave.

The Stars with deep amaze
Stand fixt in stedfast gaze,
  Bending one way their pretious influence,
And will not take their flight,
For all the morning light,
  Or *Lucifer* that often warn'd them thence ;
But in their glimmering Orbs did glow,
Untill their Lord himself bespake, and bid them go.

The Knapsack

And though the shady gloom
Had given day her room,
   The Sun himself with-held his wonted speed,
And hid his head for shame,
As his inferiour flame,
   The new-enlightn'd world no more should need ;
He saw a greater Sun appear
Then his bright Throne, or burning Axletree could bear.

The Shepherds on the Lawn,
Or ere the point of dawn,
   Sate simply chatting in a rustick row ;
Full little thought they than,
That the mighty *Pan*
   Was kindly com to live with them below ;
Perhaps their loves, or els their sheep,
Was all that did their silly thoughts so busie keep.

When such musick sweet
Their hearts and ears did greet,
   As never was by mortall finger strook,
Divinely-warbled voice
Answering the stringed noise,
   As all their souls in blisfull rapture took :
The Air such pleasure loth to lose,
With thousand echo's still prolongs each heav'nly close.

Nature that heard such sound
Beneath the hollow round
   Of *Cynthia's* seat, the Airy region thrilling,
Now was almost won
To think her part was don,
   And that her raign had here its last fulfilling ;
She knew such harmony alone
Could hold all Heav'n and Earth in happier union.

On the Morning of Christ's Nativity

The Oracles are dumm,
No voice or hideous humm
  Runs through the arched roof in words deceiving.
Apollo from his shrine
Can no more divine,
  With hollow shreik the steep of *Delphos* leaving.
No nightly trance, or breathed spell,
Inspires the pale-ey'd Priest from the prophetic cell.

The lonely mountains o're,
And the resounding shore,
  A voice of weeping heard, and loud lament ;
From haunted spring, and dale
Edg'd with poplar pale,
  The parting Genius is with sighing sent,
With flowre-inwov'n tresses torn
The Nimphs in twilight shade of tangled thickets mourn.

In consecrated Earth,
And on the holy Hearth,
  The *Lars*, and *Lemures* moan with midnight plaint,
In Urns, and Altars round,
A drear, and dying sound
  Affrights the *Flamins* at their service quaint ;
And the chill Marble seems to sweat,
While each peculiar power forgoes his wonted seat.

Peor, and *Baalim*,
Forsake their Temples dim,
  With that twice-batter'd god of *Palestine*,
And mooned *Ashtaroth*,
Heav'ns Queen and Mother both,
  Now sits not girt with Tapers holy shine,
The Libyc *Hammon* shrinks his horn,
In vain the *Tyrian* Maids their wounded *Thamuz* mourn.

The Knapsack

And sullen *Moloch* fled,
Hath left in shadows dred,
   His burning Idol all of blackest hue,
In vain with Cymbals ring,
They call the grisly king,
   In dismall dance about the furnace blue ;
The brutish gods of *Nile* as fast,
Isis and *Orus*, and the Dog *Anubis* hast.

Nor is *Osiris* seen
In *Memphian* Grove, or Green,
   Trampling the unshowr'd Grasse with lowings loud :
Nor can he be at rest
Within his sacred chest,
   Naught but profoundest Hell can be his shroud,
In vain with Timbrel'd Anthems dark
The sable-stoled Sorcerers bear his worshipt Ark.

He feels from *Juda's* land
The dredded Infants hand,
   The rayes of *Bethlehem* blind his dusky eyn ;
Nor all the gods beside,
Longer dare abide,
   Not *Typhon* huge ending in snaky twine :
Our Babe to shew his Godhead true,
Can in his swadling bands controul the damned crew.

So when the Sun in bed,
Curtain'd with cloudy red,
   Pillows his chin upon an Orient wave,
The flocking shadows pale,
Troop to th'infernall jail,
   Each fetter'd Ghost slips to his severall grave,
And the yellow-skirted *Fayes*,
Fly after the Night-steeds, leaving their Moon-lov'd maze.

On the Morning of Christ's Nativity

But see the Virgin blest,
Hath laid her Babe to rest.
  Time is our tedious Song should here have ending,
Heav'ns youngest teemed Star,
Hath fixt her polisht Car,
  Her sleeping Lord with Handmaid Lamp attending :
And all about the Courtly Stable,
Bright-harnest Angels sit in order serviceable.

JOHN MILTON

60 *Easter Day*

YE that for psalmody contend,
  Exert your trilling throats ;
And male and female voices blend
  With joy's divinest notes.

By fancy rais'd to Zion's top
  Your swelling organ join ;
And praise the Lord on every stop
  Till all your faces shine.

With sweetest breath your trumpets fill'd
  Shall forward strength and grace ;
Then all your warbling measures build
  Upon the grounding bass.

The boxen pipe, for deepness form'd,
  Involve in strains of love,
And flutes, with inspiration warm'd,
  Shall imitate the dove.

Amongst the rest arouse the harp,
  And with a master's nail ;
And from the quick vibrations carp
  The graces of the scale.

The Knapsack

The flow'rs from every bed collect,
    And on the altar lift ;
And let each silver vase be deckt
    With nature's graceful gift.

And from the steeple's summit stream
    The flag of golden gloss,
Exposing to the glancing beam
    The glorious English cross ;

And let the lads of gladness born
    The ringers be renew'd ;
And as they usher'd in the morn,
    Let them the day conclude.

CHRISTOPHER SMART

61 *Auguries of Innocence*

To see a World in a grain of sand,
And a Heaven in a wild flower,
Hold Infinity in the palm of your hand,
And Eternity in an hour.
A robin redbreast in a cage
Puts all Heaven in a rage.
A dove-house fill'd with doves and pigeons
Shudders Hell thro' all its regions.
A dog starv'd at his master's gate
Predicts the ruin of the State.
A horse misus'd upon the road
Calls to Heaven for human blood.
Each outcry of the hunted hare
A fibre from the brain does tear.
A skylark wounded in the wing,
A cherubim does cease to sing.

Auguries of Innocence

The game-cock clipt and arm'd for fight
Does the rising sun affright.
Every wolf's and lion's howl
Raises from Hell a Human soul.
The wild deer, wandering here and there,
Keeps the Human soul from care.
The lamb misus'd breeds public strife,
And yet forgives the butcher's knife.
The bat that flits at close of eve
Has left the brain that won't believe.
The owl that calls upon the night
Speaks the unbeliever's fright.
He who shall hurt the little wren
Shall never be belov'd by men.
He who the ox to wrath has mov'd
Shall never be by woman lov'd.
The wanton boy that kills the fly
Shall feel the spider's enmity.
He who torments the chafer's sprite
Weaves a bower in endless night.
The caterpillar on the leaf
Repeats to thee thy mother's grief.
Kill not the moth nor butterfly,
For the Last Judgement draweth nigh.
He who shall train the horse to war
Shall never pass the polar bar.
The beggar's dog and widow's cat,
Feed them, and thou wilt grow fat.
The gnat that sings his summer's song
Poison gets from Slander's tongue.
The poison of the snake and newt
Is the sweat of Envy's foot.
The poison of the honey-bee
Is the artist's jealousy.

The Knapsack

The prince's robes and beggar's rags
Are toadstools on the miser's bags.
A truth that's told with bad intent
Beats all the lies you can invent.
It is right it should be so ;
Man was made for joy and woe ;
And when this we rightly know,
Thro' the world we safely go.
Joy and woe are woven fine,
A clothing for the soul divine ;
Under every grief and pine
Runs a joy with silken twine.
The babe is more than swaddling-bands ;
Throughout all these human lands
Tools were made, and born were hands,
Every farmer understands.
Every tear from every eye
Becomes a babe in Eternity ;
This is caught by Females bright,
And return'd to its own delight.
The bleat, the bark, bellow, and roar
Are waves that beat on Heaven's shore.
The babe that weeps the rod beneath
Writes revenge in realms of death.
The beggar's rags, fluttering in air,
Does to rags the heavens tear.
The soldier, arm'd with sword and gun,
Palsied strikes the summer's sun.
The poor man's farthing is worth more
Than all the gold on Afric's shore.
One mite wrung from the labourer's hands
Shall buy and sell the miser's lands
Or, if protected from on high,
Does that whole nation sell and buy.

Auguries of Innocence

He who mocks the infant's faith
Shall be mock'd in Age and Death.
He who shall teach the child to doubt
The rotting grave shall ne'er get out.
He who respects the infant's faith
Triumphs over Hell and Death.
The child's toys and the old man's reasons
Are the fruits of the two seasons.
The questioner, who sits so sly,
Shall never know how to reply.
He who replies to words of Doubt
Doth put the light of knowledge out.
The strongest poison ever known
Came from Caesar's laurel crown.
Nought can deform the human race
Like to the armour's iron brace.
When gold and gems adorn the plough
To peaceful arts shall Envy bow.
A riddle, or the cricket's cry,
Is to Doubt a fit reply.
The emmet's inch and eagle's mile
Make lame Philosophy to smile.
He who doubts from what he sees
Will ne'er believe, do what you please.
If the Sun and Moon should doubt,
They'd immediately go out.
To be in a passion you good may do,
But no good if a passion is in you.
The whore and gambler, by the state
Licensed, build that nation's fate.
The harlot's cry from street to street
Shall weave Old England's winding-sheet
The winner's shout, the loser's curse,
Dance before dead England's hearse.

The Knapsack

Every night and every morn
Some to misery are born.
Every morn and every night
Some are born to sweet delight.
Some are born to sweet delight,
Some are born to endless night.
We are led to believe a lie
When we see not thro' the eye,
Which was born in a night, to perish in a night,
When the Soul slept in beams of light.
God appears, and God is Light,
To those poor souls who dwell in Night ;
But does a Human Form display
To those who dwell in realms of Day.

WILLIAM BLAKE

62 *The Recluse*

ON Man, on Nature, and on Human Life,
Musing in solitude, I oft perceive
Fair trains of imagery before me rise,
Accompanied by feelings of delight
Pure, or with no unpleasing sadness mixed ;
And I am conscious of affecting thoughts
And dear remembrances, whose presence soothes
Or elevates the Mind, intent to weigh
The good and evil of our mortal state.
—To these emotions, whencesoe'er they come,
Whether from breath of outward circumstance,
Or from the Soul—an impulse to herself—
I would give utterance in numerous verse.
Of Truth, of Grandeur, Beauty, Love, and Hope,
And melancholy Fear subdued by Faith ;
Of blessèd consolations in distress ;

The Recluse

Of moral strength, and intellectual Power ;
Of joy in widest commonalty spread ;
Of the individual Mind that keeps her own
Inviolate retirement, subject there
To Conscience only, and the law supreme
Of that Intelligence which governs all—
I sing :—' fit audience let me find though few ! '

So prayed, more gaining than he asked, the Bard—
In holiest mood.   Urania, I shall need
Thy guidance, or a greater Muse, if such
Descend to earth or dwell in highest heaven !
For I must tread on shadowy ground, must sink
Deep—and, aloft ascending, breathe in worlds
To which the heaven of heavens is but a veil.
All strength—all terror, single or in bands,
That ever was put forth in personal form—
Jehovah—with his thunder, and the choir
Of shouting Angels, and the empyreal thrones—
I pass them unalarmed.   Not Chaos, not
The darkest pit of lowest Erebus,
Nor aught of blinder vacancy, scooped out
By help of dreams—can breed such fear and awe
As fall upon us often when we look
Into our Minds, into the Mind of Man—
My haunt, and the main region of my song.
—Beauty—a living Presence of the earth,
Surpassing the most fair ideal Forms
Which craft of delicate Spirits hath composed
From earth's materials—waits upon my steps ;
Pitches her tents before me as I move,
An hourly neighbour.   Paradise, and groves
Elysian, Fortunate Fields—like those of old
Sought in the Atlantic Main—why should they be
A history only of departed things,

The Knapsack

Or a mere fiction of what never was?
For the discerning intellect of Man,
When wedded to this goodly universe
In love and holy passion, shall find these
A simple produce of the common day.
—I, long before the blissful hour arrives,
Would chant, in lonely peace, the spousal verse
Of this great consummation :—and, by words
Which speak of nothing more than what we are,
Would I arouse the sensual from their sleep
Of Death, and win the vacant and the vain
To noble raptures ; while my voice proclaims
How exquisitely the individual Mind
(And the progressive powers perhaps no less
Of the whole species) to the external World
Is fitted :—and how exquisitely, too—
Theme this but little heard of among men—
The external World is fitted to the Mind ;
And the creation (by no lower name
Can it be called) which they with blended might
Accomplish :—this is our high argument.
—Such grateful haunts foregoing, if I oft
Must turn elsewhere—to travel near the tribes
And fellowships of men, and see ill sights
Of maddening passions mutually inflamed ;
Must hear Humanity in fields and groves
Pipe solitary anguish ; or must hang
Brooding above the fierce confederate storm
Of sorrow, barricadoed evermore
Within the walls of cities—may these sounds
Have their authentic comment ; that even these
Hearing, I be not downcast or forlorn !—
Descend, prophetic Spirit ! that inspir'st
The human Soul of universal earth,
Dreaming on things to come ; and dost possess

The Recluse

A metropolitan temple in the hearts
Of mighty Poets : upon me bestow
A gift of genuine insight ; that my Song
With star-like virtue in its place may shine,
Shedding benignant influence, and secure,
Itself, from all malevolent effect
Of those mutations that extend their sway
Throughout the nether sphere !—And if with this
I mix more lowly matter ; with the thing
Contemplated, describe the Mind and Man
Contemplating ; and who, and what he was—
The transitory Being that beheld
This Vision ; when and where, and how he lived :—
Be not this labour useless.   If such theme
May sort with highest objects, then—dread Power !
Whose gracious favour is the primal source
Of all illumination,—may my Life
Express the image of a better time,
More wise desires, and simpler manners ;—nurse
My Heart in genuine freedom :—all pure thoughts
Be with me ; so shall thy unfailing love
Guide, and support, and cheer me to the end !

WILLIAM WORDSWORTH

63 Demogorgon's Last Words

THIS is the day, which down the void abysm
At the Earth-born's spell yawns for Heaven's despotism,
   And Conquest is dragged captive through the deep :
Love, from its awful throne of patient power
In the wise heart, from the last giddy hour
   Of dread endurance, from the slippery, steep,
And narrow verge of crag-like agony, springs
And folds over the world its healing wings.

The Knapsack

Gentleness, Virtue, Wisdom, and Endurance,
These are the seals of that most firm assurance
  Which bars the pit over Destruction's strength ;
And if, with infirm hand, Eternity,
Mother of many acts and hours, should free
  The serpent that would clasp her with his length ;
These are the spells by which to reassume
An empire o'er the disentangled doom.

To suffer woes which Hope thinks infinite ;
To forgive wrongs darker than death or night ;
  To defy Power, which seems omnipotent ;
To love, and bear ; to hope till Hope creates
From its own wreck the thing it contemplates ;
  Neither to change, nor falter, nor repent ;
This, like thy glory, Titan, is to be
Good, great and joyous, beautiful and free ;
This is alone Life, Joy, Empire, and Victory.

PERCY BYSSHE SHELLEY

64 *Stanzas*

OFTEN rebuked, yet always back returning
  To those first feelings that were born with me,
And leaving busy chase of wealth and learning
  For idle dreams of things which cannot be ;

To-day, I will seek not the shadowy region :
  Its unsustaining vastness waxes drear ;
And visions rising, legion after legion,
  Bring the unreal world too strangely near.

Stanzas

I'll walk, but not in old heroic traces,
  And not in paths of high morality,
And not among the half-distinguished faces,
  The clouded forms of long-past history.

I'll walk where my own nature would be leading :
  It vexes me to choose another guide :
Where the grey flocks in ferny glens are feeding ;
  Where the wild wind blows on the mountain-side.

What have those lonely mountains worth revealing ?
  More glory and more grief than I can tell :
The earth that wakes *one* human heart to feeling
  Can centre both the worlds of Heaven and Hell.

EMILY BRONTË

65   *The Phœnix and the Turtle*

LET the bird of loudest lay,
On the sole Arabian tree,
Herald sad and trumpet be,
To whose sound chaste wings obey.

But thou shrieking harbinger,
Foul precurrer of the fiend,
Augur of the fever's end,
To this troop come thou not near !

From this session interdict
Every fowl of tyrant wing,
Save the eagle, feather'd king :
Keep the obsequy so strict.

The Knapsack

Let the priest in surplice white,
That defunctive music can,
Be the death-divining swan,
Lest the requiem lack his right.

And thou treble-dated crow,
That thy sable gender mak'st
With the breath thou giv'st and tak'st,
'Mongst our mourners shalt thou go.

Here the anthem doth commence:
Love and constancy is dead;
Phœnix and the turtle fled
In a mutual flame from hence.

So they lov'd, as love in twain
Had the essence but in one;
Two distincts, division none:
Number there in love was slain.

Hearts remote, yet not asunder;
Distance, and no space was seen
'Twixt the turtle and his queen:
But in them it were a wonder.

So between them love did shine,
That the turtle saw his right
Flaming in the phœnix' sight;
Either was the other's mine.

Property was thus appall'd,
That the self was not the same;
Single nature's double name
Neither two nor one was call'd.

The Phœnix and the Turtle

Reason, in itself confounded,
Saw division grow together ;
To themselves yet either neither,
Simple were so well compounded,

That it cried, ' How true a twain
Seemeth this concordant one !
Love hath reason, reason none,
If what parts can so remain.'

Whereupon it made this threne
To the phœnix and the dove,
Co-supremes and stars of love,
As chorus to their tragic scene.

Threnos

Beauty, truth, and rarity,
Grace in all simplicity,
Here enclos'd in cinders lie.

Death is now the phœnix' nest ;
And the turtle's loyal breast
To eternity doth rest.

Leaving no posterity :
'Twas not their infirmity,
It was married chastity.

Truth may seem, but cannot be ;
Beauty brag, but 'tis not she ;
Truth and beauty buried be.

To this urn let those repair
That are either true or fair ;
For these dead birds sigh a prayer.

WILLIAM SHAKESPEARE

The Knapsack

66 *Sonnet*

THOU art indeed just, Lord, if I contend
With thee ; but, sir, so what I plead is just.
Why do sinners' ways prosper ? and why must
Disappointment all I endeavour end ?

   Wert thou my enemy, O thou my friend,
How wouldst thou worse, I wonder, than thou dost
Defeat, thwart me ? Oh, the sots and thralls of lust
Do in spare hours more thrive than I that spend,
Sir, life upon thy cause. See, banks and brakes
Now, leavèd how thick ! lacèd they are again
With fretty chervil, look, and fresh wind shakes
Them ; birds build—but not I build ; no, but strain,
Time's eunuch, and not breed one work that wakes.
Mine, O thou lord of life, send my roots rain.

GERARD MANLEY HOPKINS

67 *Prospero's Epilogue*

Now my charms are all o'erthrown,
And what strength I have's mine own ;
Which is most faint : now, 'tis true,
I must be here confin'd by you,
Or sent to Naples. Let me not,
Since I have my dukedom got
And pardon'd the deceiver, dwell
In this bare island by your spell :
But release me from my bands
With the help of your good hands.
Gentle breath of yours my sails
Must fill, or else my project fails,
Which was to please. Now I want

Prospero's Epilogue

Spirits to enforce, art to enchant ;
And my ending is despair,
Unless I be reliev'd by prayer,
Which pierces so that it assaults
Mercy itself and frees all faults.
As you from crimes would pardon'd be,
Let your indulgence set me free.

WILLIAM SHAKESPEARE

68 *Lament*

O ! WITHER'D is the garland of the war,
The soldier's pole is fall'n : young boys and girls
Are level now with men ; the odds is gone,
And there is nothing left remarkable
Beneath the visiting moon.

WILLIAM SHAKESPEARE

PART FOUR

69 Marcus Cato

MARCUS CATO is said to have been born at Tusculum, but to have been brought up and spent his time upon a farm belonging to his father in the Sabine territory, before he began to take part in war or politics. We know nothing of his ancestry, except that he himself tells us that his father, Marcus, was a good man and brave soldier, and that his grandfather, Cato, received several military rewards for his services, and that having had five horses killed under him, he received the value of them from the public treasury, as an acknowledgment of his gallantry.

It was the Roman custom to call those who had no ancestry to recommend them, but who rose by their own merits, *new* men. This name was applied to Cato, who said that he was indeed new to honours and posts of importance, but that, in respect of his brave and virtuous ancestry, he was a man of ancient family. His third name originally was not Cato, but Priscus, and was changed to Cato on account of his wisdom, for in Latin *catus* means " clever ". In appearance he was rather red-haired, and grey-eyed, peculiarities which are ill-naturedly dwelt upon by the writer of the epigram—

> Red-haired, grey-eyed, and savage-tusked as well,
> Porcius will find no welcome e'en in hell.

Accustomed as he was to hard exercise, temperate living, and frequent campaigns, his body was always both healthy and strong ; while he also practised the power of speech, thinking it a necessary instrument for a man who does not intend to live an obscure and inactive life. He consequently improved his talents in this respect by pleading causes in the neighbouring villages and towns, so that he was soon admitted to be a capable speaker, and afterwards to be a good orator. From this time all who conversed with him perceived a gravity and wisdom in his mind which qualified him to undertake the most important duties of a statesman. Not only was he so disinterested as to plead without receiving money from his clients, but he also did not think the glory which he gained in these contests to be that after which a man ought to strive, in comparison with that which is gained in battle and campaigns, in which he was so eager to distinguish himself that when quite a lad his body was covered with wounds, all in front. He himself tells us that he made his first campaign at the age of seventeen, when Hannibal was ranging through Italy uncontrolled. In battle he was prompt, steadfast, and undismayed, and was wont to address the enemy with threats and rough language, and to encourage the others to do so, as he rightly pointed out that this often cows the enemy's spirit as effectually as blows. When on the march he used to carry his own arms, and be followed by one servant who carried his provisions. It is said that he never spoke harshly to this man, no matter what food he placed before him, but that he would often help him to do his work when he was at leisure from military duty. He drank only water when campaigning, except that when suffering from parching thirst he would ask for some vinegar, and sometimes when his strength fairly failed he would drink a little wine.

Near his estate was a cottage which had once belonged to Manius Curius, who three times received the honour of a triumph. Cato used frequently to walk over and look at this cottage, and, as he observed the smallness of

Marcus Cato

the plot of ground attached to it, and the simplicity of the dwelling itself, he would reflect upon how Curius, after having made himself the first man in Rome, after conquering the most warlike nations, and driving King Pyrrhus out of Italy, used to dig this little plot of ground with his own hands, and dwelt in this little cottage, after having thrice triumphed. It was there that the ambassadors of the Samnites found him sitting by the hearth, cooking turnips, and offered him much gold ; but he sent them away, saying, " that a man who was contented with such a supper, had no need of gold, and that it was more honourable for him to conquer those who possessed gold, than to possess it himself". Cato, after leaving the cottage, full of these memories, returned to his own house and farm, and after viewing its extent and the number of slaves upon it, he increased the amount of his own daily labour, and retrenched his superfluous expenses.

When Fabius Maximus took the city of Tarentum, Cato, who was a very young lad at the time, was serving in his army. He became intimate there with one Nearchus, a philosopher of the Pythagorean school, and listened with much interest to his discourses. Hearing this man, like Plato, describe pleasure as the greatest temptation to evil, and the body as the chief hindrance to the soul, which can only free and purify itself by such a course of reasoning as removes it from and sets it above all bodily passions and feelings, he was yet more encouraged in his love of simplicity and frugality. In other respects he is said to have studied Hellenic literature late in life, and not to have read Greek books till extreme old age, when he greatly improved his style of oratory, partly by the study of Thucydides, but chiefly by that of Demosthenes. Be this as it may, his writings are full of Greek ideas and Greek anecdotes : and many of his apophthegms and maxims are literally translated from the Greek.

The Knapsack

The estate adjoining that of Cato belonged to one of the most powerful and highly born patricians of Rome, Valerius Flaccus, a man who had a keen eye for rising merit, and generously fostered it until it received public recognition. This man heard accounts of Cato's life from his servants, how he would proceed to the court early in the morning, and plead the causes of all who required his services, and then on returning to his farm would work with his servants, in winter wearing a coarse coat without sleeves, in summer nothing but his tunic, and how he used to sit at meals with his servants, eating the same loaf and drinking the same wine. Many other stories of his goodness and simplicity and sententious remarks were related to Valerius, who became interested in his neighbour, and invited him to dinner. They became intimate, and Valerius, observing his quiet and ingenuous disposition, like a plant that requires careful treatment and an extensive space in which to develop itself, encouraged and urged him to take part in the political life of Rome. On going to Rome he at once gained admirers and friends by his able pleadings in the law courts, while he obtained considerable preferment by the interest of Valerius, being appointed first military tribune, and then quæstor. After this he became so distinguished a man as to be able to compete with Valerius himself for the highest offices in the state, and they were elected together, first as consuls and afterwards as censors. Of the older Romans, Cato attached himself particularly to Fabius Maximus, a man of the greatest renown and power, although it was his disposition and mode of life which Cato especially desired to imitate. Wherefore he did not hesitate to oppose Scipio the Great, who was then a young man, but a rival and opponent of Fabius. Cato was appointed to act as his quæstor in the war in Africa, and on perceiving that Scipio was living with his usual lavish expenditure, and supplying his soldiery with extravagant pay, he sharply rebuked him, saying, " that it was not the waste of the public money that vexed him so much as the ruin of the old frugal habits of the soldiers, who were led to indulge in pleasure and luxury by receiving more pay than was necessary to supply their daily wants ". When Scipio answered that he did not require an economist for his quæstor, at a time when he was preparing to wage war on a grand scale, and reminded him that he would have to give an account to the Roman people of battles won, not of money expended, Cato left the army of Scipio, which was then being assembled in Sicily. He proceeded at once to Rome, and by adding his voice to that of Fabius in the Senate, in blame of Scipio's unspeakable waste of money, and his childish and unsoldierly love of the public games and the theatre, conduct more worthy of the president of a public festival than of the commander-in-chief of an army, prevailed upon the people to send tribunes to enquire into the charges against him, and if they proved true, to bring him back to Rome. When they arrived in Sicily, however, Scipio pointed out to them that the preparations which he had made would ensure him the victory, and that although he loved pleasant society in his hours of leisure, yet that he had never allowed his pleasures to interfere with his serious duties. The tribunes were perfectly satisfied with this explanation, and Scipio sailed for Africa.

Cato, however, gained considerable credit by his speeches on this occasion, and the Romans generally called him the new Demosthenes ; yet his manner of life was more admired than his eloquence. Cleverness of speech was a quality which nearly all the young men of the time sought to attain, but Cato was singular in his keeping up the severe traditions of his ancestors in labouring with his own hands, eating a simple dinner, lighting no fire to cook his breakfast, wearing a plain dress, living in a mean house, and neither coveting superfluities nor courting their possessors. The Romans were at this period extending their empire so much as to lose much of their own original simplicity of living, as each new conquest brought them into contact with foreign customs and new modes of life. They therefore naturally looked with admiration upon Cato, observing that while they became enervated by pleasures and broke down under labours, he on the other hand seemed unaffected by either, and that too, not only while he was young and eager for fame : but even when he was an old grey-headed man, after he had been consul and had triumphed, he yet, like a victorious athlete, still kept himself in training, and never relaxed his severe discipline. He himself tells us that he never wore a garment worth more than a hundred drachmas, that when he was general and consul he still drank the same wine as his servants, that his dinner never cost him more than thirty ases in the market, and that he only indulged himself to this extent for the good of the state, that he might be strong and able to serve his country in the field. When he was left a piece of Babylonian tapestry he at once disposed of it ; none of his rooms were whitewashed, and he never bought a slave for more than fifteen hundred drachmas, seeing that he required, not effeminate and handsome servants, but hardworking and strong men, to tend his horses and herd his cattle : and these, too, when they grew old and past work he thought it best to sell, and not feed them at his expense when they were useless. His rule was that nothing is cheap which one does not want, but that superfluities are dearly purchased even if they cost but one penny : and that it is better to buy land which can be ploughed, or where cattle can graze, than beds of flowers which require watering, and paths which have to be swept and kept in order.

Marcus Cato

These habits some ascribed to narrowness of mind, while others thought that he carried parsimony and avarice to excess in himself in order by his example to reform and restrain others. Be this as it may, I for my own part consider that his conduct in treating his slaves like beasts of burden, and selling them when old and worn out, is the mark of an excessively harsh disposition, which disregards the claims of our common human nature, and merely considers the question of profit and loss. Kindness, indeed, is of wider application than mere justice; for we naturally treat men alone according to justice and the laws, while kindness and gratitude, as though from a plenteous spring, often extend even to irrational animals. It is right for a good man to feed horses which have been worn out in his service, and not merely to train dogs when they are young, but to take care of them when they are old. When the Athenian people built the Parthenon, they set free the mules which had done the hardest work in drawing the stones up to the acropolis, and let them graze where they pleased unmolested. It is said that one of them came of its own accord to where the works were going on, and used to walk up to the acropolis with the beasts who were drawing up their loads, as if to encourage them and show them the way. This mule was, by a decree of the people of Athens, maintained at the public expense for the rest of its life. The racehorses of Kimon also, who won an Olympic victory, are buried close to the monument of their master. Many persons, too, have made friends and companions of dogs, as did Xanthippus in old times, whose dog swam all the way to Salamis beside his master's ship when the Athenians left their city, and which he buried on the promontory which to this day is called the Dog's Tomb. We ought not to treat living things as we do our clothes and our shoes, and throw them away after we have worn them out ; but we ought to accustom ourselves to show kindness in these cases, if only in order to teach ourselves our duty towards one another. For my own part I would not even sell an ox that had laboured for me because he was old, much less would I turn an old man out of his accustomed haunts and mode of life, which is as great an affliction to him as sending him into a foreign land, merely that I might gain a few miserable coins by selling one who must be as useless to his buyer as he was to his seller.

Cato, however, as if taking a perverse pleasure in flaunting his meannesses, relates that he left behind him in Spain the horse which he rode when consul there, in order to save the state the cost of carrying him over to Italy. Whether these acts of his are to be ascribed to magnanimity or narrow-mindedness the reader must decide for himself.

He was a man of wonderful temperance, in all other respects also. For example, when he was general, he only drew from the public stock three Attic bushels of wheat a month for himself and his servants, and less than three half-bushels of barley a day for his horses. When he was Governor of Sardinia, where former governors had been in the habit of charging their tents, bedding, and wearing-apparel to the province, and likewise making it pay large sums for their entertainment and that of their friends, he introduced an unheard-of system of economy. He charged nothing to the province, and visited the various cities without a carriage, walking on foot alone, attended by one single public servant carrying his robe of state and the vessel to make libations at a sacrifice. With all this he showed himself so affable and simple to those under his rule, so severe and inexorable in the administration of justice, and so vigilant and careful in seeing that his orders were duly executed, that the govern-

Marcus Cato

ment of Rome never was more feared or more loved in Sardinia than when he governed that island.

His conversation seems also to have had this character, for he was cheerful and harsh all at once, pleasant and yet severe as a companion, fond of jokes, but morose at the same time, just as Plato tells us that Sokrates, if judged merely from his outside, appeared to be only a silly man with a face like a satyr, who was rude to all he met, though his inner nature was earnest and full of thoughts that moved his hearers to tears and touched their hearts. For this reason I cannot understand how any persons can see a likeness between the orations of Lysias and those of Cato ; however, this point must be decided by those who are more skilled than myself in the comparison of oratorical styles. I shall now relate a few of his more remarkable sayings, believing that a man's real character can be better judged of by his words than by his looks, although some people hold the contrary opinion.

Once when he wished to restrain the Romans from distributing a large quantity of corn as a largesse to the people, he began his speech : " It is difficult, my fellow-citizens, to make the stomach hear reason, because it has no ears." When desiring to blame the extravagance of the Romans, he said that a city could not be safe in which a fish sold dearer than an ox. He said, too, that the Romans were like sheep, who never form opinions of their own, but follow where the others lead them. " Just so," said he, " when you are assembled together you are led by men whose advice you would scorn to take about your own private affairs." With regard to female influence he once said, " All mankind rule their wives, we rule all mankind, and we are ruled by our wives." This remark, however, is borrowed from Themistokles. He one day, when his child was instigating its mother to lay many commands upon him, said, " Wife, remember that the

The Knapsack

Athenians rule the Greeks, I rule the Athenians, you rule me, and your child rules you ; wherefore let him not abuse his power, which, though he knows it not, is greater than that of anyone else in Greece." Cato also said that the Romans fixed the price, not only of different dyes, but of different professions. " Just as the dyers," said he, " dye stuff of whatever colour they see people pleased with, so do our young men only study and apply themselves to those subjects which are praised and commended by you." He used also to beg of them, if they had become great by virtue and self-restraint, not to degenerate ; and if, on the other hand, their empire had been won by licentiousness and vice, to reform themselves, since by the latter means they had become so great as not to need any further assistance from them. Those who were always seeking office, he said, were like men who could not find their way, who always wished to walk with lictors before them to show them the road. He blamed his countrymen for often electing the same men to public offices. " You will appear," said he, " either to think that the office is not worth much, or else that there are not many worthy to fill it." Alluding to one of his enemies who led a dissolute and discreditable life, he said : " That man's mother takes it as a curse rather than a blessing if any one hopes that her son will survive her." When a certain man sold his ancestral estate, which was situated by the seashore, Cato pretended to admire him, as being more powerful than the sea itself, " for this man," said he, has " drunk up the fields which the sea itself could not swallow." When King Eumenes came to Rome the Senate received him with special honours, and he was much courted and run after. Cato, however, held himself aloof and would not go near him, and when some one said, " Yet he is an excellent man, and a good friend to Rome," he answered, " It may be so, but a king is by nature an animal that

Marcus Cato

lives on human flesh." None of those who had borne the title of king, according to Cato, were to be compared with Epameinondas, or Perikles, or Themistokles, or with Manius Curius or Hamilcar Barcas. He used to say that his enemies hated him because he began his day's work while it was still dark, and because he neglected his own affairs to attend to those of the public. He also was wont to say that he had rather his good actions should go unrewarded than that his bad ones should be unpunished ; and that he pardoned all who did wrong except himself.

When the Romans sent three ambassadors to Bithynia, one of whom was crippled by the gout, another had been trepanned and had a piece taken out of his head, and the third was thought to be a simpleton, Cato remarked that the Romans had sent an embassy which had neither feet, head, nor heart. When, for the sake of Polybius the historian, Scipio entreated Cato to exert his influence on behalf of the Achæan exiles, after a long debate in the Senate, where some advised that they should be sent back to their own country, and some that they should still be detained at Rome, he got up and said, " Have we nothing better to do than to sit all day discussing whether a parcel of old Greeks shall be buried here or in Achaia ? " A few days after the Senate had decreed the restoration of the exiles, Polybius proposed to make another application, that they should be restored to all the offices which they formerly held in Achaia. He asked Cato whether he thought that he should succeed in this second appeal to the Senate ; to which Cato answered with a smile that he was imitating Ulysses, when he returned again into the cave of the Cyclops to fetch the hat and girdle which he had left behind and forgotten. He said that wise men gained more advantage from fools, than fools from wise men ; for the wise men avoid the errors of fools, but fools cannot imitate the example of wise men. He said that he loved young men to have red cheeks rather than pale ones, and that he did not care for a soldier who used his hands while he marched and his feet while he fought, or one who snored louder in bed than he shouted in battle. When reproaching a very fat man he said, "How can this man's body be useful to his country when all parts between the neck and the groin are possessed by the belly?" Once when an epicure wished to become his friend, he said that he could not live with a man whose palate was more sensitive than his heart. He said also that the soul of a lover inhabits the body of his beloved. He himself tells us, that in his whole life he repented of three things only :—First, that he had trusted a woman with a secret. Secondly, that he had gone by water when he might have gone by land. Thirdly, that he had passed one day without having made his will. To an old man who was acting wrongly he said, "My good sir, old age is ugly enough without your adding the deformity of wickedness to it." When a certain tribune, who was suspected of being a poisoner, was endeavouring to carry a bad law, Cato remarked, "Young man, I do not know which is the worst for us, to drink what you mix, or to enact what you propose." Once when he was abused by a man of vicious life, he answered, "We are not contending upon equal terms ; you are accustomed to hearing and using bad language, while I am both unused to hearing it and unwilling to use it."

He was a good father and a good husband, and was, in his private life, an economist of no ordinary kind, as he did not despise money-making or regard it as unworthy of his abilities. For this reason I think I ought to relate how well he managed his private affairs. He married a wife who was well born, though not rich ; for he thought that though all classes might possess equally good sense, yet that a woman of noble birth would be more ashamed of doing wrong, and therefore more likely to encourage her husband to do right. He used to say that a man who beat his wife or his children laid sacrilegious hands on the holiest of things. He also said that he had rather be a good husband than a great statesman, and that what he especially admired in Sokrates the Philosopher was his patience and kindness in bearing with his ill-tempered wife and his stupid children. When his son was born, he thought that nothing except the most important business of state ought to prevent his being present while his wife washed the child and wrapped it in swaddling clothes. His wife suckled the child herself; nay she often gave her breast to the children of her slaves, and so taught them to have a brotherly regard for her own son.

As soon as he was able to learn, Cato himself taught him his letters, although he had a clever slave named Chilon, who taught many children to read. He himself declares that he did not wish a slave to reprove his son or pull his ears because he was slow at learning. He taught the boy to read, and instructed him also in the Roman law and in bodily exercises; not confining himself to teaching him to hurl the javelin, to fight in complete armour, and to ride, but also to use his fists in boxing, to endure the extremes of heat and cold, and to swim through swiftly-flowing and eddying rivers. He tells us that he himself wrote books on history with his own hands in large letters, that the boy might start in life with a useful knowledge of what his forefathers had done, and he was as careful not to use an indecent expression before his son as he would have been before the vestal virgins. He never bathed with him; which indeed seems to have been customary at Rome, as even fathers-in-law scrupled to bathe naked before their sons-in-law. In later times, however, the Romans learned from the Greeks the habit of bathing naked, and have taught the Greeks to do so even in the presence of women.

While Cato was engaged in this great work of forming his son's character and completing his education he found him eager to learn, and able to make great progress from his natural ability ; but he appeared so weak and delicate that his father was obliged to relax the stern simplicity of his own life in his favour, and allow him some indulgences in diet. The young man, although so weakly, yet proved himself a good soldier in the wars, and distinguished himself greatly in the battle in which Æmilius Paulus defeated King Perseus. Afterwards, upon the same day, he either had his sword struck from his hand or let it fall from weakness, and in his grief at the loss got together some of his friends and prevailed upon them again to charge the enemy. With great exertions they succeeded in clearing a space, and at length discovered his sword under a great heap of arms and corpses of friends and foes alike which were piled upon it. Paulus, the commander-in-chief, was much pleased with the youth's eagerness to regain his sword, and sent a letter to Cato in which he spoke in the highest terms of the courage and honourable feeling which he had shown. He afterwards married Tertia, the sister of Scipio, and had the gratification of pleasing his father as much as himself by thus allying himself with one of the noblest families in Rome. Thus was Cato rewarded for the care which he had bestowed upon his son's education.

PLUTARCH

70 *The Life of Saint Brandon*

S. BRANDON, the holy man, was a monk, and born in Ireland, and there he was abbot of a house wherein were a thousand monks, and there he had a full strait and holy

The Life of Saint Brandon

life in great penance and abstinence, and he governed his monks full virtuously. And then within short time after, there came to him a holy abbot that hight Birinus to visit him, and each of them was joyful of other. And then S. Brandon began to tell to the abbot Birinus of many wonders that he had seen in divers lands, and when Birinus heard that of S. Brandon, he began to sigh and sore weep, and S. Brandon comforted him the best wise he could, saying : Ye come hither for to be joyful with me, and therefore for God's love leave your mourning and tell me what marvels ye have seen in the great sea-ocean that compasseth all the world about, and all other waters come out of him which runneth in all parts of the earth. And then Birinus began to tell to S. Brandon and to his monks the marvels that he had seen, full sore weeping, and said : I have a son, his name is Mervok, and he was a monk of great fame, which had great desire to seek about by ship in divers countries to find a solitary place wherein he might dwell secretly, out of the business of the world, for to serve God quietly with more devotion, and I counselled him to sail into an island far in the sea, beside the mountain of stones which is full well known, and then he made him ready and sailed thither with his monks. And when he came thither he liked that place full well, where he and his monks served our Lord full devoutly.

And then Birinus saw in a vision that this monk Mervok was sailed right far eastward in the sea, more than three days' sailing, and suddenly to his seeming there came a dark cloud and overcovered them, that a great part of the day they saw no light, and as our Lord would, the cloud passed away and they saw a full fair island, and thitherward they drew. In that island was joy and mirth enough, and the earth of that island shined as bright as the sun, and there were the fairest trees and herbs that ever any man saw, and there were many precious stones shining bright, and every herb there was full of flowers, and every tree full of fruit, so that it was a glorious sight and a heavenly joy to abide there. And there, there came to them a fair young man, and full courteously he welcomed them all, and called every monk by his name, and said that they were much bound to praise the name of our Lord Jesu, that would of his grace show to them that glorious place where is ever day and never night, and this place is called Paradise terrestrial. By this island is another island wherein no man may come, and this young man said to them : Ye have been here half a year without meat, drink, or sleep, and they supposed that they had not been there the space of half an hour, so merry and joyful they were there. And the young man told them that this is the place that Adam and Eve dwelt in first and ever should have dwelled here, if that they had not broken the commandment of God. And then the young man brought them to their ship again, and said they might no longer abide there, and when they were all shipped, suddenly this young man vanished away out of their sight. And then within short time after, by the purveyance of our Lord Jesu Christ, they came to the abbey where S. Brandon dwelled, and then he with his brethren received them goodly and demanded them where they had been so long, and they said : We have been in the land of Behest tofore the gates of Paradise, whereas is ever day and never night, and they said all that the place is full delectable, for yet all their clothes smelled of that sweet and joyful place.

And then S. Brandon purposed soon after for to seek that place by God's help, and anon began to purvey for a good ship and a strong, and victualled it for seven years. And then he took his leave of all his brethren and took twelve monks with him, but ere they entered into the ship they fasted forty days and lived devoutly, and each of them received the sacrament. And when S. Brandon with his

The Life of Saint Brandon

twelve monks were entered in to the ship, there came other two of his monks and prayed him that they might sail with him, and then he said : Ye may sail with me, but one of you shall go to hell ere ye come again, but not for that they would go with him. And then S. Brandon bade the shipmen to wind up the sail and forth they sailed in God's name, so that on the morrow they were out of sight of any land. And forty days and forty nights after they sailed plat east, and then they saw an island far from them, and they sailed thitherward as fast as they could, and they saw a great rock of stone appear above all the water, and three days they sailed about it ere they could get into the place, but at the last by the purveyance of God they found a little haven and there went aland every each one. And then suddenly came a fair hound, and fell down at the feet of S. Brandon and made him good cheer in his manner, and then he bade his brethren be of good cheer, for our Lord hath sent to us his messenger to lead us into some good place. And the hound brought them into a fair hall where they found the tables spread, ready set full of good meat and drink. And then S. Brandon said graces, and then he and his brethren sat down and ate and drank of such as they found, and there were beds ready for them, wherein they took their rest after their long labour.

And on the morn they returned again to their ship, and sailed a long time in the sea after, ere they could find any land, till at last by the purveyance of God, they saw far from them a full fair island, full of green pasture, wherein were the whitest and greatest sheep that ever they saw. For every sheep was as great as an ox, and soon after came to them a goodly old man, which welcomed them and made them good cheer, and said : This is the island of sheep, and here is never cold weather, but ever summer, and that causeth the sheep to be so great and white ; they eat of the best grass and herbs that is anywhere. And then this

The Knapsack

old man took his leave of them and bade them sail forth right east, and within short time by God's grace, they should come in to a place like Paradise, wherein they should keep their Eastertide.

And then they sailed forth, and came soon after to that land, but because of little depth in some places, and in some places were great rocks, but at the last they went upon an island weening to them that they had been safe, and made thereon a fire for to dress their dinner, but S. Brandon abode still in the ship, and when the fire was right hot and the meat nigh sodden, then this island began to move, whereof the monks were afeard, and fled anon to ship and left the fire and meat behind them, and marvelled sore of the moving. And S. Brandon comforted them and said that it was a great fish named Jasconye, which laboureth night and day to put his tail in his mouth, but for greatness he may not. And then anon they sailed west three days and three nights ere they saw any land, wherefore they were right heavy, but soon after, as God would, they saw a fair island full of flowers, herbs, and trees, whereof they thanked God of his good grace, and anon they went on land, and when they had gone long in this they found a full fair well, and thereby stood a fair tree full of boughs, and on every bough sat a fair bird, and they sat so thick on the tree that unnethe any leaf of the tree might be seen. The number of them was so great, and they sang so merrily that it was a heavenly noise to hear, wherefore S. Brandon kneeled down on his knees and wept for joy, and made his prayers devoutly to our Lord God to know what these birds meant.

And then anon one of the birds fled from the tree to S. Brandon, and he with flickering of his wings made a full merry noise like a fiddle, that him seemed he heard never so joyful a melody. And then S. Brandon commanded the bird to tell him the cause why they sat so thick on the

The Life of Saint Brandon

tree and sang so merrily ; and then the bird said : Sometime we were angels in heaven, but when our master Lucifer fell down into hell for his high pride, we fell with him for our offences, some higher and some lower after the quality of the trespass, and because our trespass is but little, therefore our Lord hath set us here out of all pain, in full great joy and mirth after his pleasing, here to serve him on this tree in the best manner we can. The Sunday is a day of rest from all worldly occupation, and therefore that day all we be made as white as any snow for to praise our Lord in the best wise we may. And then this bird said to S. Brandon : That it is twelve months passed that ye departed from your abbey, and in the seventh year hereafter, ye shall see the place that ye desire to come to, and all these seven years ye shall keep your Easter here with us every year, and in the end of the seventh year ye shall come into the land of Behest. And this was on Easter day that the bird said these words to S. Brandon, and then this fowl flew again to his fellows that sat on the tree, and then all the birds began to sing evensong so merrily that it was a heavenly noise to hear. And after supper S. Brandon and his fellows went to bed and slept well, and on the morn they arose betimes, and then these birds began matins, prime, and hours, and all such service as christian men use to sing. And S. Brandon with his fellows abode there eight weeks, till Trinity Sunday was passed, and they sailed again to the island of sheep and there they victualled them well, and sith took their leave of that old man, and returned again to ship. And then the bird of the tree came again to S. Brandon and said : I am come to tell you that ye shall sail from hence into an island wherein is an abbey of twenty-four monks, which is from this place many a mile, and there ye shall hold your Christmas, and your Easter with us, like as I told you, and then this bird flew to his fellows again. And then S. Brandon and his fellows sailed forth in the ocean, and soon after fell a great tempest on them in which they were greatly troubled long time, and sore forlaboured, and after that they found by the purveyance of God an island which was far from them, and then they full meekly prayed our Lord to send them thither in safety, but it was forty days after ere they came thither, wherefore all the monks were so weary of that trouble that they set little price by their lives, and cried continually to our Lord to have mercy on them, and bring them to that island in safety. And by the purveyance of God they came at the last into a little haven, but it was so strait that unnethe the ship might come in, and after they came to an anchor, and anon the monks went to land. And when they had long walked about, at the last they found two fair wells, that one was fair and clear water, and that other was somewhat troubly and thick. And then they thanked our Lord full humbly that had brought them hither in safety, and they would fain have drunk of that water, but S. Brandon charged them they should not take without licence. For if we abstain us a while our Lord will purvey for us in the best wise. And anon after came to them a fair old man with hoar hair, and welcomed them full meekly and kissed S. Brandon, and led them by many a fair well till they came to a fair abbey, where they were received with great honour and solemn procession with twenty-four monks, all in royal copes of cloth of gold and a royal cross was before them. And then the abbot welcomed S. Brandon and his fellowship, and kissed them full meekly, and took S. Brandon by the hand and led him with his monks into a fair hall, and set them down arow upon the bench, and the abbot of the place washed all their feet with fair water of the well that they saw before, and after, led them into the fraitour and there set them among his convent. And anon there came one by the purveyance of God which served them well of meat and

The Life of Saint Brandon

drink, for every monk had set before him a fair white loaf, and white roots and herbs, which was right delicious, but they wist not what roots they were. And they drank of the water of the fair clear well that they saw before when they came first aland, which S. Brandon forbade them. And then the abbot came and cheered S. Brandon and his monks, and prayed them eat and drink for charity; for every day our Lord sendeth a goodly old man that covereth this table and setteth our meat and drink tofore us, but we know not how it cometh, ne we ordain never no meat ne drink for us, and yet we have been eighty years here, and ever our Lord, worshipped may he be, feedeth us. We be twenty-four monks in number, and every ferial day of the week he sendeth to us twelve loaves, and every Sunday and feast-day twenty-four loaves, and the bread that we leave at dinner we eat at supper, and now at your coming our Lord hath sent to us forty-eight loaves, for to make you and us merry together as brethren. And always twelve of us go to dinner whiles other twelve keep the quire, and thus have we done these eighty years, for so long have we dwelled here in this abbey. And we came hither out of the abbey of S. Patrick in Ireland, and thus as ye see our Lord hath purveyed for us, but none of us knoweth how it cometh, but God alone, to whom be given honour and laud world without end. And here in this land is ever fair weather, and none of us hath been sick sith we came hither. And when we go to mass, or to any other service of our Lord in the church, anon seven tapers of wax be set in the quire and be lighted at every time without man's hand, and so burn day and night at every hour of service, and never waste ne minish as long as we have been here, which is eighty years. And then S. Brandon went to the church with the abbot of the place, and there they said evensong together full devoutly, and then S. Brandon looked upward towards the crucifix, and saw our Lord hanging on the cross, which was made of fine crystal and curiously wrought. And in the quire were twenty-four seats for twenty-four monks, and the seven tapers burning, and the abbot's seat was made in the midst of the quire, and then S. Brandon demanded of the abbot how long they had kept that silence, that none of them spake to other, and he said : These twenty-four years we spake never one to another. And then S. Brandon wept for joy of their holy conversation. And then S. Brandon desired of the abbot that he and his monks might dwell there still with him. To whom the abbot said : Sir, that may ye not do in no wise, for our Lord hath showed to you in what manner ye shall be guided till the seven years be fulfilled, and after that term thou shalt with thy monks return into Ireland in safety, but one of the two monks that came last to you shall dwell in the island of ankers, and that other shall go quick to hell. And as S. Brandon kneeled in the church he saw a bright shining angel come in at the window, and lighted all the lights in the church, and then he flew out again at the window unto heaven, and then S. Brandon marvelled greatly how the light burned so fair and wasted not. And then the abbot said that it is written that Moses saw a bush all on afire and yet it burned not, and therefore marvel not hereof for the might of our Lord is now as great as it ever was.

And when S. Brandon had dwelled there from Christmas even till the twelfth day was passed, then he took his leave of the abbot and convent and returned with his monks to his ship, and sailed from thence with his monks toward the abbey of S. Illaries, but they had great tempests in the sea from that time till Palm-Sunday, and then they came to the island of sheep, and there were received of the old man, which brought them to a fair hall and served them. And on Shere-Thursday after supper he washed their feet and kissed them, like as our Lord did to his disciples, and

The Life of Saint Brandon

there abode till Saturday, Easter-even, and they departed
and sailed to the place where the great fish lay, and anon
they saw their caldron upon the fishes back, which they had
left there twelve months tofore, and there they kept the
service of the resurrection on the fishes back, and after,
they sailed that same day by the morning to the island
whereas the tree of birds was, and then the said bird
welcomed S. Brandon and all his fellowship, and went
again to the tree and sang full merrily, and there he and
his monks dwelled from Easter till Trinity Sunday as they
did the year before, in full great joy and mirth. And daily
they heard the merry service of the birds sitting on the
tree. And then the bird told to S. Brandon that he should
return again at Christmas to the abbey of monks, and at
Easter thither again, and the other deal of the year labour
in the ocean in full great perils, and from year to year till
the seven years be accomplished. And then shall ye come
to the joyful place of Paradise and dwell there forty days
in full great joy and mirth, and after, ye shall return home
into your own abbey in safety, and there end your life, and
come to the bliss of heaven, to which our Lord bought you
with his precious blood. And then the angel of our Lord
ordained all thing that was needful to S. Brandon and to
his monks in victuals and all other things necessary, and
then they thanked our Lord of his great goodness that he
had showed to them oft in their great need, and then
sailed forth into the great sea ocean, abiding the mercy of
our Lord in great trouble and tempests.

And soon after came to them an horrible fish which
followed the ship long time, casting so much water out of
his mouth into the ship that they supposed to have been
drowned, wherefore they devoutly prayed God to deliver
them of that great peril. And anon after, came another
fish greater than he, out of the west sea, and fought with
him, and at the last clave him into three pieces, and then

returned again. And then they thanked meekly our Lord of their deliverance from this great peril, but they were in great heaviness because their victuals were nigh spent, but by the ordinance of our Lord there came a bird and brought to them a great branch of a vine full of red grapes, by which they lived fourteen days, and then they came to a little island, wherein were many vines full of grapes, and they there landed and thanked God, and gathered as many grapes as they lived by forty days after, always sailing in the sea in many storms and tempests, and as they thus sailed, suddenly came flying towards them a great grip [1] which assailed them and was like to have destroyed them. Wherefore they devoutly prayed for help and aid of our Lord Jesu Christ. And then the bird of the tree of the island where they had holden their Easter tofore, came to the grip and smote out both his eyes, and after slew him, whereof they thanked our Lord, and then sailed forth continually till S. Peter's day, and then sang they solemnly their service in the honour of the feast. And in that place the water was so clear that they might see all the fishes that were about them, whereof they were full sore aghast, and the monks counselled S. Brandon to sing no more, for all the fishes lay then as they had slept. And then S. Brandon said : Dread ye not, for ye have kept by two Easters the feast of the Resurrection upon the great fishes back, and therefore dread ye not of these little fishes. And then S. Brandon made him ready and went to mass, and bade his monks to sing the best way they could, and then anon all the fishes awoke, and came about the ship so thick that unnethe they might see the water for the fishes, and when the mass was done all the fishes departed so as they were no more seen. And seven days they sailed always in that clear water.

And then there came a south wind and drove the ship

[1] A vulture.

The Life of Saint Brandon

northward, whereas they saw an island full dark and full of stench and smoke, and there they heard great blowing and blasting of bellows, but they might see nothing, but heard great thundering, whereof they were sore afeard, and blessed them oft. And soon after there came one starting out all burning in fire, and stared full ghastly on them with great staring eyes, of whom the monks were aghast, and at his departing from them he made the horriblest cry that might be heard, and soon there came a great number of fiends and assailed them with hooks and burning iron malles, which ran on the water, following their ship fast, in such wise that it seemed all the sea to be on fire. But by the pleasure of our Lord they had no power to hurt ne grieve them ne their ship, wherefore the fiends began to roar and cry, and threw their hooks and malles at them. And they then were sore afraid, and prayed to God for comfort and help, for they saw the fiends all about the ship, and them seemed then all the island and the sea to be on fire. And with a sorrowful cry all those fiends departed from them and returned to the place that they came from. And then S. Brandon told to them that this was a part of hell, and therefore he charged them to be steadfast in the faith, for they should yet see many a dreadful place ere they came home again. And then came the south wind, and drove them farther into the north, where they saw a hill all of fire, and a foul smoke and stench coming from thence, and the fire stood on each side of the hill like a wall all burning. And then one of his monks began to cry and weep full sore, and said that his end was come, and that he might abide no longer in the ship, and anon he leapt out of the ship into the sea, and then he cried and roared full piteously, cursing the time that he was born, and also father and mother that begat him, because they saw no better to his correction in his young age, for now I must go to perpetual pain. And then the saying of S. Brandon was verified that he said to him when he entered ; therefore it is good a man to do penance and forsake sin, for the hour of death is uncertain. And then anon the wind turned into the north and drove the ship into the south, which sailed seven days continually, and they came to a great rock standing in the sea, and thereon sat a naked man in full great misery and pain, for the waves of the sea had so beaten his body that all the flesh was gone off, and nothing left but sinews and bare bones. And when the waves were gone, there was a canvas that hung over his head which beat his body full sore with the blowing of the wind, and also there were two ox-tongues and a great stone that he sat on, which did him full great ease. And then S. Brandon charged him to tell him what he was, and he said : My name is Judas that sold our Lord Jesu Christ for thirty pence, which sitteth here thus wretchedly, howbeit I am worthy to be in the greatest pain that is, but our Lord is so merciful that he hath rewarded me better than I have deserved, for of right my place is in the burning hell, but I am here but certain times of the year, that is, from Christmas to twelfth day, and from Easter till Whitsuntide be past, and every feastful day of our Lady, and every Saturday noon till Sunday, that evensong be done, but all other times I lie still in hell in full burning fire, with Pilate, Herod, and Caiaphas, therefore accursed be the time that ever I knew them. And then Judas prayed S. Brandon to abide still there all that night, and that he would keep him there still, that the fiends should not fetch him to hell. And he said : With God's help thou shalt abide here all this night ; and then he asked Judas what cloth that was that hung over his head, and he said it was a cloth that he gave to a leper, which was bought with the money that he stole from our Lord when I bare his purse, wherefore it doth to me full great pain now, in beating my face with the blowing of the wind,

The Life of Saint Brandon

and these two ox-tongues that hang here above me I gave them sometime to two priests to pray for me, them I bought with mine own money, and therefore they ease me because the fishes of the sea gnaw on them and spare me, and this stone that I sit on, lay sometime in a desolate place where it eased no man, and I took it thence and laid it in a foul way where it did much ease to them that went by that way, and therefore it easeth me now, for every good deed shall be rewarded and every evil deed shall be punished. And the Sunday, against even, there came a great multitude of fiends, blasting and roaring and bade S. Brandon go thence that they might have their servant Judas, for we dare not come into the presence of our master but if we bring him to hell with us. And then said S. Brandon : I let not you to do your master's commandment, but by the power of our Lord Jesu Christ I charge you to leave him this night till to-morrow. They said : how darest thou help him that so sold his master for thirty pence to the Jews, and caused him also to die the most shameful death upon the cross ? And then S. Brandon charged the fiends by his passion that they should not noy him that night. And then the fiends went their way roaring and crying towards hell, to their master the great devil, and then Judas thanked S. Brandon so ruthfully, that it was pity to see, and on the morn the fiends came with a horrible noise, saying that they had that night suffered great pain because they brought not Judas and said that he should suffer double pain the six days following, and they took then Judas, trembling for fear, with them to pain. And after, S. Brandon sailed southward three days and three nights, and on the Friday they saw an island, and then S. Brandon began to sigh, and said : I see the island wherein S. Paul the hermit dwelleth, and hath dwelled there forty years without meat and drink ordained by man's hand. And when they came to the land, S. Paul came and welcomed them humbly. He was

The Knapsack

old and foregrown, so that no man might see his body, of whom S. Brandon said weeping : Now I see a man that liveth more like an angel than a man, wherefore we wretches may be ashamed that we live not better. Then S. Paul said to S. Brandon : Thou art better than I, for our Lord hath showed to thee more of his privities than he hath done to me, wherefore thou oughtest to be more praised than I. To whom S. Brandon said : We be monks, and must labour for our meat, but God hath provided for thee such meat as thou holdest thee pleased, wherefore thou art much better than I. To whom S. Paul said : Sometime I was a monk of S. Patrick's Abbey in Ireland, and was warden of the place whereas men enter into S. Patrick's purgatory, and on a day there came one to me, and I asked him what he was, and he said : I am your abbot Patrick, and charge thee that thou depart from hence to-morn early to the sea-side, and there thou shalt find a ship into which thou must enter, which God hath ordained for thee, whose will thou must accomplish. And so the next day I arose and went forth and found the ship, in which I entered, and by the purveyance of God was I brought into this island the seventh day after. And then I left the ship and went to land, and there I walked up and down a good while, and then, by the purveyance of God, there came an otter, going on his hinder feet, and brought me a flint stone and an iron to smite fire with, in his two foreclaws of his feet, and also he had about his neck great plenty of fish, which he cast down before me and went his way. And I smote fire, and made a fire of sticks, and did seethe the fish by which I lived three days, and then the otter came again and brought to me fish for other three days, and thus he hath done these fifty-one years, through the grace of God. And there was a great stone, out of which our Lord made to spring fair water, clear and sweet, whereof I drink daily, and thus have I lived one and fifty

The Life of Saint Brandon

years. And I was forty years old when I came hither, and am now one hundred and eleven years old, and abide till it please our Lord to send for me, and if it pleased him I would fain be discharged of this wretched life. And then he bade S. Brandon to take of the water of the well, and to carry into his ship: For it is time that thou depart, for thou hast a great journey to do, for thou shalt sail to an island which is forty days sailing hence, where thou shalt hold thine Easter like as thou hast done tofore, whereas the tree of birds is, and from thence thou shalt sail into the land of Behest, and shalt abide there forty days, and after return home into thy country in safety.

And then these holy men took leave each of other, and they wept both full sore, and kissed each other; and then S. Brandon entered into his ship and sailed forty days even south in full great tempest, and on Easter even came to their procurator, which made to them good cheer as he had beforetime, and from thence they came to the great fish, whereon they said matins and mass on Easter day, and when the mass was done the fish began to move and swam forth fast into the sea, whereof the monks were sore aghast which stood upon him, for it was a great marvel to see such a fish, so great as all a country, for to swim so fast in the water, but by the will of our Lord this fish set all the monks aland in the paradise of birds, all whole and sound, and then returned to the place he came from. And then S. Brandon and his monks thanked our Lord of their deliverance of the great fish, and kept their Eastertide till Trinity Sunday, like as they had done beforetime, and after this they took their ship and sailed east forty days.

And at the forty days end it began to hail right fast, and therewith came a dark mist which lasted long after, which feared S. Brandon and his monks, and they prayed to our Lord to keep and help them. And then anon came their procurator and bade them to be of good cheer, for they were come into the land of Behest. And soon after that mist passed away, and anon they saw the fairest country eastward that any man might see, and it was so clear and bright that it was a heavenly sight to behold, and all the trees were charged with ripe fruit, and herb full of flowers. In which land they walked forty days, but they could see none end of that land, and there was always day and never night, and the land temperate, ne too hot ne too cold. And at the last they came to a fair river, but they durst not go over, and there came to them a fair young man and welcomed them courteously, and called each of them by his name, and did great reverence to S. Brandon, and said to them : Be ye now joyful, for this is the land that ye have sought, but our Lord will that ye depart hence hastily and he will show to you more of his secrets when ye come again into the sea, and our Lord will that you lade your ship with the fruit of this land, and hie you hence for ye may no longer abide here, but thou shalt sail again into thine own country, and soon after thou comest home thou shalt die. And this water that thou seest here departeth the world asunder, for on that other side of this water may no man come that is in this life, and the fruit that ye see here is always thus ripe every time of the year, and always it is here light as ye now see, and he that keepeth our Lord's hests at all times shall see this land ere he pass out of this world. And then S. Brandon and his monks took of that fruit as much as they would, and also took with them great plenty of precious stones, and then took their leave, and went to ship weeping sore because they might no longer abide there. And then they took their ship and came home into Ireland in safety, whom their brethren received with great joy, giving thankings to our Lord which had kept them all those seven years from many a peril and brought them home in safety, to whom be given honour and glory, world without end. Amen. And soon after, this holy man S. Brandon waxed feeble and sick, and had but little joy of this world, but ever after his joy and mind was in the joys of heaven. And in a short time after he being full of virtues, departed out of this life to everlasting life, and was worshipfully buried in a fair abbey which he himself founded, where our Lord showeth for this holy saint many fair miracles. Wherefore let us devoutly pray to this holy saint that he pray for us to our Lord that he have mercy on us, to whom be given laud and honour and empire, world without end. Amen.

THE GOLDEN LEGEND

71 *Saint Louis*

THIS holy man, King St. Louis, loved and feared God during his life above all things, and, as is very apparent, was in consequence favoured in all his works. As I have before said that our God died for his people, so in like manner did St. Louis several times risk his life and incur the greatest dangers for the people of his realm, as shall be touched on hereafter.

The good king, being once dangerously ill at Fontainebleau, said to my Lord Louis, his eldest son, " Fair son, I beseech thee to make thyself beloved by the people of thy kingdom ; for, in truth, I should like better that a Scotsman, fresh from Scotland, or from any other distant and unknown country, should govern the subjects of my realm well and loyally, than that thou shouldst rule them wickedly and reproachfully."

The holy king loved truth so much, that even to the Saracens and infidels, although they were his enemies, he would never lie, nor break his word in any thing he had promised them, as shall be noticed hereafter. With regard to his food, he was extremely temperate ; for I never in

The Knapsack

my whole life heard him express a wish for any delicacie in eating or drinking, like too many rich men ; but he sat and took patiently whatever was set before him.

In his conversation he was remarkably chaste ; for I never heard him, at any time, utter an indecent word, nor make use of the devil's name, which, however, is now very commonly uttered by every one, by which I firmly believe is so far from being agreeable to God, that it is highly displeasing to him.

He mixed his wine with water by measure, according to the strength of it, and what it would bear. He once asked me, when at Cyprus, why I did not mix water with my wine. I answered what the physicians and surgeons had told me, that I had a large head and a cold stomach, which would not bear it. But the good king replied, that they had deceived me, and advised me to add water ; for that if I did not learn to do so when young, and was to attempt it in the decline of life, the gout and other disorders, which I might have in my stomach, would greatly increase ; or, perhaps, by drinking pure wine in my old age, I should frequently intoxicate myself ; and that it was a beastly thing for an honourable man to make himself drunk.

My good lord the king asked me at another time, if I should wish to be honoured in this world, and afterward to gain paradise ; to which I answered, that I should wish it were so. " Then," replied he, " be careful never knowingly to do or say any thing disgraceful, that should it become public, you may not have to blush, and be ashamed to say I have done this, or I have said that." In like manner he told me never to give the lie, or contradict rudely whatever might be said in my presence, unless it should be sinful or disgraceful to suffer it, for oftentimes contradiction causes coarse replies and harsh words, that bring on quarrels which create bloodshed, and are the means of the deaths of thousands.

Saint Louis

He also said, that every one should dress and equip himself according to his rank in life, and his fortune, in order that the prudent and elders of this world may not reproach him, by saying such a one has done too much, and that the youth may not remark, that such a one has done too little, and dishonours his station in society. On this subject, I remember once the good lord king, father to the king now on the throne, speaking of the pomp of dress, and the embroidered coats of arms that are now daily common in the armies. I said to the present king, that when I was in the Holy Land with his father, and in his army, I never saw one single embroidered coat or ornamented saddle in the possession of the king his father, or of any other lord. He answered, that he had done wrong in embroidering his arms ; and that he had some coats that had cost him eight hundred Parisian livres. I replied, that he would have acted better if he had given them in charity, and had his dress made of good sendal,[1] lined and strengthened with his arms, like as the king, his father, had done.

The good king, once calling me to him, said he wanted to talk with me, on account of the quickness of understanding he knew I possessed. In the presence of several, he added, " I have called these two monks, and before them ask you this question respecting God : " " Seneschal, what is God ? " " Sire," replied I, " he is so supremely good, nothing can exceed him." " In truth," answered the king, " that is well said, for your answer is written in the little book I have in my hand. I will put another question to you, whether you had rather be ' mezeau et ladre,' [2] or have committed, or be about to commit, a mortal sin ? " But I, who would not tell a lie, replied

---

[1] Sendal or cendal, is what we call taffety.
[2] These two words are synonymous, and signify lepers, of whom, at that period, there were numbers, more especially in the Holy Land.

" that I would rather have committed thirty deadly sins than be a leper."

When the two friars were gone away, he called me to him alone, making me sit at his feet, and said, " How could you dare to make the answer you did to my last question ? " When I replied, " Were I to answer it again, I should repeat the same thing," he instantly said,—" Ah, foul musart ! [1] Musart, you are deceived ; for you must know there can be no leprosy so filthy as deadly sin, and the soul that is guilty of such is like the devil in hell. It is very true," he added, " that when the leprous man is dead, he is cured of that disorder ; but when the man who has committed a deadly sin dies, he is not assured for certain that he had sufficiently repented of it before his death, to induce the goodness of God to pardon him : for which cause he must have great fears lest this leprosy of sin may endure for a length of time, even so long as God may remain in paradise.

" I therefore entreat of you, first for the love of God, and next for the affection you bear me, that you retain in your heart what I have said, and that you would much rather prefer having your body covered with the most filthy leprosy than suffer your soul to commit a single deadly sin, which is of all things the most infamous."

He then inquired if I washed the feet of the poor on Holy Thursday. On which I said, " Oh, for shame, no ; and never will I wash the feet of such fellows." " This is in truth," replied he, " very ill said, for you should never hold in disdain what God did for our instruction ; for He who is lord and master of the universe, on that same day, Holy Thursday, washed the feet of all his apostles, telling them, that he who was their master had thus done, that they, in like manner, might do the same to each other. I therefore beg of you, out of love to him first, and then

---

[1] Idler, one who amuses himself by doing nothing.

Saint Louis

from your regard to me, that you would accustom yourself to do so."

He loved every one who, with uprightness of heart, feared and loved God ; insomuch that from the great reputation he had heard of my brother Sir Gilles de Bruyn, who was not a Frenchman, for his fear and love of God, as was the truth, he appointed him constable of France.

In like manner, from the favourable report which he had heard of Master Robert de Sorbon being a courageous and discreet man, he made him one of his personal attendants, and permitted him to partake of his table. One time, as we were sitting near each other, and eating and drinking at the king's table, we conversed together in a low voice, which the good king observing, reprimanded us by saying, "You act wrong thus to whisper together ; speak out, that your companions may not suspect you are talking of them to their disadvantage, and railing at them. When eating in company, if you have any things to say that are pleasant and agreeable, say them aloud, that every one may hear them : if not, be silent."

JOHN LORD DE JOINVILLE

72 *The Trial of Jeanne d'Arc*

THE said Jeanne was then brought before us there, and we admonished and required her, under penalty of law, to take the oath that she had taken the day before ; and to swear to speak the truth, absolutely and simply, on everything which she was asked in the respect of the matter of which she was accused and defamed. To which she replied that she had taken an oath yesterday, and that should suffice.

Then we required her to swear ; for none, not even a prince, could refuse to take oath when required in matter of faith. She answered again : " I swore yesterday : that should be quite enough. You overburden me." At last she swore to speak the truth on that which concerned the faith.

Whereupon the distinguished professor of sacred theology, master Jean Beaupère, at our order and command questioned the said Jeanne as follows.

And first he exhorted her to answer truly, as she had sworn, what he should ask her. To which she replied : " You may well ask me such things, that to some I shall answer truly, and to others I shall not." And she added, " If you were well informed about me, you would wish me to be out of your hands. I have done nothing except by revelation."

Asked how old she was when she left her father's house, she said she could not vouch for her age.

Asked if in her youth she had learned any craft, she said yes, to sew and spin : and in sewing and spinning she feared no woman in Rouen. And moreover she confessed that for dread of the Burgundians she left her father's house and went to the town of Neufchâteau, in Lorraine, to the house of a certain woman called *La Rousse*, where she stayed about a fortnight. She added, too, that as long as she was at home with her father, she saw to the ordinary domestic tasks ; and that she did not go to the fields to look after the sheep and other animals.

Asked if she confessed her sins once a year, she said yes, to her own curé ; and when he was prevented, she confessed to another priest, with his permission. Sometimes, too, twice or thrice perhaps, she confessed to mendicant friars : but that was in the town of Neufchâteau. And she received the sacrament of the Eucharist at Easter.

Asked if, at other feasts than Easter, she received the said sacrament of the Eucharist, she told the interrogator to continue to the next question. Afterwards she declared that at the age of thirteen she had a voice from God to help her and guide her. And the first time she was much afraid. And this voice came towards noon, in summer, in her father's garden : and the said Jeanne had [not] fasted on the preceding day. She heard the voice on her right, in the direction of the church ; and she seldom heard it without a light. This light came from the same side as the voice, and generally there was a great light. When she came to France she often heard the voice.

Asked how she could see the light of which she spoke, since it was at the side, she made no reply, and went on to other things. She said that if she was in a wood she easily heard the voices come to her. It seemed to her a worthy voice, and she believed it was sent from God ; when she heard the voice a third time she knew that it was the voice of an angel. She said also that this voice always protected her well and that she understood it well.

Asked what instruction this voice gave her for the salvation of her soul : she said it taught her to be good and to go to church often ; and it told her that she must come to France. And, Jeanne added, Beaupère would not learn from her, this time, in what form that voice appeared to her. She further said that this voice told her once or twice a week that she should leave and come to France, and that her father knew nothing of her leaving. She said that the voice told her to come, and she could no longer stay where she was ; and the voice told her again that she should raise the siege of the city of Orleans. She said moreover that the voice told her that she, Jeanne, should go to Robert de Baudricourt, in the town of Vaucouleurs of which he was captain, and he would provide an escort for her. And the said Jeanne answered that she was a poor maid, knowing nothing of riding or fighting. She said she went to an uncle of hers, and told him she wanted to stay with him for some time; and she stayed there about eight days. And she told her uncle she must go to the said town of Vaucouleurs and so her uncle took her.

Then she said that when she reached Vaucouleurs she easily recognized Robert de Baudricourt, although she had never seen him before; and she knew him through her voice, for the voice had told her it was he. And the said Jeanne told Robert she must come to France. The said Robert twice refused to hear her and repulsed her the third time he listened to her and gave her an escort And the voice had told her that it would be so.

Then she declared that the duke of Lorraine ordered that she should be taken to him; and she went to him and told him she wished to go to France. And the duke questioned her about the recovery of his health but she said she knew nothing about that; and she spoke to him little concerning her journey. She told the duke nevertheless to send his son and some men to escort her to France, and she would pray to God for his health. She visited him with a safe conduct and returned to the town of Vaucouleurs.

She declared that, on her departure from Vaucouleurs, she wore the habit of a man, and carried a sword which Robert de Baudricourt had given her, but no other arms; and accompanied by a knight, a squire, and four servants, she reached the town of Saint Urbain, where she slept in an abbey.

She said that on her journey she passed through Auxerre, and she heard Mass in the principal church there; and from that time she frequently heard her voices, including the one already mentioned.

Required to say by what advice she took to man's dress, she several times refused to answer. Finally she answered that she charged no one with that ; and several times she answered variously.

She said that Robert de Baudricourt had sworn those who accompanied her to conduct her well and safely. " Go," said Robert to Jeanne, as she departed, " Go, and come what may."

Jeanne said furthermore that she knows very well that God loves the duke of Orleans ; and so she had more revelations concerning him than any man alive, except him whom she calls her king. She said also that it was altogether necessary to change her women's clothes for men's. She believed that her counsel said well.

She said that she sent to the English at Orleans letters telling them to depart, as shown in the copy of the letters which had been read to her in this town of Rouen, except two or three words in the copy : for example, where in this copy it read *Surrender to the Maid* it should read *Surrender to the King.* There are also these words, *body for body* and *chieftain of war*, which were not in the original letters.

After this the said Jeanne told that she went without hindrance to him whom she calls her king. And when she had arrived at Ste. Catherine de Fierbois, then she sent first to Chinon, where he whom she calls her king was. She reached Chinon towards noon and lodged at an inn ; and after dinner she went to him whom she calls king, who was at the castle. She said that when she entered her king's room she recognized him among many others by the counsel of her voice, which revealed him to her. She told him she wanted to make war on the English.

Asked whether, when the voice showed her her king, there was no light, she answered : " Pass on to the next question." Asked if she saw no angel above the king, she answered : " Spare me that. Continue." She said also that before the king put her to work he had several apparitions and beautiful revelations.

Asked what revelations and apparitions the king had, she answered : " I will not tell you. It is not now the time to tell you ; but send to the king and he will tell you."

Then Jeanne said that her voice had promised her that as soon as she should come to the king he would receive her. She said also that those of her party knew well that the voice was sent to Jeanne from God, and they saw and knew this voice. She said further that her king and several others heard and saw the voices which came to the said Jeanne ; and there were present Charles de Bourbon, and two or three others.

Then Jeanne said that there is not a day when she does not hear this voice ; and she has much need of it. She said she never asked of it any final reward but the salvation of her soul. The voice told her to remain at Saint-Denis in France, and the said Jeanne wished to remain ; but against her will the lords took her away. However, if she had not been wounded, she would not have left ; she was wounded in the trenches before Paris, after she left Saint-Denis ; but recovered in five days. Further she confessed that she caused an assault to be made before Paris.

And when she was asked if that day were a feast day, she answered she thought it certainly was.

Asked if she thought it was a good thing to do, she answered : " Pass on." When this was over, as it appeared to us sufficient for one day, we postponed the affair until the following Saturday, at eight o'clock in the morning.

THOMAS DE COURCELLES

73 *The Last Days of Dr. Donne*

I MUST here look so far back, as to tell the Reader that at his first return out of Essex, to preach his last Sermon, his

The Last Days of Dr. Donne

old friend and Physician, Dr. Fox—a man of great worth—came to him to consult his health; and that after a sight of him, and some queries concerning his distempers, he told him, "That by cordials, and drinking milk twenty days together, there was a probability of his restoration to health"; but he passionately denied to drink it. Nevertheless, Dr. Fox, who loved him most entirely, wearied him with solicitations, till he yielded to take it for ten days; at the end of which time he told Dr. Fox, "He had drunk it more to satisfy him, than to recover his health; and that he would not drink it ten days longer, upon the best moral assurance of having twenty years added to his life; for he loved it not; and was so far from fearing Death, which to others is the King of Terrors, that he longed for the day of his dissolution."

It is observed, that a desire of glory or commendation is rooted in the very nature of man; and that those of the severest and most mortified lives, though they may become so humble as to banish self-flattery, and such weeds as naturally grow there; yet they have not been able to kill this desire of glory, but that like our radical heat, it will both live and die with us; and many think it should do so; and we want not sacred examples to justify the desire of having our memory to outlive our lives; which I mention, because Dr. Donne, by the persuasion of Dr. Fox, easily yielded at this very time to have a monument made for him; but Dr. Fox undertook not to persuade him how, or what monument it should be; that was left to Dr. Donne himself.

A monument being resolved upon, Dr. Donne sent for a Carver to make for him in wood the figure of an Urn, giving him directions for the compass and height of it; and to bring with it a board, of the just height of his body. "These being got, then without delay a choice Painter was got to be in readiness to draw his picture, which was

The Knapsack

taken as followeth.—Several charcoal fires being first made in his large study, he brought with him into that place his winding-sheet in his hand, and having put off all his clothes, had this sheet put on him, and so tied with knots at his head and feet, and his hands so placed as dead bodies are usually fitted, to be shrowded and put into their coffin, or grave. Upon this Urn he thus stood, with his eyes shut, and with so much of the sheet turned aside as might shew his lean, pale, and death-like face, which was purposely turned towards the East, from whence he expected the second coming of his and our Saviour Jesus." In this posture he was drawn at his just height ; and when the picture was fully finished, he caused it to be set by his bed-side, where it continued and became his hourly object till his death, and was then given to his dearest friend and executor Dr. Henry King, then chief Residentiary of St. Paul's, who caused him to be thus carved in one entire piece of white marble, as it now stands in that Church.

And now having brought him through the many labyrinths and perplexities of a various life, even to the gates of death and the grave ; my desire is, he may rest, till I have told my Reader that I have seen many pictures of him, in several habits, and at several ages, and in several postures : and I now mention this, because I have seen one picture of him, drawn by a curious hand, at his age of eighteen, with his sword, and what other adornments might then suit with the present fashions of youth and the giddy gaieties of that age ; and his Motto then was:

> How much shall I be changed,
> Before I am changed ! [1]

And if that young, and his now dying picture were at this time set together, every beholder might say, Lord !

[1] " *Antes muerto que mudado.*" These words are supposed by a Spanish author to have been originally written on the sand by a lady promising fidelity to her lover.

The Last Days of Dr. Donne

how much is Dr. Donne already changed, before he is changed! And the view of them might give my Reader occasion to ask himself with some amazement, " Lord! how much may I also, that am now in health, be changed before I am changed; before this vile, this changeable body shall put off mortality! " and therefore to prepare for it.—But this is not writ so much for my Reader's memento, as to tell him that Dr. Donne would often in his private discourses, and often publicly in his Sermons, mention the many changes both of his body and mind; especially of his mind from a vertiginous giddiness; and would as often say, " His great and most blessed change was from a temporal to a spiritual employment "; in which he was so happy, that he accounted the former part of his life to be lost; and the beginning of it to be, from his first entering into Sacred Orders, and serving his most merciful God at his altar.

Upon Monday, after the drawing of this picture, he took his last leave of his beloved study; and, being sensible of his hourly decay, retired himself to his bed-chamber; and that week sent at several times for many of his most considerable friends, with whom he took a solemn and deliberate farewell, commending to their consideration some sentences useful for the regulation of their lives; and then dismissed them, as good Jacob did his sons, with a spiritual benediction. The Sunday following, he appointed his servants, that if there were any business yet undone, that concerned him or themselves, it should be prepared against Saturday next; for after that day he would not mix his thoughts with any thing that concerned this world; nor ever did; but, as Job, so he " waited for the appointed day of his dissolution ".

And now he was so happy as to have nothing to do but to die, to do which, he stood in need of no longer time; for he had studied it long, and to so happy a perfection, that in a former sickness he called God to witness [in his Book of Devotions written then], " He was that minute ready to deliver his soul into his hands, if that minute God would determine his dissolution." In that sickness he begged of God the constancy to be preserved in that estate for ever ; and his patient expectation to have his immortal soul disrobed from her garment of mortality, makes me confident, that he now had a modest assurance that his prayers were then heard, and his petition granted. He lay fifteen days earnestly expecting his hourly change ; and in the last hour of his last day, as his body melted away, and vapoured into spirit, his soul having, I verily believe, some revelation of the beatifical vision, he said, " I were miserable if I might not die " ; and after those words closed many periods of his faint breath by saying often, " Thy kingdom come, thy will be done." His speech, which had long been his ready and faithful servant, left him not till the last minute of his life, and then forsook him, not to serve another master—for who speaks like him,—but died before him ; for that it was then become useless to him, that now conversed with God on Earth, as Angels are said to do in Heaven, only by thoughts and looks. Being speechless, and seeing Heaven by that illumination by which he saw it, he did, as St. Stephen, " look stedfastly into it, till he saw the Son of Man standing at the right hand of God his Father " ; and being satisfied with this blessed sight, as his soul ascended, and his last breath departed from him, he closed his own eyes, and then disposed his hands and body into such a posture, as required not the least alteration by those that came to shroud him.

Thus variable, thus virtuous was the life : thus excellent, thus exemplary was the death of this memorable man.

He was buried in that place of St. Paul's Church, which he had appointed for that use some years before his death ;

and by which he passed daily to pay his public devotions to Almighty God—who was then served twice a day by a public form of prayer and praises in that place :—but he was not buried privately, though he desired it ; for, beside an unnumbered number of others, many persons of Nobility, and of eminence for Learning, who did love and honour him in his life, did shew it at his death, by a voluntary and sad attendance of his body to the grave, where nothing was so remarkable as a public sorrow.

To which place of his burial some mournful friends repaired, and, as Alexander the Great did to the grave of the famous Achilles, so they strewed his with an abundance of curious and costly flowers ; which course, they—who were never yet known—continued morning and evening for many days, not ceasing, till the stones, that were taken up in that Church, to give his body admission into the cold earth—now his bed of rest,—were again by the Mason's art so levelled and firmed as they had been formerly, and his place of burial undistinguishable to common view.

The next day after his burial, some unknown friend, some one of the many lovers and admirers of his Virtue and Learning, writ this Epitaph with a coal on the wall over his grave :

> Reader ! I am to let thee know,
> Donne's Body only lies below ;
> For, could the grave his Soul comprise,
> Earth would be richer than the Skies !

Nor was this all the honour done to his reverend ashes : for, as there be some persons that will not receive a reward for that for which God accounts himself a debtor ; persons that dare trust God with their charity, and without a witness ; so there was by some grateful unknown friend, that thought Dr. Donne's memory ought to be perpetuated, an hundred marks sent to his faithful friends [Dr. King and Dr. Montford] and Executors, towards the making of his Monument. It was not for many years known by whom ; but, after the death of Dr. Fox, it was known that it was he that sent it ; and he lived to see as lively a representation of his dead friend, as marble can express : a statue indeed so like Dr. Donne, that—as his friend Sir Henry Wotton hath expressed himself—" It seems to breathe faintly, and posterity shall look upon it as a kind of artificial miracle."

He was of stature moderately tall ; of a straight and equally-proportioned body, to which all his words and actions gave an unexpressible addition of comeliness.

The melancholy and pleasant humour were in him so contempered, that each gave advantage to the other, and made his company one of the delights of mankind.

His fancy was unimitably high, equalled only by his great wit ; both being made useful by a commanding judgment.

His aspect was cheerful, and such as gave a silent testimony of a clear knowing soul, and of a conscience at peace with itself.

His melting eye shewed that he had a soft heart, full of noble compassion ; of too brave a soul to offer injuries, and too much a Christian not to pardon them in others.

He did much contemplate—especially after he entered into his sacred calling—the Mercies of Almighty God, the Immortality of the Soul, and the Joys of Heaven : and would often say in a kind of sacred ecstacy,—" Blessed be God that he is God, only and divinely like himself."

He was by nature highly passionate, but more apt to reluct at the excesses of it. A great lover of the offices of humanity, and of so merciful a spirit, that he never beheld the miseries of mankind without pity and relief.

He was earnest and unwearied in the search of knowledge, with which his vigorous soul is now satisfied, and employed in a continual praise of that God that first breathed it into his active body : that body, which once was a Temple of the Holy Ghost, and is now become a small quantity of Christian dust :

But I shall see it re-animated.

IZAAK WALTON

74 *Lord Falkland*

BUT I must here take leave a little longer to discontinue this narration, and if the celebrating the memory of eminent and extraordinary persons, and transmitting their great virtues for the imitation of posterity, be one of the principle ends and duties of History, it will not be thought impertinent in this place to remember a loss, which no time will suffer to be forgotten, and no success or good fortune could repair ; In this unhappy battle was slain the Lord Viscount Falkland, a person of such prodigious parts of learning and knowledge, of that inimitable sweetness and delight in conversation, of so flowing and obliging a humanity and goodness to mankind, and of that primitive simplicity, and integrity of life, that if there were no other brand upon this odious and accursed Civil war, than that single loss, it must be most infamous and execrable to all posterity :

Turpe mori post te, solo non posse dolore.

Before this parliament his condition of life was so happy, that it was hardly capable of improvement ; before he came to twenty years of age, he was master of a noble fortune, which descended to him by the gift of a grandfather, without passing through his father or mother, who were then both alive, and not well enough contented to find themselves passed by in the descent : His education for some years had been in Ireland, where his father was

The Knapsack

Lord Deputy, so that when he returned into England, to the possession of his fortune, he was unintangled with any acquaintance or friends, which usually grow up by the custom of conversation, and therefore was to make a pure election of his company ; which he chose by other rules than were prescribed to the young nobility of that time ; And it cannot be denied, though he admitted some few to his friendship for the agreeableness of their natures, and their undoubted affection to him, that his familiarity and friendship for the most part was with men of the most eminent and sublime parts, and of untouched reputations in point of integrity : and such men had a title to his bosom.

He was a great cherisher of wit, and fancy, and good parts in any man, and if he found them clouded with poverty or want, a most liberal and bountiful Patron towards them, even above his fortune, of which in those administrations he was such a dispenser, as if he had been trusted with it to such uses, and if there had been the least of vice in his expense, he might have been thought too prodigal : He was constant and pertinacious in whatsoever he resolved to do, and not to be wearied by any pains that were necessary to that end, and therefore having once resolved not to see London (which he loved above all places) till he had perfectly learned the Greek tongue, he went to his own house in the country, and pursued it with that indefatigable industry, that it will not be believed, in how short a time he was master of it, and accurately read all the Greek Historians. In this time, his house being within ten miles of Oxford, he contracted familiarity and friendship with the most polite and accurate men of that University ; who found such an immenseness of wit, and such a solidity of judgement in him, so infinite a fancy bound in by a most logical ratiocination, such a vast knowledge, that he was not ignorant in any thing, yet such an excessive humility as if he had known nothing, that they frequently resorted and dwelt with him, as in a College situated in a purer air, so that his house was a University bound in a lesser volume, whither they came not so much for repose, as study : and to examine and refine those grosser propositions, which laziness and consent made current in vulgar conversation.

Many attempts were made upon him, by the instigation of his mother (who was a Lady of another persuasion in religion, and of a most masculine understanding, allayed with the passion and infirmities of her own sex) to pervert him in his piety to the Church of England, and to reconcile him to that of Rome, which they prosecuted with the more confidence, because he declined no opportunity or occasion of conference with those of that religion, whether Priests or Laiques, having diligently studied the controversies, and exactly read all or the choicest of the Greek and Latin fathers, and having a memory so stupendous, that he remembered on all occasions whatsoever he read : And he was so great an enemy to that passion and uncharitableness which he saw produced by difference of opinion in matters of religion, that in all those disputations with Priests and others of the Roman Church, he affected to manifest all possible civility to their persons, and estimation of their parts, which made them retain still some hope of his reduction, even when they had given over offering farther reasons to him to that purpose : But this charity towards them was much lessened, and any correspondence with them quite declined, when by sinister Arts they had corrupted his two younger brothers, being both children, and stolen them from his house, and transported them beyond seas, and perverted his sisters, upon which occasion he writ two large discourses against the principle positions of that Religion, with that sharpness of Style, and full

The Knapsack

weight of reason, that the Church is deprived of great jewels, in the concealment of them, and that they are not published to the world.

He was superior to all those passions and affections which attend vulgar minds, and was guilty of no other ambition, than of knowledge, and to be reputed a lover of all good men, and that made him too much a contemner of those Arts which must be indulged to in the transaction of human affairs. In the last short Parliament he was a Burgess in the House of Commons, and from the debates which were then managed with all imaginable gravity and sobriety, he contracted such a reverence to Parliaments that he thought it really impossible, that they could ever produce mischief or inconvenience to the kingdom, or that the kingdom could be tolerably happy in the intermission of them ; and from the unhappy, and unseasonable dissolution of that convention, he harboured it may be some jealousy and prejudice of the Court, towards which he was not before immoderately inclined, his father having wasted a full fortune there, in those offices and employments, by which other men use to obtain a greater. He was chosen again this Parliament to serve in the same place, and in the beginning of it, declared himself very sharply and severely against those exorbitances which had been most grievous to the State ; for he was so rigid an observer of established Laws and rules, that he could not endure the least breach or deviation from them, and thought no mischief so intolerable, as the presumption of ministers of State, to break positive rules for reason of State, or judges to transgress known Laws, upon the title of conveniency or necessity . . .

Two reasons prevailed with him to receive the seals, and but for those he had resolutely avoided them, the first, the consideration that it might bring some blemish upon the King's affairs, and that men would have believed that he had refused so great an honour and trust, because he must have been with it obliged to do somewhat else, not justifiable ; and this he made matter of conscience, since he knew the King made choice of him before other men, especially because he thought him more honest than other men ; the other was, lest he might be thought to avoid it, out of fear to do an ungracious thing to the House of Commons, who were sorely troubled at the displacing Sir Harry Vane, whom they looked upon as removed for having done them those offices they stood in need of, and the disdain of so popular an encumbrance wrought upon him next to the other, for as he had a full appetite of fame by just and generous Actions, so he had an equal contempt of it by any servile expedients, and he so much the more consented to and approved the justice upon Sir H. Vane, in his own private judgement, by how much he surpassed most men in the religious observation of a trust, the violation whereof he would not admit of any excuse for.

For these reasons he submitted to the King's command, and became his Secretary, with as humble and devout an acknowledgement of the greatness of the obligation, as could be expressed, and as true a sense of it in his heart ; yet two things he could never bring himself to whilst he continued in that office (that was to his death), for which he was contented to be reproached, as for omissions in a most necessary part of his place ; the one, employing of Spies, or giving any countenance or entertainment to them, I do not mean such emissaries as with danger will venture to view the enemies Camp, and bring intelligence of their number of quartering, or such generals as such an observation can comprehend, but those who by communication of guilt, or dissimulation of manners, wound themselves into such trust and secrets, as enabled them to make discoveries for the benefit of the State ; the other, the liberty of opening letters, upon a suspicion that they might contain matter of dangerous consequence ; for the first, he would say, such instruments must be void of all ingenuity and common honesty, before they could be of use, and afterwards they could never be fit to be credited, and that no single preservation could be worth so general a wound and corruption of human society, as the cherishing such persons would carry with it : The last he thought such a violation of the Law of nature, that no qualification by office, could justify a single person in the trespass, and though he was convinced by the necessity and iniquity of the time, that those advantages of information were not to be declined, and were necessarily to be practised, he found means to shift it from himself, when he confessed he needed excuse and pardon for the omission, so unwilling he was to resign any thing in his nature, to an obligation in his office. In all other particulars, he filled his place plentifully, being sufficiently versed in languages, to understand any that is used in business, and to make himself again understood : To speak of his integrity, and his high disdain of any bait that might seem to look towards corruption, in tanto viro, injuria virtutum fuerit.

He had a courage of the most clear and keen temper, and so far from fear, that he was not without appetite of danger, and therefore upon any occasion of action he always engaged his person in those troops which he thought by the forwardness of the Commanders to be most like to be farthest engaged, and in all such encounters he had about him a strange cheerfulness and companiableness, without at all affecting the execution that was then principally to be attended, in which he took no delight, but took pains to prevent it, where it was not by resistance necessary, insomuch that at Edgehill, when the Enemy was routed, he was like to have incurred great

Lord Falkland

peril by interposing to save those who had thrown away their arms, and against whom it may be others were more fierce for their having thrown them away, insomuch as a man might think, he came into the Field only out of curiosity to see the face of danger, and charity to prevent the shedding of blood ; yet in his natural inclination he acknowledged he was addicted to the profession of a Soldier, and shortly after he came to his fortune, and before he came to Age, he went into the Low Countries with a resolution of procuring command, and to give himself up to it, from which he was converted by the complete inactivity of that Summer ; and so he returned into England, and shortly after entered upon that vehement course of study we mentioned before, till the first Alarum from the North, and then again he made ready for the field, and though he received some repulse in the command of a troop of Horse, of which he had a promise, he went a volunteer with the Earl of Essex.

From the entrance into this unnatural war, his natural cheerfulness and vivacity grew clouded, and a kind of sadness and dejection of spirit stole upon him, which he had never been used to, yet, being one of those who believed that one battle would end all differences, and that there would be so great a victory on one side, that the other would be compelled to submit to any conditions from the victor (which supposition and conclusion generally sunk into the minds of most men, prevented the looking after many advantages which might then have been laid hold of) he resisted those indispositions, et in luctu bellum inter remedia erat : but after the King's return from Brayneforde, and the furious resolution of the two houses, not to admit any treaty for peace, those indispositions which had before touched him, grew into a perfect habit of cheerfulness, and he who had been so exactly unreserved and affable to all men, that his face and countenance was

The Knapsack

always present and vacant to his company, and held any cloudiness, and less pleasantness of the visage, a kind of rudeness or incivility, became on a sudden less communicable, and thence very sad, pale, and exceedingly affected with the spleen. In his clothes and habit, which he had intended before always with more neatness, and industry, and expense, than is usual to so great a mind, he was not now only incurious, but too negligent, and in his reception of suitors and the necessary or casual addresses to his place so quick, and sharp, and severe, that there wanted not some men (who were strangers to his nature and disposition) who believed him proud and imperious, from which no mortal man was ever more free. The truth is, as he was of a most incomparable gentleness, application, and even a demisness and submission to good, and worthy, and entire men, so he was naturally . . . adversus malos injucundus, and was so ill a dissembler of his dislike, and disinclination to ill men, that it was not possible for such not to discern it ; there was once in the House of Commons such a declared acceptation of the good service an eminent member had done to them, and as they said, to the whole kingdom, that it was moved, he being present, that the Speaker might in the name of the whole House give him thanks, and then that every member might as a testimony of his particular acknowledgement stir or move his Hat towards him, the which (though not ordered) when very many did, the Lord of Falkland (who believed the service itself not to be of that moment, and that an Honourable and generous person could not have stooped to it, for any recompense) instead of moving his Hat, stretched both his Arms out, and clasped his hands together upon the Crown of his Hat, and held it close down to his head, that all men might see how odious that flattery was to him, and the very approbation of the person, though at that time most popular.

Lord Falkland

When there was any overture or hope of peace, he would be more erect, and vigorous, and exceedingly solicitous to press any thing which he thought might promote it, and sitting amongst his friends often after a deep silence, and frequent sighs, would with a shrill and sad Accent ingeminate the word, Peace, Peace, and would passionately profess that the very Agony of the War, and the view of the calamities, and desolation the kingdom did and must endure, took his sleep from him, and would shortly break his heart. This made some think, or pretend to think, that he was so much enamoured on peace, that he would have been glad the King should have bought it at any price, which was a most unreasonable calumny, as if a man, that was himself the most punctual and precise, in every circumstance that might reflect upon conscience or Honour, could have wished the King to have committed a trespass against either ; and yet this senseless scandal made some impression upon him, or at least he used it for an excuse of the daringness of his spirit ; for at the leaguer before Gloster, when his friends passionately reprehended him for exposing his person, unnecessarily to danger, (as he delighted to visit the trenches, and nearest approaches, and to discover what the enemy did) as being so much beside the duty of his place, that it might be understood against it, he would say, merrily, that his office could not take away the privileges of his Age, and that a Secretary in war might be present at the greatest secret of danger, but withal alledged seriously that it concerned him to be more active in enterprises of hazard, than other men, that all might see that his impatiency for peace, proceeded not from pusillanimity, or fear to adventure his own person.

In the morning before the battle, as always upon Action, he was very cheerful, and put himself into the first rank of the Lord Byron's Regiment, who was then advancing upon the enemy, who had lined the hedges on both sides with Musketeers, from whence he was shot with a musket on the lower part of the belly, and in the instant falling from his horse, his body was not found till the next morning : till when there was some hope he might have been a prisoner, though his nearest friends who knew his temper, received small comfort from that imagination ; thus fell that incomparable young man, in the four and thirtieth year of his Age, having so much dispatched the business of life, that the oldest rarely attain to that immense knowledge, and the youngest enter not into the world with more innocence, and whosoever leads such a life, need not care upon how short warning it be taken from him.

EDWARD HYDE, EARL OF CLARENDON

75 *Henry Hastings*

MR. HASTINGS, by his quality, being the son, brother, and uncle to the Earls of Huntingdon, and his way of living, had the first place amongst us. He was peradventure an original in our age, or rather the copy of our nobility in ancient days in hunting and not warlike times ; he was low, very strong and very active, of a reddish flaxen hair, his clothes always green cloth, and never all worth when new five pounds. His house was perfectly of the old fashion, in the midst of a large park well stocked with deer, and near the house rabbits to serve his kitchen, many fish-ponds, and great store of wood and timber ; a bowling-green in it, long but narrow, full of high ridges, it being never levelled since it was ploughed ; they used round sand bowls, and it had a banqueting-house like a stand, a large one built in a tree. He kept all manner of sport-hounds that ran buck, fox, hare, otter, and badger, and hawks long and short winged ; he had all sorts of nets for fishing : he had a walk in the New Forest and the manor of Christ Church. This last supplied him with red deer, sea and river fish ; and indeed all his neighbours' grounds and royalties were free to him, who bestowed all his time in such sports, but what he borrowed to caress his neighbours' wives and daughters, there being not a woman in all his walks of the degree of a yeoman's wife or under, and under the age of forty, but it was extremely her fault if he were not intimately acquainted with her. This made him very popular, always speaking kindly to the husband, brother, or father, who was to boot very welcome to his house whenever he came. There he found beef pudding and small beer in great plenty, a house not so neatly kept as to shame him or his dirty shoes, the great hall strewed with marrow bones, full of hawks' perches, hounds, spaniels, and terriers, the upper sides of the hall hung with the fox-skins of this and the last year's skinning, here and there a polecat intermixed, guns and keepers' and huntsmen's poles in abundance. The parlour was a large long room, as properly furnished ; on a great hearth paved with brick lay some terriers and the choicest hounds and spaniels ; seldom but two of the great chairs had litters of young cats in them, which were not to be disturbed, he having always three or four attending him at dinner, and a little white round stick of fourteen inches long lying by his trencher, that he might defend such meat as he had no mind to part with to them. The windows, which were very large, served for places to lay his arrows, crossbows, stonebows, and other such like accoutrements ; the corners of the room full of the best chose hunting and hawking poles ; an oyster-table at the lower end, which was of constant use twice a day all the year round, for he never failed to eat oysters before dinner and supper through all seasons : the neighbouring town of Poole supplied him with them. The upper part of this

The Knapsack

room had two small tables and a desk, on the one side of which was a church Bible, on the other the Book of Martyrs; on the tables were hawks' hoods, bells, and such like, two or three old green hats with their crowns thrust in so as to hold ten or a dozen eggs, which were of a pheasant kind of poultry he took much care of and fed himself; tables, dice, cards, and boxes were not wanting. In the hole of the desk were store of tobacco-pipes that had been used. On one side of this end of the room was the door of a closet, wherein stood the strong beer and the wine, which never came thence but in single glasses, that being the rule of the house exactly observed, for he never exceeded in drink or permitted it. On the other side was a door into an old chapel not used for devotion; the pulpit, as the safest place, was never wanting of a cold chine of beef, pasty of venison, gammon of bacon, or great apple-pie, with thick crust extremely baked. His table cost him not much, though it was very good to eat at, his sports supplying all but beef and mutton, except Friday, when he had the best sea-fish as well as other fish he could get, and was the day that his neighbours of best quality most visited him. He never wanted a London pudding, and always sung it in with " my part lies therein-a". He drank a glass of wine or two at meals, very often syrup of gilliflower in his sack, and had always a tun glass without feet stood by him holding a pint of small beer, which he often stirred with a great sprig of rosemary. He was well natured, but soon angry, calling his servants bastard and cuckoldy knaves, in one of which he often spoke truth to his own knowledge, and sometimes in both, though of the same man. He lived to a hundred, never lost his eyesight, but always writ and read without spectacles, and got to horse without help. Until past fourscore he rode to the death of a stag as well as any.

THE 1st EARL OF SHAFTESBURY

76 *Colonel John Hutchinson*

HE was of a middle stature, of a slender and exactly well-proportioned shape in all parts, his complexion fair, his hair of a light brown, very thick set in his youth, softer than the finest silk, curling into loose great rings at the ends, his eyes of a lively grey, well shaped and full of life and vigour, graced with many becoming motions, his visage thin, his mouth well made, and his lips very ruddy and graceful, although the nether chap shut over the upper, yet it was in such a manner as was not unbecoming, his teeth were even and white as the purest ivory, his chin was something long, and the mould of his face, his forehead was not very high, his nose was raised and sharp, but withal he had a most amiable countenance, which carried in it something of magnanimity and majesty mixed with sweetness, that at the same time bespoke love and awe in all that saw him ; his skin was smooth and white, his legs and feet excellently well made, he was quick in his pace and turns, nimble and active and graceful in all his motions, he was apt for any bodily exercise, and any that he did became him, he could dance admirably well, but neither in youth nor riper years made any practice of it, he had skill in fencing such as became a gentleman, he had a great love of music, and often diverted himself with a viol, on which he played masterly, he had an exact ear and judgment in other music, he shot excellently in bows and guns, and much used them for his exercise, he had great judgment in paintings, graving, sculpture, and all liberal arts, and had many curiosities of value in all kinds, he took great delight in perspective glasses, and for his other rarities was not so much affected with the antiquity as the merit of the work—he took much pleasure in improvement of grounds, in planting groves and walks, and fruit-trees, in opening springs and making fish ponds ; of country recreations he loved none but hawking, and in that was very eager and much delighted for the time he used it, but soon left it off ; he was wonderfully neat, cleanly and gentle in his habit, and had a very good fancy in it, but he left off very early the wearing of anything that was costly, yet in his plainest negligent habit appeared very much a gentleman ; he had more address than force of body, yet the courage of his soul so supplied his members that he never wanted strength when he found occasion to employ it ; his conversation was very pleasant, for he was naturally cheerful, had a ready wit and apprehension ; he was eager in every thing he did, earnest in dispute, but withal very rational, so that he was seldom overcome, every thing that it was necessary for him to do he did with delight, free and unconstrained, he hated ceremonious compliment, but yet had a natural civility and complaisance to all people, he was of a tender constitution, but through the vivacity of his spirit could undergo labours, watchings and journeys, as well as any of stronger compositions ; he was rheumatic, and had a long sickness and distemper occasioned thereby two or three years after the war ended, but else for the latter half of his life was healthy though tender, in his youth and childhood he was sickly, much troubled with weakness and tooth aches, but then his spirit carried him through them ; he was very patient under sickness or pain or any common accidents, but yet upon occasions, though never without just ones, he would be very angry, and had even in that such a grace as made him to be feared, yet he was never outrageous in passion ; he had a very good faculty in persuading, and would speak very well pertinently and effectually without premeditation upon the greatest occasions that could be offered, for indeed his judgment was so nice, that he could never frame any speech beforehand to please himself, but his

invention was so ready and wisdom so habitual in all
his speeches, that he never had reason to repent himself
of speaking at any time without ranking the words beforehand, he was not talkative yet free of discourse, of a very
spare diet, not much given to sleep, an early riser when
in health, he never was at any time idle, and hated
to see any one else so, in all his natural and ordinary
inclinations and composure, there was something extraordinary and tending to virtue, beyond what I can describe,
or can be gathered from a bare dead description ; there
was a life of spirit and power in him that is not to be
found in any copy drawn from him : to sum up therefore
all that can be said of his outward frame and disposition
we must truly conclude, that it was a very handsome
and well furnished lodging prepared for the reception of
that prince, who in the administration of all excellent
virtues reigned there awhile, till he was called back to
the palace of the universal emperor.

LUCY HUTCHINSON

77 *William Cobbett*

PEOPLE have about as substantial an idea of Cobbett as
they have of Cribb. His blows are as hard, and he himself
is as impenetrable. One has no notion of him as making
use of a fine pen, but a great mutton-fist ; his style stuns
his readers, and he " fillips the ear of the public with a
three-man beetle ". He is too much for any single news-
paper antagonist ; " lays waste " a city orator or Member
of Parliament, and bears hard upon the government itself.
He is a kind of *fourth estate* in the politics of the country.
He is not only unquestionably the most powerful political
writer of the present day, but one of the best writers in the
language. He speaks and thinks plain, broad, downright

The Knapsack

English. He might be said to have the clearness of Swift, the naturalness of Defoe, and the picturesque satirical description of Mandeville ; if all such comparisons were not impertinent. A really great and original writer is like nobody but himself. In one sense, Sterne was not a wit, nor Shakespeare a poet. It is easy to describe second-rate talents, because they fall into a class, and enlist under a standard : but first-rate powers defy calculation or comparison, and can be defined only by themselves. They are *sui generis*, and make the class to which they belong. I have tried half a dozen times to describe Burke's style without ever succeeding—its severe extravagance ; its literal boldness ; its matter-of-fact hyperboles ; its running away with a subject, and from it at the same time—but there is no making it out, for there is no example of the same thing any where else. We have no common measure to refer to ; and his qualities contradict even themselves.

Cobbett is not so difficult. He has been compared to Paine ; and so far it is true there are no two writers who come more into juxtaposition from the nature of their subjects, from the internal resources on which they draw, and from the popular effect of their writings, and their adaptation (though that is a bad word in the present case) to the capacity of every reader. But still if we turn to a volume of Paine's (his Common Sense or Rights of Man), we are struck (not to say somewhat refreshed) by the difference. Paine is a much more sententious writer than Cobbett. You cannot open a page in any of his best and earlier works without meeting with some maxim, some antithetical and memorable saying, which is a sort of starting-place for the argument, and the goal to which it returns. There is not a single *bon-mot*, a single sentence in Cobbett that has ever been quoted again. If any thing is ever quoted from him, it is an epithet of abuse or a nickname. He is an excellent hand at invention in that

William Cobbett

way, and has " damnable iteration in him ". What could be better than his pestering Erskine year after year with his second title of Baron Clackmannan ? He is rather too fond of *the Sons and Daughters of Corruption*. Paine affected to reduce things to first principles, to announce self-evident truths. Cobbett troubles himself about little but the details and local circumstances. The first appeared to have made up his mind beforehand to certain opinions, and to try to find the most compendious and pointed expressions for them : his successor appears to have no clue, no fixed or leading principles, nor ever to have thought on a question till he sits down to write about it ; but then there seems no end of his matters of fact and raw materials, which are brought out in all their strength and sharpness from not having been squared or frittered down or vamped up to suit a theory—he goes on with his descriptions and illustrations as if he would never come to a stop ; they have all the force of novelty with all the familiarity of old acquaintance ; his knowledge grows out of the subject, and his style is that of a man who has an absolute intuition of what he is talking about, and never thinks of any thing else. He deals in premises and speaks to evidence—the coming to a conclusion and summing up (which was Paine's *forte*) lies in a smaller compass. The one could not compose an elementary treatise on politics to become a manual for the popular reader ; nor could the other in all probability have kept up a weekly journal for the same number of years with the same spirit, interest, and untired perseverance. Paine's writings are a sort of introduction to political arithmetic on a new plan : Cobbett keeps a day-book and makes an entry at full of all the occurrences and troublesome questions that start up throughout the year. Cobbett, with vast industry, vast information, and the utmost power of making what he says intelligible, never seems to get at the beginning or come to the end of any question : Paine, in a few short sentences, seems by his peremptory manner " to clear it from all controversy, past, present, and to come ". Paine takes a bird's-eye view of things. Cobbett sticks close to them, inspects the component parts, and keeps fast hold of the smallest advantages they afford him. Or, if I might here be indulged in a pastoral allusion, Paine tries to enclose his ideas in a fold for security and repose : Cobbett lets *his* pour out upon the plain like a flock of sheep to feed and batten. Cobbett is a pleasanter writer for those to read who do not agree with him ; for he is less dogmatical, goes more into the common grounds of fact and argument to which all appeal, is more desultory and various, and appears less to be driving at a previous conclusion than urged on by the force of present conviction. He is therefore tolerated by all parties, though he has made himself by turns obnoxious to all ; and even those he abuses read him. The Reformers read him when he was a Tory, and the Tories read him now that he is a Reformer. He must, I think, however, be *caviare* to the Whigs.

If he is less metaphysical and poetical than his celebrated prototype, he is more picturesque and dramatic. His episodes, which are numerous as they are pertinent, are striking, interesting, full of life and *naïveté*, minute, double measure running over, but never tedious—*nunquam sufflaminandus erat*. He is one of those writers who can never tire us, not even of himself ; and the reason is, he is always " full of matter ". He never runs to lees, never gives us the vapid leavings of himself, is never " weary, stale, and unprofitable ", but always setting out afresh on his journey, clearing away some old nuisance, and turning up new mould. His egotism is delightful, for there is no affectation in it. He does not talk of himself for lack of something to write about, but because some circumstance that has happened to himself is the best possible illustration of the

William Cobbett

subject, and he is not the man to shrink from giving the best possible illustration of the subject from a squeamish delicacy. He likes both himself and his subject too well. He does not put himself before it, and say—" admire me first "—but places us in the same situation with himself, and makes us see all that he does. There is no blindman's-buff, no conscious hints, no awkward ventriloquism, no testimonies of applause, no abstract, senseless self-complacency, no smuggled admiration of his own person by proxy : it is all plain and above-board. He writes himself plain William Cobbett, strips himself quite as naked as any body would wish—in a word, his egotism is full of individuality, and has room for very little vanity in it. We feel delighted, rub our hands, and draw our chair to the fire, when we come to a passage of this sort : we know it will be something new and good, manly and simple, not the same insipid story of self over again. We sit down at table with the writer, but it is to a course of rich viands, flesh, fish, and wild-fowl, and not to a nominal entertainment, like that given by the Barmecide in the Arabian Nights, who put off his visitors with calling for a number of exquisite things that never appeared, and with the honour of his company. Mr. Cobbett is not a *make-believe* writer. His worst enemy cannot say that of him. Still less is he a vulgar one. He must be a puny, common-place critic indeed, who thinks him so. How fine were the graphical descriptions he sent us from America : what a transatlantic flavour, what a native *gusto*, what a fine *sauce-piquante* of contempt they were seasoned with ! If he had sat down to look at himself in the glass, instead of looking about him like Adam in Paradise, he would not have got up these articles in so capital a style. What a noble account of his first breakfast after his arrival in America ! It might serve for a month. There is no scene on the stage more amusing. How well he paints the gold and scarlet plumage of the American birds, only to lament more pathetically the want of the wild wood-notes of his native land ! The groves of the Ohio that had just fallen beneath the axe's stroke " live in his description ", and the turnips that he transplanted from Botley " look green " in prose ! How well at another time he describes the poor sheep that had got the tick, and had tumbled down in the agonies of death ! It is a portrait in the manner of Bewick, with the strength, the simplicity, and feeling of that great naturalist. What havoc he makes, when he pleases, of the curls of Dr. Parr's wig and of the Whig consistency of Mr. —— ! His Grammar too is as entertaining as a story-book. He is too hard upon the style of others, and not enough (sometimes) on his own.

As a political partisan, no one can stand against him. With his brandished club, like Giant Despair in the Pilgrim's Progress, he knocks out their brains ; and not only no individual, but no corrupt system could hold out against his powerful and repeated attacks, but with the same weapon, swung round like a flail, that he levels his antagonists, he lays his friends low, and puts his own party *hors de combat*. This is a bad propensity, and a worse principle in political tactics, though a common one. If his blows were straight forward and steadily directed to the same object, no unpopular Minister could live before him ; instead of which he lays about right and left, impartially and remorselessly, makes a clear stage, has all the ring to himself, and then runs out of it, just when he should stand his ground. He throws his head into his adversary's stomach, and takes away from him all inclination for the fight, hits fair or foul, strikes at every thing, and as you come up to his aid or stand ready to pursue his advantage, trips up your heels or lays you sprawling, and pummels you when down as much to his heart's content as ever the Yanguesian carriers belaboured Rosinante with their pack-

William Cobbett

staves. "*He has the back-trick simply the best of any man in Illyria.*" He pays off both scores of old friendship and new-acquired enmity in a breath, in one perpetual volley, one raking fire of "arrowy sleet" shot from his pen. However his own reputation or the cause may suffer in consequence, he cares not one pin about that, so that he disables all who oppose, or who pretend to help him. In fact, he cannot bear success of any kind, not even of his own views or party; and if any principle were likely to become popular, would turn round against it to shew his power in shouldering it on one side. In short, wherever power is, there is he against it: he naturally butts at all obstacles, as unicorns are attracted to oak-trees, and feels his own strength only by resistance to the opinions and wishes of the rest of the world. To sail with the stream, to agree with the company is not his humour. If he could bring about a Reform in Parliament, the odds are that he would instantly fall foul of and try to mar his own handy-work; and he quarrels with his own creatures as soon as he has written them into a little vogue—and a prison. I do not think this is vanity or fickleness so much as a pugnacious disposition, that must have an antagonist power to contend with, and only finds itself at ease in systematic opposition. If it were not for this, the high towers and rotten places of the world would fall before the battering-ram of his hard-headed reasoning: but if he once found them tottering, he would apply his strength to prop them up, and disappoint the expectations of his followers. He cannot agree to any thing established, nor to set up any thing else in its stead. While it is established, he presses hard against it, because it presses upon him, at least in imagination. Let it crumble under his grasp, and the motive to resistance is gone. He then requires some other grievance to set his face against. His principle is repulsion, his nature contradiction: he is made up of mere antipathies, an Ishmaelite indeed without a

The Knapsack

fellow. He is always playing at *hunt-the-slipper* in politics. He turns round upon whoever is next him. The way to wean him from any opinion, and make him conceive an intolerable hatred against it, would be to place somebody near him who was perpetually dinning it in his ears. When he is in England, he does nothing but abuse the Borough-mongers, and laugh at the whole system : when he is in America, he grows impatient of freedom and a republic. If he had stayed there a little longer, he would have become a loyal and a loving subject of his Majesty King George IV. He lampooned the French Revolution when it was hailed as the dawn of liberty by millions : by the time it was brought into almost universal ill-odour by some means or other (partly no doubt by himself) he had turned, with one or two or three others, staunch Buonapartist. He is always of the militant, not of the triumphant party : so far he bears a gallant shew of magnanimity ; but his gallantry is hardly of the right stamp. It wants principle : for though he is not servile or mercenary, he is the victim of self-will. He must pull down and pull in pieces : it is not his disposition to do otherwise. It is a pity ; for with his great talents he might do great things, if he would go right forward to any useful object, make thorough-stitch work of any question, or join hand and heart with any principle. He changes his opinions as he does his friends, and much on the same account. He has no comfort in fixed principles : as soon as any thing is settled in his own mind, he quarrels with it. He has no satisfaction but in the chase after truth, runs a question down, worries and kills it, then quits it like vermin, and starts some new game, to lead him a new dance, and give him a fresh breathing through bog and brake, with the rabble yelping at his heels, and the leaders perpetually at fault. This he calls sport-royal. He thinks it as good as cudgel-playing or single-stick, or any thing else that has life in it. He likes

William Cobbett

the cut and thrust, the falls, bruises, and dry blows of an argument : as to any good or useful results that may come of the amicable settling of it, any one is welcome to them for him. The amusement is over, when the matter is once fairly decided.

There is another point of view in which this may be put. I might say that Mr. Cobbett is a very honest man with a total want of principle, and I might explain this paradox thus. I mean that he is, I think, in downright earnest in what he says, in the part he takes at the time ; but in taking that part, he is led entirely by headstrong obstinacy, caprice, novelty, pique or personal motive of some sort, and not by a stedfast regard for truth, or habitual anxiety for what is right uppermost in his mind. He is not a fee'd, time-serving, shuffling advocate (no man could write as he does who did not believe himself sincere)—but his under-standing is the dupe and slave of his momentary, violent, and irritable humours. He does not adopt an opinion " deliberately or for money " ; yet his conscience is at the mercy of the first provocation he receives, of the first whim he takes in his head ; he sees things through the medium of heat and passion, not with reference to any general principles, and his whole system of thinking is deranged by the first object that strikes his fancy or sours his temper.— One cause of this phenomenon is perhaps his want of a regular education. He is a self-taught man, and has the faults as well as excellences of that class of persons in their most striking and glaring excess. It must be acknowledged that the Editor of the Political Register (the *two-penny trash*, as it was called, till a bill passed the House to raise the price to sixpence) is not " the gentleman and scholar " : though he has qualities that, with a little better manage-ment, would be worth (to the public) both those titles. For want of knowing what has been discovered before him, he has not certain general landmarks to refer to, or a general standard of thought to apply to individual cases. He relies on his own acuteness and the immediate evidence, without being acquainted with the comparative anatomy or philosophical structure of opinion. He does not view things on a large scale or at the horizon (dim and airy enough perhaps)—but as they affect himself, close, palpable, tangible. Whatever he finds out, is his own, and he only knows what he finds out. He is in the constant hurry and fever of gestation : his brain teems incessantly with some fresh project. Every new light is the birth of a new system, the dawn of a new world to him. He is continually outstripping and overreaching himself. The last opinion is the only true one. He is wiser to-day than he was yesterday. Why should he not be wiser to-morrow than he was to-day ?—Men of a learned education are not so sharp-witted as clever men without it : but they know the balance of the human intellect better ; if they are more stupid, they are more steady ; and are less liable to be led astray by their own sagacity and the overweening petulance of hard-earned and late-acquired wisdom. They do not fall in love with every meretricious extravagance at first sight, or mistake an old battered hypothesis for a vestal, because they are new to the ways of this old world. They do not seize upon it as a prize, but are safe from gross imposition by being as wise and no wiser than those who went before them.

Paine said on some occasion—" What I have written, I have written "—as rendering any farther declaration of his principles unnecessary. Not so Mr. Cobbett. What he has written is no rule to him what he is to write. He learns something every day, and every week he takes the field to maintain the opinions of the last six days against friend or foe. I doubt whether this outrageous inconsistency, this headstrong fickleness, this understood want of all rule and method, does not enable him to go on with the spirit, vigour, and variety that he does. He is not pledged to repeat himself. Every new Register is a kind of new Prospectus. He blesses himself from all ties and shackles on his understanding ; he has no mortgages on his brain ; his notions are free and unincumbered. If he was put in trammels, he might become a vile hack like so many more. But he gives himself " ample scope and verge enough ". He takes both sides of a question, and maintains one as sturdily as the other. If nobody else can argue against him, he is a very good match for himself. He writes better in favour of Reform than any body else ; he used to write better against it. Wherever he is, there is the tug of war, the weight of the argument, the strength of abuse. He is not like a man in danger of being *bed-rid* in his faculties—He tosses and tumbles about his unwieldy bulk, and when he is tired of lying on one side, relieves himself by turning on the other. His shifting his point of view from time to time not merely adds variety and greater compass to his topics (so that the Political Register is an armoury and magazine for all the materials and weapons of political warfare), but it gives a greater zest and liveliness to his manner of treating them. Mr. Cobbett takes nothing for granted as what he has proved before ; he does not write a book of reference. We see his ideas in their first concoction, fermenting and overflowing with the ebullitions of a lively conception. We look on at the actual process, and are put in immediate possession of the grounds and materials on which he forms his sanguine, unsettled conclusions. He does not give us samples of reasoning, but the whole solid mass, refuse and all.

> ———" He pours out all as plain
> As downright Shippen or as old Montaigne."

This is one cause of the clearness and force of his writings. An argument does not stop to stagnate and muddle in his brain, but passes at once to his paper. His ideas are served up, like pancakes, hot and hot. Fresh theories give him fresh courage. He is like a young and lusty bridegroom that divorces a favourite speculation every morning and marries a new one every night. He is not wedded to his notions, not he. He has not one Mrs. Cobbett among all his opinions. He makes the most of the last thought that has come in his way, seizes fast hold of it, rumples it about in all directions with rough strong hands, has his wicked will of it, takes a surfeit, and throws it away.—Our author's changing his opinions for new ones is not so wonderful : what is more remarkable is his facility in forgetting his old ones. He does not pretend to consistency (like Mr. Coleridge) ; he frankly disavows all connexion with himself. He feels no personal responsibility in this way, and cuts a friend or principle with the same decided indifference that Antipholis of Ephesus cuts Ægeon of Syracuse. It is a hollow thing. The only time he ever grew romantic was in bringing over the relics of Mr. Thomas Paine with him from America to go a progress with them through the disaffected districts. Scarce had he landed in Liverpool when he left the bones of a great man to shift for themselves ; and no sooner did he arrive in London than he made a speech to disclaim all participation in the political and theological sentiments of his late idol, and to place the whole stock of his admiration and enthusiasm towards him to the account of his financial speculations, and of his having predicted the fate of paper-money. If he had erected a little gold statue to him, it might have proved the sincerity of this assertion : but to make a martyr and a patron-saint of a man, and to dig up " his canonized bones " in order to expose them as objects of devotion to the rabble's gaze, asks something that has more life and spirit in it, more mind and vivifying soul, than has to do with any calculation of pounds, shillings, and pence ! The fact is, he *ratted* from his own project. He found the thing not so ripe as he had expected. His heart failed him : his enthusiasm fled, and he made his retractation. His admiration is short-lived : his contempt only is rooted, and his resentment lasting.—The above was only one instance of his building too much on practical *data*. He has an ill habit of prophesying, and goes on, though still deceived. The art of prophesying does not suit Mr. Cobbett's style. He has a knack of fixing names and times and places. According to him, the Reformed Parliament was to meet in March, 1818—it did not, and we heard no more of the matter. When his predictions fail, he takes no farther notice of them, but applies himself to new ones—like the country-people who turn to see what weather there is in the almanac for the next week, though it has been out in its reckoning every day of the last.

Mr. Cobbett is great in attack, not in defence : he cannot fight an up-hill battle. He will not bear the least punishing. If any one turns upon him (which few people like to do) he immediately turns tail. Like an overgrown school-boy, he is so used to have it all his own way, that he cannot submit to any thing like competition or a struggle for the mastery ; he must lay on all the blows, and take none. He is bullying and cowardly ; a Big Ben in politics, who will fall upon others and crush them by his weight, but is not prepared for resistance, and is soon staggered by a few smart blows. Whenever he has been set upon he has slunk out of the controversy. The Edinburgh Review made (what is called) a dead set at him some years ago, to which he only retorted by an eulogy on the superior neatness of an English kitchen-garden to a Scotch one. I remember going one day into a bookseller's shop in Fleet-street to ask for the Review ; and on my expressing my opinion to a young Scotchman, who stood behind the counter, that Mr. Cobbett might hit as hard in his reply, the North Briton said with some alarm—" But you don't

The Knapsack

think, Sir, Mr. Cobbett will be able to injure the Scottish nation?" I said I could not speak to that point, but I thought he was very well able to defend himself. He, however, did not, but has borne a grudge to the Edinburgh Review ever since, which he hates worse than the Quarterly. I cannot say I do.

WILLIAM HAZLITT

PART FIVE

78 *Lollai, lollai, litil child*

Lollai, lollai, litil child !
 Whi wepistou so sore ?
Nedis mostou wepe,
 Hit was iyarkid [1] the yore
Ever to lib in sorow,
 And sich and mourne evere,
As thin eldren did er this,
 Whil hi alivès were.
  Lollai, lollai, litil child,
   Child, lolai, lullow !
  Into uncuth world
   Icommen so ertow [2].

Bestis and thos foules,
 The fisses in the flode,
And euch schef [3] alives
 Makid of bone and blode,
Whan hi commith to the world
 Hi doth ham silf sum gode,
Al bot the wrech brol [4]
 That is of Adamis blode.
  Lollai, lollai, litil child !
   To kar ertow bemette ;
  Thou nost noght this worldis wild
   Bifor the is isette.

[1] *iyarkid*, prepared, ordained. [2] *ertow*, art thou.
[3] *schef*, creature. [4] *brol*, child.

The Knapsack

Child, if it betidith
 That thou ssalt thrive and the [1],
Thench thou wer ifostred
 Up thi moder kne ;
Ever hab mund [2] in thi hert
 Of thos thingès thre,
Whan thou commist, whan thou art,
 And what ssal com of the.
  Lollai, lollai, litil child,
   Child, lollai, lollai !
   With sorow thou com into this world,
   With sorow ssalt wend awai.

Ne tristou to this world ;
 Hit is thi ful fo.
The rich he makith pouer,
 The porè rich also.
Hit turneth wo to wel,
 And ekè wel to wo.
Ne trist no man to this world,
 Whil hit turnith so.
  Lollai, lollai, litil child !
   The fote is in the whele.
   Thou nost whoder turne
   To wo other wele.

Child, thou ert a pilgrim
 In wikidnis ibor ;
Thou wandrest in this fals world ;
 Thou lokè the befor.
Deth ssal com with a blast
 Ute of a wel dim horre [3],
Adamis kin dun to cast,

---

[1] *the,* prosper.   [2] *mund,* memory.
     [3] *horre,* mist, fog, cloud.

Lollai, lollai, litil child

Him silf hath ido befor.
  Lollai, lollai, litil child !
    So wo the worth Adam
  In the lond of Paradis
    Throgh wikidnes of Satan.

Child, thou nert a pilgrim,
  Bot an uncuthe gist ;
Thi dawès[1] beth itold ;
  Thi iurneis beth icast.
Whoder thou salt wend,
  North other est,
Deth the sal betide,
  With bitter bale in brest.
    Lollai, lollai, litil child !
      This wo Adam the wroght,
  Whan he of the appil ete,
    And Eve hit him betacht[2].

ANON

79 *I sing of a Maiden*

I SING of a maiden
  That is makèles[3],
King of all kinges
  To her sone sche ches[4].
He cam also stille
  There his moder was,
As dew in Aprille
  That fallyt on the grass.
He cam also stille
  To his moderès bour,

[1] *dawès,* days.   [2] *betacht,* gave.
[3] *makèles,* without a mate.   [4] *ches,* chose.

287

The Knapsack

As dew in Aprille
  That fallyt on the flour.
He cam also stille
  There his moder lay,
As dew in Aprille
  That fallyt on the spray.
Moder and maiden
  Was never non but sche ;
Well may swich a lady
  Godès moder be.

ANON

80 *Western Wind*

WESTERN wind, when will thou blow,
  The small rain down can rain ?
Christ, if my love were in my arms
  And I in my bed again !

ANON

81 *The Maidens came*

THE maidens came
  When I was in my mother's bower ;
I had all that I would.
  The bailey beareth the bell away ;
  The lily, the rose, the rose I lay.
The silver is white, red is the gold ;
The robes they lay in fold.
  The bailey beareth the bell away ;
  The lily, the rose, the rose I lay.
And through the glass window shines the sun.
How should I love, and I so young ?
  The bailey beareth the bell away ;
  The lily, the lily, the rose I lay.

ANON

The Cherry-tree Carol

JOSEPH was an old man,
 and an old man was he,
When he wedded Mary,
 in the land of Galilee.

Joseph and Mary walked
 through an orchard good,
Where was cherries and berries,
 so red as any blood.

Joseph and Mary walked
 through an orchard green,
Where was berries and cherries,
 as thick as might be seen.

O then bespoke Mary,
 so meek and so mild :
' Pluck me one cherry, Joseph,
 for I am with child.'

O then bespoke Joseph,
 with words most unkind :
' Let him pluck thee a cherry
 that brought thee with child.'

O then bespoke the babe,
 within his mother's womb :
' Bow down then the tallest tree,
 for my mother to have some.'

Then bowed down the highest tree
 unto his mother's hand ;
Then she cried, ' See, Joseph,
 I have cherries at command.'

The Knapsack

'O eat your cherries, Mary,
  O eat your cherries, now ;
O eat your cherries, Mary,
  that grow upon the bough.'

As Joseph was a walking,
  he heard an angel sing :
'This night shall be born
  our heavenly king.

'He neither shall be born
  in housen nor in hall,
Nor in the place of Paradise,
  but in an ox's stall.

'He neither shall be clothed
  in purple nor in pall,
But all in fair linen,
  as were babies all.

'He neither shall be rocked
  in silver nor in gold,
But in a wooden cradle,
  that rocks on the mould.

'He neither shall be christened
  in white wine nor red,
But with fair spring water,
  with which we were christened.'

Then Mary took her babe,
  and sat him on her knee,
Saying, 'My dear son, tell me
  what this world will be.'

The Cherry-tree Carol

' O I shall be as dead, mother,
    as the stones in the wall ;
O the stones in the streets, mother,
    shall mourn for me all.

' Upon Easter-day, mother,
    my uprising shall be ;
O the sun and the moon, mother,
    shall both rise with me.'

ANON

83   *She is gentle and also wise*

SHE is gentle and also wise ;
Of all other she beareth the prize,
    That ever I saw.

To hear her sing, to see her dance !
She will the best herself advance,
    That ever I saw.

To see her fingers that be so small !
In my conceit she passeth all
    That ever I saw.

Nature in her hath wonderly wrought.
Christ never such another bought,
    That ever I saw.

I have seen many that have beauty,
Yet is there none like to my lady
    That ever I saw.

Therefore I dare this boldly say,
I shall have the best and fairest may
    That ever I saw.

ANON

84 *To Mistress Margaret Hussey*

Merry Margaret,
  As midsummer flower,
Gentle as falcon
  Or hawk of the tower,
With solace and gladness,
Much mirth and no madness ;
All good and no badness,
So joyously,
So maidenly,
So womanly,
Her demeaning
In every thing
Far far passing
That I can endite
Or suffice to write
Of merry Margaret,
  As midsummer flower,
Gentle as falcon
  Or hawk of the tower.

As patient and as still,
And as full of good will,
As fair Isaphill,
Coliander,
Sweet pomander,
Good Cassander,
Steadfast of thought,
Well made, well wrought.
Far may be sought
Erst that ye can find
So courteous, so kind,

To Mistress Margaret Hussey

As merry Margaret,
    This midsummer flower,
Gentle as falcon
    Or hawk of the tower.

JOHN SKELTON

85   *To Mistress Isabel Pennell*

By Saint Mary, my lady,
Your mammy and your daddy
Brought forth a goodly baby.

My maiden Isabel,
Reflaring rosabel,
The flagrant camomel,

The ruddy rosary,
The sovereign rosemary,
The pretty strawberry,

The columbine, the nepte [1],
The ieloffer [2] well set,
The proper violet,

Ennewèd [3] your colour
Is like the daisy flower
After the April shower.

Star of the morrow gray,
The blossom on the spray,
The freshest flower of May,

Maidenly demure,
Of womanhood the lure ;
Wherefore I make you sure

[1] *nepte*, mint.   [2] *ieloffer*, gilliflower.   [3] *Ennewèd*, freshly tinted.

293

The Knapsack

It were an heavenly health,
It were an endless wealth,
A life for God himself,

To hear this nightingale
Among the birdès small
Warbling in the vale,

' Dug, dug, jug, jug !
Good year and good luck !'
With ' Chuck, chuck, chuck, chuck !'

JOHN SKELTON

86 *Spring, the sweet Spring*

SPRING, the sweet Spring, is the year's pleasant king ;
Then blooms each thing, then maids dance in a ring.
Cold doth not sting, the pretty birds do sing,
Cuckoo, jug, jug, pu we, to witta woo.

The palm and may make country houses gay,
Lambs frisk and play, the shepherds pipe all day,
And we hear aye birds tune this merry lay,
Cuckoo, jug, jug, pu we, to witta woo.

The fields breathe sweet, the daisies kiss our feet,
Young lovers meet, old wives a-sunning sit,
In every street these tunes our ears do greet,
Cuckoo, jug, jug, pu we, to witta woo.
    Spring, the sweet Spring !

THOMAS NASHE

The Passionate Shepherd

87 *The Passionate Shepherd*

COME live with me and be my Love,
And we will all the pleasures prove
That hills and valleys, dale and field,
And all the craggy mountains yield.

There will we sit upon the rocks
And see the shepherds feed their flocks,
By shallow rivers, to whose falls
Melodious birds sing madrigals.

There will I make thee beds of roses
And a thousand fragrant posies,
A cap of flowers, and a kirtle
Embroider'd all with leaves of myrtle.

A gown made of the finest wool,
Which from our pretty lambs we pull,
Fair linéd slippers for the cold,
With buckles of the purest gold.

A belt of straw and ivy buds
With coral clasps and amber studs :
And if these pleasures may thee move,
Come live with me and be my Love.

Thy silver dishes for thy meat
As precious as the gods do eat,
Shall on an ivory table be
Prepared each day for thee and me.

The shepherd swains shall dance and sing
For thy delight each May morning :
If these delights thy mind may move,
Then live with me and be my Love.

CHRISTOPHER MARLOWE

The Knapsack

88 *Autolycus' Song*

LAWN as white as driven snow ;
Cyprus black as e'er was crow ;
Gloves as sweet as damask roses ;
Masks for faces and for noses ;
Bugle bracelet, necklace amber,
Perfume for a lady's chamber ;
Golden quoifs and stomachers,
For my lads to give their dears :
Pins and poking-sticks of steel,
What maids lack from head to heel :
Come buy of me, come ; come buy, come buy ;
Buy, lads, or else your lasses cry :
Come buy.

WILLIAM SHAKESPEARE

89 *Desdemona's Song*

THE poor soul sat sighing by a sycamore tree,
   Sing all a green willow ;
Her hand on her bosom, her head on her knee,
   Sing willow, willow, willow :
The fresh streams ran by her, and murmur'd her moans ;
   Sing willow, willow, willow ;
Her salt tears fell from her, and soften'd the stones ;
   Sing willow, willow, willow ;
   Sing all a green willow must be my garland.
Let nobody blame him ; his scorn I approve,—
I call'd my love false love ; but what said he then ?
   Sing willow, willow, willow :
If I court moe women, you'll couch with moe men.

WILLIAM SHAKESPEARE

90 *Where the Bee Sucks*

WHERE the bee sucks, there suck I :
In a cowslip's bell I lie ;
There I couch when owls do cry.
On the bat's back I do fly
After summer merrily.
Merrily, merrily shall I live now
Under the blossom that hangs on the bough.

WILLIAM SHAKESPEARE

91 *Epilogue to a Midsummer Night's Dream*

Now the hungry lion roars,
  And the wolf behowls the moon ;
Whilst the heavy ploughman snores,
  All with weary task fordone.
Now the wasted brands do glow,
  Whilst the screech-owl, screeching loud,
Puts the wretch that lies in woe
  In remembrance of a shroud.
Now it is the time of night
  That the graves, all gaping wide,
Every one lets forth his sprite,
  In the church-way paths to glide :
And we fairies, that do run
  By the triple Hecate's team,
From the presence of the sun,
  Following darkness like a dream,
Now are frolic : not a mouse
Shall disturb this hallow'd house :
I am sent with broom before,
To sweep the dust behind the door.

Enter OBERON *and* TITANIA *with their train.*

The Knapsack

OBE. Through the house give glimmering light,
    By the dead and drowsy fire :
Every elf and fairy sprite,
    Hop as light as bird from brier ;
And this ditty, after me,
Sing, and dance it trippingly.

TITA. First, rehearse your song by rote,
To each word a warbling note :
Hand in hand, with fairy grace,
Will we sing, and bless this place.

                              [Song and dance.

OBE. Now, until the break of day,
Through this house each fairy stray.
To the best bride-bed will we,
Which by us shall blessed be ;
And the issue there create
Ever shall be fortunate.
So shall all the couples three
Ever true in loving be ;
And the blots of Nature's hand
Shall not in their issue stand ;
Never mole, hare lip, nor scar,
Nor mark prodigious, such as are
Despised in nativity,
Shall upon their children be.
With this field-dew consecrate,
Every fairy take his gait :
And each several chamber bless,
Through this palace, with sweet peace ;
And the owner of it blest
Ever shall in safety rest.
    Trip away ;
    Make no stay ;
Meet me all by break of day.

WILLIAM SHAKESPEARE

92 *Come unto these Yellow Sands*

Come unto these yellow sands,
   And then take hands :
Curtsied when you have, and kiss'd—
   The wild waves whist ;
Foot it featly here and there ;
And, sweet sprites, the burthen bear.
     Hark, hark !
              Bow-wow.
  The watch-dogs bark :
              Bow-wow.
  Hark, hark ! I hear
  The strain of strutting chanticleer
  Cry, Cock-a-diddle-dow.

             WILLIAM SHAKESPEARE

93 *Full Fathom Five*

Full fathom five thy father lies ;
   Of his bones are coral made ;
Those are pearls that were his eyes :
   Nothing of him that doth fade
But doth suffer a sea-change
Into something rich and strange.
Sea-nymphs hourly ring his knell :
             Ding-dong.
Hark ! now I hear them,—Ding-dong, bell.

             WILLIAM SHAKESPEARE

94 *Spring and Winter*

WHEN daisies pied and violets blue
   And lady-smocks all silver-white
And cuckoo-buds of yellow hue
   Do paint the meadows with delight,
The cuckoo then, on every tree,
Mocks married men ; for thus sings he,
                    Cuckoo ;
Cuckoo, cuckoo : O word of fear,
Unpleasing to a married ear !

When shepherds pipe on oaten straws
   And merry larks are ploughmen's clocks,
When turtles tread, and rooks, and daws,
   And maidens bleach their summer smocks,
The cuckoo then, on every tree,
Mocks married men ; for thus sings he,
                    Cuckoo ;
Cuckoo, cuckoo : O word of fear,
Unpleasing to a married ear !

When icicles hang by the wall
   And Dick the shepherd blows his nail
And Tom bears logs into the hall
   And milk comes frozen home in pail,
When blood is nipp'd and ways be foul,
Then nightly sings the staring owl,
                    Tu-whit tu-who ;
A merry note,
While greasy Joan doth keel the pot.

When all aloud the wind doth blow
   And coughing drowns the parson's saw
And birds sit brooding in the snow
   And Marian's nose looks red and raw,

Spring and Winter

When roasted crabs hiss in the bowl,
Then nightly sings the staring owl,
                    Tu-whit tu-who ;
A merry note,
While greasy Joan doth keel the pot.

WILLIAM SHAKESPEARE

95   *Who is Silvia?*

WHO is Silvia ? what is she,
    That all our swains commend her ?
Holy, fair and wise is she ;
    The heaven such grace did lend her,
That she might admired be.

Is she kind as she is fair ?
    For beauty lives with kindness.
Love doth to her eyes repair,
    To help him of his blindness,
And, being help'd, inhabits there.

Then to Silvia let us sing,
    That Silvia is excelling ;
She excels each mortal thing
    Upon the dull earth dwelling :
To her let us garlands bring.

WILLIAM SHAKESPEARE

96   *You spotted Snakes*

YOU spotted snakes with double tongue,
    Thorny hedgehogs, be not seen ;
Newts and blind-worms, do no wrong,
    Come not near our fairy queen.

Philomel, with melody
Sing in our sweet lullaby ;
Lulla, lulla, lullaby, lulla, lulla, lullaby :
    Never harm,
    Nor spell nor charm,
Come our lovely lady nigh ;
So, good night, with lullaby.

Weaving spiders, come not here ;
    Hence, you long-legg'd spinners, hence !
Beetles black, approach not near ;
    Worm nor snail, do no offence.
    Philomel, with melody,
    Sing in our sweet lullaby ;
Lulla, lulla, lullaby, lulla, lulla, lullaby :
    Never harm,
    Nor spell nor charm,
Come our lovely lady nigh ;
So, good night, with lullaby.

WILLIAM SHAKESPEARE

97 *Over Hill, Over Dale*

OVER hill, over dale,
    Thorough bush, thorough brier,
Over park, over pale,
    Thorough flood, thorough fire,
I do wander every where,
Swifter than the moonès sphere ;
And I serve the fairy queen,
To dew her orbs upon the green.
The cowslips tall her pensioners be :
In their gold coats spots you see ;

Over Hill, Over Dale

Those be rubies, fairy favours,
In those freckles live their savours :
I must go seek some dewdrops here
And hang a pearl in every cowslip's ear.

WILLIAM SHAKESPEARE

98 *Under the Greenwood Tree*

UNDER the greenwood tree
  Who loves to lie with me,
  And turn his merry note
  Unto the sweet bird's throat ;
Come hither, come hither, come hither :
    Here shall he see
    No enemy
But winter and rough weather.

Who doth ambition shun
  And loves to live i' the sun,
  Seeking the food he eats
  And pleas'd with what he gets,
Come hither, come hither, come hither :
    Here shall he see
    No enemy
But winter and rough weather.

WILLIAM SHAKESPEARE

99 *O Mistress Mine*

O MISTRESS mine, where are you roaming ?
O, stay and hear ; your true love's coming,
  That can sing both high and low :
Trip no further, pretty sweeting ;
Journeys end in lovers meeting,
  Every wise man's son doth know.

What is love ? 'tis not hereafter ;
Present mirth hath present laughter ;
   What's to come is still unsure :
In delay there lies no plenty ;
Then come kiss me, sweet and twenty,
   Youth's a stuff will not endure.

WILLIAM SHAKESPEARE

100 *Come Away, Come Away, Death*

COME away, come away, death,
   And in sad cypress let me be laid ;
Fly away, fly away, breath ;
   I am slain by a fair cruel maid.
My shroud of white, stuck all with yew,
     O, prepare it !
My part of death, no one so true
     Did share it.

Not a flower, not a flower sweet,
   On my black coffin let there be strown ;
Not a friend, not a friend greet
   My poor corpse, where my bones shall be thrown :
A thousand thousand sighs to save,
     Lay me, O, where
Sad true lover never find my grave,
     To weep there !

WILLIAM SHAKESPEARE

101 *When that I was and a Little Tiny Boy*

WHEN that I was and a little tiny boy,
   With hey, ho, the wind and the rain,
A foolish thing was but a toy,
   For the rain it raineth every day.

When that I was and a Little Tiny Boy

But when I came to man's estate,
  With hey, ho, the wind and the rain,
'Gainst knaves and thieves men shut their gate,
  For the rain it raineth every day.

But when I came, alas ! to wive,
  With hey, ho, the wind and the rain,
By swaggering could I never thrive,
  For the rain it raineth every day.

But when I came unto my beds,
  With hey, ho, the wind and the rain,
With toss-pots still had drunken heads,
  For the rain it raineth every day.

A great while ago the world begun,
  With hey, ho, the wind and the rain,
But that's all one, our play is done,
  And we'll strive to please you every day.
                    WILLIAM SHAKESPEARE

102 *What shall he have that kill'd the Deer ?*

WHAT shall he have that kill'd the deer ?
His leather skin and horns to wear.
      Then sing him home ;
Take thou no scorn to wear the horn ;
It was a crest ere thou wast born :
      Thy father's father wore it,
      And thy father bore it :
The horn, the horn, the lusty horn
Is not a thing to laugh to scorn.

                    WILLIAM SHAKESPEARE

103 *When Daffodils begin to peer*

WHEN daffodils begin to peer,
  With heigh ! the doxy over the dale,
Why, then comes in the sweet o' the year ;
  For the red blood reigns in the winter's pale.

The white sheet bleaching on the hedge,
  With heigh ! the sweet birds, O, how they sing !
Doth set my pugging tooth on edge ;
  For a quart of ale is a dish for a king.

The lark, that tirra-lirra chants,
  With heigh ! with heigh ! the thrush and the jay
Are summer songs for me and my aunts,
  While we lie tumbling in the hay.

But shall I go mourn for that, my dear ?
  The pale moon shines by night :
And when I wander here and there,
  I then do most go right.

If tinkers may have leave to live,
  And bear the sow-skin bowget,
Then my account I well may give,
  And in the stocks avouch it.

WILLIAM SHAKESPEARE

104 *Orpheus with his Lute*

ORPHEUS with his lute made trees,
And the mountain tops that freeze,
  Bow themselves when he did sing :
To his music plants and flowers
Ever sprung ; as sun and showers
  There had made a lasting spring.

Song

Are burnt out : no heat, no light.
Now remains ; 'tis ever night.
  Love is dead, let lovers' eyes,
    Lock'd in endless dreams,
    Th' extreme of all extremes,
    Ope no more, for now Love dyes.
Now Love dyes, implying
Love's martyrs must be ever, ever dying.

JOHN FORD

109   *Hymn to Diana*

QUEEN and huntress, chaste and fair,
  Now the sun is laid to sleep ;
Seated in thy silver chair
  State in wonted manner keep :
    Hesperus entreats thy light,
    Goddess excellently bright.

Earth, let not thy envious shade
  Dare itself to interpose ;
Cynthia's shining orb was made
  Heaven to clear when day did close ;
    Bless us then with wishèd sight,
    Goddess excellently bright.

Lay thy bow of pearl apart,
  And thy crystal shining quiver
Give unto the flying hart
  Space to breathe, how short soever,
    Thou that mak'st a day of night,
    Goddess excellently bright.

BEN JONSON

110 *Charm*

THE owl is abroad, the bat, and the toad,
  And so is the cat-a-mountain ;
The ant and the mole sit both in a hole,
  And the frog peeps out o' the fountain.
The dogs they do bay, and the timbrels play,
  The spindle is now a-turning ;
The moon it is red, and the stars are fled,
  But all the sky is a-burning :
The ditch is made, and our nails the spade,
With pictures full, of wax and of wool ;
Their livers I stick with needles quick ;
There lacks but the blood to make up the flood.
Quickly, dame, then, bring your part in !
Spur, spur, upon little Martin,
Merrily, merrily, make him sail,
A worm in his mouth and a thorn in his tail,
Fire above, and fire below,
With a whip in your hand, to make him go !

BEN JONSON

111 *Cupid and my Campaspe Play'd*

CUPID and my Campaspe play'd
At cards for kisses ; Cupid paid :
He stakes his quiver, bow, and arrows,
His mother's doves, and team of sparrows ;
Loses them too ; then down he throws
The coral of his lip, the rose
Growing on's cheek (but none knows how) ;
With these, the crystal of his brow,
And then the dimple on his chin ;
All these did my Campaspe win :

Cupid and my Campaspe Play'd

And last he set her both his eyes—
She won, and Cupid blind did rise.
　　O Love ! has she done this to thee ?
　　What shall, alas ! become of me ?

JOHN LYLY

112 *Pack, Clouds, Away*

PACK, clouds, away, and welcome day,
　　With night we banish sorrow ;
Sweet air blows soft, mount larks aloft
　　To give my love good-morrow !
Wings from the wind to please her mind,
　　Notes from the lark I'll borrow ;
Bird, prune thy wing, nightingale sing,
　　To give my Love good-morrow ;
　　　To give my Love good-morrow
　　　Notes from them both I'll borrow.

Wake from thy nest, Robin-red-breast,
　　Sing, birds, in every furrow ;
And from each hill, let music shrill
　　Give my fair Love good-morrow !
Blackbird and thrush in every bush,
　　Stare, linnet, and cock-sparrow !
You pretty elves, amongst yourselves
　　Sing my fair Love good-morrow ;
　　　To give my Love good-morrow
　　　Sing, birds, in every furrow.

THOMAS HEYWOOD

The Knapsack

113 *Dirge*

CALL for the robin-redbreast and the wren,
Since o'er shady groves they hover,
And with leaves and flowers do cover
The friendless bodies of unburied men.
Call unto his funeral dole
The ant, the field mouse, and the mole,
To rear him hillocks that shall keep him warm,
And (when gay tombs are robbed) sustain no harm ;
But keep the wolf far thence, that's foe to men,
For with his nails he'll dig them up again.

JOHN WEBSTER

114 *Sweet Echo*

SWEET echo, sweetest nymph, that liv'st unseen
　　Within thy airy shell,
　　By slow Meander's margent green,
And in the violet-imbroider'd vale,
　　Where the love-lorn nightingale
Nightly to thee her sad song mourneth well ;
Canst thou not tell me of a gentle pair
　　That likest thy Narcissus are ?
　　　O, if thou have
　　Hid them in some flow'ry cave,
　　　Tell me but where,
Sweet queen of parley, daughter of the sphere ?
So mayst thou be translated to the skies,
And give resounding grace to all heav'ns harmonies.

JOHN MILTON

312

115 *To Gather Flowers Sappha went*

To gather flowers Sappha went,
    And homeward she did bring
Within her lawnie continent
    The treasure of the Spring.

She smiling blusht, and blushing smil'd
    And sweetly blushing thus,
She lookt as she'd been got with child
    By young Favonius.

Her apron gave (as she did pass)
    An odour more divine,
More pleasing too, than ever was
    The lap of Proserpine.

ROBERT HERRICK

116 *To Meadows*

YE have been fresh and green,
    Ye have been fill'd with flowers ;
And ye the walks have been
    Where maids have spent their hours.

You have beheld how they
    With wicker arks did come,
To kiss and bear away
    The richer cowslips home.

You've heard them sweetly sing,
    And seen them in a round ;
Each virgin, like a spring,
    With honeysuckles crown'd.

The Knapsack

But now, we see none here,
　Whose silvery feet did tread,
And with dishevelled hair
　Adorn'd the smoother mead.

Like unthrifts, having spent
　Your stock and needy grown,
You're left here to lament
　Your poor estates alone.

ROBERT HERRICK

117 Upon a Maid

HERE she lies (in bed of spice)
Fair as Eve in Paradise :
For her beauty it was such
Poets could not praise too much.
Virgins come, and in a ring
Her supremest requiem sing ;
Then depart, but see ye tread
Lightly, lightly o'er the dead.

ROBERT HERRICK

118 The Mower to the Glo-worms

YE living Lamps by whose dear light
The Nightingale does sit so late,
And studying all the Summer-night,
Her matchless Songs does meditate ;

Ye Country Comets, that portend
No War, nor Princes funeral,
Shining unto no higher end
Then to presage the Grasses fall ;

The Mower to the Glo-worms

Ye glo-worms, whose officious Flame
To wandering Mowers shows the way,
That in the Night have lost their aim,
And after foolish Fires do stray ;

Your courteous Lights in vain you waste,
Since *Juliana* here is come,
For She my mind hath so displac'd,
That I shall never find my home.

ANDREW MARVELL

119 *Hope*

MY banks they are furnish'd with bees,
  Whose murmur invites one to sleep ;
My grottos are shaded with trees,
  And my hills are white-over with sheep.
I seldom have met with a loss,
  Such health do my fountains bestow ;
My fountains all border'd with moss,
  Where the hare-bells and violets grow.

Not a pine in my grove is there seen,
  But with tendrils of woodbine is bound ;
Not a beech's more beautiful green,
  But a sweet-briar entwines it around,
Not my fields, in the prime of the year,
  More charms than my cattle unfold ;
Not a brook that is limped and clear,
  But it glitters with fishes of gold.

One would think she might like to retire
  To the bow'r I have labour'd to rear :
Not a shrub that I heard her admire,
  But I hasted and planted it there.

The Knapsack

O how sudden the jesamine strove
  With the lilac to render it gay !
Already it calls for my love,
  To prune the wild branches away.

WILLIAM SHENSTONE

120 *Ode to Evening*

If aught of Oaten Stop, or Pastoral Song,
May hope, O pensive *Eve*, to soothe thine Ear,
  Like thy own brawling Springs,
  Thy Springs, and dying Gales,

O *Nymph* reserv'd, while now the bright-hair'd Sun
Sits in yon western Tent, whose cloudy Skirts,
  With Brede ethereal wove,
  O'erhang his wavy Bed :

Now Air is hush'd, save where the weak-ey'd Bat,
With short shrill Shriek flits by on leathern Wing,
  Or where the Beetle winds
  His small but sullen Horn,

As oft he rises 'midst the twilight Path,
Against the Pilgrim borne in heedless Hum :
  Now teach me, *Maid* compos'd,
  To breathe some soften'd Strain,

Whose Numbers stealing thro' thy darkning Vale,
May not unseemly with its Stillness suit,
  As musing slow, I hail
  Thy genial lov'd Return !

For when thy folding star arising shews
His paly Circlet, at his warning Lamp
  The fragrant *Hours*, and *Elves*
  Who slept in Buds the Day,

And many a *Nymph* who wreaths her Brows with Sedge,
And sheds the fresh'ning Dew, and lovelier still,
  The *Pensive Pleasures* sweet
  Prepare thy shadowy Car.

Ode to Evening

Then let me rove some wild and heathy Scene,
Or find some Ruin 'midst its dreary Dells,
    Whose Walls more awful nod
    By thy religious Gleams.
Or if chill blust'ring Winds, or driving Rain,
Prevent my willing Feet, be mine the Hut,
    That from the Mountain's side,
    Views Wilds, and swelling Floods,
And Hamlets brown, and dim-discover'd Spires,
And hears their simple Bell, and marks o'er all
    Thy Dewy Fingers draw
    The gradual dusky Veil.
While *Spring* shall pour his Show'rs, as oft he wont,
And bathe thy breathing Tresses, modest *Eve* !
    While *Summer* loves to sport,
    Beneath thy ling'ring Light :
While sallow *Autumn* fills thy Lap with Leaves,
Or *Winter* yelling thro' the troublous Air,
    Affrights thy shrinking Train,
    And rudely rends thy Robes.
So long regardful of thy quiet Rule,
Shall *Fancy, Friendship, Science,* smiling *Peace,*
    Thy gentlest Influence own,
    And love thy fav'rite Name !

WILLIAM COLLINS

121   *To the Evening Star*

THOU fair-hair'd angel of the evening,
Now, whilst the sun rests on the mountains, light
Thy bright torch of love ; thy radiant crown
Put on, and smile upon our evening bed !
Smile on our loves, and while thou drawest the
Blue curtains of the sky, scatter thy silver dew

317

L*

The Knapsack

On every flower that shuts its sweet eyes
In timely sleep.   Let thy west wind sleep on
The lake ; speak silence with thy glimmering eyes,
And wash the dusk with silver.   Soon, full soon,
Dost thou withdraw ; then the wolf rages wide,
And the lion glares thro' the dun forest :
The fleeces of our flocks are cover'd with
Thy sacred dew : protect them with thine influence.

WILLIAM BLAKE

122 Song

How sweet I roam'd from field to field
   And tasted all the summer's pride,
Till I the prince of love beheld,
   Who in the sunny beams did glide !

He show'd me lilies for my hair,
   And blushing roses for my brow ;
He led me through his gardens fair
   Where all his golden pleasures grow.

With sweet May dews my wings were wet,
   And Phœbus fir'd my vocal rage ;
He caught me in his silken net,
   And shut me in his golden cage.

He loves to sit and hear me sing,
   Then, laughing, sports and plays with me
Then stretches out my golden wing,
   And mocks my loss of liberty.

WILLIAM BLAKE

123 *Introduction to Songs of Innocence*

PIPING down the valleys wild
Piping songs of pleasant glee,
On a cloud I saw a child,
And he laughing said to me :

' Pipe a song about a Lamb ! '
So I piped with merry cheer.
' Piper, pipe that song again ' ;
So I piped : he wept to hear.

' Drop thy pipe, thy happy pipe ;
Sing thy songs of happy cheer ' :
So I sang the same again,
While he wept with joy to hear.

' Piper, sit thee down and write
In a book, that all may read.'
So he vanish'd from my sight,
And I pluck'd a hollow reed,

And I made a rural pen,
And I stain'd the water clear,
And I wrote my happy songs
Every child may joy to hear.

WILLIAM BLAKE

124 *Infant Joy*

'I HAVE no name :
I am but two days old.'
What shall I call thee ?
'I happy am,
Joy is my name,'
Sweet joy befall thee !

Pretty Joy !
Sweet Joy, but two days old,
Sweet Joy I call thee :
Thou dost smile,
I sing the while,
Sweet joy befall thee !

WILLIAM BLAKE

125 *Laughing Song*

WHEN the green woods laugh with the voice of joy,
And the dimpling stream runs laughing by ;
When the air does laugh with our merry wit,
And the green hill laughs with the noise of it ;

When the meadows laugh with lively green,
And the grasshopper laughs in the merry scene ;
When Mary and Susan and Emily
With their sweet round mouths sing, ' Ha, ha, he ! '

When the painted birds laugh in the shade,
Where our table with cherries and nuts is spread,
Come live, and be merry, and join with me,
To sing the sweet chorus of ' Ha, ha, he ! '

WILLIAM BLAKE

Nurse's Song

126 *Nurse's Song*

WHEN the voices of children are heard on the green,
And laughing is heard on the hill,
My heart is at rest within my breast,
And everything else is still.

' Then come home, my children, the sun is gone down,
And the dews of night arise ;
Come, come, leave off play, and let us away
Till the morning appears in the skies.'

' No, no, let us play, for it is yet day,
And we cannot go to sleep ;
Besides, in the sky little birds fly,
And the hills are all cover'd with sheep.'

' Well, well, go and play till the light fades away,
And then go home to bed.'
The little ones leaped, and shouted, and laugh'd,
And all the hills echoèd.

WILLIAM BLAKE

127 *The Shepherd*

How sweet is the Shepherd's sweet lot !
From the morn to the evening he strays ;
He shall follow his sheep all the day,
And his tongue shall be filled with praise.

For he hears the lamb's innocent call,
And he hears the ewe's tender reply ;
He is watchful while they are in peace,
For they know when their Shepherd is nigh.

WILLIAM BLAKE

128 *The Chimney Sweeper*

WHEN my mother died I was very young,
And my father sold me while yet my tongue
Could scarcely cry, ' 'Weep ! 'weep ! 'weep ! 'weep ! '
So your chimneys I sweep, and in soot I sleep.

There's little Tom Dacre, who cried when his head
That curl'd like a lamb's back, was shav'd : so I said,
' Hush, Tom ! never mind it, for, when your head's bare
You know that the soot cannot spoil your white hair.'

And so he was quiet, and that very night,
As Tom was a-sleeping, he had such a sight !—
That thousands of sweepers, Dick, Joe, Ned, and Jack,
Were all of them lock'd up in coffins of black.

And by came an Angel, who had a bright key,
And he open'd the coffins and set them all free ;
Then down a green plain leaping, laughing, they run,
And wash in a river, and shine in the sun.

Then naked and white, all their bags left behind,
They rise upon clouds and sport in the wind ;
And the Angel told Tom, if he'd be a good boy,
He'd have God for his father, and never want joy.

And so Tom awoke ; and we rose in the dark,
And got with our bags and our brushes to work.
Tho' the morning was cold, Tom was happy and warm ;
So if all do their duty, they need not fear harm.

WILLIAM BLAKE

129 *The Echoing Green*

THE sun does arise,
And make happy the skies ;
The merry bells ring
To welcome the Spring ;
The skylark and thrush,
The birds of the bush,
Sing louder around
To the bells' cheerful sound,
While our sports shall be seen
On the echoing Green.

Old John, with white hair,
Does laugh away care,
Sitting under the oak,
Among the old folk.
They laugh at our play,
And soon they all say :
' Such, such were the joys
When we all, girls and boys,
In our youth-time were seen
On the echoing Green.'

Till the little ones, weary,
No more can be merry ;
The sun does descend,
And our sports have an end.
Round the laps of their mothers
Many sisters and brothers,
Like birds in their nest,
Are ready for rest,
And sport no more seen
On the darkening Green.

WILLIAM BLAKE

The Knapsack

130 *Spring*

Sound the flute !
Now it's mute.
Birds delight,
Day and night ;
Nightingale
In the dale,
Lark in sky,
Merrily,
Merrily, merrily, to welcome in the year.

Little boy
Full of joy ;
Little girl,
Sweet and small ;
Cock does crow,
So do you ;
Merry voice,
Infant noise,
Merrily, merrily, to welcome in the year.

Little lamb,
Here I am ;
Come and lick
My white neck ;
Let me pull
Your soft wool ;
Let me kiss
Your soft face :
Merrily, merrily, we welcome in the year.

WILLIAM BLAKE

Kubla Khan : or, A Vision in a Dream

131   *Kubla Khan : or, A Vision in a Dream*

IN Xanadu did Kubla Khan
   A stately pleasure-dome decree :
Where Alph, the sacred river, ran
Through caverns measureless to man
     Down to a sunless sea.

So twice five miles of fertile ground
With walls and towers were girdled round :
And there were gardens bright with sinuous rills
Where blossomed many an incense-bearing tree ;
And here were forests ancient as the hills
Enfolding sunny spots of greenery.

But oh ! that deep romantic chasm which slanted
Down the green hill athwart a cedarn cover !
A savage place ! as holy and enchanted
As e'er beneath a waning moon was haunted
By woman wailing for her demon lover !
And from this chasm, with ceaseless turmoil seething,
As if this earth in fast thick pants were breathing,
A mighty fountain momently was forced :
Amid whose swift half-intermitted burst
Huge fragments vaulted like rebounding hail,
Or chaffy grain beneath the thresher's flail :
And mid these dancing rocks at once and ever
It flung up momently the sacred river.
Five miles meandering with a mazy motion
Through wood and dale the sacred river ran,
Then reached the caverns measureless to man,
And sank in tumult to a lifeless ocean :
And mid this tumult Kubla heard from far
Ancestral voices prophesying war !

The Knapsack

The shadow of the dome of pleasure
Floated midway on the waves ;
Where was heard the mingled measure
From the fountain and the caves.
It was a miracle of rare device,
A sunny pleasure-dome with caves of ice !

A damsel with a dulcimer
In a vision once I saw :
It was an Abyssinian maid,
And on a dulcimer she play'd,
Singing of Mount Abora.
Could I revive within me
Her symphony and song,
To such a deep delight 'twould win me,
That with music loud and long,
I would build that dome in air,
That sunny dome ! those caves of ice !
And all who heard should see them there
And all should cry, Beware ! Beware !
His flashing eyes, his floating hair !
Weave a circle round him thrice,
And close your eyes with holy dread,
For he on honey-dew hath fed,
And drunk the milk of Paradise.

SAMUEL TAYLOR COLERIDGE

132 *An Invocation*

HEAR, sweet Spirit, hear the spell,
Lest a blacker charm compel !
So shall the midnight breezes swell
With thy deep long-lingering knell.

An Invocation

And at evening evermore,
In a chapel on the shore,
Shall the chaunter, sad and saintly,
Yellow tapers burning faintly,
Doleful masses chaunt for thee,
    Miserere Domine !

Hush ! the cadence dies away
  On the quiet moonlight sea :
The boatmen rest their oars and say,
    Miserere Domine !

SAMUEL TAYLOR COLERIDGE

133 *The Solitary Reaper*

BEHOLD her, single in the field,
Yon solitary Highland Lass !
Reaping and singing by herself ;
Stop here, or gently pass !
Alone she cuts, and binds the grain,
And sings a melancholy strain ;
O listen ! for the Vale profound
Is overflowing with the sound.

No Nightingale did ever chant
More welcome notes to weary bands
Of travellers in some shady haunt,
Among Arabian sands ;
A voice so thrilling ne'er was heard
In spring-time from the Cuckoo-bird,
Breaking the silence of the seas
Among the farthest Hebrides.

The Knapsack

Will no one tell me what she sings ?
Perhaps the plaintive numbers flow
For old, unhappy, far-off things,
And battles long ago :
Or is it some more humble lay,
Familiar matter of to-day ?
Some natural sorrow, loss, or pain,
That has been, and may be again !

Whate'er the theme, the Maiden sang
As if her song could have no ending ;
I saw her singing at her work,
And o'er the sickle bending :—
I listened, motionless and still ;
And as I mounted up the hill,
The music in my heart I bore,
Long after it was heard no more.

WILLIAM WORDSWORTH

134 *Ode on a Grecian Urn*

THOU still unravish'd bride of quietness,
    Thou foster-child of silence and slow time,
Sylvan historian, who canst thus express
    A flowery tale more sweetly than our rhyme :
What leaf-fring'd legend haunts about thy shape
    Of deities or mortals, or of both,
        In Tempe or the dales of Arcady ?
    What men or gods are these ?   What maidens loth ?
What mad pursuit ?   What struggle to escape ?
        What pipes and timbrels ?   What wild ecstasy ?

Ode on a Grecian Urn

2

Heard melodies are sweet, but those unheard
   Are sweeter ; therefore, ye soft pipes, play on ;
Not to the sensual ear, but, more endear'd,
   Pipe to the spirit ditties of no tone :
Fair youth, beneath the trees, thou canst not leave
   Thy song, nor ever can those trees be bare ;
     Bold Lover, never, never canst thou kiss,
Though winning near the goal—yet, do not grieve ;
   She cannot fade, though thou hast not thy bliss,
     For ever wilt thou love, and she be fair !

3

Ah, happy, happy boughs ! that cannot shed
   Your leaves, nor ever bid the Spring adieu ;
And, happy melodist, unwearied,
   For ever piping songs for ever new ;
More happy love ! more happy, happy love !
   For ever warm and still to be enjoy'd,
     For ever panting, and for ever young ;
All breathing human passion far above,
   That leaves a heart high-sorrowful and cloy'd,
     A burning forehead, and a parching tongue.

4

Who are these coming to the sacrifice ?
   To what green altar, O mysterious priest,
Lead'st thou that heifer lowing at the skies,
   And all her silken flanks with garlands drest ?
What little town by river or sea shore,
   Or mountain-built with peaceful citadel,
     Is emptied of this folk, this pious morn ?
And, little town, thy streets for evermore
   Will silent be ; and not a soul to tell
Why thou art desolate, can e'er return.

5

O Attic shape ! Fair attitude ! with brede
Of marble men and maidens overwrought,
With forest branches and the trodden weed ;
   Thou, silent form, dost tease us out of thought
As doth eternity : Cold Pastoral !
When old age shall this generation waste,
   Thou shalt remain, in midst of other woe
Than ours, a friend to man, to whom thou say'st,
   ' Beauty is truth, truth beauty,'—that is all
   Ye know on earth, and all ye need to know.

JOHN KEATS

135 *La Belle Dame Sans Merci*

A BALLAD

I

O, WHAT can ail thee, knight-at-arms,
   Alone and palely loitering ?
The sedge has wither'd from the lake,
   And no birds sing.

II

O, what can ail thee, knight-at-arms !
   So haggard and so woe-begone ?
The squirrel's granary is full,
   And the harvest's done.

III

I see a lilly on thy brow,
   With anguish moist and fever dew ;
And on thy cheeks a fading rose
   Fast withereth too.

La Belle Dame Sans Merci

IV

I met a lady in the meads,
  Full beautiful—a faery's child,
Her hair was long, her foot was light,
  And her eyes were wild.

V

I made a garland for her head,
  And bracelets too, and fragrant zone ;
She look'd at me as she did love,
  And made sweet moan.

VI

I set her on my prancing steed,
  And nothing else saw all day long ;
For sidelong would she bend, and sing
  A faery's song.

VII

She found me roots of relish sweet,
  And honey wild, and manna dew,
And sure in language strange she said—
  ' I love thee true.'

VIII

She took me to her elfin grot,
  And there she wept and sigh'd full sore,
And there I shut her wild wild eyes
  With kisses four.

IX

And there she lulled me asleep
  And there I dream'd—Ah ! woe betide !
The latest dream I ever dream'd
  On the cold hill side.

X

I saw pale kings and princes too,
  Pale warriors, death-pale were they all ;
Who cried—' La Belle Dame sans Merci
  Hath thee in thrall ! '

XI

I saw their starved lips in the gloam,
  With horrid warning gaped wide,
And I awoke and found me here,
  On the cold hill's side.

XII

And this is why I sojourn here
  Alone and palely loitering,
Though the sedge is wither'd from the lake,
  And no birds sing.

JOHN KEATS

136 Song

' A widow bird sate mourning for her love
  Upon a wintry bough ;
The frozen wind crept on above,
  The freezing stream below.

' There was no leaf upon the forest bare,
  No flower upon the ground,
And little motion in the air
  Except the mill-wheel's sound.'

PERCY BYSSHE SHELLEY

The Cloud

137 *The Cloud*

I BRING fresh showers for the thirsting flowers,
    From the seas and the streams ;
I bear light shade for the leaves when laid
    In their noonday dreams.
From my wings are shaken the dews that waken
    The sweet buds every one,
When rocked to rest on their mother's breast,
    As she dances about the sun.
I wield the flail of the lashing hail,
    And whiten the green plains under,
And then again I dissolve it in rain,
    And laugh as I pass in thunder.

I sift the snow on the mountains below,
    And their great pines groan aghast ;
And all the night 'tis my pillow white,
    While I sleep in the arms of the blast.
Sublime on the towers of my skiey bowers,
    Lightning my pilot sits ;
In a cavern under is fettered the thunder,
    It struggles and howls at fits ;
Over earth and ocean, with gentle motion,
    This pilot is guiding me,
Lured by the love of the genii that move
    In the depths of the purple sea ;
Over the rills, and the crags, and the hills,
    Over the lakes and the plains,
Wherever he dream, under mountain or stream,
    The Spirit he loves remains ;
And I all the while bask in Heaven's blue smile,
    Whilst he is dissolving in rains.

The Knapsack

The sanguine Sunrise, with his meteor eyes,
  And his burning plumes outspread,
Leaps on the back of my sailing rack,
  When the morning star shines dead ;
As on the jag of a mountain crag,
  Which an earthquake rocks and swings,
An eagle alit one moment may sit
  In the light of its golden wings.
And when Sunset may breathe, from the lit sea beneath,
  Its ardours of rest and of love,
And the crimson pall of eve may fall
  From the depth of Heaven above,
With wings folded I rest, on mine aëry nest,
  As still as a brooding dove.

That orbèd maiden with white fire laden,
  Whom mortals call the Moon,
Glides glimmering o'er my fleece-like floor,
  By the midnight breezes strewn ;
And wherever the beat of her unseen feet,
  Which only the angels hear,
May have broken the woof of my tent's thin roof,
  The stars peep behind her and peer ;
And I laugh to see them whirl and flee,
  Like a swarm of golden bees,
When I widen the rent in my wind-built tent,
  Till the calm rivers, lakes, and seas,
Like strips of the sky fallen through me on high,
  Are each paved with the moon and these.

I bind the Sun's throne with a burning zone,
  And the Moon's with a girdle of pearl ;
The volcanoes are dim, and the stars reel and swim,
  When the whirlwinds my banner unfurl.

The Cloud

From cape to cape, with a bridge-like shape,
    Over a torrent sea,
Sunbeam-proof, I hang like a roof,—
    The mountains its columns be.
The triumphal arch through which I march
    With hurricane, fire, and snow,
When the Powers of the air are chained to my chair,
    Is the million-coloured bow ;
The sphere-fire above its soft colours wove,
    While the moist Earth was laughing below.

I am the daughter of Earth and Water,
    And the nursling of the Sky ;
I pass through the pores of the ocean and shores ;
    I change, but I cannot die.
For after the rain when with never a stain
    The pavilion of Heaven is bare,
And the winds and sunbeams with their convex gleams
    Build up the blue dome of air,
I silently laugh at my own cenotaph,
    And out of the caverns of rain,
Like a child from the womb, like a ghost from the tomb,
    I arise and unbuild it again.

PERCY BYSSHE SHELLEY

138   *Evening : Ponte al Mare, Pisa*

I

THE sun is set ; the swallows are asleep ;
    The bats are flitting fast in the gray air ;
The slow soft toads out of damp corners creep,
    And evening's breath, wandering here and there
Over the quivering surface of the stream,
Wakes not one ripple from its summer dream.

The Knapsack

II

There is no dew on the dry grass to-night,
  Nor damp within the shadow of the trees ;
The wind is intermitting, dry, and light ;
  And in the inconstant motion of the breeze
The dust and straws are driven up and down,
And whirled about the pavement of the town.

III

Within the surface of the fleeting river
  The wrinkled image of the city lay,
Immovably unquiet, and forever
  It trembles, but it never fades away ;
Go to the . . .
You, being changed, will find it then as now.

IV

The chasm in which the sun has sunk is shut
  By darkest barriers of cinereous cloud,
Like mountain over mountain huddled—but
  Growing and moving upwards in a crowd,
And over it a space of watery blue,
Which the keen evening star is shining through.

PERCY BYSSHE SHELLEY

139 *To Night*

I

SWIFTLY walk o'er the western wave,
  Spirit of Night !
Out of the misty eastern cave,
Where, all the long and lone daylight,
Thou wovest dreams of joy and fear,
Which make thee terrible and dear,—
  Swift be thy flight !

To Night

II

Wrap thy form in a mantle gray,
    Star-inwrought !
Blind with thine hair the eyes of Day ;
Kiss her until she be wearied out,
Then wander o'er city, and sea, and land,
Touching all with thine opiate wand—
    Come, long-sought !

III

When I arose and saw the dawn,
    I sighed for thee ;
When light rode high, and the dew was gone,
And noon lay heavy on flower and tree,
And the weary Day turned to his rest,
Lingering like an unloved guest,
    I sighed for thee.

IV

Thy brother Death came, and cried,
    Wouldst thou me ?
Thy sweet child Sleep, the filmy-eyed,
Murmured like a noontide bee,
Shall I nestle near thy side ?
Wouldst thou me ?—And I replied,
    No, not thee !

V

Death will come when thou art dead,
    Soon, too soon—
Sleep will come when thou art fled ;
Of neither would I ask the boon
I ask of thee, belovèd Night—
Swift be thine approaching flight,
    Come soon, soon !

PERCY BYSSHE SHELLEY

140 *To* ——

MUSIC, when soft voices die,
Vibrates in the memory—
Odours, when sweet violets sicken,
Live within the sense they quicken.

Rose leaves, when the rose is dead,
Are heaped for the belovèd's bed ;
And so thy thoughts, when thou art gone,
Love itself shall slumber on.

PERCY BYSSHE SHELLEY

141 *The Indian Serenade*

I

I ARISE from dreams of thee
In the first sweet sleep of night.
When the winds are breathing low,
And the stars are shining bright :
I arise from dreams of thee,
And a spirit in my feet
Hath led me—who knows how ?
To thy chamber window, Sweet !

II

The wandering airs they faint
On the dark, the silent stream—
The Champak odours fail
Like sweet thoughts in a dream ;
The nightingale's complaint,
It dies upon her heart ;—
As I must on thine,
Oh, belovèd as thou art !

The Indian Serenade

III

Oh lift me from the grass !
I die ! I faint ! I fail !
Let thy love in kisses rain
On my lips and eyelids pale.
My cheek is cold and white, alas !
My heart beats loud and fast ;—
Oh ! press it to thine own again,
Where it will break at last.

PERCY BYSSHE SHELLEY

142 *A Lament*

I

O WORLD ! O life ! O time !
On whose last steps I climb,
    Trembling at that where I had stood before ;
When will return the glory of your prime ?
        No more—Oh, never more !

II

Out of the day and night
A joy has taken flight ;
    Fresh spring, and summer, and winter hoar,
Move my faint heart with grief, but with delight
        No more—Oh, never more !

PERCY BYSSHE SHELLEY

143 *The Mermaidens' Vesper-Hymn*

TROOP home to silent grots and caves !
    Troop home ! and mimic as you go
The mournful winding of the waves
    Which to their dark abysses flow.

The Knapsack

At this sweet hour, all things beside
    In amorous pairs to covert creep ;
The swans that brush the evening tide
    Homeward in snowy couples keep.

In his green den the murmuring seal
    Close by his sleek companion lies ;
While singly we to bedward steal,
    And close in fruitless sleep our eyes.

In bowers of love men take their rest,
    In loveless bowers we sigh alone,
With bosom-friends are others blest,—
    But we have none ! but we have none !

GEORGE DARLEY

144 *Song*

I

A SPIRIT haunts the year's last hours
Dwelling amid these yellowing bowers :
    To himself he talks ;
For at eventide, listening earnestly,
At his work you may hear him sob and sigh
    In the walks ;
    Earthward he boweth the heavy stalks
Of the mouldering flowers :
    Heavily hangs the broad sunflower
        Over its grave i' the earth so chilly ;
    Heavily hangs the hollyhock,
        Heavily hangs the tigerlily.

Song

The air is damp, and hushed, and close,
As a sick man's room when he taketh repose
    An hour before death ;
My very heart faints and my whole soul grieves
At the moist rich smell of the rotting leaves,
    And the breath
    Of the fading edges of box beneath,
And the year's last rose.
    Heavily hangs the broad sunflower
      Over its grave i' the earth so chilly ;
    Heavily hangs the hollyhock,
      Heavily hangs the tigerlily.
              ALFRED LORD TENNYSON

145 *Now sleeps the crimson petal* . . .

Now sleeps the crimson petal, now the white ;
Nor waves the cypress in the palace walk ;
Nor winks the gold fin in the porphyry font :
The fire-fly wakens : waken thou with me.

Now droops the milk-white peacock like a ghost,
And like a ghost she glimmers on to me.

Now lies the Earth all Danaë to the stars,
And all thy heart lies open unto me.

Now slides the silent meteor on, and leaves
A shining furrow, as thy thoughts in me.

Now folds the lily all her sweetness up,
And slips into the bosom of the lake :
So fold thyself, my dearest, thou, and slip
Into my bosom and be lost in me.
              ALFRED LORD TENNYSON

146 *To Helen*

HELEN, thy beauty is to me
   Like those Nicéan barks of yore
That gently, o'er a perfumed sea,
   The weary way-worn wanderer bore
   To his own native shore.

On desperate seas long wont to roam,
   Thy hyacinth hair, thy classic face,
Thy Naiad airs have brought me home
   To the glory that was Greece,
   And the grandeur that was Rome.

Lo ! in yon brilliant window niche
   How statue-like I see thee stand,
   The agate lamp within thy hand !
Ah, Psyche, from the regions which
   Are Holy Land !

EDGAR ALLAN POE

147 *The Valley of Unrest*

ONCE it smiled, a silent dell
Where the people did not dwell ;
They had gone unto the wars,
Trusting to the mild-eyed stars,
Nightly, from their azure towers,
To keep watch above the flowers,
In the midst of which all day
The red sunlight lazily lay.
Now each visitor shall confess
The sad valley's restlessness.

The Valley of Unrest

Nothing there is motionless—
Nothing save the airs that brood
Over the magic solitude.
Ah, by no wind are stirred those trees
That palpitate like the chill seas
Around the misty Hebrides !
Ah, by no wind those clouds are driven,
That rustle through the unquiet Heaven
Uneasily, from morn till even,
Over the violets that there lie
In myriad types of the human eye—
Over the lilies there that wave
And weep above a nameless grave !
They wave :—from out their fragrant tops
Eternal dews come down in drops.
They weep :—from off their delicate stems
Perennial tears descend in gems.

EDGAR ALLAN POE

148 Song from Golden Wings

GOLD wings across the sea !
Grey light from tree to tree,
Gold hair beside my knee,
I pray thee come to me,
Gold wings !

The water slips,
The red-bill'd moorhen dips.
Sweet kisses on red lips ;
Alas ! the red rust grips,
And the blood-red dagger rips,
Yet, O knight, come to me !

343

The Knapsack

Are not my blue eyes sweet?
The west wind from the wheat
Blows cold across my feet;
Is it not time to meet
Gold wings across the sea?

White swans on the green moat,
Small feathers left afloat
By the blue-painted boat;
Swift running of the stoat,
Sweet gurgling note by note
Of sweet music.

O gold wings,
Listen how gold hair sings,
And the Ladies' Castle rings,
Gold wings across the sea.

I sit on a purple bed,
Outside, the wall is red,
Thereby the apple hangs,
And the wasp, caught by the fangs,

Dies in the autumn night,
And the bat flits till light,
And the love-crazed knight

Kisses the long wet grass:
The weary days pass,—
Gold wings across the sea.

Gold wings across the sea!
Moonlight from tree to tree,
Sweet hair laid on my knee,
O, sweet knight, come to me.

Song from Golden Wings

> Gold wings, the short night slips,
> The white swan's long neck drips,
> I pray thee, kiss my lips,
> Gold wings across the sea !

WILLIAM MORRIS

149 *Mirage*

THE hope I dreamed of was a dream,
  Was but a dream ; and now I wake,
Exceeding comfortless, and worn, and old,
  For a dream's sake.

I hang my harp upon a tree,
  A weeping willow in a lake ;
I hang my silent harp there, wrung and snapt
  For a dream's sake.

Lie still, lie still, my breaking heart ;
  My silent heart, lie still and break :
Life, and the world, and mine own self, are changed
  For a dream's sake.

CHRISTINA ROSSETTI

150 *Spring and Fall*

TO A YOUNG CHILD

MÁRGARÉT, are you gríeving
Over Goldengrove unleaving ?
Leáves, líke the things of man, you
With your fresh thoughts care for, can you ?
Áh ! ás the heart grows older
It will come to such sights colder
By and by, nor spare a sigh
Though worlds of wanwood leafmeal lie ;

And yet you will weep and know why.
Now no matter, child, the name :
Sórrow's spríngs áre the same.
Nor mouth had, no nor mind, expressed
What heart heard of, ghost guessed :
It ís the blight man was born for,
It is Margaret you mourn for.

GERARD MANLEY HOPKINS

151 *Pied Beauty*

GLORY be to God for dappled things—
  For skies of couple-colour as a brinded cow ;
    For rose-moles all in stipple upon trout that swim ;
Fresh-firecoal chestnut-falls ; finches' wings ;
  Landscape plotted and pieced—fold, fallow, and plough ;
    And áll trádes, their gear and tackle and trim.

All things counter, original, spare, strange ;
  Whatever is fickle, freckled (who knows how ?)
    With swift, slow ; sweet, sour ; adazzle, dim ;
He fathers-forth whose beauty is past change :
                Praise him.

GERARD MANLEY HOPKINS

152 *Felix Randal*

FELIX RANDAL the farrier, O he is dead then ? my duty
    all ended,
Who have watched his mould of man, big-boned and hardy-
    handsome
Pining, pining, till time when reason rambled in it and
    some
Fatal four disorders, fleshed there, all contended ?

Landscapes

Moon cold or moon hot. The road winds in
Listlessness of ancient war,
Languor of broken steel,
Clamour of confused wrong, apt
In silence. Memory is strong
Beyond the bone. Pride snapped,
Shadow of pride is long, in the long pass
No concurrence of bone.

(v) *Cape Ann*

O QUICK quick quick, quick hear the song-sparrow,
Swamp-sparrow, fox-sparrow, vesper-sparrow
At dawn and dusk. Follow the dance
Of the goldfinch at noon. Leave to chance
The Blackburnian warbler, the shy one. Hail
With shrill whistle the note of the quail, the bob-white
Dodging by bay-bush. Follow the feet
Of the walker, the water-thrush. Follow the flight
Of the dancing arrow, the purple martin. Greet
In silence the bullbat. All are delectable. Sweet sweet
    sweet
But resign this land at the end, resign it
To its true owner, the tough one, the sea-gull.
The palaver is finished.

T. S. ELIOT

PART SIX

WITH the two thousand camels, given us in July by General Allenby, we calculated that we could afford to send up to Azrak, for operations about Deraa, an expedition of four hundred and fifty camel corps of the Arab regular army, four Arab Vickers, twenty Arab Hotchkiss, a French battery of four mountain Q.F. ·65 guns, two British aeroplanes, three British armoured cars with necessary tenders, a demolition company of Egyptian Camel Corps and a section of camel-Ghurkas. Besides these, Sherif Nasir and myself had our private body-guards of Arab camel-men. This made our total force one thousand strong, and its prospects were so sure that we made no provision (and had no means) for getting it back again. The supply problem, especially in petrol and ammunition, was a very great one, and we lived from hand to mouth, without, however, ever being in serious need.

The force left Ab el-Lissan in detachments early in September, and concentrated, without accident, to time at Azrak on the twelfth of the month. The distance from Akaba to Azrak was two hundred and ninety miles, and we used the wells of Jefer, Bair and Ammari on the way. At Azrak we had meant to collect the Rualla and descend in force on the Hauran, with direct assault on Deraa, which was only held by five hundred rifles—but this plan was spoiled by the unfortunate outburst of the King of

The Knapsack

Hejaz against Jaafar Pasha and the senior officers of the Northern Army, since the crisis he provoked upset the whole local temper, and delayed me in Ab el-Lissan till September 4. As a result, the Rualla never came together, and we had to modify our schemes. In the end, we decided to carry out a flying attack on the northern, western and southern railways at Deraa, with our regular troops, the Rualla horse under Khalid and Trad Shaalan, and such Hauran peasants as should be brave enough to declare for us.

As we sat at Azrak we put in a strong bluff towards Amman. Money was sent to Mithgal with very secret instructions to collect barley dumps for us and the British, in our combined surprise attack against Amman and Salt on the 18th. The Beni Sakhr were to mass at Ziza to help us. The rumour of this, and the rumour of our simultaneous intention on Deraa, confirmed by other factors supplied them from Palestine, kept the Turks' eyes fixed on the Jordan and east of it, where their lines were very long, expensive in men, and, despite their best efforts, inevitably vulnerable to a force of our mobility and range.

On the 13th we left Azrak and marched over the long Gian el-Khunna into the basalt screes of Jebel Druse. The Egyptian and Ghurka units were sent westward to cut the Amman line by Mafrak, but, owing to a misunderstanding with their guides, never got so far. However, our Bristol Fighter the same day brought down a German two-seater in flames near Um-el-Jimal : so all was well. We got to Umtaiye, thirteen miles south-east of Deraa, on the 15th. This (and its neighbour Um el-Surab) were our forward bases, as about them were many cisterns of water of last year's rain. We were at once joined by the male population of the nearest villages, and by Sheikh Talal el-Hareidhin of Tafas, the finest fighter of the

Destruction of the Fourth Turkish Army

Hauran, who had come to me in Azrak in 1917. He had agreed to be our guide, and marched with us till he died near Deraa, helping us day and night, our sponsor and backer in every village. But for his energy, courage and honesty, things would have gone hard with us many times.

It was still necessary for us to cut the railway between Deraa and Amman, not only to give colour to our supposed attack on the Fourth Army, but to prevent the reinforcement of Deraa from the south. It was our plan to put ourselves between Deraa and Palestine, to force the enemy to reinforce the former from the latter. Had we merely moved troops from Amman to Deraa we should be doing Palestine no good, and should probably have been rounded up and caught ourselves. The only unit now in hand to do this cutting—since the army must go forward at once—were the armoured cars, which are not ideal for the purpose, as you are almost as shut in to them as the enemy are shut out. However, we went down in all the cars we had to the railway and took a post of open-mouthed Turks too suddenly for them to realise that we were hostile. The post commanded a very pleasant four-arched bridge (kilo. 149) about twenty-five metres long and six metres high, with a flattering white marble inscription to Abd el-Hamid. We wrecked all this with one hundred and fifty pounds of gun-cotton, and did what we could to the station.

On the way back we had a mishap to one of the cars, and a vile road, so did not catch our army till after dawn on the 17th, going down to the line near Tell Arar, five miles north of Deraa. We suppressed a little post and some Kurdish cavalry, and put our demolition party on the line. The French blew up part of the bridge, and the Egyptians, working up the line towards Ghazale, did six hundred pairs of rails before dusk on our new " tulip " system.[1] Meanwhile we climbed to the top of Tell Arar, which commanded a complete view of Deraa, about four miles off, and we realised that there were nine enemy machines on the aerodrome. Our Bristol had been badly shot about, so they had no competition to fear, and for a time they did what they liked to us with bombs and machine-gunning. We had luck, and used our mountain guns and Hotchkiss for what they were worth, but were getting much the worst of it, till our only surviving machine, a B.E. 12 from Azrak, turned up and sailed into the middle of the show. We watched with very mixed feelings, for the four Turkish two-seaters and their four scouts were all of them much more than its equal in the air : however, by good hap or skill, the B.E. came through them and led the whole circus of them away westward, and after to Ghazale, in pursuit, while we took advantage of our respite to organise and send off a mixed column to Mezerib, to cut the Palestine line. Just after this was done, the B.E. came back again with its attendant swarm, and telling us that it had finished its petrol, landed near us and turned over on to its back in the rough, while a Halberstadt came down and scored a direct hit on it with a bomb. Our

[1] After long experiment we found this the cheapest and most destructive demolition for a line with steel sleepers. Dig a hole midway between the tracks under a mid-rail sleeper, and work out the ballast from the hollow section of the sleeper. Put in two slabs of guncotton, return the ballast to the hole, and light. If the charge is properly laid, and not in contact with the sleeper, a 12-inch fuse is enough. The gas expansion arches the sleeper eighteen inches above the rail, draws the metals six inches towards one another, humps them three inches above the horizontal, and twists the web from the bottom inwards. It drives a trough a foot deep across the formation. This three-dimension distortion of the rails is impossible to straighten, and they have to be cut or scrapped. A gang of four men can lay twenty " tulips " in an hour on easy ballast, and for each two slabs (and single fuse) you ruin a sleeper, a yard of bank and two rails. The effect of a long stretch of line planted with these " tulips " is most beautiful, since no two look just alike.

Destruction of the Fourth Turkish Army

them with all arms as they marched out later, and bent the head of their column back towards Tell Arar. When Sherif Bey, the Turkish Commander of the Lancer rearguard in the village, saw this he ordered that the inhabitants be killed. These included some twenty small children (killed with lances and rifles), and about forty women. I noticed particularly one pregnant woman, who had been forced down on a saw-bayonet. Unfortunately, Talal, the Sheikh of Tafas, who, as mentioned, had been a tower of strength to us from the beginning, and who was one of the coolest and boldest horsemen I have ever met, was in front with Auda abu Tayi and myself when we saw these sights. He gave a horrible cry, wrapped his headcloth about his face, put spurs to his horse, and, rocking in the saddle, galloped at his full speed into the midst of the retiring column, and fell, himself and mare, riddled with machine-gun bullets, among their lance points.

With Auda's help we were able to cut the enemy column into three. The third section, with German machine-gunners, resisted magnificently, and got off, not cheaply, with Jemal Pasha in his car in their midst. The second and leading portions, after a bitter struggle, we wiped out completely. We ordered " no prisoners " and the men obeyed, except that the reserve company took two hundred and fifty men (including many German A.S.C.[1]) alive. Later, however, they found one of our men with a fractured thigh who had been afterwards pinned to the ground by two mortal thrusts with German bayonets. Then we turned our Hotchkiss on the prisoners and made an end of them, they saying nothing. The common delusion that the Turk is a clean and merciful fighter led some of the British troops to criticise Arab methods a little later—but they had not entered Turaa or Tafas, or watched the Turks swing their wounded by the hands and feet into a

[1] Army Service Corps.

burning railway truck, as had been the lot of the Arab army at Jerdun. As for the villagers, they and their ancestors have been for five hundred years ground down by the tyranny of these Turks.

Our Rualla horse were then sent on straight to Deraa, with orders to scatter any Turkish formations met with on the road, and to occupy the place. They had two or three fights on their way down, and took Deraa station at a whirlwind gallop, riding over all the trenches, and blotting out the enemy elements that still tried to hold the place. Next morning they brought us three hundred mule-mounted infantry prisoners, and about two hundred infantry men and two guns. The Turks and Germans had unfortunately burnt their stores before we took it.

The regular troops spent that night—a very uneasy night it was—at Sheikh Saad. We did not yet know that we had won, since there was always a risk of our being washed away by a great wave of the enemy in retreat. I went out to see our Haurani horse, near Sheikh Miskin, where they were tenaciously clinging on to the great Turkish column from Deraa, giving much more than they were getting. At midnight I was back in Sheikh Saad, and found Nasir and Nuri just off for Deraa : we had a race, in which my camel-corps beat the headquarters horses and joined Trad Shaalan in Deraa village at dawn. We had some little work to do then in making the necessary local arrangements.

Afterwards I rode out westwards till I met the outposts of the Fourth Division (British) and guided them into Deraa. They only stayed there one night and early on the 29th they left for Damascus, after assigning to us the duty of right-flank guard. Accordingly, we marched up the Hejaz line, which suited us very well, for first our three hundred Rualla and Abu Tayi horse, and then our nine

Destruction of the Fourth Turkish Army

hundred Rualla camels, caught up with our Hauran cavalry harassing the Turkish Deraa column near Mesmiye.

The aeroplanes had reported this column as six thousand strong. At Sheikh Miskin on the second day it looked about five thousand strong. At Mesmiye it was said to be three thousand strong, and at Kiswe, where our horse headed them into General Gregory's Brigade, there were about two thousand of them. The whole of this gradual attrition was the work of the irregulars, since the Arab Regular Army, not being skilled camel-men, marched little faster than the British cavalry, and never came into action after Deraa. The Kiswe fight was a satisfactory affair. The Turks came along the valley of the Hejaz line, in a long, straggling column, halting every few miles to bring their guns into action against the Arabs. Nasir knew that the leading brigade of the Fourth Division was nearing Khan Denun, so he galloped forward with his slaves, and Nuri Shaalan and his slaves, about thirty in all, headed the Turkish column off between Jebel Mania and the trees of Khiata, and threw himself into the trees to delay them till the British were ready. The British had not seen or heard of this enemy column, and were in order of march, but as soon as they had learned what was forward they got their cavalry to north, west, and south of them, and opened on them with their Horse Artillery. It was just sunset when the affair began, but before it was too dark to see, the Turks were a scattered mob, running up the steep slopes of Mania and over it, in their ignorance that the Wuld Ali and Abu Tayi were waiting for them there in force. This ended the history of the Fourth Army. Old Auda, tired of slaughter, took the last six hundred prisoners. In all we killed nearly five thousand of them, captured about eight thousand (as we took them we stripped them, and sent them to the nearest village, where they will be put to work on the land till further notice) and counted spoils of about one hundred and fifty machine guns and from twenty-five to thirty guns.

Our horse rode on that evening (September 30) into Damascus, where the burning ammunition dumps turned night into day. Away back at Kiswe the glare was painful, and the roar and reverberation of the explosions kept us all awake. In Damascus, Shukri el-Ayubi and the town council had proclaimed the King of the Arabs and hoisted the Arab flag as soon as Mustafa Kemal and Jemal had gone. The Turk and German morale was so low that they had marched out beneath the Arab flag without protest: and so good was the civil control that little or no looting took place.

T. E. LAWRENCE

157 *The Landing at V Beach*

THE men told off for this landing were: The Dublin Fusiliers, the Munster Fusiliers, half a battalion of the Hampshire Regiment, and the West Riding Field Company.

Three companies of the Dublin Fusiliers were to land from towed lighters, the rest of the party from a tramp steamer, the collier *River Clyde*. This ship, a conspicuous seamark at Cape Helles throughout the rest of the campaign, had been altered to carry and land troops. Great gangways or entry ports had been cut in her sides on the level of her between decks, and platforms had been built out upon her sides below these, so that men might run from her in a hurry. The plan was to beach her as near the shore as possible, and then drag or sweep the lighters, which she towed, into position between her and the shore, so as to make a kind of boat bridge from her to the beach. When the lighters were so moored as to make this bridge,

The Landing at V Beach

he entry ports were to be opened, the waiting troops
vere to rush out on to the external platforms, run from
hem on to the lighters, and so to the shore. The ship's
upper deck and bridge were protected with boiler plate
ind sandbags, and a casemate for machine guns was
built upon her fo'c'sle, so that she might reply to the
enemy's fire.

Five picket-boats, each towing five boats or launches
full of men, steamed alongside the *River Clyde* and went
ahead when she grounded. She took the ground rather
to the right of the little beach, some four hundred yards
from the ruins of Sedd-el-Bahr Castle, before the Turks
had opened fire ; but almost as she grounded, when the
picket-boats with their tows were ahead of her, only
twenty or thirty yards from the beach, every rifle and
machine gun in the castle, the town above it, and in the
curved, low, strongly trenched hill along the bay, began
a murderous fire upon ship and boats. There was no
question of their missing. They had their target on the
front and both flanks at ranges between a hundred and
three hundred yards in clear daylight, thirty boats bunched
together and crammed with men and a good big ship.
The first outbreak of fire made the bay as white as a rapid,
for the Turks fired not less than ten thousand shots a minute
for the first few minutes of that attack. Those not killed
in the boats at the first discharge jumped overboard to
wade or swim ashore. Many were killed in the water,
many, who were wounded, were swept away and drowned ;
others, trying to swim in the fierce current, were drowned
by the weight of their equipment. But some reached the
shore, and these instantly doubled out to cut the wire
entanglements, and were killed, or dashed for the cover
of a bank of sand or raised beach which runs along the
curve of the bay. Those very few who reached this
cover were out of immediate danger, but they were only

The Knapsack

a handful. The boats were destroyed where the grounded.

Meanwhile the men of the *River Clyde* tried to mak their bridge of boats by sweeping the lighters into positio and mooring them between the ship and the shore. The were killed as they worked, but others took their places the bridge was made, and some of the Munsters dashec along it from the ship and fell in heaps as they ran. As second company followed, the moorings of the lighter broke or were shot ; the men leaped into the water, and were drowned or killed, or reached the beach and wer killed, or fell wounded there, and lay under fire, gettin wound after wound till they died ; very, very few reachec the sandbank. More brave men jumped aboard the lighters to remake the bridge ; they were swept away o shot to pieces. The average life on those boats was some three minutes long, but they remade the bridge, and the third company of the Munsters doubled down to death along it under a storm of shrapnel which scarcely a man survived. The big guns in Asia were now shelling the *River Clyde*, and the hell of rapid fire never paused. More men tried to land, headed by Brigadier-General Napier, who was instantly killed, with nearly all his followers. Then for long hours the remainder stayed on board, down below in the grounded steamer, while the shots beat on her plates with a rattling clang which never stopped. Her twelve machine guns fired back, killing any Turk who showed ; but nothing could be done to support the few survivors of the landing, who now lay under cover of the sandbank on the other side of the beach. It was almost certain death to try to leave the ship, but all through the day men leaped from her (with leave or without it) to bring water or succour to the wounded on the boats or beach. A hundred brave men gave their lives thus ; every man there earned the Cross

hat day. A boy earned it by one of the bravest deeds
of the war, leaping into the sea with a rope in his teeth
to try to secure a drifting lighter.

The day passed thus, but at nightfall the Turks' fire
paused, and the men came ashore from the *River Clyde*,
almost unharmed. They joined the survivors on the
beach, and at once attacked the old fort and the village
above it. These works were strongly held by the enemy.
All had been ruined by the fire from the fleet, but in the
rubble and ruin of old masonry there were thousands of
hidden riflemen backed by machine guns. Again and
again they beat off our attacks, for there was a bright
moon and they knew the ground, and our men had to
attack uphill over wire and broken earth and heaped
stones in all the wreck and confusion and strangeness of
war at night in a new place. Some of the Dublins and
Munsters went astray in the ruins, and were wounded
far from their fellows, and so lost. The Turks became
more daring after dark ; while the light lasted they were
checked by the *River Clyde's* machine guns, but at midnight
they gathered unobserved and charged. They came right
down on to the beach, and in the darkness and moonlight
much terrible and confused fighting followed. Many were
bayoneted, many shot, there was wild firing and crying,
and then the Turk attack melted away, and their machine
guns began again. When day dawned, the survivors of
the landing party were crouched under the shelter of the
sandbank ; they had had no rest ; most of them had
been fighting all night ; all had landed across the corpses
of their friends. No retreat was possible, nor was it
dreamed of, but to stay there was hopeless. Lieut.-
Colonel Doughty-Wylie gathered them together for an
attack ; the fleet opened a terrific fire upon the ruins of
the fort and village, and the landing party went forward
again, fighting from bush to bush and from stone to stone,

till the ruins were in their hands. Shells still fell amon
them, single Turks, lurking under cover, sniped them an
shot them ; but the landing had been made good, an
V beach was secured to us.

This was the worst and the bloodiest of all the landing

JOHN MASEFIELD

158 *The Battle of Jutland*

THINGS seemed as peaceful as could be on the afternoon
of Tuesday, May 30th, when Maurice Bethell and I wen
ashore for a round of golf at Bruntsfield near Edinburgh
After a thoroughly enjoyable game over this course, whose
delightful inland surroundings reflected all the charm o
early summer, we adjourned for tea to " Rospletha "—
the little house I had rented on the side of the links—and
then found our way down to Queensferry Pier at the
regulation hour of 6 p.m., in order to catch the routine
boat.

While we stood waiting on the pier amid a throng of
fellow-officers, all eyes were suddenly drawn in the direction
of the *Lion*, from whose masthead there floated a string
of flags with this message to all ships—" Raise steam for
22 knots and bank fires at half an hour's notice." Next,
observing the significance of the fact that this signal was
being made to the seaplane-carrier ships, we not unnaturally
concluded that a Pemberton-Billing benefit or air-raid
picnic was about to develop. In this state of mind we
reached our various ships. Before another half an hour
had elapsed the bustling activity and constant changes of
signals on board the flagship produced throughout the
other ships that atmosphere of suppressed excitement
which is the herald of great events. Clearly some further
change of plans was in the air. Another half-hour, and
then up went those flags for the last time that evening,

The Battle of Jutland

bearing the message—" Raise steam for full speed with all despatch."

There was now not a shadow of doubt that something considerably more than an air-picnic was impending.

At nightfall the entire force based on the Firth of Forth steamed out of harbour. It consisted of the following units :

(a) The First and Second Battle-Cruiser Squadrons, composed of H.M.S. *Lion*, *Princess Royal*, *Tiger*, *Queen Mary*, and *Australia*, *New Zealand*, *Indefatigable*.

(b) A squadron of battleships of the *Queen Elizabeth* class, consisting of H.M.S. *Barham*, *Warspite*, *Valiant*, *Malaya*. The *Queen Elizabeth* was unfortunately in dock at the time.

(c) Twelve light cruisers : the *Southampton*, *Nottingham*, *Birmingham*, *Dublin*, *Galatea*, *Inconstant*, *Phaeton*, *Cordelia*, *Falmouth*, *Birkenhead*, *Gloucester*, *Yarmouth*.

(d) The 1st and 13th Flotillas of destroyers, led respectively by the *Fearless* and the *Champion*, and eight destroyers from the Harwich Force temporarily attached.

A TABULATED LIST OF DESTROYERS WITH ADMIRAL BEATTY'S FORCE

13th Flotilla.	Harwich Force.	1st Flotilla.
Nestor	*Lydiard*	*Acheron*
Onslow	*Liberty*	*Ariel*
Nomad	*Landrail*	*Attack*
Nicator	*Laurel*	*Hydra*
Narborough	*Moorsom*	*Badger*
Obdurate	*Morris*	*Goshawk*
Petard	*Turbulent*	*Defender*
Pelican	*Termagant*	*Lizard*
Nerissa		*Lapwing*
Moresby		

(e) The seaplane-carrier ship *Engadine*.

Steaming at high speed eastwards in the direction of the Skagerrack, the force found itself at noon on the following day (May 31st) in a position approximately

120 miles west of the north coast of Jutland. The disposition of the force was as follows :

The 5th Battle Squadron N.N.W. five miles from *Lion* screened by *Fearless* and nine destroyers of the 1st Flotilla. The 2nd Battle-Cruiser Squadron was stationed E.N.E. three miles from *Lion*. The *Lion* and 1st Battle-Cruiser Squadron were screened by the *Champion* and ten destroyers of the 13th Flotilla, with *Turbulent* and *Termagant*. Light cruisers were screening on a bearing E.N.E. and W.S.W. Centre of screen S.S.E. from *Lion*. It was a glorious sunny day, the sea almost a dead calm, the atmosphere clear and conducive to good visibility.

Nothing worth recording occurred until 2.30 p.m., when the light cruisers, who, together with the seaplane-carrier ship, had been thrown out in advance as scouts, reported " Smoke ahead ! "—which smoke they were shortly afterwards able to diagnose as that of the enemy's battle-cruisers, who were bearing E.N.E.

At 3 p.m. the light cruisers spread to the east and formed a screen in front of the Battle-Cruiser Squadron and 5th Battle Squadron. At 3.30 the signal was hoisted : " Enemy in sight ! "

Almost simultaneously the enemy, who had been steaming north, altered course to S.E.

Admiral Beatty steered a course to cut the enemy off and prevent him rounding Horn Reef.

At this moment the " enemy " comprised the following ships :

(*a*) Five battle-cruisers, *viz. Lutzow, Derfflinger, Seydlitz, Moltke, Von der Tann.*

(*b*) Two light cruisers.

(*c*) A flotilla of fifteen destroyers.

Admiral Beatty formed battle line on a course parallel to that of the enemy, placing the *Champion* and twelve destroyers (*i.e.* eight of the 13th Flotilla, two of the

The Battle of Jutland

10th Flotilla, and two of the 9th Flotilla) half a mile ahead in order that their smoke might not interfere with his gunnery.

At 3.48 p.m. both sides opened fire almost simultaneously at 18,500 yards, and Admiral Beatty reduced speed to 21 knots, in order that the battleships of the *Queen Elizabeth* class might close up on him. Being only 24-knot ships, they had been left behind when the speed was increased to 27 knots by the Admiral on sighting the enemy.

In order to make certain our exact rate of speed, and thereby to obtain accurate data for their calculations, the Germans made an unsuccessful attempt to send a wireless signal ordering the British Fleet to steam at 23 knots.

From 4 o'clock onwards, the *Lion* and battle-cruisers altered course on two or three occasions one point to throw the enemy off the range. At 4·5 (approx.) H.M.S. *Indefatigable* was hit by three shells falling together. She blew up and sank almost immediately.

When the action commenced, the *Nestor* was about half a mile ahead of the battle-cruisers, from which position we had the best point of vantage for observing the enemy's salvoes falling around the *Lion*. The enemy's shooting appeared good, and it was clear that he was concentrating on Admiral Beatty's flagship.

Shortly after 4 p.m. the admiral signalled that the flotilla of destroyers ahead was to attack the enemy's battle-cruisers with torpedoes. " Captain D " in the *Champion* immediately repeated this order, adding that the *Nestor* and her division were to lead the attack. The attacking destroyers of the 13th, 10th, and 9th Flotillas were as follows : *Nestor*, *Nomad*, *Nicator*, *Narborough*, *Pelican*, *Petard*, *Obdurate*, *Nerissa*, with *Moorsom* and *Morris* of the 10th Flotilla (Harwich Force), *Turbulent* and *Termagant* of the 9th Flotilla (Harwich Force). The *Onslow* was detached on special service with *Engadine*.

The Knapsack

I immediately hoisted the signal for full speed and ordered the destroyers to form a single line astern of me. Then, shaping course a point and a half in towards the enemy, we ran full speed at 35 knots for half an hour, in order to reach an advantageous position on the enemy's bows, such as would enable me to launch the torpedo attack with the greatest possible prospect of success.

On drawing out to this position, we observed the enemy's fifteen destroyers coming out with the object of making a similar torpedo attack on our battle-cruisers.

At 4.40 p.m., having reached the desired position, I turned to N. (approximately fourteen points to port), followed in succession by the rest of the destroyers, with this objective : (*a*) to frustrate the intended torpedo attack by enemy destroyers on our battle-cruisers by intercepting them and bringing them to action ; (*b*) to push home our torpedo attack on the enemy's battle-cruisers.

The German destroyers then immediately turned on a course parallel to ours, and the destroyer action thus commenced at a range of 10,000 yards. I promptly manœuvred to close this range.

At 4.45 the *Nomad*, my immediate follower, was hit in the boiler-room and hauled out of line disabled. We in the *Nestor* got the range very quickly, and pumped in three or four salvoes from our 4-in. guns. Two German destroyers disappeared beneath the surface, and though it is unreasonable definitely to claim the credit of sinking a given ship where many are concerned, my control officer is still prepared to affirm that the *Nestor's* guns accounted for one of them.

At 4.50 p.m. the enemy's destroyers turned tail and fled. Pursued by the British they divided themselves into two portions, one half of which made for the head, while the other took cover under the tail, of the German battle-cruiser line. It must be remembered that although they

The Battle of Jutland

were numerically superior to us, the enemy's destroyers were neither so large nor so heavily armed.

The British boats promptly turned to chase the enemy's fleeing T.B.D.'s, and while I proceeded with my division, now reduced to two boats (*i.e. Nestor* and *Nicator*), after those of the enemy's destroyers who were making for the head of the battle-cruiser line, the other two divisions of the T.B.D.'s went after the remaining, and larger, portion of the German destroyers.

Just then the enemy's battle-cruisers altered course four points to port, that is, forty-five degrees to the left. Most probably this manœuvre was prompted by the warning splashes that marked the discharge of the British torpedoes, of which the *Nestor* had just fired her first two.[1]

Thus I found myself with the solitary *Nicator* hot in the track of the fleeing destroyers and now rapidly approaching the head of the German battle-cruiser line, who were not slow in giving us an extremely warm welcome from their secondary armament. At a distance of 3,000 to 4,000 yards the *Nestor* fired her third torpedo and immediately afterwards at 4.58 turned away eight points to starboard, in order to get clear of the danger zone and to regain the line of the British battle-cruisers.

Suddenly from behind the head of the enemy's line there came a German light cruiser, who opened hot fire and straddled us. It was just about 5 o'clock when two boilers were put out of action by direct hits. From the bridge I saw at once that something of the kind had happened. A huge cloud of steam was rising from the

[1] It is quite likely that one of these torpedoes actually struck the *Lutzow*. She was subsequently sunk, and her survivors at Wilhelmshaven, whilst in conversation with *Nestor's* men, told them that a torpedo from *Nestor's* division had struck them; this so reduced their speed that they became an easy prey to the 5th Battle Squadron's gunfire.

boiler-room, completely enshrouding the whole ship, and it was painfully apparent that our speed was dropping every second. Our speed died away gradually, until at 5.30 p.m. we came to a dead stop.

Nothing daunted, the engine-room staff applied themselves with all the means in their power to the work of setting the engines in motion. But it was all without avail. The damage was of a nature which required, above all, time. Before anything could be done, the boilers had to be cooled off, and all pipes were in the overheated condition that results from a high-speed run.

The German light cruiser having crippled us, almost immediately turned back and rejoined her own battle-cruisers.

Seeing our plight the *Petard* (Lieutenant-Commander E. C. O. Thompson), now returning from the chase of the major portion of the German flotilla, gallantly offered a tow; but I had no hesitation in refusing an offer which would have meant the exposure of two ships to the danger that properly belonged to one.

Curiously enough, when our speed gave out, we found ourselves brought to a standstill at a spot only two miles west of the *Nomad*, our only comrade in misfortune.

But though crippled, we had guns that were still intact, and a hostile destroyer, swooping down on what she thought an easy prey, was greeted with volleys of salvoes from our invaluable semi-automatic guns. After such a warm reception, the German destroyer sheered off posthaste.

While lying helpless and broken down, we saw the opposing forces of battle-cruisers retracing their tracks to the N.W., fighting on parallel courses. The rival squadrons quickly disappeared behind the horizon, engaged furiously, and we were now left with the ocean to ourselves. But it was not to be for long. Fifteen minutes later my yeoman-of-signals reported : " German battleships on the horizon, shaping course in our direction." This was more than I had ever bargained for, and, using my own glasses, I was dumbfounded to see that it was in truth the main body of the German High Sea Fleet, steaming at top speed in a N.W. direction and following the wake of their own battle-cruisers.

Their course necessarily led them first past the *Nomad*, and in another ten minutes the slaughter began. They literally smothered the destroyer with salvoes. Of my divisional mate nothing could be seen : great columns of spray and smoke alone gave an indication of her whereabouts. I shall never forget the sight, and mercifully it was a matter of a few minutes before the ship sank ; at the time it seemed impossible that any one on board could have survived.

Of what was in store for us there was now not the vestige of a doubt, and the problem was, how to keep all hands occupied for the few minutes that remained before the crash must come.

While the sub-lieutenant and myself were " ditching " all charts, confidential books, and documents, the first lieutenant and the men were executing my orders in providing biscuit and water for the boats ; lowering these to the water's edge ; hoisting out Carley floats ; and generally preparing for the moment when we should be obliged to leave the ship.

These orders were rapidly executed, and there was still time on our hands ; for nothing had as yet happened. By a brilliant inspiration, Bethell then suggested to me that the cables might be ranged on deck—ostensibly for use in case of a friendly tow, but in reality to keep the men busy to the last. This suggestion I readily accepted, and the hands were still thus employed when the end came.

The Knapsack

From a distance of about five miles, the Germans commenced with their secondary armament, and very soon we were enveloped in a deluge of shell fire. Any reply from our own guns was absolutely out of the question at a range beyond the possibilities of our light shells ; to have answered any one of our numerous assailants would have been as effective as the use of a peashooter against a wall of steel. Just about this time we fired our last torpedo at the High Sea Fleet and it was seen to run well.

It was a matter of two or three minutes only before the *Nestor*, enwrapped in a cloud of smoke and spray, the centre of a whirlwind of shrieking shells, received not a few heavy and vital hits, and the ship began slowly to settle by the stern and then to take up a heavy list to starboard.

Her decks now showed the first signs of havoc amongst life and limb.

It was clear that the doomed *Nestor* was sinking rapidly, and at that moment I gave my last order as her commander, " Abandon ship."

The motor-boat and Carley floats were quickly filled ; and as the dinghy was badly broken up by shell fire, there seemed to remain for me only the possibility of a place in the whaler.

Bethell was standing beside me, and I turned to him with the question, " Now where shall *we* go ? " His answer was only characteristic of that gallant spirit, " To Heaven, I trust, sir ! "

At that moment he turned aside to attend to a mortally wounded signalman and was seen no more amidst a cloud of fumes from a bursting shell.

I clambered into the whaler, where I found about eight others waiting, and we remained alongside until the last possible moment, hailing the partially submerged ship

The Battle of Jutland

vigorously, in the unlikely event of any survivors being still on board. Finally we pushed off clear.

The whaler, however, had also been hit, probably at the same time as the dinghy, and before we had gone half a dozen strokes she filled and sank. We then struck out, I luckily having my " Miranda " life-saving waistcoat on, for the well-loaded motor-boat, lying some fifty yards ahead of the *Nestor*, where some of us were pulled in, the rest supporting themselves by holding on to the gunwale.

Looking now towards the *Nestor*, we saw the water lapping over the decks, and the forecastle high in the air, still the target of the German gun-layers, some of whose projectiles fell uncomfortably near us in the motor-boat and rafts.

In about three minutes, the destroyer suddenly raised herself into an absolutely perpendicular position, and thus slid down, stern first, to the bottom of the North Sea, leaving a quantity of oil and wreckage to mark the spot where she had last rested.

As she sank, her sharp stem and stockless anchors alone visible, we gave our gallant but cruelly short-lived *Nestor* three rousing cheers and sang " God Save the King."

A reverential pause followed, broken almost immediately by the voice of a typical " A.B.," " Are we down-'earted ? No ! " Then " Wot abart ' Tipperary ' ? " His words and spirit were infectious, and all joined lustily in the chorus of that hackneyed but inspiring modern war song.

The song was thus in no small degree responsible for a frame of mind in which it was possible calmly to face the situation of finding oneself afloat, sixty-odd miles from the nearest shore, in an overladen, leaking, and broken-down motor-boat, with nothing in sight except the enemy's High Sea Fleet vanishing in the distance.

It was now about 5.30 p.m. and the weather was still

calm and fine, but the slightly freshening breeze increased my anxieties as to the length of time the motor-boat would remain afloat.

In about fifteen minutes' time we saw a division of German destroyers shoot out from the rear of the battle fleet and steam towards us at high speed. Rapidly closing, one of them picked us up and carried off our motor-boat as a prize ; while another took the men off the Carley floats. Once aboard, the wounded were placed in the ward-room, the officers in the captain's cabin, and the rest of the men in the stokeholds and engine-rooms.

The captain of the destroyer, which turned out to be the S 15, sent for me and interviewed me on the bridge. He saw that I was wet through from my immersion, but never offered me a change of clothes. He interrogated me without gaining any information, and his manner all through was typically Prussian and discourteous. We were, however, fed until our arrival at Wilhelmshaven the following evening.

What occurred from the moment we were shut down in the captain's cabin until we disembarked next evening can only be a matter of conjecture from the movements of the propellers, supplemented by the observations of Dr. Alexander Joe, who was once called forward about 8.30 p.m. to minister to two British seamen, picked up from the *Indefatigable*. But by putting two and two together, we gathered that our captor was escorting the " lame ducks " of the High Sea Fleet back to the base ; further, from the intermittent firing of the guns overhead and from the many sudden and rapid reversings and alternating movements of the engines, we inferred that, if the main battle had ceased, destroyer attacks were in progress on both sides.

Lying on top of the captain's bunk in semi-darkness, with clothes slowly drying on me, weary and feeling that one had reached the end, no wonder if I began to reflect about the immediate future. How was it all going to end? Assuming that the British sank this German T.B.D.—an eventuality one's patriotism demanded and thoroughly expected, because she was one of an old type and no kind of match for any of our destroyers—should we pull through, after a scuffle with the sentry, another bath in the North Sea, and with the remote chance of being picked up by a British destroyer in the dark? Probably not. On the other hand, if the German destroyer came through unscathed, one would emerge from the business with a whole skin, with a certainty of a dreary spell of captivity, but with the hope of serving under the White Ensign at a future date.

And so the long-drawn torture of this ghastly night crept on until the first tinge of dawn found its way into the cabin, and with a silent prayer of heartfelt gratitude for the miraculous preservation of my life, I sank into sleep from sheer exhaustion.

At 7.30 a.m. the sub-lieutenant of the destroyer came below, and after ordering some breakfast for us, announced that the battle was over and that the destroyer was shaping course for Wilhelmshaven.

THE HON. BARRY BINGHAM, V.C.

159 *The Retreat from St. Quentin*

IT was now dusk, and with dusk came peace and silence. And at dusk this was our position :—The front rim of the redoubt was in the enemy's possession. The counter-attack company had disappeared. The company-keeps still held out with a few men in each. The inner ring of the redoubt was held by one company, and the remnants of three. B. had survived with one of his officers. But several officers in the three front companies had been either killed, wounded, or captured. There were probably two hundred men still surviving in the battalion.

In the darkness the colonel and I walked up to the line. As we went along the road, the stillness was abruptly broken by the sounds of three or four shots, screams and curses. We flung ourselves on the roadside, our revolvers ready. We shouted : " Who goes there ? " English voices answered, and the sergeant-major went to investigate. Two German privates had walked into a sentry on the road, *coming from behind us.* No one could understand what they said, and they were sent back to brigade headquarters. And I don't remember that any one of us was perturbed by the incident, eerie though it was.

Just after one o'clock in the day, we received long-awaited instructions from the brigade : The battalion in reserve was to deliver a counter-attack. The line of deployment was given, and the direction of attack. The battalion was to leave its position at 12.45, and the guns were to start a creeping barrage at 1.33 a.m.

The whole thing was a ghastly failure. The night was black, and the battalion attacking was unfamiliar with the ground it had to cover. We waited hours for a sign of their approach. About two o'clock a stray officer came to us, having lost his company. Eventually, about four o'clock, one company did appear. It went forward in the darkness, but got dispersed and uncontrollable in the effort to deploy into attack formation. Dawn found us as dusk had found us, with the sole difference that some two hundred men of the counter-attack battalion had found refuge in our redoubt, and in the keeps in front.

I think by then we were past hope or despair. We regarded all events with an indifference of weariness, knowing that with the dawn would come another attack.

The Retreat from St. Quentin

We distributed ammunition, reorganized our Lewis guns, and waited dully, without apprehension.

Again the morning was thickly misty. Our own artillery fire was desultory and useless. Under cover of the mist, the enemy massed in battle formation, and the third attack commenced about 7 a.m. We only heard a babel in the mist. Now our artillery was firing short among our men in the redoubt. About ten o'clock the enemy penetrated our left flank, presumably in the gap between us and the battalion on our left, which was still in position. Machine-gun fire began to harass us from that direction, somewhere in the ruins of the village. We never heard from the battalion on our right, and a runner I sent there did not return. I think they must have withdrawn about ten o'clock.

This new attack petered out. I fancy it was only half-hearted on the part of the enemy—probably only a demonstration to see if we intended to make a determined resistance, or to fight only a rearguard action. Finding the resistance determined enough, they evidently retired to prepare the real thing.

This fourth attack was delivered about midday. The mist still persisted thinly. One could perhaps see objects fifty yards away. I don't know what resistance the platoon-keeps offered. They were in a hopeless position, and would easily have been swamped in a massed attack.

Shortly after midday, the enemy came in direct contact with the inner ring of the redoubt.

We fired like maniacs. Every round of ammunition had been distributed. The Lewis guns jammed ; rifle bolts grew stiff and unworkable with the expansion of heat.

In the lull before noon, the colonel and I had left the dugout, in which we were beginning to feel like rats in a trap, and had found an old gun-pit about two hundred and fifty yards further back, and here we established our

The Knapsack

headquarters. An extraordinary thing happened. The gun-pit was dug out of the bank on the roadside. About two o'clock one of our guns, evidently assuming that Roupy had been evacuated, began to pound the road between Roupy and Fluquières. One of these shells landed clean on the road edge of our pit. We were all hurled to the ground by the explosion, but, on recovering ourselves, found only one casualty : the colonel had received a nasty gash in the forearm. We then went two hundred to three hundred yards across the open, away from the road, and found a smaller over-grown pit. The colonel refused to regard his wound as serious ; but he soon began to feel dizzy, and was compelled to go back to the dressing-station. I was then left in charge of the battalion.

It was now about 2.30. The attack still persisted in a guerilla fashion. But the enemy was massing troops in the trenches already taken. At 4 p.m. the intensity of the attack deepened suddenly. A new intention had come into the enemy's mind : he was directing his attack on the flanks of our position in an effort to close round us like pincers. On the left he made use of cover offered by the ruined village, and eventually brought machine-guns to bear against us from our left rear. On the right he made use of the trenches evacuated by the Inniskillings.

In the height of this attack, while my heart was heavy with anxiety, I received a message from the brigade. Surely reinforcements were coming to our aid ! Or was I at length given permission to withdraw ? Neither : it was a rhetorical appeal to hold on to the last man. I rather bitterly resolved to obey the command.

Another hour passed. The enemy pressed on relentlessly with a determined, insidious energy, reckless of cost. Our position was now appallingly precarious. I therefore resolved to act independently, and do as perhaps I should have done hours earlier. I ordered B. to organize a withdrawal. This message despatched, I lay on my belly in the grass and watched through my field-glasses every minute trickling of the enemy's progress. Gradually they made their way round the rim of the redoubt, bombing along the traverses. And now we only held it as lips might touch the rim of a saucer. I could see the heads of my men, very dense and in a little space. And on either side, incredibly active, gathered the grey helmets of the Germans. It was like a long bowstring along the horizon, and our diminished forces the arrow to be shot into a void. A great many hostile machine-guns had now been brought up, and the plain was sprayed with hissing bullets. They impinged and spluttered about the little pit in which I crouched.

I waited anxiously for B. to take the open. I saw men crawl out of the trenches, and lie flat on the parados, still firing at the enemy. Then, after a little while, the arrow was launched. I saw a piteous band of men rise from the ground, and run rapidly towards me. A great shout went up from the Germans : a cry of mingled triumph and horror. " Halt Eenglisch ! " they cried, and for a moment were too amazed to fire ; as though aghast at the folly of men who could plunge into such a storm of death. But the first silent gasp of horror expended, then broke the crackling storm. I don't remember in the whole war an intenser taste of hell. My men came along spreading rapidly to a line of some two hundred yards length, but bunched here and there. On the left, by the main road, the enemy rushed out to cut them off. Bayonets clashed there. Along the line men were falling swiftly as the bullets hit them. Each second they fell, now one crumpling up, now two or three at once. I saw men stop to pick up their wounded mates, and as they carried them along, themselves get hit and fall with their inert burdens. Now they were near me, so I rushed out of my pit and ran with them to the line of trenches some three hundred yards behind.

It seemed to take a long time to race across those few hundred yards. My heart beat nervously, and I felt infinitely weary. The bullets hissed about me, and I thought : then this is the moment of death. But I had no emotions. I remembered having read how in battle men are hit, and never feel the hurt till later, and I wondered if I had yet been hit. Then I reached the line. I stood petrified, enormously aghast. *The trench had not been dug, and no reinforcements occupied it.* It was as we had passed it on the morning of the 21st, the sods dug off the surface, leaving an immaculately patterned " mock " trench. A hundred yards on the right a brigade machine-gun had taken up a position, and was already covering our retreat. I looked about me wildly, running along the line and signalling to the men to drop as they reached the slender parapet of sods. But the whole basis of my previous tactics had been destroyed. I should never have ordered my men to cross that plain of death, but for the expectation that we were falling back to reinforce a new line. We found an empty mockery, and I was in despair. But I must steady the line. On the actual plain the men obeyed my signals, and crouched in the shallow trench. But even as they crouched, the bullets struck them. On the road, the straight white road leading to the western safety, there was something like a stampede. S. and the sergeant-major went and held it with pointed revolvers. But it was all useless—hopeless. On the right, I saw the enemy creeping round. They would soon enfilade us, and then our shallow defence would be a death-trap. I accordingly gave the signal to withdraw, bidding the two Lewis guns to cover us as long as possible. Once more we rose and scattered in retreat. It would be about seven hundred yards to the next trenches—the village line round Fluquières —and this we covered fairly well, sections occasionally halting to give covering fire. The enemy had not yet ventured from the redoubt, and our distance apart was now great enough to make his fire of little effect. And I think as we moved up the slope towards the village we must have been in " dead " ground, so far as the enemy advancing on the right was concerned.

We reached Fluquières, which lay on the top of the slope, and found there some deep trenches on each side of the road at the entrance of the village. Further to the left, I found certain London troops commanded by a major. One of my Lewis guns still remained intact, and this I placed to fire down the straight road to Roupy. The enemy had now left the redoubt and were advancing in line formation.

We were at Fluquières about an hour. The enemy evidently did not intend to rest content with his capture of the redoubt. It was just beginning to get dusk. Earlier we had noticed sporadic contact lights go up. But now they shot into the sky from all along the plain. Low-flying aeroplanes hovered over the advancing line, and their wireless messages soon put the German guns on to us. Big black high-explosive shells began to fall on our position, making our tired flesh shudder. I now began to be amazed at the advancing contact lights. They did not merely stretch in a line in front of us : *they encircled us like a horse-shoe, the points of which seemed* (and actually were) *miles behind us.* On the right the enemy was enfilading us with machine-gun fire.

I searched for the major commanding the troops on my left, but could not find him. By this time I was determined to act, and therefore gave the order to withdraw. The men filed through the village, gathering fresh ammunition from a dump at the cross-roads. From the village the road went up a slope leading to Aubigny. The enemy's fire soon followed us, and we proceeded along the ditches on each side of the road.

Three-quarters of the way up the slope I observed a trench running at right angles to the road on each side of it. I ordered the London men to go to the left, my own to the right, there to reorganize into companies. The twilight was now fairly deep, and I thought that with evening the enemy's advance would stay. The major I had seen in Fluquières now appeared again, and cursed me for giving the order to retire. I was too tired to argue, and even then a gust of machine-gun fire swept above our heads. They were going to attack again. We could hear them moving in the semi-darkness. Something else we could hear too—the throb of a motor-cycle behind us. It was a despatch rider, and when he drew level to us, he stopped his machine and came towards me with a message. I opened it. It ordered all troops east of the Aubigny defences to retire through Ham.

I was glad. I believe I thought then that it was the end of our share of the battle. I went to the men, and assembled them in companies, and in close artillery formation we retired across country due west. We came to the Aubigny defences, manned by fresh troops, about a mile further on, and then we gathered on the road again and marched wearily along. I remember coming to a water-tank, where we all drank our fill—our mouths were swollen with thirst. When we reached Ham, an officer met us and ordered us to proceed to Muille Villette, about two miles further on, and there billet for the night. Ham, as we walked through its cobbled streets, seemed very hollow and deserted. The last time we had seen it, it had been a busy market-town, full of civilians. Now only a few sinister looters went about the empty houses with candles. We saw one fellow come out of a door with a

The Retreat from St. Quentin

and innumerable bolsters on little carts, some hand-pulled, some yoked to bony horses. They tied cows behind. There were old men, many old women, a few young women, but no young men. They and their like proceeded with us along the western road.

We had gone perhaps five miles when an orderly on horseback overtook us with orders. We were to report to the —th Division at Freniches.

This we eventually did, and a fat staff colonel studied a map, and then told me to take my battalion to Esmery-Hallon, a village four miles due north, and there take up a defensive position. This was more than I expected. I explained that my men had been fighting continuously for forty-eight hours, and were beaten and spiritless. But I received no comfort : the situation demanded that every available man should be used to the bitter end. I hardly dared to face my men : but I think they were too tired to mind where they went. We turned off at a right angle, and slowly marched on. The road led through a beautiful patch of country, steeped in a calm, liquid sunshine. We tilted our bodies forward, and forced our weary muscles to act.

About two miles south of Esmery-Hallon, an officer (a lieutenant) appeared on a motor-cycle. He was in command of a scrap lot—transport men, cobblers, returned leave men, etc. He seemed to have the impression that the enemy were upon us, and wanted me to deploy and take up a position facing east. I explained that we were much too tired to do any such thing. He expostulated. Did I realize this, that, and the other ? I explained that I had cause to realize such things better than he did. He raved. I told him finally that I didn't care a damn, but that I had orders to defend Esmery-Hallon, and thither I must go. He went off in a rage, seeming incredibly silly and fussy to us all.

391

The Knapsack

Esmery-Hallon is a small village perched on a detached conical hill, overlooking the plain on all sides. The defence was simply arranged. Two companies of engineers were entrenched in front of the village. I sent a lookout on to the top of the church tower, and extended my men astraddle the hill on each side of the village, north and south. The men on the south found a ditch, which made an admirable trench. The men on the north extended over the ploughed land, and dug shallow pits for shelter. We had no machine-guns or Lewis guns, but every man had a rifle and a decent amount of ammunition. I established my headquarters on the north side by a quarry, where I had a wide view of the plain.

The day was very still, and the distant rattle of machine-gun fire carried to us. A few enemy shells fell ineffectively about the landscape. I got into touch with a major of the Inniskillings in command of one hundred and fifty men on my right, and we co-ordinated defences on that wing. My left wing was in the air, so to speak—not a soul visible for miles.

When our dispositions were finally made, I returned to the quarry edge. My servant T. had already been away to search the village, and now came laden with samples of red wine and cider which he had found in a cellar. So I sent him back to the village with other men, telling them to search for food also. They soon returned with bottles of red wine and a large tin of army biscuits. Evidently there was any amount of wine, but I was afraid to distribute it among the men for fear lest on fasting stomachs it should make them drunk. So S. and I each took a wine glass, and starting at different points, we began to go a round of the men. Each man lay curled up in his shallow pit, resting. To each we gave a glass of wine and a few biscuits. They took it thankfully. There was a lull in the distant fighting: I don't remember any noise of fire during that hour. The sun was warm and seemed to cast a golden peace on the scene. A feeling of unity with the men about me suddenly suffused my mind.

It was nearly two o'clock when we got settled. About this time I interrupted a message which gave me the useful information that the enemy had been seen in Ham at 10 a.m. I guessed that the silence meant they were now consolidating along the Somme Canal. Later in the afternoon a cavalry patrol trotted up to our position. Officer, men, and horses all looked very debonair and well fed. The officer was very condescending towards me, but made a message of the information I gave him, thought it would not be worth while venturing further on to the plain, so rode away back, harness jingling, the sun shining on well-polished accoutrements.

About five o'clock, I judged that we were to be left alone for the night, and made my plans accordingly. I sent the following message to B., who was in charge of the men on the right of the village : " We hold on to our present positions unless otherwise ordered. When it is getting dark close your men in a little to form about 7 or 8 pickets. From these pickets send standing patrols out about 150 yards, or to any good observation point within warning distance. Any show of resistance should drive off any enemy patrols. But as far as I can make out the Boche is still east of the canal. Should you be attacked by overwhelming numbers, withdraw fighting in a due westerly direction under your own arrangements. I should do the same in case of need. I suggest you come up to have a look at our position before dark."

But just after dark, I received orders to relieve the Royal Engineers in front of the village. I regretted this order, but had to obey it. We now found ourselves in freshly dug

The Knapsack

trenches on the flat of the plain, our view to the left and right obstructed by woods.

Included in the orders mentioned was a message to the effect that advance parties of the French would probably arrive that night, and the positions would be shown to them. This message filled us with wild hope; we became almost jaunty.

But the night was very cold, and heavily wet with dew. We improved the trenches, and stamped about, flapping our arms in an effort to keep warm. I sat with L., bravest and brightest of my runners, on a waterproof sheet beneath a tree in the centre of our position. We waited for the dawn: it was weird, phantasmagorical. Again the fateful mist. As it cleared a little, the woods near us hung faintly in the whiteness.

At 8 a.m. we began to observe troops retreating in front of us. They came in little groups down the road, or straggled singly over the landscape. The mist gradually lifted. We heard machine-gun fire fairly near, somewhere on the right. The stragglers informed us that the enemy had crossed the canal in the early dawn, and was advancing in considerable force. We waited patiently. At 9 a.m. the enemy came into touch with our fellows on the left, and here we rebutted him successfully. At 9.30 the troops on our right were reported to be withdrawing. About ten o'clock, there happened one of those sudden episodes, which would be almost comic with their ludicrous *bouleversement* were they not so tragic in their results. Seemingly straight from the misty sky itself, but in reality from our own guns, descended round after round of shrapnel bursting terrifically just above our heads, and spraying leaden showers upon us. Simultaneously, from the woods on out right there burst a fierce volley of machine-gun fire, hissing and spluttering among us. We just turned and fled into the shelter of the village buildings. I shouted to my men to make for the position by the quarry. We scuttled through gardens and over walls. By the time we reached the quarry we had recovered our nerve. We extended and faced the enemy, who were advancing skilfully over the plain on our left. We on our part were a scrap lot composed of various units. We hastily reorganized into sections. Retreat was inevitable. Then followed a magnificent effort of discipline. A major took charge of the situation, and we began to retire with covering fire, section by section, in perfect alternation.

We were now on a wide expanse of plain, sloping gently westward. We stretched over this—a thin line of men, perhaps a thousand yards long. We were approaching the Nesle-Noyon Canal. When within a few hundred yards of the canal, we closed inwards to cross a bridge (Ramecourt). At the other end of the bridge stood a staff officer, separating the men like sheep as they crossed, first a few to the left, then a few to the right. Here I got separated from the majority of my men, finding myself with only fifteen. We were told to proceed along the bank of the canal until we found an unoccupied space, and there dig in.

As we crossed the bridge, we saw for the first time the sky-blue helmets of French troops peeping above a parapet. I think our eyes glistened with expectation of relief.

We went perhaps half a mile along the bank of the canal, and there I halted my attenuated company. The sun was now blazing hotly above our heads. We dropped to the ground, utterly exhausted. Presently some of the men began spontaneously to dig. R., the only officer left with me, also took a pick and joined the men. I began to feel ashamed just then, for I would willingly have died. I took a spade (there was a dump of such things just by us) and began to shovel the earth loosened by R. I seemed to be lifting utterly impossible burdens. My flesh seemed to move uneasily through iron bands ; my leaden lids drooped smartingly upon my eyes.

We dug about three feet deep, and then ceased, incapable of more. At the foot of the bank there was a small pool of water. The enemy was not now in sight, so we plunged our hot faces and hands into its weedy freshness, and took off our boots and socks, and bathed our aching feet.

In the evening, about 5 p.m., a few skirmishing patrols appeared on the horizon. But our artillery was now active and fairly accurate, and machine-guns swept the plain. The patrols retired, without having advanced any distance. A large German aeroplane, with a red belly, floated persistently above our line. We fired hundreds of shots at it, but without effect. T., my servant, nearly blew my head off in his efforts.

We had gathered a lot of sun-scorched hemlock and bedded the bottom of our trenches ; and when night came on we posted sentries, and huddled down to the bedding. The night was clear, and I gazed unblinkingly at the fierce stars above me, my aching flesh forbidding sleep. Later, I must have dozed in a wakeful stupor.

The next daybreak, that of the 25th, was less misty. Bread and bully-beef had come up during the night, and we fed to get warmth into our bodies. But the sun was soon up, and we began to feel almost cheerful once again. There was no immediate sign of the enemy, and I walked along to the bridge we had crossed the previous day to glean some information of our intentions ; but the only plan seemed to be the obvious one of holding on to our positions. I noticed some engineers were there ready to blow up the bridge if need be.

About 8 a.m. we saw little groups of enemy cavalry appear on the horizon. Through my glasses I could see

The Retreat from St. Quentin

them consulting maps, pointing, trotting fussily about. Our artillery was planting some kind of scattered barrage on the plain, and an occasional near shot made the horsemen scamper. We watched them rather amusedly till ten o'clock and then we saw signs of infantrymen. They came from the direction of Esmery-Hallon, and at first seemed in fairly dense formation. But they extended as they cut the sky-line, and we soon perceived them advancing in open order. As they got nearer, they began to organize short rushes, a section at a time.

We were now well stocked with ammunition—there were piles of it laid about—and as soon as the advancing troops were within anything like range, we began to " pot " them. In fact, the whole thing became like a rifle-gallery entertainment at a fair. But still they came on. Now we could see them quite plainly—could see their legs working like dancing bears, and their great square packs bobbing up and down as they ran. Occasionally one dropped.

Immediately in front of our trench, about eight hundred yards away, there was a little copse of perhaps fifty trees. This they reached about eleven o'clock and halted there. If only our flanks held out, I guessed they would never get further, for between the copse and our rifles and Lewis guns there was not a shred of cover ; and we were well entrenched, with a wide canal in front of us.

Of course, the artillery was busy all the while : not methodically, but thickly enough to give the day the appearance of a conventional battle. But then the unexpected (really we had no cause longer to regard it as unexpected), the fatal thing happened. A battery of ours shortened its range, and got our position exactly " taped." The shells fell thick and fast, right into our backs. We were, remember, dug in on the top of a bank, perhaps fifteen feet high. All along this bank the shells plunged. Immediately on our right, not fifty yards away, a shell landed cleanly into a trench, and when the smoke cleared there remained nothing, absolutely nothing distinguishable, where a moment ago had been five or six men. We grovelled like frightened, cowed animals. Still the shells fell : and there was no means of stopping them. I glanced distractedly round ; men on the right were running under cover of the bank away to the right. Other men on the left were retreating to the left. I resolved to get out of it. Immediately behind us, fifty yards away, was a large crescent-shaped mound, very steep, like a railway embankment, and perhaps sixty feet high. It occurred to me that from there we should command, and command as effectively as ever, the plain in front of us. I made my intention known, and at a given signal we leapt down the bank, and across the intervening fifty yards. We were evidently in sight, for a hail of machine-gun bullets made dusty splutters all round us as we ran. But we reached the mound without a casualty, and climbed safely on to it. There I found a few men already in occupation, commanded by a colonel, under whose orders I then placed myself.

The enemy's artillery fire now increased in volume. I saw a cow hit in a field behind us, and fall funnily with four rigid legs poking up at the sky.

At 3.30 we saw the French retiring on the right, about a thousand yards away. They were not running, but did not seem to be performing any methodic withdrawal. We then fell into one of those awful states of doubt and indecision. What was happening ? What should we do ? There was angry, ominous rifle-fire on our immediate left. About 4 p.m. there was a burst of machine-gun fire on our immediate right. I noticed that the stray bullets were coming over our heads. This meant that the enemy was advancing from the right.

I then saw English troops withdrawing, about six hundred

The Retreat from St. Quentin

yards away on the right—evidently the troops that had been defending the bridge. I did not hear any explosion, and so far as I know the bridge remained intact.

At 4.15 I saw the colonel with his men suddenly leave his position on my immediate left. Although I was within sight—within calling distance—he did not give me an order. I was now alone on the mound with my fifteen men.

I did not wait long. I resolved to act on my own initiative once more. We had now moved off the maps I possessed and might as well be in an unknown wilderness. I resolved to proceed due west, taking the sun as a guide. We moved down the back slope of the mound. At the foot we found a stream or off-flow from the canal, about ten feet wide and apparently very deep. As we hesitated, looking for a convenient crossing, a machine-gun a few hundred yards away opened fire on us. There were a good few trees about which must have obstructed the firer's view : the cut twigs, newly budded, fell into the water. We hesitated no longer : we plunged into the stream. The men had to toss their rifles across, many of which landed short and were lost. The sight of these frightened men plunging into the water effected one of those curious stirrings of the memory that call up some vivid scene of childhood : I saw distinctly the water-rats plunging at dusk into the mill-dam at Thornton-le-Dale, where I had lived as a boy of ten.

The water sucked at my clothes as I met it, and filled my field-boots. They seemed weighted with lead now as I walked, and oozed for hours afterwards.

We came out facing a wide plain, climbing gently westward. Machine-gun and rifle-fire still played about us. We could see a church steeple on the horizon due west, and I told the men to scatter and make for that steeple. Shrapnel was bursting in the sky, too high to be effective. We ran a little way, but soon got too tired. A., a faithful orderly, had stayed with me, and soon we walked over the fields as friends might walk in England. We came across French machine-gunners, who looked at us curiously, asked for news of the situation, but did not seem very perturbed.

We eventually came to the village on the horizon (probably Solente). An officer of the engineers stood by the side of his horse at the cross-roads, smoking a cigarette. He asked me why I was retreating. The question seemed silly : " We shall have to fight every inch of the way back again," he said. " These Frenchmen will never hold them." I went on, too tired to answer.

Here I saw for the first time a new post stuck on the roadside. It had on it an arrow and " Stragglers Post " in bold letters. So I was a straggler. I felt very bitter and full of despair.

I followed the road indicated by the arrow. It was dotted with small parties of men, all dejected and weary. We trudged along till we came to the village of Carrepuits. Military police met us at the entrance, and told us to report to the Traffic Control in a house a few hundred yards away. It was now getting dusk. I went into the cottage indicated, and here found an officer, very harassed and bored. Men were collected, and separated into the divisions they belonged to, and then given orders to report to such and such a place. I found a party of about fifty men of my division, and was instructed to take them and report to a divisional headquarters situated in a certain street in Roye.

I have forgotten that walk : it was only about two miles, but our utter dejection induced a kind of unconsciousness in us. It would be between ten and eleven o'clock when we got to Roye. I reported to a staff officer, who sent me off to the town major to get billets. The town major I found distracted, unable to say where I should find a billet. Apparently the town was packed with stragglers.

The Retreat from St. Quentin

We peered into two great gloomy marquees, floored densely with recumbent men. Meanwhile two other officers joined me with their men, and together we went off to search on our own. We found a magnificent house, quite empty, and here we lodged the men. Some kind of rations had been found. They soon had blazing wood fires going, and seemed happy in a way.

The town major had indicated a hut, where we officers might get rest, and perhaps some food. We went round, tired and aching though we were; we lifted the latch and found ourselves in a glowing room. A stove roared in one corner—and my teeth were chattering with cold, my clothes still being sodden—and a lamp hung from the roof. A large pan of coffee simmered on the stove, and the table was laden with bread, tinned-foods, butter; food, food, food. I hadn't had a bite since early morning, and then not much.

I forget, if I ever knew, who or what the two occupants were, but they were not stragglers. Roye had been their station for some time. One of them was fat, very fat, with a tight, glossy skin. I don't remember the other. We explained that we would like a billet for the night—anything would do so long as it was warmth. They were sorry: they had no room. Could they spare us some rations? They were sorry: this was all they had got till to-morrow noon. We stood very dejected, sick at our reception. "Come away!" I said. "Before I go away," cried one of my companions, "I would just like to tell these blighters what I think of them." He cursed them, and then we walked away, back to the men's billet. I looked in at my fellows; most of them were naked, drying their clothes at the fire. Some slept on the floor.

We went upstairs into an empty room. Two of us agreed to make a fire, while the other, the one who had given vent to his feelings, volunteered to go off in search

of food. We split up wood we found in the house, and li
a fire. I took off my clothes to dry them, and sat on a
bench in my shirt. If I had been asked then what I most
desired, besides sleep, I think I would have said: French
bread, butter, honey, and hot milky coffee.

The forager soon turned up. God only knows where
he got that food from : we did not ask him. But it was
French bread, butter, honey, and hot milky coffee in
a champagne bottle ! We cried out with wonder : we
almost wept. We shared the precious stuff out, eating
and drinking with inexpressible zest.

As we supped we related our experiences. I forget
their names ; I don't think I ever knew them. Were they
of the Border Regiment ? I'm not sure ; but they were
Northerners. They had been trapped in a sunken road,
with a Boche machine-gun at either end, and Boche calling
on them to surrender. I don't think either of them was
more than twenty years old : they were fresh and boyish,
and had been faced with this dilemma. They put it to
the vote : there, with death literally staring them in the
face, they solemnly called on the men to show hands as
to whether they would surrender, or make a run for it.
They had voted unanimously for the run. Half of them
perished in the attempt. But here, a few hours afterwards,
were the survivors, chatting over a blazing wood fire,
passing a bottle of coffee round, very unperturbed, not
in any way self-conscious. We stacked the fire high and
stretched ourselves on the floor in front of it, and slept for
a few hours.

We were up at six the next morning, the 26th of March,
and reporting to the Assistant Provost-Marshal, who was
reorganizing stragglers. We congregated in the Town
Square, and I was amazed at the numbers there. The
streets were thickly congested with infantrymen from

several divisions, with French armoured cars, cavalry, and staff officers. We fell in by divisions, and presently marched off, a column a mile or two in length. Cavalry protected our flanks and rear from surprise.

At Villers-les-Roye, I found B., the man who had been separated from me at Ramecourt Bridge. We were glad to be united again, and from there proceeded together. B. had had orders to go to a place called La Neuville, where the first-line transport awaited us. We were now passing through the battlefields of 1916, and everywhere was desolate and ruined. We marched on as far as Hangest-en-Santerre, where we met our battalion cookers loaded with a welcome meal. Just as we had devoured this, and were starting on our way again, we were met by a staff colonel, who, after inquiring who we were, ordered us to turn back and proceed to Folies, where our brigade was reorganizing.

We could but mutely obey, but with dull despair and an aching bitterness. We had never thought since leaving Roye but that we were finally out of the mêlée. To turn back meant, we knew, that we might still be very much in it. We crossed country to Folies, about two miles away, in a blazing sun. There we found the details of the brigade, consisting mostly of returned leave men, already holding a line of trenches. We were told to reinforce them.

Here the second-in-command rejoined the battalion and assumed command. My endurance was broken, and I was ordered down to the transport lines. I pointed out that the men were as weary as I, and should on no account be ordered into action again. It was useless : no man could be spared. But there was not much more for them to bear. Good hot food came up to them again at dusk. The night was warm and restful.

On the morning of the 27th, the enemy had possession

The Knapsack

of Bouchoir, a village about one mile to the south-east. He began to advance during the morning, and a skirmishing fight went on during that day and the next; and during this time the battalion was withdrawn from the line without suffering any serious casualties.

But I had gone back with the transport officer on the 26th. I mounted the transport-sergeant's horse, and in a dazed sort of way galloped westward in the dusk. I arrived half-dead at La Neuville, and slept there for twelve hours or more. The next day we went to Braches, and thence on foot to Rouvrel. About here, the country was yet unscathed by war, and very beautiful. On a bank by the roadside, I took *Walden* out of my pocket, where it had been forgotten since the morning of the 21st, and there began to read it. At Rouvrel the rest of the battalion rejoined us the next day. On the 29th I set off on horse-back with the transport to trek down the valley of the Somme.

When evening came and the hills of Moreuil were faint in the twilight, we were still travelling along the western road. No guns nor any clamour of war could be heard: a great silence filled the cup of misty hills. My weary horse drooped her head as she ambled along, and I, too, was sorrowful. To our north-east lay the squat towers of Amiens, a city in whose defence we had endured hardships until flesh had been defeated, and the brave heart broken. My mind held a vague wonder for her fate—a wonder devoid of hope. I could not believe in the avail of any effort. Then I listened to the rumbling cart, and the quiet voices of the men about me. The first stars were out when we reached Guignemicourt, and there we billeted for the night. In this manner we marched by easy stages down the valley of the Somme, halting finally at Salenelle, a village near Valery, and there we rested four days.

HERBERT READ

Illumination

160 *Illumination*

FOR the next two days still we are likely to be safe from any sudden alarm. We are settling down ; many are unpacking their books and best uniforms, others are setting out a photograph or two on their tables. My quarters are seething with people ; all the neighbours come in and out ; an old woman has just been in begging for brandy. This morning I was the witness of a scene which in itself perhaps has no significance, but yet seems to me to come home both to myself and others. A few weeks ago there was a large litter of kittens in the house ; they have become a nuisance now, for there is no milk for them. A fifteen-year-old lad who is on service here seems to have got instructions to destroy the superfluous ones. While I was writing in my room I saw him carrying them across the yard, and, before I could guess his intention, dashing them one after the other with incredible speed against the wall of a shed, where they remained lying ; then whistling and swinging his arms as usual he returned to the kitchen, where the food was just being set out, sat down with the others, and began to eat heartily. But one kitten quite unlike the others, a bluish-grey kitten with a white head, breast, and legs, and a light silvery fringe on the back of its neck, was only stunned and began to recover little by little. It attempted a few unsteady steps, sat down, washed itself for a while behind the ears, as if that would help it to come to its senses ; then crept across the yard into the house. Now I noticed for the first time that it was bleeding from the chin ; otherwise it seemed unhurt. Somewhat hesitatingly it went in through the kitchen door and looked around. When it saw the people eating at the table it tried to jump on to the bench, and after a few attempts succeeded ; then it sat still for a while. At last it rubbed itself cajolingly against the elbow of its murderer, who was comfortably eating. From my concealed position I had a good view of him, and I lost nothing that followed. When he became aware of the kitten he still went on eating for a little ; then all at once he seemed to be struggling with nausea, gulped once or twice and pushed away his spoon. As soon as the others were gone he touched the kitten cautiously, as if he were afraid of it or doubted its physical presence. Finally he lifted it on to the table with extreme care, as if it were of porcelain, and crumbled up for it what was left of his meat and bread. It ate a little, and that made him visibly happy. When the housewife came in he began to talk to her urgently ; I caught several times the word " Matchka ", and when he said it he would always point towards the kitten. The woman gazed at it in silence and went away again. Then the lad went out into the yard to his work. He took up the dead kittens with the same care he had shown to the living, and carried them away. It seems to me that something in his nature has changed ; his face is more alert, his step firmer, and I have not heard him whistling since. To-morrow the Austrian Crown Prince is coming to review the troops at Lemhény. I reported myself as indisposed and asked to be allowed to remain in Kézdi-Almás. It has become very windy and cold.

28th *November*.

The bluish-grey kitten has died to-day, and, as I have a free hour left, I must set down the brief story of its sufferings ; it has been part of my day's experience in any case. Early yesterday morning I was awakened by a soft whimpering and growling. In the great room the Hungarian lad was crouching on the floor, with a tremulous expression trying the kitten by turns with a dish of water and one of milk. During the night it had vomited blood, and in the morning bile. It paid no attention to the milk, but kept gazing steadily at the water. As I went near it slowly lifted its head like a tired and sorrowful human being. Its skull seemed to have shrunk, the gold-rimmed amber yellow of the eyes was dimmed, its nose was very hot. It was clearly suffering from fever and a burning thirst. Whimpering and growling by turns it approached the water with its nose, but as soon as it touched it shrank back with an angry noise ; obviously the attempt to drink caused it pain. Yet its raging thirst always drove it back again to the water. Suddenly it dipped one of its fore-paws in, then the other ; finally it tried to get in altogether, but the dish was much too small. A large basin was filled ; with all the burning heat of its body the kitten laid itself down in the water and remained peacefully resting for a while.

Meanwhile the farmer's wife had come in ; children and neighbours arrived ; a circle of curiosity and pity closed round the poor beast and its anguish. Only yester-day it had been heedlessly thrown out ; but now no one thought of ending its suffering by a speedy death ; they all discovered that it was a delightful little kitten, and were full of counsels and specifics for curing it. As if through its sufferings it had been brought into sacred proximity with them, they felt almost a reverent feeling before it, the children especially. And in reality there was something worthy of admiration in the bearing of the tiny kitten, something hardly to be described, which lifted it above its sufferings ; a sort of pride, a consciousness of its native wild grace which death could bit by bit wear down or suddenly crush, but could never bend. Ignoring its misery, it strove to remain true to its nature ; shaken already by the pangs of dissolution, it retained its dignity and kept its head gracefully inclined as before ; and thir

The Knapsack

impressed them all far more deeply, it is certain, than even its suffering. Some spiritual meaning is hidden here, and the ancient Egyptians knew very well why they considered the cat sacred and punished those who killed it.

But the villagers of Kézdi-Almás very soon exhausted all their good advice, and at last looked full of expectation towards me. Dehm, who came in just then, advised morphia; I suggested atropine as well. We had the kitten lifted out of its bath, and injected a tiny drop of the solution in its leg, at which one of the little girls screamed. But Matchka did not even twitch, so filled was its body with internal pain. After three minutes it made towards a patch of sunshine which fell into the room, stretched itself out comfortably, laid its head along its front paws and went to sleep; sometimes it growled softly in its dreams. We found it there much later, when the sun had long gone away; then began again its vain journeys to the water. We repeated the injection three times stronger. After that the kitten was very gay at first, almost skittish, cutting strangely impudent capers, as if incipient derangement were already altering its nature; but it still remained beautiful in the harmony of its movements. Suddenly it sprang up on me and rubbed its nose against my face. I lifted it and laid it down at my feet; it growled but made no resistance, and fell asleep at once. Wakening at two o'clock I examined it by the light of my pocket-torch; it was twitching slightly in its sleep. Curled cosily in a ball, its head was resting on my left foot. My position was uncomfortable, and I tried to draw my foot away; but then it began to growl angrily and even made as if to bite my toe. So I summoned the courtesy which is due by us to a dying creature and lay still. Forced thus into quietness by the little creature, I presently noticed a change in myself as well, a curious inner stillness and heightening of my faculties, such as the monks, I believe, call concentration. My body felt lighter, my thoughts came more freely and with more certainty than usual. Vivid intuitions of the nature of certain diseases thronged up first ; I knew suddenly that I could handle them much more simply in future. All the time I remained aware that Matchka was responsible for this heightened state, and never have I been more convinced that we are insensibly led to ourselves not only by human beings, spirits, and planets, but often by animals and plants as well, yes, even by inanimate matter, from all of which finally goes out what in theology is called grace. And now all the good things which I had heard or read about cats flew through my mind in a rapid and clear procession ; last of all the touching myth of a great flood which my mother had often related to me. On the limitless storm-swept waters a cradle had been seen with a child sleeping in it. There was a cat in the cradle as well, and every time that it threatened to capsize the alert cat would spring to the other side so as to restore the balance, until finally the little boat remained hanging in the branches of a great oak. The flood sank, the cradle was rescued, and baby and cat were found alive and unhurt. As no one knew who the little boy's parents were, the people gave him the name of Dold, which means treetop, and he became the sire of a great and famous people.

These recollections started a whole train of thought which after wandering far at last came back to the immediate everyday things which were most occupying me at the moment. All at once I was quite certain that the key of the ambulance van was lying in one of the big leather cases, among bandages and instruments ; very probably I had mislaid it there myself. Rid at last of this anxiety, I began to nod in spite of myself, and slept until Rehm wakened me bringing in my morning tea. I had a search made for the key at once ; they found it, right enough, in the place I had thought of. But Matchka did not waken again. While I was getting up her breathing grew more difficult, then came a sudden, sharp wail, and a final deep, almost comfortable respiration.

At that moment the orderly brought the command to fall in. The review of the troops at Lemhény had been cancelled. We packed our things. How lucky that the key had been found ! Our fine uniforms were discarded, the photographs disappeared into our haversacks. The Hungarian boy was kneeling beside the dead kitten and stroking it and crying. There is always beauty at the moment when a ray from eternity strikes upon our gross natures—we should reverence every illumination, every transfiguring terror—I could vouch that this boy will never lift his hand again against a living creature—may God give each of us his animal and his sin to awaken him. But there must be other kinds of illumination, out of which, from far purer terrors, a deed goes up like a star.

Snow-clouds cover the sky. The frost has set in, the sunflower is misted with rime. The seeds are now frozen fast, the bird will have a job to pick them out. To the east there is a dull rattle of rifle-firing. It is four o'clock. We are to march off for Kézdi-Vásárhely.

HANS CAROSSA

161 *All the Interim*

THEY moved back to Bus in the afternoon, marching through fine, steady rain. Days passed, and the weather showed no signs of mending ; and as they settled down to the routine of a battalion holding the line, the attack, without fading from their minds, no longer seemed an imminent trial, becoming only a vague probability of the future. It had certainly been delayed. The colours, with which they had been so gaily bedecked, became a little

an N.C.O. checking some minor fault, someone asking a simple question of his fellow, someone's personal sense of irksomeness becoming audible in grumbled oaths. But for the most part it was a silent half-hour, except for the regular beat of the feet on the stone sets ; the outside men of each four slithering now and again on the too acute camber.

John Ball regained a certain quietness and an indifference to what might be, as his loaded body moved forward unchoosingly as part of a mechanism, another mile or so.

They passed a small building, lying back from the road, that appeared deserted, its roof and nearer wall damaged at some time and now repaired with boarding. Perhaps they'd had some kind of fire, at all events it looked sordid and unloved. He drew back into his but lately lifted gloom.

There was a temporary halt where a light railway met the road. Trucks filled with very new clean deal planking, stakes of pine, stacked neatly up, wooden frames, bales of wire-netting and other wire, hedge-hog like, in balls ; a rigid medley thrown about—iron and wood and iron, made evidently to some precise requirement, shaped to some usage yet unknown to any of that halting company ; who looked on wonderingly, with half-inquisitive, half-fearful, glancing. Anyway, they wouldn't have railways very near the line—would they? They went on again more feebly, more pain in the soles of the feet—that renewal, and increase of aching, which comes after the brief halting. The sky maintained its clear serenity, no cloud at all sailed on its vastness at noon. John Ball stretched his neck to ease the pain of his valise-straps chafing, his eyes looked involuntarily, with his head's tilting. There spread before him on the blue warp above as though by a dexterous, rapid shuttling, unseen, from the nether-side, a patterning of intense white ; each separate bright breaking through, sudden and with deliberate placing—a slow spreading out, a loss of compact form, drifting into an indeterminate mottling. He marvelled at these foreign clouds. There seemed in the whole air above but from no sensible direction, or point, a strong droning, as if a million bees were hiving to the stars.

They gazed upwards as they went, their ill-guided feet stumbling stupidly over filled-in circular roughnesses pitting the newly-mended road. Ten minutes passed uneventfully and in silence.

Close in left—large hole to right of road.

As each congested file skirted that cavity, apprehensive eyes glanced sideways, turned in unison, as though at a saluting base.

Eyes front can't you—open out again in those fours.

That hole was wide and very deeply conical—the hard cut stones split and dislodged lay all about for many yards, they had to step over the fragments as they passed. A message reached Mr. Jenkins, who halted them—the platoon in front moved on—leaving them standing. When they started again the platoon behind did not move with them.

One running back from No. 6 saluted.

Open out in two ranks, sir—road block in centre, sir.

Men were busy here shovelling rubble into a great torn upheaval in the paving. A splintered tree scattered its winter limbs, spilled its life low on the ground. They stepped over its branches and went on. A cyclist slid in haste from his machine, saluted, handed a written message to the Company Commander, received back an initialled slip, again saluted—sped on wheels away.

Must increase the pace a bit sergeant. Be careful not to close on the people in front—we march by sections after we pass—X 18 b 5—four, yes, after we pass the large house—there—by the bend. You see it—no—yes, that one.

Strange New Things

Moving by section of platoon their way inclined more south and right, well shielded by trees. They became comforted in their mood and talked to each other and smoked. They asked of each other why there seemed in that place the sickly smell of pineapple. John Ball was puzzled, why in his mouth and throat there seemed to be the astringency of Parrish's Food—Aunt Woodman in Norwood kept it in bottles.

A sharp inclination right, along a watery byway, open to all the world, winding the recession of mangolds. A man with his puttees fastened at the ankle, without tunic, his cap at a tilt, emerged upon the landscape and took water in a flexible green canvas bucket from the ditch, where a newly painted board, bearing a map reference, marked the direction of a gun-position. Tall uprights at regular intervals, to the north-east side of this path were hung with a sagging netting—in its meshes painted bits of rag, bleached with rain and very torn, having all the desolation peculiar to things that functioned in the immediate past but which are now no longer serviceable, either by neglect or by some movement of events.

At a forking of the path were buildings, farm buildings, like any others. The leading platoon carried on, took the way left.

No. 7 closed its sections and waited.

You bunch together before a tarred door. Chalk scrawls on its planking—initials, numbers, monograms, signs, hasty, half erased, of many regiments. Scratched out dates measuring the distance back to antique beginnings.

Dragoons—one troop.

4th Hussars—" D " Squadron No. 3 Troop.

Numerals crossed slanting indecipherable allocations earlier still.

More clear, and very newly chalked, you read the title of your entering, and feel confident, as one who reads his

The Knapsack

own name in a church pew. " 2 platoons, B Company ",
in large, ill-formed calligraphy, countermanding the
shadowy ciphering of the previous occupants. Lance-
Corporal Lewis pushed open the door—and you file in.

The straw was grey and used and not so plentiful as
the heaped-up hay of their morning's rising.

All right in here—comfortable—let them get some rest—
we parade at five o'clock.

Reveille ?—no—five this evening.

Scattered recumbent round the walls within, they
listened with eagerness, the truth stole upon them. That
night would be spent in some other place.

The more contriving had already sought out nails and
hooks on which to hang their gear for the night, and to
arrange, as best they might, their allotted flooring.

They would make order, for however brief a time, and
in whatever wilderness.

Anyway, get what rest you can. I'll be along at 4.30—
yes, everything, I'm afraid. There was talk of dumping
valises—yes, we're taking them in. I think greatcoats
folded—they may change that—waterproof capes worn.

Very good, sir.

Oh, I forgot, there will be a rifle-inspection in an hour's
time—yes, at 3.45.

I see, sir, I'll get 'em on their rifles at once. Sergeant
Snell's salute had not to it the usual perfection.

Some sleep if you can, sergeant.

He walked slowly across the yard, meeting John Ball
at the gate, carrying a mess-tin of water.

Have you a match, Ball ?

Confusedly he put his mess-tin down, to search his
pockets. Mr. Jenkins tapped the end of a cigarette on
the broken gate-post, his head turned away and toward
the lane, toward the shielded batteries, toward the sagging

was using his front gun on me most of the time. On my way back I spotted a flock of Fokkers about three thousand feet above me. I didn't know what was going on, but it looked to me as if the thing to do was to suck those Fokkers down on me and then there would be plenty of our machines up above to come down on them and get some easy picking. I knew I was a good way over but I thought sure there would be a squadron of Dolphins about in addition to the S. E.s, so I climbed for all I was worth and waited for the Huns to see me and come down. Archie put up a burst as a signal and I didn't have long to wait. I turned towards the lines and two of them came down. I put my nose down and waited for them to catch up. As soon as one of them opened fire I pulled up in a long zoom and turned. One Hun overshot and I found myself level with the other one. He half rolled and I did a skid turn and opened up on him. He wasn't much of a pilot because I got about a hundred and fifty rounds into him. He went into a dive. But that first lad was all that could be expected. He got a burst in my right wing on his first crack and now he was stalling up under me and the first thing I knew about it was when I saw his tracer going by. I half rolled and sprayed a few rounds at him and went on down out of it too. I was getting worried about where the rest of the boys were and couldn't see any signs of an S. E. Three Huns came down on me from above and played their new game. They try to fight in threes. They have some prearranged method of attack by which one sits on your tail while the other two take time about shooting from angles. They were all three firing and all I could do was to stay in a tight bank and pray. I thought I was gone. One of them pulled up and then came straight down to finish me off. I turned towards him and forced him to pull up to keep from overshooting. As soon as I saw his nose go by, I put mine down, for I saw it was time to think more about rescuing the decoy than holding any bag for the rest of them. One Hun was on my tail in a flash and we were both doing about two hundred and fifty. I turned around to see what he was doing and as soon as his tracer showed up close, I pulled straight up. He tried to pull up but overshot and went on by, about fifty feet from me. I was close enough to see his goggles and note all the details of his plane, which was black and white checked with a white nose. I waved to him and I think he waved back, tho I'm not sure. I tried to turn my guns on him but he went up like an elevator and tried to turn back to get on my tail. I put my nose down again and we more or less repeated. The rest of his crew didn't seem to be in a fighting mood and only picked at me from a distance, so I got away. I had to come back on the carpet and I shot up some infantry on the ground, but it was too hot for me and I zigzagged on home. I felt fine then but before I got back I was shivering so I could hardly land. And I haven't been feeling right since. My heart seems to be trying to stunt all the time.

These present quarters aren't much and the food down here is terrible. Bully beef, boiled potatoes and Brussels sprouts. I've never been able to understand those people who go out into the woods with a tent and a frying pan and have such a wonderful time. And now that I am actually in possession of a tent and a frying pan, I understand that form of exercise much less. Bring back, oh, bring back, my shower and breakfast in bed! True, I can't really call this roughing it, with a valet to bring me hot water when there is any water, and a good chef to cook for me when there is anything to cook, and a bartender to shake up a drink when there is anything to shake ; but this is closer to nature than my table of organization calls for. Don't bother about my liberty, give me a suite !

War Birds

A general came over to see us the other day. I was down at the hangars and he walked up unannounced and we started conversing. I didn't know who he was as his insignia wasn't showing on his flying suit and he spoke so familiarly of various matters that I thought he was a captain and we had quite a little argument about these new Hun planes. It turned out that he was the general in London who fixed it up for us to come out with Bish. These British great moguls are the finest in the world. They make Lord Chesterfield appear like a truck driver for polish. He invited me over to his château for dinner next week.

AN UNKNOWN AVIATOR

164 *Pajaro Negro (The Black Bird)*

I CANNOT tell for certain whether it was a magpie or a crow that our boys picked up somewhere among the bushes along the stream during those first spring days. What I do know is that the bird began by greatly resenting captivity, and showed it by ferociously pecking at the hands of its captor.

With a playful allusion to the Fascist aeroplanes, which were called " blackbirds " by our men, it was known as " nuestro pajaro negro ". The boys were amused at the bird's still uncertain gait ; pretending to let it go, they would catch it again with their caps when, too heavy for its young wings, it endeavoured to escape with a flutter and a jump. Within a few days, however, a quite different relationship was established between our pajaro negro and the men of the fourth company. The little bird's heart no longer beat so wildly and tumultuously against their horny hands and the crafty, beady eyes lost their

The Knapsack

expression of panic fear. In the trenches the boys vied with each other in their search for grasshoppers; noticing that their pajaro negro was scared by the perpetual twitching of these insects, they rammed their fat green bodies into its ever hungry, wide-open beak only after depriving them of their legs. At nights the bird slept warmly in the dug-outs half buried in the mops of the militiamen's unkempt hair. Our pajaro negro soon became the mascot of the company, and was shown to every stranger with much pride. Nevertheless, one fact was incontrovertible: the bird belonged to Juan Antonio who had picked it up. He, too, had taught it to march with little mincing steps to his word of command: " Left right, one two, one two," and when Juan Antonio was on duty in the foremost trench, the bird sat on his shoulders. It seemed to have a dim awareness of what was happening, and had a particular aversion to machine-gun fire. When machine-guns began to patter on the other side it ruffled its feathers, looked sideways, and gave an angry, mischievous croak in the direction of the enemy—Kra, kra. If I happened to be passing by just then, Juan Antonio would stop me and say with a happy smile: " Can you hear, *teniente*? It's saying *No pasaran, no pasaran.*"

This state of things lasted several weeks, and I have a strong suspicion that when Carlos Suarez was making up the list of the company in red and black ink with all the meticulous care which he was wont to use in his bookkeeping days in Madrid, he also wrote down our pajaro negro, simply as militiaman number so and so. One morning I was giving my usual theoretical instruction to the men who were off duty in the second line. By then the sun was shining pitilessly and a number of the militiamen who had been on duty that night were only giving a drowsy look to the bullet trajectories that I was drawing on the company's blackboard. The arrival of the post

426

Pajaro Negro (The Black Bird)

was a welcome excuse for breaking off. Our comrades withdrew in groups towards their shelters. Whoever was able to read was never without a few mates, who peered over his shoulder and read with him, and whoever was innocent of the art had his letter read out to him word for word by the more scholarly comrades. No letter had come for me and I was sitting on a stone staring out in front of me a trifle sad and bored. I was startled out of my meditations by the rude sound of curses and abuse. Rows had been an extremely rare occurrence during the ten months we had already spent at the front, and it was therefore with amazement that I saw what looked like a scuffle outside the shelter at the farther end of the trench. I rose in haste and made for the scene of the disturbance ; but already the men were moving up towards me and the little gipsy was in the vanguard carrying the dead body of our pajaro negro in his open hand. All he said was " assassinau " (murdered). From the confusion and excitement of voices all raised at once, I gathered that Juan Antonio himself had wrung the neck of his bird. I looked at him in astonishment ; he had been given a black eye, his hair was in disorder, and his face was covered in mud—the very image of a street urchin who had had a beating but who refused nevertheless to admit that he was in the wrong. All I could get out of him was, " With my bird I do as I like, and if I want to wring its neck, I wring its neck ; if they want to shoot me for it, let them go ahead."

The boys of the company were pressing round me, curious to know what I should say. I was more and more at a loss to know what to think, and wishing to gain time stooped down and picked up a crumpled sheet of note-paper that the wind had blown at my feet.

Automatically I smoothed out the sheets until suddenly I saw from the opening words that the letter was addressed

The Knapsack

to Juan Antonio. I then began to read attentively. It was a typical peasant's letter without capitals, commas, or full stops, full of grammatical errors in which the v's and b's were mixed up, the h's were absent wherever they belonged, and suddenly reappeared at unexpected places. I think I can remember its contents almost word for word : " dear juan antonio", his father wrote, " we are glad to hear that all is well with you and are pleased to let you know that all is well with me too and your little sister pepita is well too and so is carmen and your little brothers juanito and carlo and felipe and quintin are also doing fine and so are your friends pepe and antonio and so is your girl rosita and all of them greet you." Up to this point the letter was very clearly written. Then a couple of lines were scratched out as if the writer had hesitated what to write next. The letter continued, " and we regret to have to write that your mother is not so well because last week the blackbirds came over our village and bombed us and we all fled together in the fields, but your mother ran back to save the cow in the byre and when she got back to the field the blackbirds shot with their machine-guns and they hit your mother in the shoulder and your mother wants to know whether the captain would approve if you could come home for a few days on leave because she suffers great pain but that if it is not possible it is also all right because we are all suffering and struggling together for the cause (por la causa) and pepita and carmen and juanito and carlo and felipe wish to greet you and your friends too and also your girl and your father and mother embrace you and wish you all good luck from your father antonio."

When I had finished reading the letter I saw that Juan Antonio had turned away and was sobbing very gently, his face pressed against the breastwork. I said to the others, " Let him be, his mother has been wounded by

Pajaro Negro (The Black Bird)

the pajaros negros." They dispersed, and the little gipsy hurled the body of the blackbird over the breastwork in the direction of the enemy.

JEF LAST

165 *Illusion : 1915*

THE French house I sought was seen, as I turned a corner, remote in a diminishing avenue of noble trees. Below the hush of midsummer was the vibration of many wings. The bees were in the limes. I could smell the nectar of that tree ; it is full summer when the limes are flowering and the bees get drunk. I found that a pleasant confirmation of the season, for to me that summer was hardly authentic. The house was set deeply in a long perspective of foliage, as though I stood in the June of one year and saw distantly the pale ghost of the old château in a silent June of the past. I wanted to reach that house, but it looked as though I could get no nearer to it than the murmuring summer in which I stood. I could only look back to where it was secluded in the silence of a forgotten year.

A confusing idea, but then it was a confusing summer— a summer doubtful with its aspect of immemorial continuity, yet suggesting bleakly a subtle yet disastrous interruption in the life of the earth, as though everything appeared to be the same, but we were being cheated with only the bright illusion of familiar things. What had been always behind them had gone. It was June, 1915. If in one of the arbors about me, where stood white statues pensive with ancient secrets they would never disclose, I had surprised a furbelowed lady who ought to have been living only in a picture by Watteau, she might have been more startled than myself. I should have felt that I was the intruder, and should have withdrawn at once from a June which did not belong to me. Not my June. Not a lady for me, but only for a gentleman in satin breeches and a brocaded coat. And from one of those arbors, in a scene which was still and haunted, a figure did suddenly emerge. It came out briskly, gave me a direct but not a startled look, and turned towards the château. It had a cockney face, and its khaki dress was unrelieved by any ornament except the blue-and-white armlet of a British signaller. It seemed to have no doubt about its year.

So I judged that, after all, I might not be lost in another age. Anyhow, others were lost there with me ; or perhaps in a celestial dreaminess the gods had become careless and had muddled the sunlights and affairs of far different times. For a Sikh, with a rifle which was only a toy in his giant's grasp—a giant in a black beard—was patrolling the balustrade of that French house above a moat in which waterlilies floated. The Indian sentry reached the limit of his beat and paused to regard the figure of Aphrodite, who stood below him with a foot coyly poised over the water she had been about to enter since Louis Soleil was king. War ? Not even though a bearded Sikh was contemplating Aphrodite. There was no war. There was but an occasional and inexplicable flutter of the air. The air sometimes shook ; the summer day was quite peaceful, but it was not accurately fitted to the earth, it was not quite firm on its base. There was a sense of insecurity in it, as though it might be withdrawn from us because it was a mistake, being the summer of another page and place.

Nor did the interior of the château reassure. The frail old furniture was understandable, and the ormolu, the crystal candelabra hanging from a painted ceiling, and the tapestries—they gave the right suggestion, for a summer noon, of the serene continuity of pleasant human things.

Illusion : 1915

The ladies of the house looked down into the room from their frames of heavy gilt, which hung on the walls, and one of them, the portrait near me, of a girl of 1779, seemed as surprised as myself to observe soldiers below intent upon typewriters, and the coming and going of British officers.

One of the officers came to me. He knew my name, and met me as if I were one of that household, though I had never seen him before. " They telephoned from head-quarters about you this morning. We were beginning to think you were lost. The battalion you want is some-where near Neuve Chapelle, but you'd never find it. It's rather altered up there, since the attack, and it's an un-attractive corner. But we've got a guide for you—here he is, too. Lieutenant Jones . . ."

The lieutenant was boyish, and had the awkward candor of shyness. He smiled, and said, " I offered to take you before I knew where you wanted to go. Shall we start at once ? It's fairly quiet there now, so we'd better get it over."

We had a brief run by car through an uninhabited country, and then, for no reason that I could see—but perhaps reason was not there—the officer hid the car by a hedge and said we must walk. We took a straight road through an avenue of poplar trees. There was a stagnant ditch on either side of it and limited views of level meadows. The hot sun was there, but if his light had been green, and so the land had had that sinister complexion of the spectral vistas we may see through coloured glass, it could not have been more forbidding. It was an earth changed in nature. We were alone in it. There was enchantment here, and we had no clue. We approached a large pool of blood and separated to walk round it. Its extent alarmed me, but, except that my guide must have seen it to have avoided it, he gave no other sign that he admitted its existence. It lay in front of an estaminet. The door

The Knapsack

of the inn was open, and beside the door was a chair ; but nobody was in the chair ; nobody sat in it contemplating that mystery in the middle of the road. The estaminet was deserted. There were houses and sunlight but no people.

The distance was thudding heavily. The horizon was loose, perhaps, and was bumping on the earth. Ahead of us, almost lost in a clump of trees, were the red roofs of secretive farm buildings. There were ragged gaps in the tiles. As we neared the farm there was a crash, as though a boiler plate had fallen from a great height on to paving stones and was at once inert. Two columns of black smoke, which had not been there before, stood over the farm. The road, which was scattered with holes, continued straight on with indifference, though a tree had been lifted by its roots athwart it. There was a row of trees that were bundles of white splinters, and beyond them we came upon the first men. Six were lying on the ground, and two other men were bent over them. The faces of the men on the ground were averted and their eyes closed. They did not want to look at us or at anything else.

The ugly but intermittent sounds were not so distant as they had been when we reached another group of farm buildings, scattered among plantations near a road crossing. The trees about them were motionless in the sleeping afternoon, as though guarding a secret. The walls of one of the old barns, a structure so weathered that its rufous brickwork had the surface of dusty gray stone, were riven, and the edges of the new gaps were bright red. From somewhere not so far away there came a noise which might have been of an idle boy rattling a stick along a fence. An officer, to my surprise, came to a door of a barn which I had thought was empty. " Come in," he cried. " They spray that road with a machine-gun. Can't you hear it ? "

Under the rafters of that partially dismantled building

Illusion : 1915

was a man who laughed when he saw me, though we had not met for years. His amusement was caused, most likely, by my unexpected appearance, which he accepted as another absurd feature of the common phantasy. He himself, an Oriental scholar, in that place, as a soldier, was not easily believable ; but I took him in as one of the irrelevances which are quite consistent anyhow in prolonged and vivid nightmares. It was the last place where one would have expected to see him, yet there he was ; and he laughed again, as he came forward, because his quizzical temper thoroughly relished the waywardness of this resort and this coincidence. His blue eyes were merry.

"Have you gone mad, too ? " he asked. "What brings you here ? " He gossiped, presently, about our circumstances. "There's a war on up here, but who's making it, except ourselves, beats me. I think it is between us and the spooks. You haven't noticed any so-called Germans about, have you ? I haven't seen one yet "—he flinched and grimaced at an explosion outside—" but that sort of thing all day long has to be accounted for."

We set off together for his own place, which he said was near, though long before we reached it—mainly through a serpenting trench—my sense of direction became dizzy and was restricted merely to up and down. The earth was decrepitating in the heat ; that was rifle fire. The deep drain meandered aimlessly, with yellow charlock and scarlet poppies vivid overhead against the blue sky. We climbed out to hurry across a road, and entered another drain, which traversed the foundations of extensive ruins, and there we waited, on our hands and knees, while the ruin ahead of us was smashed a little more. When the dust and smoke had settled a little we hurried along, and soon emerged into a village.

Nobody else was in it. It seemed proper to find it was deserted. It was acrid with damp mortar and smouldering fires. Some of the houses lay piled across the street. That village had come to its end, and the only proof that life had ever known it was a child's doll stretched out on its back in an attitude of abandoned grief near the mummied carcass of a cow. We went across the churchyard—just one vacant Gothic arch of the church was standing—and strode over gray rubble, splintered coffin boards, and a few disinterred sleepers in nightgowns who had come to the surface again, indifferent as to how they slept. As we got through that square a spasmodic growling sped at us through the silence and burst in violence by the Gothic arch. We descended hurriedly a long flight of stone steps to a cellar. My friend Reynolds then sat on a soap box and laughed once more, a little too long. "This is my home," he said. "I share it with a surgeon. I think he'll lend you a bed for the night." Reynolds pointed to a stretcher in the corner.

The cellar was immense and gloomy, and our privacy was a corner of it, screened by some sacking from the battalion aid post, which was the remainder of the cellar. Just then we had the place to ourselves. Reynolds was eager for news ; yet as I began to speak the cellar shook in a series of spasms, and a tin bowl on the floor trembled and whined. We waited, and soon the cellar became deep in the still earth again.

"We're all right here," Reynolds speculated, " because if that stairway goes there's another way out. Perhaps I'd better show you where it is."

We had a look round, and saw the other stairway, a pile of bandages, and a wine-bin in which there was nothing but a cat which was glad to meet us. Then there was no more to do but to return to the kitchen table. That was loaded with documents, neatly piled under shell-noses. Reynolds took his tunic off, inspected the topmost documents, and filled his pipe.

Illusion : 1915

" Now you've seen this place, perhaps you'd hardly believe the trouble I took to get from India to it," he said. " They said men were badly wanted, so I supposed I ought to be quick. The results surprised me. My patience had to mount a lot of monuments—it was patience which sat on a monument, wasn't it ?—well, I was kept waiting a devil of a time on each one I came to. Authority is a funny old dear, and tried to keep me from the delights of this hole as long as possible. But one day I got as near to this as Marseilles, and I was despondent because I thought all would be over before I could have some. . . . Orderly ! "

" Sir ! "

" Bring two drinks. I say, have you seen Major Weston to-day ? "

" No, sir. He was killed last night, sir."

Reynolds rose and stared at me. Then he sat down again. " Bring the drinks, Richard," he said.

He sat, while waiting the return of the orderly, playing a tattoo on the table. Then he spoke to himself. " There it is," he said. He murmured across to me in doubt. " I tell you I *spoke* to him last night. I *spoke* to him." He looked at me as though I ought to confirm that a little conversation with another man might sometimes fail to render him invulnerable.

The orderly returned, methodical as at a London counter, and then silently vanished as though he had passed through a wall.

" Well, here we are," said Reynolds, in a subdued way. " I was telling you how I got here, in a hurry, to join in the war before it was over. They shunted me in trains and lorries about France for weeks. I began to believe they had attached me to a battalion which didn't exist. Everybody knew promptly where it was, but it was never there, though sometimes it had been. I did find it at

The Knapsack

last, though, and reported myself. The adjutant said,
' But where's your sword? You can't parade without a
sword.' So I went to a farm, and sent to London for a
sword, and slept in an outhouse under some fowls while
waiting for it. At length it came, and I reported myself
again. ' You've got a sword,' said the adjutant. ' You
cannot parade with a sword. The order is that all swords
must be returned.'

" It is all like that," Reynolds assured me. " The only
thing to do here is to shut off your intelligence and hope
that the next thing to happen won't be as idiotic as everything which has happened before. I got into frightful
difficulties at first through trying to be reasonable. One
day some headquarters or another sent a stern demand to
know why we were using so much chloride of lime. I
suppose they thought we were stealing it. I don't know.
Anyhow, a divisional headquarters has no reason to use
chloride of lime. So I told them what we did with it.
That made matters worse. That made them suspicious.
The colonel told me I'd better send an officer up to the
latrines just to satisfy them with a report. The young
officer was gone so long that when I remembered the
chloride of lime again, because the report had to be made,
I got nervous, and went to look for him. There had been
a bit of shelling. I found him. He was in a crater. We
had to waste some more chloride of lime."

Here Reynolds' narrative was interrupted. There was
a shuffling on the stairs, and a whispering, " Take 'is legs."
" I got 'im." A little group of soldiers moved across the
cellar and laid one of their number on a bench. The
others arranged themselves along the same form in various
attitudes of lassitude and weary indifference. They were
muddy, gaunt, and unshaven ; all that was clean and
bright about them was some bandages. Several attempted
cigarettes with a slowness which allowed a match to burn

out before it was used. They paid no attention to us and, after a steady glance at that array of cripples who seemed resigned to anything that could happen, Reynolds called out to them that the medical officer was expected in at once. They did not answer. Some of them turned reproachful eyes on us, but they neither spoke nor moved. Other footsteps sounded on the stairs, hard and deliberate, and the M.O. and two assistants entered. Reynolds watched the scene for a while, called out that if help were wanted we could give a hand, and readjusted more privily the canvas screen.

" That goes on all day, off and on, if it's only a quiet day. When they're busy I clear out—I can't stand being looked at like that, when I can't do anything. We haven't had as many to-day. But I don't like the look of that fellow on his back. His feet are too loose. Sometimes the feet tell you more than a man's face."

There was groaning in the far corner, and Reynolds waited. He began his tattoo on the table. We sat, looking at the floor.

" No." (It was the voice of the M.O.) " No. Leave that man. You other fellows all right now ? Better make your way to the transport while it's quiet. You'll do till you get to the hospital. Lucky beggars. Hop it. Off you go."

The shuffling began again, and when that had ceased we heard the Medical Officer instructing his men where to put the soldier who remained. The doctor came over for a gossip with Reynolds before venturing out, and then once more we had the gloom to ourselves.

" Can you make anything of it ? " asked Reynolds, with an inconsequence which was not altogether innocent.

" I find it a bit bewildering."

" There's no sense in it, none at all. Those fellows who have just gone out to hobble through shell-bursts in the hope of finding salvation—I wonder what they make of it ? They never say a word about it. You might as well ask the horses—but some of the horses sweat through funk. It's very queer. Once a horse has had a dose of it, he trembles whenever he hears a gun. Trembles and sweats. But he goes into it when told, all of a lather, and so do we—all of a lather."

" It seemed to me when on my way here," I told him, " that the whole thing was just an illusion. The country didn't look real. Sometimes I wondered whether it was there, or whether I was there."

" I know. Most of the fellows feel that way. But don't be fooled by it. It's as real as stupidity. At first you think it's all rather an imbecile joke. That's why some of the best of the young uns die too soon. They go about showing it no respect, just as though the silly business was only pretending to be there. But there it is, all right. It is fatuous moonshine stuff, but it has got us in irons, and so you'll jolly well find. Here comes its Hermes—one of its envoys."

A despatch rider entered, saluted, handed over his token out of the blue, and went. Reynolds read the message, sighed, and placed it on one of the piles. " You get the notion, too, that you are lost in it, that nobody knows where you are, and could never find you. But the gods have got us taped. They know all about us, and if they told you to put your head in a bag you'd have to do it. You can get killed for two reasons—for being an idiot, and for refusing to be an idiot.

" One day, when we were just back in some particularly unpleasing rest billets—most of our rest, by the way, was shelled to hell—the colonel came to me. ' Look here,' he said, ' the general has sent a message that a French colonel is to visit us on urgent business, though I don't know what he wants, and we are to treat him mighty fine. But there's no food fit to eat. He'll be here to-night. Just scout around for something tasty, will you? Luckily we can make him drunk, if he's that way inclined. And, I say, I wish you'd let him have your bed. His A.D.C. may have mine, as yours is the best.'

"We blessed those Frenchmen for nuisances, but we made ready for them, and our mess cook made a really presentable table of the stuff we had. Then we waited, wondering what these fellows were going to be like, for we'd seen nothing of the French, but had a huge respect for their military qualities. Most of us were only civilians turned soldiers. I think even our colonel had been a solicitor, in another life. Only the adjutant was a regular. So we were a bit nervous about it.

"At length he came, this French colonel—a tall, portly man in a blue uniform and brown bulging gaiters, accompanied by a slender young officer, very stiff and correct. The French colonel had one of those hunting horns round his shoulder—you know the sort of thing—you see the curly instrument in comic prints of French sportsmen out after partridges. He didn't take that trumpet off. Only his cap. His bald head was pale, but his big round face was red and very hearty, with lots of chin, and a long grizzled moustache which would have been straight and fierce if he hadn't laughed so much. He laughed, and stamped with one foot, or patted his sides with both hands, very free and friendly, and then pulled out his moustache. A cheery card. But his pale young A.D.C. was prim. Prim and silent. Never said a word. Smiled faintly and ironically when spoken to. 'Yes?' he would say. Only that. Seemed to think that it was all rather a bore.

"Not a word about the business of their visit. Only rich laughter about nothing in particular. We began dinner. The French colonel wore his hunting horn. We pretended not to see the thing—we sort of behaved as though a hunting horn at dinner was the custom of the country, especially in war, and we didn't want our curiosity to betray our ignorance. The young French officer hardly looked up, and if he did it was to stare at the wall over the head of the man opposite. I suppose he found the crudities of a British table unentertaining, but that duty was duty.

"His colonel was different. He was enjoying himself— we happened to have a Burgundy of a good year—and our young fellows played up to him on behalf of the regiment and the good name of England. After one bout of merriment, which was so happy that we all joined in, that stout Frenchman rose, put one foot on his chair, and blew a tantara on the horn. Then he sat down again and went on.

"Of course we took no notice of the fanfare. Pretended we had heard nothing. The French colonel's A.D.C. paid no attention to it, either. We thought perhaps it might be the custom of the Frenchman's regiment, some ancient right won in battle. Now it was the proper thing for the colonel of that regiment to do—to wind the horn at intervals during dinner. Maintain a link with the glorious past.

"That lusty colonel was full of funny stories, and at the end of a good one, when he'd got us all going, he'd rise from his chair and give a fanfare solemnly. I noticed our orderlies looked a bit surprised, but they didn't laugh. As for our own colonel, he was so polite that he appeared to have been as deaf to it as the young French officer.

"The fun got very lively after dinner, and I must say our youngsters thoroughly enjoyed this Gascon, who was certainly enjoying himself. He loudly approved our whiskey. Then, in a sentimental mood, he mentioned his wife. Ah ! He would show why France would fight, but yes, till not a German was this side of the Rhine ; that

Illusion : 1915

heard another word about it. Never knew why they called. What do you make of that?"

I didn't attempt to make anything of it. As an episode of the world of war it was as meet and proper as an Oriental scholar making British reports on chloride of lime in the cellar of a French farm. While Reynolds and I sat smiling at each other, filling our pipes, the tin bowl on the floor began to complain again. It trembled and whined. The cellar began to be convulsive. Somebody fell headlong down the stairway.

H. M. TOMLINSON

H. M. Tomlinson

PART SEVEN

166 *I have a gentil cok*

I HAVE a gentil cok
  Croweth me day ;
He doth me risen erly
  My matines for to say.

I have a gentil cok ;
  Comen he is of grete ;
His comb is of red corel,
  His tail is of get.

I have a gentil cok ;
  Comen he is of kinde ;
His comb is of red corel,
  His tail is of inde [1].

His leggès ben of asour,
  So gentil and so smale ;
His sporès arn of silver white
  Into the wortèwale [2].

His eynen arn of cristal,
  Loken [3] all in aumber ;
And every night he percheth him
  In mine ladyes chaumber.

ANON

[1] *inde*, indigo.   [2] *wortèwale*, the skin of the claws.
           [3] *loken*, set ; lit., locked.

167 *My lady went to Canterbury*

My lady went to Canterbury,
 The saint to be her boot ;
She met with Kate of Malmesbury :
 Why sleepest thou in an apple root ?

Nine mile to Michaelmas,
 Our dame began to brew ;
Michael set his mare to grass,
 Lord, so fast it snew !

For you, love, I brake my glass,
 Your gown is furred with blue ;
The devil is dead, for there I was ;
 Iwis it is full true.

And if ye sleep, the cock will crow,
 True heart, think what I say ;
Jackanapes will make a mow,
 Look, who dare say him nay ?

I pray you have me now in mind,
 I tell you of the matter ;
He blew his horn against the wind ;
 The crow goeth to the water.

Yet I tell you mickle more ;
 The cat lieth in the cradle ;
I pray you keep true heart in store ;
 A penny for a ladle.

My lady went to Canterbury

I swear by Saint Katharine of Kent,
    The goose goeth to the green ;
All our doggès tail is brent,
    It is not as I ween.

Tirlery lorpin, the laverock sang,
    So merrily pipes the sparrow,
The cow brake loose, the rope ran home,
    Sir, God give you good-morrow !

ANON

168   *Tom o' Bedlam*

FROM the hag and hungry goblin
That into rags would rend ye
And the spirit that stan' by the naked man
In the Book of Moons defend ye !
That of your five sound senses
You never be forsaken
Nor travel from yourselves with Tom
Abroad to beg your bacon.
    Nor never sing " Any food, any feeding,
    Money, drink or clothing " :
    Come dame or maid, be not afraid,
    Poor Tom will injure nothing.

Of thirty bare years have I
Twice twenty been enragéd
And of forty bin three times fifteen
In durance soundly cagéd
In the lordly lofts of Bedlam
On stubble soft and dainty,
Brave bracelets strong, sweet whips ding dong,
With wholesome hunger plenty.
    And now I sing, &c.

The Knapsack

With a thought I took for Maudlin
And a cruse of cockle pottage
With a thing thus—tall, (sky bless you all),
I fell into this dotage.
I slept not since the conquest,
Till then I never wakéd
Till the roguish boy of love where I lay
Me found and stripped me naked.
　　And made me sing, &c.

When short I have shorn my sowce face
And swigged my hornéd barrel
In an oaken inn do I pawn my skin
As a suit of gilt apparel.
The moon's my constant mistress
And the lonely owl my marrow
The flaming drake and the night-crow make
Me music to my sorrow.
　　While there I sing, &c.

The palsy plague these pounces,
When I prig your pigs or pullen,[1]
Your culvers [2] take, or mateless make
Your chanticlere, and sullen.
When I want provant [3] with Humfrey
I sup, and when benighted
To repose in Paul's with waking souls
I never am affrighted.
　　But still do I sing, &c.

I know more than Apollo,
For oft when he lies sleeping
I behold the stars at mortal wars
And the wounded welkin weeping ;

---

[1] chickens.　　　　[2] doves.　　　　[3] provender.

Tom o'Bedlam

The moon embrace her shepherd
And the queen of love her warrior,
While the first doth horn the star of the morn
And the next the heavenly Farrier.
    While I do sing, &c.

The Gipsy Snap and Tedro
Are none of Tom's comrados.
The punk I scorn and the cutpurse sworn
And the roaring-boys bravadoes.
The sober, white, and gentle,
Me trace, or touch, and spare not ;
But those that cross Tom's Rhinoceros
Do what the panther dare not.
    Although I sing, &c.

With an host of furious fancies
Whereof I am commander
With a burning spear, and a horse of air,
To the wilderness I wander.
By a knight of ghosts and shadows
I summoned am to tourney
Ten leagues beyond the wide world's end.
Me thinks it is no journey.
    All while I sing, &c.

ANON

169 *I once was a Maid*

I ONCE was a maid, tho' I cannot tell when,
And still my delight is in proper young men :
Some one of a troop of dragoons was my daddie,
No wonder I'm fond of a sodger laddie.
    Sing, lal de lal, &c.

The Knapsack

The first of my loves was a swaggering blade,
To rattle the thundering drum was his trade ;
His leg was so tight, and his cheek was so ruddy,
Transported I was with my sodger laddie.

But the godly old chaplain left him in the lurch ;
The sword I forsook for the sake of the church :
He ventur'd the soul, and I risked the body,
'Twas then I proved false to my sodger laddie.

Full soon I grew sick of my sanctified sot,
The regiment at large for a husband I got ;
From the gilded spontoon to the fife I was ready,
I askèd no more but a sodger laddie.

But the peace it reduc'd me to beg in despair,
Till I met my old boy in a Cunningham fair ;
His rags regimental, they flutter'd so gaudy,
My heart it rejoic'd at a sodger laddie.

And now I have liv'd—I know not how long,
And still I can join in a cup and a song ;
But whilst with both hands I can hold the glass steady,
Here's to thee, my hero, my sodger laddie !

ROBERT BURNS

170 *Holy Willie's Prayer*

O THOU, wha in the Heavens dost dwell,
Wha, as it pleases best thysel',
Sends ane to heaven and ten to hell,
    A' for thy glory,
And no for ony guid or ill
      They've done afore thee !

Holy Willie's Prayer

Lord, mind Gawn Hamilton's deserts,
He drinks, an' swears, an' plays at cartes,
Yet has sae mony takin' arts
   Wi' grit an' sma',
Frae God's ain priest the people's hearts
   He steals awa'.

An' when we chasten'd him therefor,
Thou kens how he bred sic a splore
As set the warld in a roar
   O' laughin' at us ;
Curse thou his basket and his store,
   Kail and potatoes.

Lord, hear my earnest cry an' pray'r,
Against that presbyt'ry o' Ayr ;
Thy strong right hand, Lord, make it bare
   Upo' their heads ;
Lord, weigh it down, and dinna spare,
   For their misdeeds.

O Lord my God, that glib-tongu'd Aiken,
My very heart and soul are quakin',
To think how we stood sweatin', shakin',
   An' piss'd wi' dread,
While he, wi' hingin' lips and snakin',
   Held up his head.

Lord, in the day of vengeance try him ;
Lord, visit them wha did employ him,
And pass not in thy mercy by them,
   Nor hear their pray'r :
But, for thy people's sake, destroy them,
   And dinna spare.

The Knapsack

But, Lord, remember me and mine
Wi' mercies temp'ral and divine,
That I for gear and grace may shine
    Excell'd by nane,
And a' the glory shall be thine,
        Amen, Amen !

ROBERT BURNS

171 *Mrs. Harris's Petition*

TO THEIR

EXCELLENCIES

THE

Lords Justices of IRELAND.

The Humble Petition of Frances Harris,

Who must Starve, and Die a Maid if it miscarries.

Anno 1700.

Humbly Sheweth.

THAT I went to warm my self in Lady *Betty*'s Chamber,
    because I was cold,
And I had in a Purse, seven Pound, four Shillings and
    six Pence, besides Farthings, in Money, and Gold ;
So because I had been buying things for my *Lady* last
    Night,
I was resolved to tell my Money, to see if it was right :
Now you must know, because my Trunk has a very bad
    Lock,
Therefore all the Money, I have, which, *God* knows,
    is a very small Stock,
I keep in a Pocket ty'd about my Middle, next my
    Smock.

Mrs. Harris's Petition

So when I went to put up my Purse, as *God* would have
  it, my Smock was unript,
And, instead of putting it into my Pocket, down it slipt :
Then the Bell rung, and I went down to put my *Lady*
  to Bed,
And, *God* knows, I thought my Money was as safe as
  my Maidenhead.
So when I came up again, I found my Pocket feel very light,
But when I search'd, and miss'd my Purse, *Lord !* I
  thought I should have sunk outright :
Lord ! Madam, says *Mary*, how d'ye do ? Indeed, says I,
  never worse ;
But pray, *Mary*, can you tell what I have done with my
  Purse !
Lord help me, said *Mary*, I never stirr'd out of this Place !
Nay, said I, I had it in Lady *Betty*'s Chamber, that's a plain
  Case.
So *Mary* got me to Bed, and cover'd me up warm,
However, she stole away my Garters, that I might do
  my self no Harm :
So I tumbl'd and toss'd all Night, as you may very well
  think,
But hardly ever set my Eyes together, or slept a Wink.
So I was a-dream'd, methought, that we went and search'd
  the Folks round,
And in a Corner of Mrs. *Dukes*'s Box, ty'd in a Rag, the
  Money was found.
So next Morning we told *Whittle*, and he fell a Swearing ;
Then my Dame *Wadgar* came, and she, you know, is
  thick of Hearing ;
Dame, said I, as loud as I could bawl, do you know what
  a Loss I have had ?
Nay, said she, my Lord *Collway*'s Folks are all very sad,
For my Lord *Dromedary* comes a *Tuesday* without fail ;
Pugh ! said I, but that's not the Business that I ail.

The Knapsack

Says *Cary*, says he, I have been a Servant this Five and
  Twenty Years, come Spring,
And in all the Places I liv'd, I never heard of such a
  Thing.
Yes, says the *Steward*, I remember when I was at my
  Lady *Shrewsbury*'s,
Such a thing as this happen'd, just about the time of
  Goosberries.
So I went to the Party suspected, and I found her full of
  Grief ;
(Now you must know, of all Things in the World, I hate
  a Thief.)
However, I was resolv'd to bring the Discourse slily
  about,
Mrs. *Dukes*, said I, here's an ugly Accident has happen'd
  out ;
'Tis not that I value the Money three Skips of a Louse ;
But the Thing I stand upon, is the Credit of the House ;
'Tis true, seven Pound, four Shillings, and six Pence,
  makes a great Hole in my Wages,
Besides, as they say, Service is no Inheritance in these Ages.
Now, Mrs. *Dukes*, you know, and every Body under-
  stands,
That tho' 'tis hard to judge, yet Money can't go without
  Hands.
The *Devil* take me, said she, (blessing her self,) if I ever
  saw't !
So she roar'd like a *Bedlam*, as tho' I had call'd her all
  to naught ;
So you know, what could I say to her any more,
I e'en left her, and came away as wise as I was before.
Well : But then they would have had me gone to the
  Cunning Man ;
No, said I, 'tis the same Thing, the *Chaplain* will be here
  anon.

Mrs. Harris's Petition

So the *Chaplain* came in ; now the Servants say, he is my
  Sweet-heart,

Because he's always in my Chamber, and I always take
  his Part ;

So, as the *Devil* would have it, before I was aware, out I
  blunder'd,

Parson, said I, can you cast a *Nativity*, when a Body's
  plunder'd ?

(Now you must know, he hates to be call'd *Parson*, like
  the *Devil*.)

Truly, says he, Mrs. *Nab*, it might become you to be
  more civil :

If your Money be gone, as a Learned *Divine* says, d'ye see,

You are no *Text* for my Handling, so take that from me :

I was never taken for a *Conjurer* before, I'd have you to
  know.

Lord, said I, don't be angry, I'm sure I never thought
  you so ;

You know, I honour the Cloth, I design to be a *Parson*'s
  Wife,

I never took one in *Your Coat* for a *Conjurer* in all my
  Life.

With that, he twisted his Girdle at me like a Rope, as
  who should say,

Now you may go hang your self for me, and so went away.

Well ; I thought I should have swoon'd ; *Lord*, said I,
  what shall I do ?

I have lost my *Money*, and shall lose my *True-Love* too.

Then my *Lord* call'd me ; *Harry*, said my *Lord*, don't cry,

I'll give something towards thy Loss ; and says my *Lady*,
  so will I.

Oh but, said I, what if after all my Chaplain won't
  come to ?

For that, he said, (an't please your *Excellencies*) I must
  Petition You.

459

The Knapsack

The Premises tenderly consider'd, I desire your *Excellencies* Protection,
And that I may have a Share in next *Sunday*'s Collection :
And over and above, that I may have your *Excellencies* Letter,
With an Order for the *Chaplain* aforesaid ; or instead of Him, a Better :
And then your poor *Petitioner*, both Night and Day,
Or the *Chaplain*, (for 'tis his *Trade*) as in Duty bound, shall ever *Pray*.

JONATHAN SWIFT

172 *A Description of a City Shower*

October, 1710.

CAREFUL Observers may fortel the Hour
(By sure Prognosticks) when to dread a Show'r :
While Rain depends, the pensive Cat gives o'er
Her Frolicks, and pursues her Tail no more.
Returning Home at Night, you'll find the Sink
Strike your offended Sense with double Stink.
If you be wise, then go not far to Dine,
You'll spend in Coach-hire more than save in Wine.
A coming Show'r your shooting Corns presage,
Old Aches throb, your hollow Tooth will rage.
Sauntring in Coffee-house is *Dulman* seen ;
He damns the Climate, and complains of Spleen.

MEAN while the South rising with dabbled Wings,
A Sable Cloud a-thwart the Welkin flings,
That swill'd more Liquor than it could contain,
And like a Drunkard gives it up again.
Brisk *Susan* whips her Linen from the Rope,
While the first drizzling Show'r is born aslope,

A Description of a City Shower

Such is that Sprinkling which some careless Quean
Flirts on you from her Mop, but not so clean.
You fly, invoke the Gods ; then turning, stop
To rail ; she singing, still whirls on her Mop.
Not yet, the Dust had shun'd th' unequal Strife,
But aided by the Wind, fought still for Life ;
And wafted with its Foe by violent Gust,
'Twas doubtful which was Rain, and which was Dust.
Ah ! where must needy Poet seek for Aid,
When Dust and Rain at once his Coat invade ;
His only Coat, where Dust confus'd with Rain,
Roughen the Nap, and leave a mingled Stain.

Now in contiguous Drops the Flood comes down,
Threat'ning with Deluge this *Devoted* Town.
To Shops in Crouds the dagged Females fly,
Pretend to cheapen Goods, but nothing buy.
The Templer spruce, while ev'ry Spout's a-broach,
Stays till 'tis fair, yet seems to call a Coach.
The tuck'd-up Sempstress walks with hasty Strides,
While Streams run down her oil'd Umbrella's Sides.
Here various Kinds by various Fortunes led,
Commence Acquaintance underneath a Shed.
Triumphant Tories, and desponding Whigs,
Forget their Fewds, and join to save their Wigs.

Box'd in a Chair the Beau impatient sits,
While Spouts run clatt'ring o'er the Roof by Fits ;
And ever and anon with frightful Din
The Leather sounds, he trembles from within.
So when *Troy* Chair-men bore the Wooden Steed,
Pregnant with *Greeks*, impatient to be freed,
(Those Bully *Greeks*, who, as the Moderns do,
Instead of paying Chair-men, run them thro'.)
Laoco'n struck the Outside with his Spear,
And each imprison'd Hero quak'd for Fear.

The Knapsack

Now from all Parts the swelling Kennels flow,
And bear their Trophies with them as they go :
Filth of all Hues and Odours seem to tell
What Street they sail'd from, by their Sight and Smell.
They, as each Torrent drives, with rapid Force
From *Smithfield*, or St. *Pulchre*'s shape their Course,
And in huge Confluent join at *Snow-Hill* Ridge,
Fall from the *Conduit* prone to *Holborn-Bridge*.
Sweepings from Butchers Stalls, Dung, Guts, and Blood,⎫
Drown'd Puppies, stinking Sprats, all drench'd in Mud, ⎬
Dead Cats and Turnip-Tops come tumbling down the ⎭
   Flood.

Jonathan Swift

173   *Baucis and Philemon*

Imitated from the Eighth Book of OVID.

In antient Times, as Story tells,
The Saints would often leave their Cells.
And strole about, but hide their Quality,
To try good People's Hospitality.

It happen'd on a Winter Night,
As Authors of the Legend write ;
Two Brother Hermits, Saints by Trade.
Taking their *Tour* in Masquerade ;
Disguis'd in tatter'd Habits, went
To a small Village down in *Kent* ;
Where, in the Strolers Canting Strain,
They beg'd from Door to Door in vain ;
Try'd ev'ry Tone might Pity win,
But not a Soul would let them in.

Our wand'ring Saints in woful State,
Treated at this ungodly Rate,

Baucis and Philemon

Having thro' all the Village pass'd,
To a small Cottage came at last ;
Where dwelt a good old honest Yeoman,
Call'd, in the Neighbourhood, *Philemon.*
Who kindly did the Saints invite
In his Poor Hut to pass the Night ;
And then the Hospitable Sire
Bid *Goody Baucis* mend the Fire ;
While He from out of Chimney took
A Flitch of Bacon off the Hook ;
And freely from the fattest Side
Cut out large Slices to be fry'd :
Then stept aside to fetch 'em Drink,
Fill'd a large Jug up to the Brink ;
And saw it fairly twice go round ;
Yet (what is wonderful) they found,
'Twas still replenished to the Top,
As if they ne'er had toucht a Drop.
The good old Couple was amaz'd,
And often on each other gaz'd ;
For both were frighted to the Heart
And just began to cry ;—What ar't !
Then softly turn'd aside to view,
Whether the Lights were burning blue.
The gentle *Pilgrims* soon aware on't,
Told 'em their Calling, and their Errant :
Good Folks, you need not be afraid,
We are but *Saints,* the Hermits said ;
No Hurt shall come to You, or Yours ;
But, for that Pack of churlish Boors,
Not fit to live on Christian Ground,
They and their Houses shall be drown'd :
Whilst you shall see your Cottage rise,
And grow a Church before your Eyes.

The Knapsack

THEY scarce had Spoke ; when, fair and soft,
The Roof began to mount aloft ;
Aloft rose ev'ry Beam and Rafter,
The heavy Wall climb'd slowly after.

THE Chimney widen'd, and grew higher,
Became a Steeple with a Spire.

THE Kettle to the Top was hoist,
And there stood fast'ned to a Joist :
But with the Upside down, to shew
Its Inclinations for below ;
In vain ; for a Superior Force
Apply'd at Bottom, stops its Course,
Doom'd ever in Suspence to dwell,
'Tis now no Kettle, but a Bell.

A wooden Jack, which had almost
Lost, by Disuse, the Art to Roast,
A sudden Alteration feels,
Increas'd by new Intestine Wheels :
And, what exalts the Wonder more,
The Number made the Motion slow'r :
The Flyer, tho't had Leaden Feet,
Turn'd round so quick, you scarce cou'd see't ;
But slacken'd by some secret Power,
Now hardly moves an Inch an Hour.
The Jack and Chimney near ally'd,
Had never left each other's Side ;
The Chimney to a Steeple grown,
The Jack wou'd not be left alone,
But up against the Steeple rear'd,
Became a Clock, and still adher'd :
And still its Love to Household Cares
By a shrill Voice at Noon declares,
Warning the Cook-maid, not to burn
That Roast-meat which it cannot turn.

Baucis and Philemon

THE Groaning Chair began to crawl
Like an huge Snail along the Wall ;
There stuck aloft, in Publick View,
And with small Change, a Pulpit grew.

THE Porringers, that in a Row
Hung high, and made a glitt'ring Show,
To a less Noble Substance chang'd,
Were now but Leathern Buckets rang'd.

THE Ballads pasted on the Wall,
Of *Joan of France*, and *English Moll*,
Fair *Rosamond*, and *Robin Hood*,
The *Little Children in the Wood* :
Now seem'd to look abundance better,
Improv'd in Picture, Size, and Letter ;
And high in Order plac'd, describe
The Heraldry of ev'ry Tribe.

A Bedstead of the Antique Mode,
Compact of Timber many a Load,
Such as our Ancestors did use,
Was Metamorphos'd into Pews ;
Which still their antient Nature keep ;
By lodging Folks dispos'd to Sleep.

THE Cottage by such Feats as these,
Grown to a Church by just Degrees,
The Hermits then desir'd their Host
To ask for what he fancy'd most :
Philemon, having paus'd a while,
Return'd 'em Thanks in homely Stile ;
Then said ; my House is grown so Fine
Methinks, I still wou'd call it mine :
I'm Old, and fain wou'd live at Ease,
Make me the *Parson*, if you please.

The Knapsack

He spoke, and presently he feels,
His Grazier's Coat fall down his Heels ;
He sees, yet hardly can believe,
About each Arm a Pudding-sleeve ;
His Wastcoat to a Cassock grew,
And both assum'd a Sable Hue ;
But being Old, continu'd just
As Thread-bare, and as full of Dust.
His Talk was now of *Tythes* and *Dues*,
Cou'd smoak his Pipe, and read the News ;
Knew how to preach old Sermons next,
Vampt in the Preface and the Text ;
At Christnings well could act his Part,
And had the Service all by Heart ;
Wish'd Women might have Children fast,
And thought whose *Sow* had *farrow'd* last :
Against *Dissenters* wou'd repine,
And stood up firm for *Right Divine* :
Found his Head fill'd with many a System,
But Classick Authors—he ne'er miss'd 'em.

Thus having furbish'd up a Parson,
Dame *Baucis* next, they play'd their Farce on :
Instead of Home-spun Coifs were seen,
Good Pinners edg'd with Colberteen :
Her Petticoat transform'd apace,
Became Black Sattin, Flounc'd with Lace.
Plain *Goody* would no longer down,
'Twas *Madam*, in her Grogram Gown.
Philemon was in great Surprize,
And hardly could believe his Eyes,
Amaz'd to see Her look so Prim,
And she admir'd as much at Him.

Baucis and Philemon

THUS, happy in their Change of Life,
Were several Years this Man and Wife,
When on a Day, which prov'd their last,
Discoursing on old Stories past,
They went by chance, amidst their Talk,
To the Church-yard, to take a walk ;
When *Baucis* hastily cry'd out ;
My Dear, I see your Forehead sprout :
Sprout, quoth the Man, What's this you tell us ?
I hope you don't believe me Jealous :
But yet, methinks, I feel it true ;
And re'ly, Yours is budding too—
Nay,—now I cannot stir my Foot :
It feels as if 'twere taking Root.

DESCRIPTION would but tire my Muse :
In short, they both were turn'd to *Yews*.
Old Good-man *Dobson* of the Green
Remembers he the Trees has seen ;
He'll talk of them from Noon till Night,
And goes with Folks to shew the Sight :
On *Sundays*, after Ev'ning Prayer.
He gathers all the Parish there ;
Points out the Place of either *Yew* ;
Here *Baucis*, there *Philemon* grew.
Till once, a Parson of our Town,
To mend his Barn, cut *Baucis* down ;
At which, 'tis hard to be believ'd,
How much the other Tree was griev'd,
Grew Scrubby, dy'd a-top, was stunted :
So, the next Parson stub'd and burnt it.

JONATHAN SWIFT

174 *Triumphal March*

STONE, bronze, stone, steel, stone, oakleaves, horses' heels
Over the paving.
And the flags. And the trumpets. And so many eagles.
How many? Count them. And such a press of people.
We hardly knew ourselves that day, or knew the City.
This is the way to the temple, and we so many crowding
    the way.
So many waiting, how many waiting? what did it matter,
    on such a day?
Are they coming? No, not yet. You can see some eagles.
        And hear the trumpets.
Here they come. Is he coming?
The natural wakeful life of our Ego is a perceiving.
We can wait with our stools and our sausages.
What comes first? Can you see? Tell us. It is

      5,800,000 rifles and carbines,
        102,000 machine guns,
         28,000 trench mortars,
         53,000 field and heavy guns,
I cannot tell how many projectiles, mines and fuses,
         13,000 aeroplanes,
         24,000 aeroplane engines,
         50,000 ammunition waggons
now 55,000 army waggons,
         11,000 field kitchens,
          1,150 field bakeries

What a time that took. Will it be he now? No.
Those are the golf club Captains, these the Scouts,
And now the *société gymnastique de Poissy*
And now come the Mayor and the Liverymen. Look
There he is now, look:

Triumphal March

There is no interrogation in his eyes
Or in the hands, quiet over the horse's neck,
And the eyes watchful, waiting, perceiving, indifferent.
O hidden under the dove's wing, hidden in the turtle's
      breast,
Under the palmtree at noon, under the running water
At the still point of the turning world.   O hidden.

Now they go up to the temple.   Then the sacrifice.
Now come the virgins bearing urns, urns containing
Dust
Dust
Dust of dust, and now
Stone, bronze, stone, steel, stone, oakleaves, horses' heels
Over the paving.

That is all we could see.   But how many eagles? and how
      many trumpets!
(And Easter Day, we didn't get to the country,
So we took young Cyril to church.   And they rang a bell
And he said right out loud, *crumpets*.)
        Don't throw away that sausage,
It'll come in handy.   He's artful.   Please, will you
Give us a light?
Light
Light
Et les soldats faisaient la haie?   ILS LA FAISAIENT.

T. S. ELIOT

The Knapsack

175 *Billy in the Darbies*

Good of the Chaplain to enter Lone Bay
And down on his marrow-bones here and pray
For the likes just o' me, Billy Budd.—But look :
Through the port comes the moon-shine astray !
It tips the guard's cutlass and silvers this nook ;
But 'twill die in the dawning of Billy's last day.
A jewel-block they'll make of me to-morrow,
Pendant pearl from the yard-arm-end
Like the ear-drop I gave to Bristol-Molly—
Oh, 'tis me, not the sentence, they'll suspend.
Ay, Ay, all is up ; and I must up too
Early in the morning, aloft from alow.
On an empty stomach, now, never it would do.
They'll give me a nibble—bit o' biscuit ere I go.
Sure, a messmate will reach me the last parting cup ;
But turning heads away from the hoist and the belay,
Heaven knows who will have the running of me up !
No pipe to those halyards—But aren't it all sham ?
A blur's in my eyes ; it is dreaming that I am.
A hatchet to my panzer ? all adrift to go ?
The drum roll to grog, and Billy never know ?
But Donald he has promised to stand by the plank ;
So I'll shake a friendly hand ere I sink.
But—no ! It is dead then I'll be, come to think.
I remember Taff the Welshman when he sank.
And his cheek it was like the budding pink.
But me, they'll lash me in hammock, drop me deep
Fathoms down, fathoms down, how I'll dream fast asleep.
I feel it stealing now. Sentry, are you there ?
Just ease these darbies at the wrist,
And roll me over fair.
I am sleepy, and the oozy weeds about me twist.

HERMAN MELVILLE

176 *The War Song of Dinas Vawr*

THE mountain sheep are sweeter,
But the valley sheep are fatter ;
We therefore deemed it meeter
To carry off the latter.
We made an expedition ;
We met a host and quelled it ;
We forced a strong position,
And killed the men who held it.

On Dyfed's richest valley,
Where herds of kine were browsing,
We made a mighty sally,
To furnish our carousing.
Fierce warriors rushed to meet us ;
We met them, and o'erthrew them :
They struggled hard to beat us ;
But we conquered them, and slew them.

As we drove our prize at leisure,
The king marched forth to catch us :
His rage surpassed all measure,
But his people could not match us.
He fled to his hall-pillars ;
And, ere our force we led off,
Some sacked his house and cellars,
While others cut his head off.

We there, in strife bewildering,
Spilt blood enough to swim in :
We orphaned many children,
And widowed many women.

The Knapsack

The eagles and the ravens
We glutted with our foemen :
The heroes and the cravens,
The spearmen and the bowmen.

We brought away from battle,
And much their land bemoaned them,
Two thousand head of cattle,
And the head of him who owned them :
Ednyfed, King of Dyfed,
His head was borne before us ;
His wine and beasts supplied our feasts,
And his overthrow, our chorus.

THOMAS LOVE PEACOCK

177 *Llyn-y-Dreiddiad-Vrawd*

THE POOL OF THE DIVING FRIAR

GWENWYNWYN withdrew from the feasts of his hall :
He slept very little, he prayed not at all :
He pondered, and wandered, and studied alone ;
And sought, night and day, the philosopher's stone.

He found it at length, and he made its first proof
By turning to gold all the lead of his roof :
Then he bought some magnanimous heroes, all fire,
Who lived but to smite and be smitten for hire.

With these on the plains like a torrent he broke ;
He filled the whole country with flame and with smoke ;
He killed all the swine, and he broached all the wine ;
He drove off the sheep, and the beeves, and the kine ;

Llyn-y-Dreiddiad-Vrawd

He took castles and towns ; he cut short limbs and lives ;
He made orphans and widows of children and wives :
This course many years he triumphantly ran,
And did mischief enough to be called a great man.

When, at last, he had gained all for which he had striven,
He bethought him of buying a passport to heaven ;
Good and great as he was, yet he did not well know,
How soon, or which way, his great spirit might go.

He sought the grey friars, who beside a wild stream,
Refected their frames on a primitive scheme ;
The gravest and wisest Gwenwynwyn found out,
All lonely and ghostly, and angling for trout.

Below the white dash of a mighty cascade,
Where a pool of the stream a deep resting-place made,
And rock-rooted oaks stretched their branches on high,
The friar stood musing, and throwing his fly.

To him said Gwenwynwyn, ' Hold, father, here's store,
For the good of the church, and the good of the poor ' ;
Then he gave him the stone ; but, ere more he could speak,
Wrath came on the friar, so holy and meek.

He had stretched forth his hand to receive the red gold,
And he thought himself mocked by Gwenwynwyn the Bold ;
And in scorn of the gift, and in rage at the giver,
He jerked it immediately into the river.

Gwenwynwyn, aghast, not a syllable spake ;
The philosopher's stone made a duck and a drake ;
Two systems of circles a moment were seen,
And the stream smoothed them off, as they never had been.

The Knapsack

Gwenwynwyn regained, and uplifted his voice,
' Oh friar, grey friar, full rash was thy choice ;
The stone, the good stone, which away thou hast thrown,
Was the stone of all stones, the philosopher's stone.'

The friar looked pale, when his error he knew ;
The friar looked red, and the friar looked blue ;
And heels over head, from the point of a rock,
He plunged, without stopping to pull off his frock.

He dived very deep, but he dived all in vain,
The prize he had slighted he found not again ;
Many times did the friar his diving renew,
And deeper and deeper the river still grew.

Gwenwynwyn gazed long, of his senses in doubt,
To see the grey friar a diver so stout ;
Then sadly and slowly his castle he sought,
And left the friar diving, like dabchick distraught.

Gwenwynwyn fell sick with alarm and despite,
Died, and went to the devil, the very same night ;
The magnanimous heroes he held in his pay
Sacked his castle, and marched with the plunder away.

No knell on the silence of midnight was rolled
For the flight of the soul of Gwenwynwyn the Bold.
The brethren, unfeed, let the mighty ghost pass,
Without praying a prayer, or intoning a mass.

The friar haunted ever beside the dark stream ;
The philosopher's stone was his thought and his dream :
And day after day, ever head under heels
He dived all the time he could spare from his meals.

Llyn-y-Dreiddiad-Vrawd

He dived, and he dived, to the end of his days,
As the peasants oft witnessed with fear and amaze.
The mad friar's diving-place long was their theme,
And no plummet can fathom that pool of the stream.

And still, when light clouds on the midnight winds ride,
If by moonlight you stray on the lone river-side,
The ghost of the friar may be seen diving there,
With head in the water, and heels in the air.

T. L. Peacock

178   *Broom, Green Broom*

There was an old man and he lived in a wood,
   And his trade it was making of broom, of broom,
And he had a naughty boy, Jack, to his son,
    And he lay in bed till 'twas noon, 'twas noon,
      And he lay in bed till 'twas noon.
The father was vext and sorely perplext,
   With passion he enters the room, the room,
' Come, sirrah,' he cried, ' I'll leather your hide,
    If you will not go gather green broom, green broom,
      If you will not go gather green broom.'

Master Jack being sly, he got up by and bye,
   And went into the town to cry, ' Broom, green broom.'
So loud did he call, and so loudly did bawl,
    ' Pretty maids, do you want any broom, green broom ?
      Pretty maids, do you want any broom ? '

A lady looked out of her lattice so high,
   And spied Jack a-selling of broom, green broom,
Says she, ' You young blade, won't you give up your trade,
    And marry a maid in full bloom, full bloom ?
      And marry a maid in full bloom ? '

The Knapsack

So they sent for the parson without more delay,
  And married they were in the room, the room,
There was eating and drink, and says Jack, with a wink,
  'This is better than cutting of broom, green broom,
    This is better than cutting of broom.'

ANON

179 *Poor Old Horse*

My clothing was once of the linsey woolsey fine,
My tail it grew at length, my coat did likewise shine;
But now I'm growing old; my beauty does decay,
My master frowns upon me; one day I heard him say,
  Poor old horse : poor old horse.

Once I was kept in the stable snug and warm,
To keep my tender limbs from any cold or harm;
But now, in open fields, I am forced for to go,
In all sorts of weather, let it be hail, rain, freeze, or snow.
  Poor old horse : poor old horse.

Once I was fed on the very best corn and hay
That ever grew in yon fields, or in yon meadows gay;
But now there's no such doing can I find at all,
I'm glad to pick the green sprouts that grow behind yon
  wall.
  Poor old horse : poor old horse.

" You are old, you are cold, you are deaf, dull, dumb and
  slow,
You are not fit for anything, or in my team to draw.
You have eaten all my hay, you have spoiled all my straw.
So hang him, whip, stick him, to the huntsman let him go."
  Poor old horse : poor old horse.

Poor Old Horse

My hide unto the tanners then I would freely give,
My body to the hound dogs, I would rather die than live,
Likewise my poor old bones that have carried you **many**
     a mile,
Over hedges, ditches, brooks, bridges, likewise gates and
     stiles.

Poor old horse : poor old horse.

ANON

180 *Casey Jones*

COME all you rounders if you want to hear
The story of a brave engineer ;
Casey Jones was the hogger's name,
On a big eight-wheeler, boys, he won his fame.
Caller called Casey at half-past four,
He kissed his wife at the station door,
Mounted to the cabin with orders in his hand,
And took his farewell trip to the promised land.

  Casey Jones, he mounted to the cabin,
  Casey Jones, with his orders in his hand !
  Casey Jones, he mounted to the cabin,
  Took his farewell trip into the promised land.

Put in your water and shovel in your coal,
Put your head out the window, watch the drivers roll,
I'll run her till she leaves the rail,
'Cause we're eight hours late with the Western Mail !
He looked at his watch and his watch was slow,
Looked at the water and the water was low,
Turned to his fireboy and said,
' We'll get to 'Frisco, but we'll all be dead ! '

(Refrain)

The Knapsack

Casey pulled up Reno Hill,
Tooted for the crossing with an awful shrill,
Snakes all knew by the engine's moans
That the hogger at the throttle was Casey Jones.
He pulled up short two miles from the place,
Number Four stared him right in the face,
Turned to his fireboy, said ' You'd better jump,
'Cause there's two locomotives going to bump ! '

(Refrain)

Casey said, just before he died,
' There's two more roads I'd like to ride.'
Fireboy said, ' What can they be ? '
' The Rio Grande and the Old S.P.'
Mrs. Jones sat on her bed a-sighing,
Got a pink that Casey was dying,
Said, ' Go to bed, children ; hush your crying,
'Cause you'll get another papa on the Salt Lake line.'

Casey Jones !   Got another papa !
Casey Jones, on the Salt Lake Line !
Casey Jones !   Got another papa !
Got another papa on the Salt Lake Line !

ANON

181   *The Rebel*

OH, I'm a good old rebel, that's what I am,
And for this land of freedom, I don't give a damn ;
I'm glad I fought agin her, I only wish we'd won,
And I ain't axed any pardon for anything I've done.

I fought with old Bob Lee for three years about,
Got wounded in four places and starved at Point Lookout.
I caught the rheumatism a-campin' in the snow,
And I killed a chance of Yankees and I wish I'd killed some
    mo' !

478

The Rebel

Three hundred thousand Yankees is dead in Southern dust,
We got three hundred thousand before they conquered us ;
They died of Southern fever, of Southern steel and shot—
I wish they was three million instead of what we got.

I hate the Constitution, this great republic, too ;
I hate the nasty eagle, and the uniform so blue ;
I hate their glorious banner, and all their flags and fuss.
Those lying, thieving Yankees, I hate 'em wuss and wuss.

I hate the Yankee nation and everything they do ;
I hate the Declaration of Independence, too ;
I hate the glorious Union, 'tis dripping with our blood ;
I hate the striped banner, I fought it all I could.

I won't be reconstructed !   I'm better now than them ;
And for a carpetbagger, I don't give a damn ;
So I'm off for the frontier, soon as I can go,
I'll prepare me a weapon and start for Mexico.

I can't take up my musket and fight them now no mo',
But I'm not goin' to love 'em, and that is certain sho' ;
And I don't want no pardon for what I was or am,
I won't be reconstructed and I don't give a damn.

INNES RANDOLPH

182   *Poor but Honest*

SHE was poor, but she was honest,
    Victim of the squire's whim :
First he loved her, then he left her,
    And she lost her honest name.

The Knapsack

Then she ran away to London,
    For to hide her grief and shame ;
There she met another squire,
    And she lost her name again.

See her riding in her carriage,
    In the Park and all so gay :
All the nibs and nobby persons
    Come to pass the time of day.

See the little old-world village
    Where her aged parents live,
Drinking the champagne she sends them ;
    But they never can forgive.

In the rich man's arms she flutters,
    Like a bird with broken wing :
First he loved her, then he left her,
    And she hasn't got a ring.

See him in the splendid mansion,
    Entertaining with the best,
While the girl that he has ruined,
    Entertains a sordid guest.

See him in the House of Commons,
    Making laws to put down crime,
While the victim of his passions
    Trails her way through mud and slime.

Standing on the bridge at midnight,
    She says : ' Farewell, blighted Love.'
There's a scream, a splash—Good Heavens !
    What is she a'doing of ?

Poor but Honest

Then they drag her from the river,
  Water from her clothes they wrang,
For they thought that she was drownded;
  But the corpse got up and sang:

' It's the same the whole world over;
  It's the poor what gets the blame,
It's the rich what gets the pleasure.
  Ain't it all a blooming shame?'

ANON

183 *Sally in our Alley*

OF all the girls that are so smart
  There's none like pretty Sally;
She is the darling of my heart,
  And she lives in our alley.
There is no lady in the land
  Is half so sweet as Sally;
She is the darling of my heart,
  And she lives in our alley.

Her father he makes cabbage-nets
  And through the streets does cry them;
Her mother she sells laces long
  To such as please to buy them:
But sure such folks could ne'er beget
  So sweet a girl as Sally!
She is the darling of my heart,
  And she lives in our alley.

When she is by, I leave my work,
  I love her so sincerely;
My master comes like any Turk,
  And bangs me most severely—

The Knapsack

But let him bang his bellyful,
   I'll bear it all for Sally ;
She is the darling of my heart,
   And she lives in our alley.

Of all the days that's in the week
   I dearly love but one day—
And that's the day that comes betwixt
   A Saturday and Monday ;
For then I'm dressed all in my best
   To walk abroad with Sally ;
She is the darling of my heart,
   And she lives in our alley.

My master carries me to church,
   And often am I blamed
Because I leave him in the lurch
   As soon as text is named ;
I leave the church in sermon-time
   And slink away to Sally ;
She is the darling of my heart,
   And she lives in our alley.

When Christmas comes about again
   O then I shall have money ;
I'll hoard it up, and box and all
   I'll give it to my honey :
And would it were ten thousand pounds,
   I'd give it all to Sally ;
She is the darling of my heart,
   And she lives in our alley.

My master and the neighbours all
   Make game of me and Sally,
And, but for her, I'd better be
   A slave and row a galley ;

Sally in our Alley

But when my seven long years are out
  O then I'll marry Sally,—
O then we'll wed, and then we'll bed,
  But not in our alley !

HENRY CAREY

184 *By Way of Preface*

How pleasant to know Mr. Lear ! '
  Who has written such volumes of stuff !
Some think him ill-tempered and queer,
  But a few think him pleasant enough.

His mind is concrete and fastidious,
  His nose is remarkably big ;
His visage is more or less hideous,
  His beard it resembles a wig.

He has ears, and two eyes, and ten fingers,
  Leastways if you reckon two thumbs ;
Long ago he was one of the singers,
  But now he is one of the dumbs.

He sits in a beautiful parlour,
  With hundreds of books on the wall ;
He drinks a great deal of Marsala,
  But never gets tipsy at all.

He has many friends, laymen and clerical,
  Old Foss is the name of his cat :
His body is perfectly spherical,
  He weareth a runcible hat.

The Knapsack

When he walks in a waterproof white,
　　The children run after him so !
Calling out, ' He's come out in his night-
　　gown, that crazy old Englishman, oh ! '

He weeps by the side of the ocean,
　　He weeps on the top of the hill ;
He purchases pancakes and lotion,
　　And chocolate shrimps from the mill.

He reads but he cannot speak Spanish,
　　He cannot abide ginger-beer :
Ere the days of his pilgrimage vanish,
　　How pleasant to know Mr. Lear !

EDWARD LEAR

185   *The Jumblies*

I

THEY went to sea in a Sieve, they did,
　　In a Sieve they went to sea :
In spite of all their friends could say,
On a winter's morn, on a stormy day,
　　In a Sieve they went to sea !
And when the Sieve turned round and round,
And every one cried, ' You'll all be drowned ! '
They called aloud, ' Our Sieve ain't big,
But we don't care a button ! we don't care a fig !
　　In a Sieve we'll go to sea ! '
　　　Far and few, far and few,
　　　　Are the lands where the Jumblies live ;
　　　Their heads are green, and their hands are blue,
　　　　And they went to sea in a Sieve.

The Jumblies

II

They sailed away in a Sieve, they did,
  In a Sieve they sailed so fast,
With only a beautiful pea-green veil
Tied with a riband by way of a sail,
  To a small tobacco-pipe mast ;
And every one said, who saw them go,
' O won't they be soon upset, you know !
For the sky is dark, and the voyage is long,
And happen what may, it's extremely wrong
  In a Sieve to sail so fast ! '
    Far and few, far and few,
      Are the lands where the Jumblies live ;
      Their heads are green, and their hands are blue,
      And they went to sea in a Sieve.

III

The water it soon came in, it did,
  The water it soon came in ;
So to keep them dry, they wrapped their feet
In a pinky paper all folded neat,
  And they fastened it down with a pin,
And they passed the night in a crockery-jar,
And each of them said, ' How wise we are !
Though the sky be dark, and the voyage be long,
Yet we never can think we were rash or wrong,
  While round in our Sieve we spin ! '
    Far and few, far and few,
      Are the lands where the Jumblies live ;
      Their heads are green, and their hands are blue,
      And they went to sea in a Sieve.

The Knapsack

IV

And all night long they sailed away;
  And when the sun went down,
They whistled and warbled a moony song
To the echoing sound of a coppery gong,
  In the shade of the mountains brown.
'O Timballoo! How happy we are,
When we live in a Sieve and a crockery-jar,
And all night long in the moonlight pale,
We sail away with a pea-green sail,
  In the shade of the mountains brown!'
    Far and few, far and few,
      Are the lands where the Jumblies live;
      Their heads are green, and their hands are blue,
        And they went to sea in a Sieve.

V

They sailed to the Western Sea, they did,
  To a land all covered with trees,
And they bought an Owl, and a useful Cart,
And a pound of Rice, and a Cranberry Tart,
  And a hive of silvery Bees.
And they bought a Pig, and some green Jack-daws,
And a lovely Monkey with lollipop paws,
And forty bottles of Ring-Bo-Ree,
  And no end of Stilton Cheese.
    Far and few, far and few,
      Are the lands where the Jumblies live;
      Their heads are green, and their hands are blue,
        And they went to sea in a Sieve.

The Jumblies

VI

And in twenty years they all came back,
  In twenty years or more,
And every one said, ' How tall they've grown !
For they've been to the Lakes, and the Torrible Zone,
  And the hills of the Chankly Bore ' ;
And they drank their health, and gave them a feast
Of dumplings made of beautiful yeast ;
And every one said, ' If we only live,
We too will go to sea in a Sieve,—
  To the hills of the Chankly Bore ! '
    Far and few, far and few,
      Are the lands where the Jumblies live ;
     Their heads are green, and their hands are blue,
      And they went to sea in a Sieve.

EDWARD LEAR

186   *The Dong with a Luminous Nose*

WHEN awful darkness and silence reign
Over the great Gromboolian plain,
  Through the long, long, wintry nights ;—
    When the angry breakers roar
    As they beat on the rocky shore ;—
  When Storm-clouds brood on the towering heights
   Of the Hills of the Chankly Bore :—

Then, through the vast and gloomy dark,
There moves what seems a fiery spark,
  A lonely spark with silvery rays
    Piercing the coal-black night,—
    A meteor strange and bright :—
  Hither and thither the vision strays,
    A single lurid light.

The Knapsack

Slowly it wanders,—pauses,—creeps,—
Anon it sparkles,—flashes and leaps ;
And ever as onward it gleaming goes
A light on the Bong-tree stems it throws.
And those who watch at that midnight hour
From Ha'l or Terrace, or lofty Tower,
Cry, as the wild light passes along,—
     " The Dong !—the Dong !
   " The wandering Dong through the forest goes !
     " The Dong ! the Dong !
  " The Dong with a luminous Nose ! "

    Long years ago
  The Dong was happy and gay,
Till he fell in love with a Jumbly Girl
  Who came to those shores one day.
For the Jumblies came in a Sieve, they did,—
Landing at eve near the Zemmery Fidd
   Where the Oblong Oysters grow,
  And the rocks are smooth and gray.
And all the woods and the valleys rang
With the Chorus they daily and nightly sang,—
 " *Far and few, far and few,*
   Are the lands where the Jumblies live ;
   Their heads are green, and their hands are blue,
   And they went to sea in a sieve."

Happily, happily passed those days !
  While the cheerful Jumblies staid ;
They danced in circlets all night long,
To the plaintive pipe of the lively Dong,
  In moonlight, shine or shade.
For day and night he was always there
By the side of the Jumbly Girl so fair,
With her sky-blue hands, and her sea-green hair.

The Dong with a Luminous Nose

Till the morning came of that hateful day
When the Jumblies sailed in their sieve away,
And the Dong was left on the cruel shore
Gazing—gazing for evermore,—
Ever keeping his weary eyes on
That pea-green sail on the far horizon,—
Singing the Jumbly Chorus still
As he sate all day on the grassy hill,—

> " *Far and few, far and few,*
> *Are the lands where the Jumblies live ;*
> *Their heads are green, and their hands are blue,*
> *And they went to sea in a sieve.*"

But when the sun was low in the West,
  The Dong arose and said,—
  " What little sense I once possessed
  Has quite gone out of my head ! "
And since that day he wanders still
By lake and forest, marsh and hill,
Singing—" O somewhere, in valley or plain
Might I find my Jumbly Girl again !
For ever I'll seek by lake and shore
Till I find my Jumbly Girl once more ! "

    Playing a pipe with silvery squeaks,
    Since then his Jumbly Girl he seeks.
    And because by night he could not see,
    He gathered the bark of the Twangum Tree
      On the flowery plain that grows.
      And he wove him a wondrous Nose,—
    A Nose as strange as a Nose could be !

The Knapsack

Of vast proportions and painted red,
And tied with cords to the back of his head.
 —In a hollow rounded space it ended
 With a luminous lamp within suspended,
  All fenced about
  With a bandage stout
   To prevent the wind from blowing it out ;—
 And with holes all round to send the light,
 In gleaming rays on the dismal night.

And now each night, and all night long,
Over those plains still roams the Dong ;
And above the wail of the Chimp and Snipe
You may hear the squeak of his plaintive pipe
While ever he seeks, but seeks in vain
To meet with his Jumbly Girl again ;
Lonely and wild—all night he goes,—
The Dong with a luminous Nose !
And all who watch at the midnight hour,
From Hall or Terrace, or lofty Tower,
Cry, as they trace the Meteor bright,
Moving along through the dreary night,—
 " This is the hour when forth he goes,
 The Dong with a luminous Nose !
 Yonder—over the plain he goes ;
  He goes !
  He goes ;
 The Dong with a luminous Nose ! "

EDWARD LEAR

The Owl and the Pussy Cat

THE Owl and the Pussy-Cat went to sea
  In a beautiful pea-green boat.
They took some honey, and plenty of money
  Wrapped up in a five-pound note.
The Owl looked up to the stars above,
  And sang to a small guitar,
' O lovely Pussy ! O Pussy, my love,
What a beautiful Pussy you are,
      You are,
      You are !
What a beautiful Pussy you are ! '

Pussy said to the Owl, ' You elegant fowl !
  How charmingly sweet you sing !
O let us be married ! too long we have tarried :
  But what shall we do for a ring ? '
They sailed away, for a year and a day,
  To the land where the Bong-Tree grows,
And there in a wood a Piggy-wig stood,
  With a ring at the end of his nose,
      His nose,
      His nose !
With a ring at the end of his nose.

' Dear Pig, are you willing to sell for one shilling
  Your ring ? ' Said the Piggy, ' I will.'
So they took it away, and were married next day
  By the Turkey who lives on the hill.
They dinèd on mince, and slices of quince,
  Which they ate with a runcible spoon ;

The Knapsack

And hand in hand, on the edge of the sand
They danced by the light of the moon,
The moon,
The moon,
They danced by the light of the moon.

EDWARD LEAR

188 *Little Birds are Playing*

LITTLE Birds are playing
Bagpipes on the shore,
Where the tourists snore :
' Thanks ! ' they cry.   ' 'Tis thrilling !
Take, oh, take, this shilling !
Let us have no more ! '

Little Birds are bathing
Crocodiles in cream,
Like a happy dream :
Like, but not so lasting—
Crocodiles, when fasting,
Are not all they seem !

Little Birds are choking
Baronets with bun,
Taught to fire a gun :
Taught, I say, to splinter
Salmon in the winter—
Merely for the fun.

Little Birds are hiding
Crimes in carpet-bags,
Blessed by happy stags :

Little Birds are Playing

Blessed, I say, though beaten—
Since our friends are eaten
    When the memory flags.

Little Birds are tasting
    Gratitude and gold,
    Pale with sudden cold ;
Pale, I say, and wrinkled—
When the bells have tinkled,
    And the Tale is told.

CHARLES LUTWIDGE DODGSON (LEWIS CARROLL)

189 'You are old, Father William'

' You are old, Father William,' the young man said,
  ' And your hair has become very white ;
And yet you incessantly stand on your head—
  Do you think, at your age, it is right ? '

' In my youth,' Father William replied to his son,
  ' I feared it might injure the brain ;
But now that I'm perfectly sure I have none,
  Why, I do it again and again.'

' You are old,' said the youth, ' as I mentioned before,
  And have grown most uncommonly fat ;
Yet you turned a back-somersault in at the door—
  Pray, what is the reason of that ? '

' In my youth,' said the sage, as he shook his grey locks,
  ' I kept all my limbs very supple
By the use of this ointment—one shilling the box—
  Allow me to sell you a couple ? '

The Knapsack

'You are old,' said the youth, 'and your jaws are too
   weak
  For anything tougher than suet ;
Yet you finished the goose, with the bones and the beak—
  Pray how did you manage to do it ? '

'In my youth,' said his father, 'I took to the law,
  And argued each case with my wife ;
And the muscular strength, which it gave to my jaw,
  Has lasted the rest of my life.'

'You are old,' said the youth, 'one would hardly suppose
  That your eye was as steady as ever ;
Yet you balanced an eel on the end of your nose—
  What made you so awfully clever ? '

I have answered three questions, and that is enough,'
  Said his father ; 'don't give yourself airs !
Do you think I can listen all day to such stuff ?
  Be off, or I'll kick you downstairs ! '

     CHARLES LUTWIDGE DODGSON (LEWIS CARROLL)

190 *Ode on the Death of a Favourite Cat*

   'TWAS on a lofty vase's side
   Where China's gayest art had dyed
     The azure flowers, that blow ;
   Demurest of the tabby kind,
   The pensive Selima reclined,
     Gazed on the lake below.

Ode on the Death of a Favourite Cat

Her conscious tail her joy declared ;
The fair round face, the snowy beard,
　　The velvet of her paws,
Her coat, that with the tortoise vies,
Her ears of jet, and emerald eyes
　　She saw ; and purred applause.

Still had she gazed ; but 'midst the tide
Two angel forms were seen to glide,
　　The Genii of the stream :
Their scaly armour's Tyrian hue
Through richest purple to the view
　　Betrayed a golden gleam.

The hapless Nymph with wonder saw :
A whisker first and then a claw
　　With many an ardent wish,
She stretched in vain to reach the prize.
What female heart can gold despise ?
　　What Cat's averse to fish ?

Presumptuous Maid ! with looks intent
Again she stretched, again she bent,
　　Nor knew the gulf between.
(Malignant Fate sat by and smiled)
The slippery verge her feet beguiled,
　　She tumbled headlong in.

Eight times emerging from the flood
She mewed to every watry God,
　　Some speedy aid to send.
No Dolphin came, no Nereid stirred :
Nor cruel Tom, nor Susan heard.
　　A Favourite has no friend !

The Knapsack

From hence, ye Beauties, undeceived,
Know, one false step is ne'er retrieved,
    And be with caution bold.
Not all that tempts your wandering eyes
And heedless hearts, is lawful prize ;
    Nor all, that glisters, gold.

THOMAS GRAY

191 *Macavity :   The Mystery Cat*

MACAVITY'S a Mystery Cat : he's called the Hidden Paw—
For he's the master criminal who can defy the Law.
He's the bafflement of Scotland Yard, the Flying Squad's
    despair :
For when they reach the scene of crime—*Macavity's not there !*

Macavity, Macavity, there's no one like Macavity,
He's broken every human law, he breaks the law of gravity.
His powers of levitation would make a fakir stare,
And when you reach the scene of crime—*Macavity's not
    there !*
You may seek him in the basement, you may look up in
    the air—
But I tell you once and once again, *Macavity's not there !*

Macavity's a ginger cat, he's very tall and thin ;
You would know him if you saw him, for his eyes are
    sunken in.
His brow is deeply lined with thought, his head is highly
    domed ;
His coat is dusty from neglect, his whiskers are uncombed.
He sways his head from side to side, with movements like
    a snake ;
And when you think he's half asleep, he's always wide
    awake.

Macavity : The Mystery Cat

Macavity, Macavity, there's no one like Macavity,
For he's a fiend in feline shape, a monster of depravity.
You may meet him in a by-street, you may see him in the
    square—
But when a crime's discovered, then *Macavity's not there !*

He's outwardly respectable. (They say he cheats at cards.)
And his footprints are not found in any file of Scotland
    Yard's.
And when the larder's looted, or the jewel-case is rifled,
Or when the milk is missing, or another Peke's been stifled,
Or the greenhouse glass is broken, and the trellis past
    repair—
Ay, there's the wonder of the thing ! *Macavity's not there !*

And when the Foreign Office find a Treaty's gone astray,
Or the Admiralty lose some plans and drawings by the way,
There may be a scrap of paper in the hall or on the stair—
But it's useless to investigate—*Macavity's not there !*
And when the loss has been disclosed, the Secret Service say :
' It must have been Macavity ! '—but he's a mile away.
You'll be sure to find him resting, or a-licking of his thumbs,
Or engaged in doing complicated long division sums.

Macavity, Macavity, there's no one like Macavity,
There never was a Cat of such deceitfulness and suavity.
He always has an alibi, and one or two to spare :
At whatever time the deed took place—MACAVITY WASN'T
    THERE !
And they say that all the Cats whose wicked deeds are
    widely known
(I might mention Mungojerrie, I might mention Griddle-
    bone)
Are nothing more than agents for the Cat who all the time
Just controls their operations : the Napoleon of Crime !

T. S. ELIOT

PART EIGHT

1779

Jan. 1. Storm all night. The may-pole is blown-down. Thatch & tiles damaged. Great damage is done both by sea & land.

Jan. 4. Water froze in my chamber-window.

Jan. 10. My therm^r is broken.

Jan. 16. Sowed the great mead in part, & all Berriman's field (laid down last year with grass-seeds) with good peat-ashes.

Jan. 17. Ice on ponds is very thick.

Jan. 22. Bees come-out, & gather on the snowdrops. Many gnats in the air.

Jan. 29. Out of the wind there is frost; but none where the S. wind blows.

Jan. 30. Tulips begin to peep.

Feb. 7. Lambs come very fast. Bats appear. Field-pease are sowing.

Feb. 9. The garden works well: sowed pease, & planted beans. Crocus's blow.

Feb. 12. The dry season lasted from Dec. 14 to Feb. 12. This whole time was very still; & even the frosty part of it very moderate: the barom^r was up at 30 great part of the time. We have experienced no such winter since the year 1750.

Feb. 14. The hazels are finely illuminated with their male-bloom.

Feb. 15. A vivid Aurora : a red belt from East to West.

Feb. 16. Crocus's blow-out. When the vernal crocus blows, the autumnal crocus peeps out of the ground. Bees gather on the crocuss.

Feb. 17. Bees rob each other, & fight.

Feb. 20. Field-crickets have opened their holes, & stand in the mouths of them basking in the sun ! They do not usually appear 'til March.

Feb. 23. Drivers use the summer track. Roads dusty.

Feb. 26. Pilewort [lesser celandine] Summer-like.

Feb. 27. The gardener begins to mow my Brother's grass-walks.

Feb. 28. Gossamer abound. Frogs swarm in the ditches. Spawn.

Mar. 6. Radishes pulled in the cold ground.

Mar. 13. The roads in a most dusty, smothering condition.

Mar. 14. Small rain. Quick-set hedges begin to leaf. Dust is laid.

Mar. 17. Tussilago farfara [coltsfoot]. Stellaria holostia [greater stitchwort].

Mar. 25. Picturesque, partial fogs, looking like seas, islands, rivers, harbours, &c. ! ! Vivid Auroras.

Mar. 26. Made an asparagus bed : that which was made last spring was spoiled for want of rain. Planted potatoes ; sowed carrots.

Mar. 30. *Bombylius medius :* many appear down the long Lithe. *Field-crickets* bask at the mouths of their holes : they seem to be yet in their pupa-state ; as yet they show no wings.

Apr. 2. Efts appear.

Apr. 10. The beeches on the hanger begin to show leaves.

Apr. 11. Ivy-berries are ripe : the birds eat them, & stain the walks with their dung.

An English Year

Apr. 14. Two cuckows appear in my outlet. The mole-cricket jars. The wry-neck appears, & pipes.

Apr. 15. Thunder-like clouds in the W. at break of day. Nightingale sings in my outlet. Blackcap sings. Dark clouds to the W. & N.W. Lightening.

Apr. 17. Rain greatly wanted. No spring corn comes up. The dry weather has now lasted four months; from the 15th of Decemr 1778. Apple-trees blow this year a full month sooner than last year. The hanger is pretty well in full leaf : last year not 'til May 15. Musca meridiana.

Apr. 18. Some young grass-hoppers appear : they are very minute.

Apr. 21. Lathraea squammaria, in the Church-litten coppice near the bridge among the hasel-stems, is out of bloom.

Apr. 23. The caterpillars of some phalaenae attack the foliage of the apricots again.

Apr. 24. Hail, stormy, strong wind. The wind broke-off the great elm in the churchyard short in two : the head of which injured the yew-tree. The garden is much damaged by the wind. Many tulips & other flowers are injured by the hail. *Footnotes.* The lightening on friday morning shivered the masts of the Terrible man of war in Portsmouth harbour. The field-crickets in the short Lithe have cast their skins, are much encreased in bulk, show their wings, being now arrived at their ἡλιϰια. 'Til this alteration they are in their pupa-state, but are alert, & eat ; yet cannot chirp, nor propagate their kind.

Apr. 26. Opened the leaves of the Apricot-trees, & killed many hundreds of caterpillars which infest their foliage. These insects would lay the tree bare. They roll the leaves up in a kind of web. N.B. By care & attention the leaves were saved this year.

Apr. 28. Five *long-legged plovers, charadrius himantopus,* were shot at Frinsham-pond. There were three brace in all. These are the most rare of all British birds. Their legs are marvellously long for the bulk of their bodies. To be in proportion of weight for inches the legs of the *Flamingo* should be more than 10 feet in length.

Apr. 30. Two swifts seen at Puttenham in Surrey. Bank-martins on the heaths all the way to London.

May 1. A pair of Creepers (Certhia) build at one end of the parsonage-house at Greatham, [near Selborne] behind some loose plaster. It is very amusing to see them run creeping up the walls with the agility of a mouse. They take great delight in climbing up steep surfaces, & support themselves in their progress with their tails, which are long, & stiff & inclined downwards.

May 3. Shower of snow. The snow lay but a small time. Began to turn my horses into my field lain down last year with rye-grass & dutch-clover. Wheat looks wretchedly.

May 5. The swifts which dashed-by on saturday last have not appeared since ; & were therefore probably on their passage.

May 8. A good crop of rye-grass in the field sown last year ; but the white clover takes only in patches. Sowed 4 pounds more of white clover, & a willow basket of hay-seeds. [*Later.*] The white clover since is spread all over the field.

May 22. Nightingales have eggs. They build a very inartificial nest with dead leaves, & dry stalks. Their eggs are of a dull olive colour. A boy took my nest with five eggs : but the cock continues to sing : so probably they will build again.

May 24. Fiery lily blows : orange lily blows.

May 26. The nightingale continues to sing ; & therefore is probably building again.

May 28. Young pheasants !

An English Year

May 31. Cut my *Saint foin*, the 12th crop. The smoke lies low over the fields. Glow-worms begin to appear.

June 1. In Mr Richardson's garden ripe scarlet strawberries every day ; large artichokes, pease, radishes, beans just at hand. Bramshot soil is a warm, sandy loam. Small cauliflowers. Wheat shoots into ear. Barley & pease are good on the sands. The sands by liming, & turniping produce as good corn as the clays. *Footnote.* Many large edible chestnut-trees which grew on the turnpike road near Bramshot-place were cut this spring for repairs : but they are miserably shaky, & make wretched timber. They are not only shaky, but what the workmen call *cup-shaky*, coming apart in great plugs, & round pieces as big as a man's leg. The timber is grained like oak, but much softer.

June. 6. Sparrows take possession of the martins nests. When we shot the cock, the hen soon found another male ; & when we killed the hen, the cock soon procured another mate ; & so on for three or four times.

June 19. Farmer Turner cut my great meadow. He bought the crop. Wood-strawberries begin to ripen.

June 22. Farmer Turner housed his hay : it should, I think, have lain a day longer.

June 23. Golden-crowned wrens, & creepers bring-out their broods.

June 24. Things in the garden do not grow. Clap of thunder. Vine-bloom smells fragrantly.

June 26. Cold black solstice.

July 3. Hops are remarkably bad, covered with aphides, & honey-dews.

July 7. Vipers are big with young.

July 9. A surprizing humming of bees all over the common, tho' none can be seen ! This is frequently the case in hot weather.

July 11. By the number of swifts round the church

The Knapsack

which seem to be encreased to more than 30, their young ones must be come out.

July 12. Apricots, the young tree, ripen. Mossed [mulched] the hills of the white cucumbers to keep them moist.

July 13. Therm^r 79 ! The grass-mowers complain of the heat.

July 14. Dwarf elder blows. Red martagons begin to blow. Large kidney beans bud for bloom. Grapes swell.

July 25. Puff-balls come up in my grass-plot, & walks : they came from the common in the turf. There are many fairy-rings in my walks, in these the puff-balls thrive best. The fairy-rings alter & vary in their shape.

July 27. Planted out in trenches four rows of celeri.

Aug. 7. Rain, rain, rain. Wheat under the hedges begins to grow.

Aug. 10. Wheat lies in a bad way. Peaches, & plums rot. Wheat grows. Flying ants swarm in millions. Inches of rain 3 [hundredths].

Aug. 17. Much wheat housed. Drank tea at the hermitage.

Aug. 21. Sun, brisk air, sweet even. Many people have finished wheat-harvest.

Aug. 23. Sun, clouds, thunder shower, red even : Great blackness.

Aug. 27. Full moon. My well is shallow & the water foul.

Aug. 29. House-crickets are heard in all the gardens, & court-yards. One came to my kitchen-hearth.

Aug. 30–*Sept.* 8. Harvest is nearly at an end on the downs.

Aug. 31. The grass burns.

Sept. 2. Partridges innumerable. Barley-harvest finished here.

Sept. 6. The trufle-hunter trie's my brother's groves ;

but finds few trufles, & those very small. They want moisture.

Sept. 7. No mushrooms for want of more moisture.

Sept. 9. The greens of the turneps in light shallow land are quite withered away for want of moisture.

Sept. 10. Gloomy, still, sultry, soft showers.

Sept. 11. The rain that fell in my absence was 73 (hundredths].

Sept. 13. Gathered-in the filberts, a large crop.

Sept. 25. Full moon. No mushrooms have appeared all this month. I find that the best crop is usually in Aug : & if they are not taken then, the season for catchup [ketchup] is lost. Many other fungi.

Sept. 27. Gathered-in the pears. The Cardillac-tree bore five bushels. Apples are few ; & the crop of grapes small.

Sept. 28. Grapes are rich, & sweet.

Oct. 3. Began lighting fires in the parlor.

Oct. 4. Mushrooms abound. Made catchup.

Oct 12. Bad fevers near Chichester.

Oct. 13. Small showers, sun.

Oct. 15–27. Heavy clouds, rain. One martin at Lewes.

Oct. 16. Vast rain with strong wind for near 24 hours. *Footnote*. Thomas Hoar kept the measure of the rain during my absence.

Oct. 18. Mrs Snooke's black grapes are very fine. Ponds are very low.

Oct. 20. Many libellulae in copulation. Rooks frequent their nest-trees very much.

Oct. 23. Whitings, & herrings. Timothy, the old tortoise at this house, weighs 6 pounds 9 ounces & an half averdupoise. It weighed last year, Oct. 2, an ounce & an half more. But perhaps the abstemious life that it lives at this season may have reduced it's bulk : for tortoises seem to eat nothing for some weeks before they lay-up.

However this enquiry shews, that these reptiles do not, as some have imagined, continue to grow as long as they live. This poor being has been very torpid for some time ; but it does not usually retire under ground 'til the middle of next month.

Oct. 24.   Many hornets about the vines.

Oct. 28.   Sheep-ponds on the downs are all filled by the rains.   A great beast-market this day at Arundel.

Nov. 2.   My well is risen very fast.

Nov. 5.   On this day many house-martins were seen playing about the side of the hanger.

Nov. 18.   Frost, ice, snow, grey, bright.

Nov. 23.   An eclipse of the moon, total but not central.

Nov. 25.   Mrs Snooke's old tortoise retired under the ground.

Nov. 28.   The ground is glutted with water.

Nov. 29.   Snow was halfshoe-deep on the hill.   Distant lightening.

Dec. 2.   Vast condensations in the great parlor : the grate, the marble-jams, the tables, the chairs, the walls are covered with dew.   [*Later.*]   This inconvenience may be prevented by keeping the window-shutters, & the door close shut in such moist seasons.

Dec. 13.   Much thunder.   Great hail at Faringdon.

Dec. 22.   Ground covered with snow.

Dec. 25.   Vast rime, strong frost, bright, & still, fog. The hanging woods when covered with a copious rime appear most beautiful & grotesque.

Dec. 26.   Most beautiful rimes.

GILBERT WHITE

Spring in the Country

193 *Spring in the Country*

THE weather now changed, and the rest of Easter week was wet and cold. So much rain came down, that the floods, when thus reinforced, rose again, and remained at their former level for twenty-four hours, after which they fell rapidly. At the same time, as often happens in April, the summer warmth set in. Within a week of St. Thomas's Sunday [1] began that marvellous season, not always clement at its opening, at which Nature awakens from sleep and begins to live a full, young, rapid life ; the season of universal movement and excitement, of sound and colour and fragrance. I was too young then to understand it and appreciate it in detail ; but I felt new life in myself and became a part of Nature. Not till I had grown to maturity and recalled this time, did I consciously appreciate all its enchanting spell and poetic beauty. But I then recognized what I had before dimly guessed at, when I greeted spring in our house at Ufa, in our poor little garden, and in the muddy streets. At Sergéyevka, our arrival had been too late : I saw there only the end of spring, when Nature had reached her full development and full splendour, and the constant change and forward movement had stopped.

The sad death of the old miller soon passed from my mind, crushed down and crowded out by new and powerful impressions. My heart and mind were full ; some mysterious business seemed to weigh on me and make me anxious ; I felt a mysterious desire to go somewhere. And yet, in reality, I went nowhere and did nothing ; I neither read nor wrote. It was impossible to read and write, when the birch buds were bursting and the fragrant bird-cherries breaking into blossom—when the crinkled

[1] " Low Sunday " in the English Church calendar.

The Knapsack

leaflets, as they opened, threw a veil of whitish down over the black gooseberry bushes—when the larks hung all day right over the court-yard, pouring out a stream of unvarying song till it died away in the sky, a song which caught at my heart and affected me to tears—when all the slopes were covered with crocuses, purple and blue and white and yellow, and the funnel-shaped grass-blades and close-sheathed flower-buds stole everywhere out of the ground—when ladybirds and beetles of every kind came out into the kindly light, and white and yellow butterflies began to flash past, and bees and bumble-bees to buzz—when there was movement in the water, noise on the earth, and the very air trembled—when the sunbeams quivered, as they made their way through the moist atmosphere filled with the elements of life. How much business I had, how many anxieties! Twice every day I had to visit the wood and make sure that the jackdaws were sitting on their nests; I had to listen to their incessant cawing; I had to watch the lilac-leaves opening to let out the plum-coloured clusters of the coming blossom —the finches and warblers establishing themselves in the gooseberry bushes and barberries—the ant-heaps waking to life and movement, where first a few ants showed themselves and then multitudes poured forth and began their labours—the swallows flashing past and diving into their old nests under the eaves—the clucking hen brooding over her tiny chickens, while the kite made circles and floated above them. Oh, I had business enough and cares enough! I ceased to run about the court-yard; I did not roll eggs on the ground, or swing with my sister, or play with Soorka. I walked, or more often I stood still; I seemed depressed and uneasy; I walked and looked and, for a wonder, was silent; I was tanned like a gipsy by the sun and wind. My sister laughed at me; Yevséitch was astonished that I did not play in the proper way or

Spring in the Country

ask leave to go to the mill, but was always walking and then standing stock-still. " What can there be you have not seen there, my little falcon ? " he used to ask. My mother, too, did not understand the state I was in, and used to look at me anxiously. I got more sympathy from my father : he often went with me to the garden, to look at the birds in the bushes, and explained to me that they were beginning to build their nests. Or we went to the Jackdaw Wood, where he was very angry with the jackdaws for killing the tops of the birches by breaking off twigs to make their clumsy nests ; he even threatened to destroy them. How charmed he was when he saw the lungwort for the first time ! He showed me how to twitch off the purple flowers and suck the sweet white stalks. He was even more delighted when he heard in the distance, also for the first time, the song of the mocking-bird. " There, Seryozha," he said to me, " all the birds will start singing now : the mocking-bird is the first to begin. And presently, when the bushes are in leaf, our nightingales will begin too ; and then life will be still more cheerful at Bagrovo."

That time also came at last : the grass grew green, the trees and bushes put forth their leaves, and the nightingales began to sing. Night and day they sang, never ceasing. By day their song did not strike me as wonderful : I even said that the larks sang as well ; but in the late evening or at night, when universal silence began to reign, under the light of the fading sunset-glow or the glitter of the stars, the song of the nightingales was an excitement and joy to me, and for a time prevented me from sleeping. There were a great number of the birds, and they evidently came close to the house at night. One corner of our bedroom ran out towards the bend of the river, close to the bushes swarming with nightingales, so that their calls and rapid cadences came loudly through the shuttered windows on two sides. My mother used to send out at night to frighten them away. I had never before believed my aunt when she said that her rest was disturbed by the nightingales. I don't know if my father's promise came true, that life would be more cheerful at Bagrovo ; nor can I say whether I was at this time in what could be called high spirits ; but this I know, that the thought of that time has been, throughout my whole life, a source of quiet happiness in my heart.

SERGHEI AKSAKOFF

194 *A Boy's Animism*

THE first intimations of the feeling are beyond recall ; I only know that my memory takes me back to a time when I was unconscious of any such element in nature, when the delight I experienced in all natural things was purely physical. I rejoiced in colours, scents, sounds, in taste and touch : the blue of the sky, the verdure of earth, the sparkle of sunlight on water, the taste of milk, of fruit, of honey, the smell of dry or moist soil, of wind and rain, of herbs and flowers ; the mere feel of a blade of grass made me happy ; and there were certain sounds and perfumes, and above all certain colours in flowers, and in the plumage and eggs of birds, such as the purple polished shell of the tinamou's egg, which intoxicated me with delight. When, riding on the plain, I discovered a patch of scarlet verbenas in full bloom, the creeping plants covering an area of several yards, with a moist, green sward sprinkled abundantly with the shining flower-bosses, I would throw myself from my pony with a cry of joy to lie on the turf among them and feast my sight on their brilliant colour.

A Boy's Animism

It was not, I think, till my eighth year that I began to be distinctly conscious of something more than this mere childish delight in nature. It may have been there all the time from infancy—I don't know ; but when I began to know it consciously it was as if some hand had surreptitiously dropped something into the honeyed cup which gave it at certain times a new flavour. It gave me little thrills, often purely pleasurable, at other times startling, and there were occasions when it became so poignant as to frighten me. The sight of a magnificent sunset was sometimes almost more than I could endure and made me wish to hide myself away. But when the feeling was roused by the sight of a small and beautiful or singular object, such as a flower, its sole effect was to intensify the object's loveliness. There were many flowers which produced this effect in but a slight degree, and as I grew up and the animistic sense lost its intensity, these too lost their magic and were almost like other flowers which had never had it. There were others which never lost what for want of a better word I have just called their magic, and of these I will give an account of one.

I was about nine years old, perhaps a month or two more, when during one of my rambles on horseback I found at a distance of two or three miles from home, a flower that was new to me. The plant, a little over a foot in height, was growing in the shelter of some large cardoon thistle, or wild artichoke, bushes. It had three stalks clothed with long, narrow, sharply-pointed leaves, which were downy, soft to the feel like the leaves of our great mullein, and pale green in colour. All three stems were crowned with clusters of flowers, the single flower a little larger than that of the red valerian, of a pale red hue and a peculiar shape, as each small pointed petal had a fold or twist at the end. Altogether it was slightly singular in appearance and pretty, though not to be compared with scores of other flowers of the plains for beauty. Nevertheless, it had an extraordinary fascination for me, and from the moment of its discovery it became one of my sacred flowers. From that time onwards, when riding on the plain, I was always on the look-out for it, and as a rule I found three or four plants in a season, but never more than one at any spot. They were usually miles apart.

On first discovering it I took a spray to show to my mother, and was strangely disappointed that she admired it merely because it was a pretty flower, seen for the first time. I had actually hoped to hear from her some word which would have revealed to me why I thought so much of it : now it appeared as if it was no more to her than any other pretty flower and even less than some she was peculiarly fond of, such as the fragrant little lily called Virgin's Tears, the scented pure white and the rose-coloured verbenas, and several others. Strange that she who alone seemed always to know what was in my mind and who loved all beautiful things, especially flowers, should have failed to see what I had found in it !

No doubt in cases of this kind, when a first impression and the emotion accompanying it endures through life, the feeling changes somewhat with time ; imagination has worked on it and has had its effect ; nevertheless, the endurance of the image and emotion serves to show how powerfully the mind was moved in the first instance.

I have related this case because there were interesting circumstances connected with it ; but there were other flowers which produced a similar feeling, which, when recalled, bring back the original emotion ; and I would gladly travel many miles any day to look again at any one of them. The feeling, however, was evoked more powerfully by trees than by even the most supernatural

A Boy's Animism

of my flowers; it varied in power according to time and place and the appearance of the tree or trees, and always affected me most on moonlight nights. Frequently, after I had first begun to experience it consciously, I would go out of my way to meet it, and I used to steal out of the house alone when the moon was at its full to stand, silent and motionless, near some group of large trees, gazing at the dusky green foliage silvered by the beams; and at such times the sense of mystery would grow until a sensation of delight would change to fear, and the fear increase until it was no longer to be borne, and I would hastily escape to recover the sense of reality and safety indoors, where there was light and company. Yet on the very next night I would steal out again and go to the spot where the effect was strongest, which was usually among the large locust or white acacia trees, which gave the name of Las Acacias to our place. The loose feathery foliage on moonlight nights had a peculiar hoary aspect that made this tree seem more intensely alive than others, more conscious of my presence and watchful of me.

I never spoke of these feelings to others, not even to my mother, notwithstanding that she was always in perfect sympathy with me with regard to my love of nature. The reason of my silence was, I think, my powerlessness to convey in words what I felt; but I imagine it would be correct to describe the sensation experienced on those moonlight nights among the trees as similar to the feeling a person would have if visited by a supernatural being, if he was perfectly convinced that it was there in his presence, albeit silent and unseen, intently regarding him, and divining every thought in his mind. He would be thrilled to the marrow, but not terrified if he knew that it would take no visible shape nor speak to him out of the silence.

This faculty or instinct of the dawning mind is or has

always seemed to me essentially religious in character ; undoubtedly it is the root of all nature-worship, from fetishism to the highest pantheistic development. It was more to me in those early days than all the religious teaching I received from my mother. Whatever she told me about our relations with the Supreme Being I believed implicitly, just as I believed everything else she told me, and as I believed that two and two make four and that the world is round in spite of its flat appearance ; also that it is travelling through space and revolving round the sun instead of standing still, with the sun going round it, as one would imagine. But apart from the fact that the powers above would save me in the end from extinction, which was a great consolation, these teachings did not touch my heart as it was touched and thrilled by something nearer, more intimate, in nature, not only in moonlit trees or in a flower or serpent, but, in certain exquisite moments and moods and in certain aspects of nature, in " every grass " and in all things, animate and inanimate.

W. H. HUDSON

195 *Morning in the Woods*

EVERY morning was a cheerful invitation to make my life of equal simplicity, and I may say innocence, with Nature herself. I have been as sincere a worshipper of Aurora as the Greeks. I got up early and bathed in the pond : that was a religious exercise, and one of the best things which I did. They say that characters were engraven on the bathing tub of king Tching-thang to this effect : " Renew thyself completely each day ; do it again, and again, and forever again." I can understand that. Morning brings back the heroic ages. I was as much affected by the faint hum of a mosquito making its invisible and unimaginable tour through my apartment at earliest dawn, when I was sitting with door and windows open, as I could be by any trumpet that ever sang of fame. It was Homer's requiem; itself an Iliad and Odyssey in the air, singing its own wrath and wanderings. There was something cosmical about it; a standing advertisement, till forbidden, of the ever-lasting vigour and fertility of the world. The morning, which is the most memorable season of the day, is the awakening hour. Then there is least somnolence in us; and for an hour, at least, some part of us awakes which slumbers all the rest of the day and night. Little is to be expected of that day, if it can be called a day, to which we are not awakened by our Genius, but by the mechanical nudgings of some servitor, are not awakened by our own newly-acquired force and aspirations from within, accompanied by the undulations of celestial music, instead of factory bells, and a fragrance filling the air—to a higher life than we fell asleep from; and thus the darkness bear its fruit, and prove itself to be good, no less than the light. That man who does not believe that each day contains an earlier, more sacred, and auroral hour than he has yet profaned, has despaired of life, and is pursuing a descending and darkening way. After a partial cessation of his sensuous life, the soul of man, and his Genius tries again what noble life it can make. All memorable events, I should say, transpire in morning time and in a morning atmosphere. The Vedas say, "All intelligences awake with the morning." Poetry and art, and the fairest and most memorable of the actions of men, date from such an hour. All poets and heroes, like Memnon, are the children of Aurora, and emit their music at sunrise. To him whose elastic and vigorous thought keeps pace with the sun, the day is a perpetual morning. It matters not what the clocks say or the attitudes and labours of men. Morning is when I am awake and there is a dawn in me. Moral reform is the effort to throw off sleep. Why is it that men give so poor an account of their day if they have not been slumbering? They are not such poor calculators. If they had not been overcome with drowsiness they would have performed something. The millions are awake enough for physical labour; but only one in a million is awake enough for effective intellectual exertion, only one in a hundred millions to a poetic or divine life. To be awake is to be alive. I have never yet met a man who was quite awake. How could I have looked him in the face?

We must learn to reawaken and keep ourselves awake, not by mechanical aids, but by an infinite expectation of the dawn, which does not forsake us in our soundest sleep. I know of no more encouraging fact than the unquestionable ability of man to elevate his life by a conscious endeavour. It is something to be able to paint a particular picture, or to carve a statue, and so to make a few objects beautiful; but it is far more glorious to carve and paint the very atmosphere and medium through which we look, which morally we can do. To affect the quality of the day, that is the highest of arts. Every man is tasked to make his life, even in its details, worthy of the contemplation of his most elevated and critical hour. If we refused, or rather used up, such paltry information as we get, the oracles would distinctly inform us how this might be done.

I went to the woods because I wished to live deliberately, to front only the essential facts of life, and see if I could not learn what it had to teach, and not, when I came to die, discover that I had not lived. I did not wish to live what was not life, living is so dear; nor did I wish to practise resignation, unless it was quite necessary. I wanted to live deep and suck out all the marrow of life, to live so sturdily and Spartan-like as to put to rout all that was not life, to cut a broad swath and shave close, to drive

Morning in the Woods

life into a corner, and reduce it to its lowest terms, and, if it proved to be mean, why then to get the whole and genuine meanness of it, and publish its meanness to the world ; or if it were sublime, to know it by experience, and be able to give a true account of it in my next excursion. For most men, it appears to me, are in a strange uncertainty about it, whether it is of the devil or of God, and have *somewhat hastily* concluded that it is the chief end of man here to " glorify God and enjoy Him forever".

HENRY DAVID THOREAU

196 *On the Margin of a Lake*

THE country for some way eastward of Festiniog is very wild and barren, consisting of huge hills without trees or verdure. About three miles' distance, however, there is a beautiful valley, which you look down upon from the southern side of the road, after having surmounted a very steep ascent. This valley is fresh and green and the lower parts of the hills on its farther side are, here and there, adorned with groves. At the eastern end is a deep, dark gorge, or ravine, down which tumbles a brook in a succession of small cascades. The ravine is close by the road. The brook after disappearing for a time shows itself again far down in the valley, and is doubtless one of the tributaries of the Tan y Bwlch river, perhaps the very same brook the name of which I could not learn the preceding day in the vale.

As I was gazing on the prospect an old man driving a peat cart came from the direction in which I was going. I asked him the name of the ravine and he told me it was Ceunant Coomb or hollow-dingle coomb. I asked the name of the brook, and he told me that it was called the brook of the hollow-dingle coomb, adding that it ran under Pont Newydd, though where that was I knew not. Whilst he was talking with me he stood uncovered. Yes, the old peat driver stood with his hat in his hand whilst answering the questions of the poor, dusty foot-traveller. What a fine thing to be an Englishman in Wales !

In about an hour I came to a wild moor ; the moor extended for miles and miles. It was bounded on the east and south by immense hills and moels. On I walked at a round pace, the sun scorching me sore, along a dusty, hilly road, now up, now down. Nothing could be conceived more cheerless than the scenery around. The ground on each side of the road was mossy and rushy— no houses—instead of them were peat stacks, here and there, standing in their blackness. Nothing living to be seen except a few miserable sheep picking the wretched herbage, or lying panting on the shady side of the peat clumps. At length I saw something which appeared to be a sheet of water at the bottom of a low ground on my right. It looked far off—" Shall I go and see what it is ? " thought I to myself. " No," thought I. " It is too far off "—so on I walked till I lost sight of it, when I repented and thought I would go and see what it was. So I dashed down the moory slope on my right, and presently saw the object again—and now I saw that it was water. I sped towards it through gorse and heather, occasionally leaping a deep drain. At last I reached it. It was a small lake. Wearied and panting I flung myself on its bank and gazed upon it.

There lay the lake in the low bottom, surrounded by the heathery hillocks ; there it lay quite still, the hot sun reflected upon its surface, which shone like a polished blue shield. Near the shore it was shallow, at least near that shore upon which I lay. But farther on, my eye, practised in deciding upon the depths of waters, saw reason to suppose that its depth was very great. As I gazed upon it my mind indulged in strange musings. I thought of the afanc, a creature which some have supposed to be the harmless and industrious beaver, others the frightful and destructive crocodile. I wondered whether the afanc was the crocodile or the beaver, and speedily had no doubt that the name was originally applied to the crocodile.

" Oh, who can doubt," thought I, " that the word was originally intended for something monstrous and horrible ? Is there not something horrible in the look and sound of the word afanc, something connected with the opening and shutting of immense jaws, and the swallowing of writhing prey ? Is not the word a fitting brother of the Arabic timsah, denoting the dread horny lizard of the waters ? Moreover, have we not the voice of tradition that the afanc was something monstrous ? Does it not say that Hu the Mighty, the inventor of husbandry, who brought the Cumry from the summer-country, drew the old afanc out of the lake of lakes with his four gigantic oxen ? Would he have had recourse to them to draw out the little harmless beaver ? Oh, surely not. Yet have I no doubt that when the crocodile had disappeared from the lands, where the Cumric language was spoken, the name afanc was applied to the beaver, probably his successor in the pool, the beaver now called in Cumric Llost-lydan, or the broad-tailed, for tradition's voice is strong that the beaver has at one time been called the afanc." Then I wondered whether the pool before me had been the haunt of the afanc, considered both as crocodile and beaver. I saw no reason to suppose that it had not. " If crocodiles," thought I, " ever existed in Britain, and who shall say that they have not, seeing that their remains have been discovered, why should they not have haunted this pool ? If beavers ever existed in Britain, and do not tradition and Giraldus say that they have, why should they not have existed in this pool ?

The Knapsack

" At a time almost inconceivably remote, when the hills around were covered with woods, through which the elk and the bison and the wild cow strolled, when men were rare throughout the lands and unlike in most things to the present race—at such a period—and such a period there has been—I can easily conceive that the afanc-crocodile haunted this pool, and that when the elk or bison or wild cow came to drink of its waters the grim beast would occasionally rush forth, and seizing his bellowing victim, would return with it to the deeps before me to luxuriate at his ease upon its flesh.   And at a time less remote, when the crocodile was no more, and though the woods still covered the hills, and wild cattle strolled about, men were more numerous than before, and less unlike the present race, I can easily conceive this lake to have been the haunt of the afanc-beaver, that he here built cunningly his house of trees and clay, and that to this lake the native would come with his net and his spear to hunt the animal for his precious fur.   Probably if the depths of that pool were searched relics of the crocodile and the beaver might be found, along with other strange things connected with the periods in which they respectively lived.   Happy were I if for a brief space I could become a Cingalese that I might swim out far into that pool, dive down into its deepest part and endeavour to discover any strange things which beneath its surface may lie."   Much in this guise rolled my thoughts as I lay stretched on the margin of the lake.

GEORGE BORROW

197 *Nature and Art*

I HAVE begun to take off a pretty view of part of the village, and have no doubt but the drawing of choice portions and aspects of external objects is one of the

Nature and Art

varieties of study requisite to build up an artist, who should be a magnet to all kinds of knowledge ; though, at the same time, I can't help seeing that the general characteristics of Nature's beauty not only differ from, but are, in some respects, opposed to those of Imaginative Art ; and *that*, even in those scenes and appearances where she is loveliest, and most universally pleasing.

Nature, with mild reposing breadths of lawn and hill, shadowy glades and meadows, is sprinkled and showered with a thousand pretty eyes, and buds, and spires, and blossoms gemm'd with dew, and is clad in living green. Nor must be forgotten the motley clouding, the fine meshes, the aerial tissues, that dapple the skies of spring ; nor the rolling volumes and piled mountains of light ; nor the purple sunset blazon'd with gold and the translucent amber. Universal nature wears a lovely gentleness of mild attraction ; but the leafy lightness, the thousand repetitions of little forms, which are part of its own genuine perfection (and who would wish them but what they are ?), seem hard to be reconciled with the unwinning severity, the awfulness, the ponderous globosity of Art.

Milton, by one epithet, draws an oak of the largest girth I ever saw, " Pine and *monumental* oak " : I have just been trying to draw a large one in Lullingstone ; but the poet's tree is huger than any in the park : there, the moss, and rifts, and barky furrows, and the mouldering grey (tho' that adds majesty to the lord of forests) mostly catch the eye, before the grasp and grapple of the roots, the muscular belly and shoulders, the twisted sinews.

Many of the fine pictures of the thirteenth, fourteenth, and two following centuries, which our modern addlepates grin at for Gothic and barbarous, do seem to me, I confess, much deteriorated by the faces, though exquisitely drawn, looking like portraits, which many of them are ; and from the naked form, thwarted with fringes, and belts, and trappings, being generally neglected or ill expressed, through a habit of disproportioned attention to secondary things, as the stuff and texture of draperies, etc.; which ended at last in the Dutch school; with this damning difference; that in the fine old works the heads are always most elaborated—on the Flemish canvas, the least finished of any part; and yielding to the perfected polish of pots and stew-pans; a preference most religiously observed by the cleverest disciples of that style at present. An instance of this appeared in the last exhibition, where was a painting in which, against the sky and distance, beautiful, intense, and above the Dutch perception, there came a woman's head; hard to tell whether quite neglected, or laboriously muzzled—the least perfect object in the piece, with a careful avoidance of all shape, roundness, and outline. But nature is not like this. I saw a lovely little rustic child this evening, which took my fancy so much that I long, with to-morrow's light (God sparing me), to make a humble attempt to catch some of its graces. If I can at all succeed it will be nothing Dutch or boorish.

Temporal Creation, whose beauties are in their kind perfect, and made and adapted by the benevolent Author to please all eyes and gladden all hearts, seems to differ from images of the mind, as that beautiful old picture in the last British Gallery (I forget the name; it is that I miscalled Garofalo) differs from the conceptions of the Sistine Chapel, or the tomb of the Medici: were both called suddenly into breath, the simple shepherds would, I think, as they ought, modestly withdraw themselves from the stupendous majesty of Buonarroti's *Night*.

So, among our poets, Milton is abstracted and eternal. That arch-alchemist, let him but touch a history, yea a dogma of the schools, or a technicality of science, and it becomes poetic gold. Has an old chronicle told, perhaps marred an action? Six words from the blind old man reinvigorate it beyond the living fact; so that we may say the spectators themselves saw only the wrong side of the tapestry. If superior spirits could be fancied to enact a masque of one of the greatest of those events which have transpired on earth, it would resemble the historical hints and allusions of our bard. I must be called mad to say it but I do believe his stanzas will be read in Heaven: and to be yet more mad—to foam at the mouth, I will declare my conviction that the *St. George* of Donatello, the *Night* of Michelangelo, and *The Last Supper* of Da Vinci are as casts and copies, of which, when their artists had obtained of God to conceive the Idea, an eternal mould was placed above the tenth sphere, beyond changes and decay.

Terrestrial spring showers blossoms and odours in profusion, which, at some moments, " Breathe on earth the air of Paradise "; indeed sometimes, when the spirits are in Heav'n, earth itself, as in emulation, blooms again into Eden; rivalling those golden fruits which the poet of Eden sheds upon his landscape, having stolen [them] from that country where they grow without peril of frost, or drought, or blight—" But not in this soil ".

Still, the perfection of nature is not the perfection of severest art: they are two things. The former we may liken to an easy, charming colloquy of intellectual friends; the latter is " Imperial Tragedy ". *That* is graceful humanity; *this* is Plato's Vision; who, somewhere in untracked regions, primigenous Unity, above all things holds his head and bears his forehead among the stars, tremendous to the gods!

If the *Night* could get up and walk, and were to take a swim to the white cliffs, and after the fashion of Shakespeare's tragicomic mixtures, were amusing herself with a huge bit of broken tobacco-pipe, I think about half a dozen whiffs would blow down the strongest beech and oak at Windsor, and the pipe-ashes chance to make a big bonfire of the forest !

General nature is wisely and beneficently adapted to refresh the senses and soothe the spirits of general *observers*. We find hundreds in raptures when they get into the fields, who have not the least relish for grand art. General nature is simple and lovely ; but, compared with the loftier vision, it is the shrill music of the " Little herd grooms, Keeping their beasts in the budded brooms ; And crowing in pipes made of green corn," to the sound of the chant and great organ, pealing through dusky aisles and reverberating in the dome ; or the trombone, and drums, and cymbals of the banner'd march. Everywhere curious, articulate, perfect and inimitable of structure, like her own entomology, Nature does yet leave a space for the soul to climb above her steepest summits. As, in her own dominion, she swells from the herring to leviathan, from the hodmandod to the elephant, so, divine Art piles mountains on her hills, and continents upon those mountains.

However, creation sometimes pours into the spiritual eye the radiance of Heaven : the green mountains that glimmer in a summer gloaming from the dusky yet bloomy east ; the moon opening her golden eye, or walking in brightness among innumerable islands of light, not only thrill the optic nerve, but shed a mild, a grateful, an unearthly lustre into the inmost spirits, and seem the interchanging twilight of that peaceful country, where there is no sorrow and no night. . . .

SAMUEL PALMER

NOT a footstep was to be heard on any of the paths.   Somewhere in one of the tall trees, making a stage in its height, an invisible bird, desperately attempting to make the day seem shorter, was exploring with a long, continuous note the solitude that pressed it on every side, but it received at once so unanimous an answer, so powerful a repercussion of silence and of immobility that, one would have said, it had arrested for all eternity the moment which it had been trying to make pass more quickly.   The sunlight fell so implacably from a fixed sky that one was naturally inclined to slip away out of the reach of its attentions, and even the slumbering water, whose repose was perpetually being invaded by the insects that swarmed above its surface, while it dreamed, no doubt, of some imaginary maelstrom, intensified the uneasiness which the sight of that floating cork had wrought in me, by appearing to draw it at full speed across the silent reaches of a mirrored firmament ; now almost vertical, it seemed on the point of plunging down out of sight, and I had begun to ask myself whether, setting aside the longing and the terror that I had of making her acquaintance, it was not actually my duty to warn Mlle. Swann that the fish was biting—when I was obliged to run after my father and grandfather, who were calling me, and were surprised that I had not followed them along the little path, climbing up hill towards the open fields, into which they had already turned.   I found the whole path throbbing with the fragrance of hawthorn-blossom. The hedge resembled a series of chapels, whose walls were no longer visible under the mountains of flowers that were heaped upon their altars ; while, underneath, the sun cast a square of light upon the ground, as though it had shone in upon them through a window ; the scent that swept out over me from them was as rich, and as circumscribed in its range, as though I had been standing before the Lady-altar, and the flowers, themselves adorned also, held out each its little bunch of glittering stamens with an air of inattention, fine, radiating " nerves " in the flamboyant style of architecture, like those which, in church, framed the stair to the rood-loft or closed the perpendicular tracery of the windows, but here spread out into pools of fleshy white, like strawberry-beds in spring. How simple and rustic, in comparison with these, would seem the dog-roses which, in a few weeks' time, would be climbing the same hillside path in the heat of the sun, dressed in the smooth silk of their blushing pink bodices, which would be undone and scattered by the first breath of wind.

But it was in vain that I lingered before the hawthorns, to breathe in, to marshal before my mind (which knew not what to make of it), to lose in order to rediscover their invisible and unchanging odour, to absorb myself in the rhythm which disposed their flowers here and there with the lightheartedness of youth, and at intervals as unexpected as certain intervals of music ; they offered me an indefinite continuation of the same charm, in an inexhaustible profusion, but without letting me delve into it any more deeply, like those melodies which one can play over a hundred times in succession without coming any nearer to their secret. I turned away from them for a moment so as to be able to return to them with renewed strength. My eyes followed up the slope which, outside the hedge, rose steeply to the fields, a poppy that had strayed and been lost by its fellows, or a few cornflowers that had fallen lazily behind, and decorated the ground here and there with their flowers like the border of a tapestry, in which may be seen at intervals hints of the rustic theme which appears triumphant in the panel itself ; infrequent still, spaced apart as the scattered houses which

warn us that we are approaching a village, they betokened
to me the vast expanse of waving corn beneath the fleecy
clouds, and the sight of a single poppy hoisting upon its
slender rigging and holding against the breeze its scarlet
ensign, over the buoy of rich black earth from which it
sprang, made my heart beat as does a wayfarer's when he
perceives, upon some low-lying ground, an old and broken
boat which is being caulked and made sea-worthy, and
cries out, although he has not yet caught sight of it, " The
Sea ! "

And then I returned to my hawthorns, and stood before
them as one stands before those masterpieces of painting
which, one imagines, one will be better able to " take in "
when one has looked away, for a moment, at something
else ; but in vain did I shape my fingers into a frame, so
as to have nothing but the hawthorns before my eyes ; the
sentiment which they aroused in me remained obscure and
vague, struggling and failing to free itself, to float across
and become one with the flowers. They themselves offered
me no enlightenment, and I could not call upon any other
flowers to satisfy this mysterious longing. And then, inspiring me with that rapture which we feel on seeing a
work by our favourite painter quite different from any of
those that we already know, or, better still, when some one
has taken us and set us down in front of a picture of which
we have hitherto seen no more than a pencilled sketch, or
when a piece of music which we have heard played over
on the piano bursts out again in our ears with all the
splendour and fullness of an orchestra, my grandfather
called me to him, and, pointing to the hedge of Tanson-
ville, said : " You are fond of hawthorns ; just look at this
pink one ; isn't it pretty ? "

And it was indeed a hawthorn, but one whose flowers
were pink, and lovelier even than the white. It, too, was
in holiday attire, for one of those days which are the only

true holidays, the holy days of religion, because they are not appointed by any capricious accident, as secular holidays are appointed, upon days which are not specially ordained for such observances, which have nothing about them that is essentially festal—but it was attired even more richly than the rest, for the flowers which clung to its branches, one above another, so thickly as to leave no part of the tree undecorated, like the tassels wreathed about the crook of a rococo shepherdess, were every one of them " in colour ", and consequently of a superior quality, by the aesthetic standards of Combray, to the " plain ", if one was to judge by the scale of prices at the " stores " in the Square, or at Camus's, where the most expensive biscuits were those whose sugar was pink. And for my own part I set a higher value on cream cheese when it was pink, when I had been allowed to tinge it with crushed strawberries. And these flowers had chosen precisely the colour of some edible and delicious thing, or of some exquisite addition to one's costume for a great festival, which colours, inasmuch as they make plain the reason for their superiority, are those whose beauty is most evident to the eyes of children, and for that reason must always seem more vivid and more natural than any other tints, even after the child's mind has realized that they offer no gratification to the appetite, and have not been selected by the dressmaker. And, indeed, I had felt at once, as I had felt before the white blossom, but now still more marvelling, that it was in no artificial manner, by no device of human construction, that the festal intention of these flowers was revealed, but that it was Nature herself who had spontaneously expressed it (with the simplicity of a woman from a village shop, labouring at the decoration of a street altar for some procession) by burying the bush in these little rosettes, almost too ravishing in colour, this rustic " pompadour ". High up on the branches, like so many of those tiny rose-

The Hawthorns

trees, their pots concealed in jackets of paper lace, whose slender stems rise in a forest from the altar on the greater festivals, a thousand buds were swelling and opening, paler in colour, but each disclosing as it burst, as at the bottom of a cup of pink marble, its blood-red stain, and suggesting even more strongly than the full-blown flowers the special, irresistible quality of the hawthorn-tree, which, wherever it budded, wherever it was about to blossom, could bud and blossom in pink flowers alone. Taking its place in the hedge, but as different from the rest as a young girl in holiday attire among a crowd of dowdy women in every-day clothes, who are staying at home, equipped and ready for the " Month of Mary ", of which it seemed already to form a part, it shone and smiled in its cool, rosy garments, a Catholic bush indeed, and altogether delightful.

MARCEL PROUST

PART NINE

WHAT makes us specially at home with the Greeks is that they made their world their home ; the common spirit of homeliness unites us both. In ordinary life we like best the men and families that are homely and contented in themselves, not desiring what is outside and above them, and so it is with the Greeks. They certainly received the substantial beginnings of their religion, culture, their common bonds of fellowship, more or less from Asia, Syria and Egypt ; but they have so greatly obliterated the foreign nature of this origin, and it is so much changed, worked upon, turned round, and altogether made so different, that what they, as we, prize, know, and love in it, is essentially their own. For this reason, in the history of Greek life, when we go further back and seem constrained so to go back, we find we may do without this retrogression and follow within the world and manners of the Greeks, the beginnings, the germination, and the progress of art and science up to their maturity, even seeing the origin of their decay—and this completely comprehended within their own range. For their spiritual development requires that which is received or foreign, as matter or stimulus only ; in such they have known and borne themselves as men that were free. The form which they have given to the foreign principle is this characteristic breath of spirituality, the spirit of freedom and of beauty which can in the one aspect be regarded as form, but which in another and higher sense is simply substance.

They have thus not only themselves created the substantial in their culture and made their existence their own, but they have also held in reverence this their spiritual rebirth, which is their real birth. The foreign origin they have, so to speak, thanklessly forgotten, putting it in the background—perhaps burying it in the darkness of the mysteries which they have kept secret from themselves. They have not only done this, that is they have not only used and enjoyed all that they have brought forth and formed, but they have become aware of and thankfully and joyfully placed before themselves this at-homeness (Heimathlichkeit) in their whole existence, the ground and origin of themselves, not merely existing in it, possessing and making use of it. For their mind, when transformed in this spiritual new birth, is just the living in their life, and also the becoming conscious of that life as it has become actual. They represent their existence as an object apart from themselves, which manifests itself independently and which in its independence is of value to them ; hence they have made for themselves a history of everything which they have possessed and have been. Not only have they represented the beginning of the world—that is, of gods and men, the earth, the heavens, the wind, mountains and rivers—but also of all aspects of their existence, such as the introduction of fire and the offerings connected with it, the crops, agriculture, the olive, the horse, marriage, property, laws, arts, worship, the sciences, towns, princely races, etc. Of all these it is pleasingly represented through tales how they have arisen in history as their own work.

It is in this veritable homeliness, or, more accurately, in the spirit of homeliness, in this spirit of ideally being-at-home-with-themselves in their physical, corporate, legal,

The World of Thought

moral and political existence ; it is in the beauty and the freedom of their character in history, making what they are to be also a sort of Mnemosyne with them, that the kernel of thinking liberty rests ; and hence it was requisite that Philosophy should arise amongst them. Philosophy is being at home with self, just like the homeliness of the Greek ; it is man's being at home in his mind, at home with himself. If we are at home with the Greeks, we must be at home more particularly in their Philosophy ; not, however, simply as it is with them, for Philosophy is at home with itself, and we have to do with Thought, with what is most specially ours, and with what is free from all particularity. The development and unfolding of thought has taken place with them from its earliest beginning, and in order to comprehend their Philosophy we may remain with them without requiring to seek for further and external influences.

But we must specify more particularly their character and point of view. The Greeks have a starting-point in history as truly as they have arisen from out of themselves : this starting-point, comprehended in thought, is the oriental substantiality of the natural unity between the spiritual and the natural. To start from the self, to live in the self, is the other extreme of abstract subjectivity, when it is still empty, or rather has made itself to be empty ; such is pure formalism, the abstract principle of the modern world. The Greeks stand between both these extremes in the happy medium ; this therefore is the medium of beauty, seeing that it is both natural and spiritual, but yet that the spiritual still remains the governing, determining subject. Mind immersed in nature is in substantial unity with it, and in so far as it is consciousness, it is essentially sensuous perception : as subjective consciousness it is certainly form-giving, though it is devoid of measure. For the Greeks, the substantial unity of nature and spirit was a fundamental principle, and thus being in the possession and knowledge of this, yet not being overwhelmed in it, but having retired into themselves, they have avoided the extreme of formal subjectivity, and are still in unity with themselves. Thus it is a free subject which still possesses that original unity in content, essence and substratum, and fashions its object into beauty. The stage reached by Greek consciousness is the stage of beauty. For beauty is the ideal ; it is the thought which is derived from Mind, but in such a way that the spiritual individuality is not yet explicit as abstract subjectivity that has then in itself to perfect its existence into a world of thought. What is natural and sensuous still pertains to this subjectivity, but yet the natural form has not equal dignity and rank with the other, nor is it predominant as is the case in the East. The principle of the spiritual now stands first in rank, and natural existence has no further value for itself, in its existent forms, being the mere expression of the Mind shining through, and having been reduced to be the vehicle and form of its existence. Mind, however, has not yet got itself as a medium whereby it can represent itself in itself, and from which it can form its world.

Thus free morality could and necessarily did find a place in Greece, for the spiritual substance of freedom was here the principle of morals, laws and constitutions.. Because the natural element is, however, still contained in it, the form taken by the morality of the state is still affected by what is natural ; the states are small individuals in their natural condition, which could not unite themselves into one whole. Since the universal does not exist in independent freedom, that which is spiritual still is limited. In the Greek world what is potentially and actually eternal is realized and brought to consciousness through Thought ; but in such a way that subjectivity confronts it in a determination which is still accidental, because it is still essentially related to what is natural ; and in this we find the reason as promised above, for the fact that in Greece the few alone are free.

The measureless quality of substance in the East is brought, by means of the Greek mind, into what is measureable and limited ; it is clearness, aim, limitation of forms, the reduction of what is measureless, and of infinite splendour and riches, to determinateness and individuality. The riches of the Greek world consist only of an infinite quantity of beautiful, lovely and pleasing individualities in the serenity which pervades all existence ; those who are greatest among the Greeks are the individualities—the connoisseurs in art, poetry, song, science, integrity and virtue. If the serenity of the Greeks, their beautiful gods, statues, and temples, as well as their serious work, their institutions and acts, may seem—compared to the splendour and sublimity, the colossal forms of oriental imagination, the Egyptian buildings of Eastern kingdoms—to be like child's play, this is the case yet more with the thought that comes into existence here. Such thought puts a limit on this wealth of individualities as on the oriental greatness, and reduces it into its one simple soul, which, however, is in itself the first source of the opulence of a higher ideal world, of the world of Thought.

GEORG WILHELM FRIEDRICH HEGEL

200 *The Last Journey*

THERE is another question, which will probably throw light on our present enquiry if you and I can agree about it : Ought the philosopher to care about the pleasures— if they are to be called pleasures—of eating and drinking ?

Certainly not, answered Simmias.

The Knapsack

And what about the pleasures of love—should he care for them?

By no means.

And will he think much of the other ways of indulging the body, for example, the acquisition of costly raiment, or sandals, or other adornments of the body? Instead of caring about them, does he not rather despise anything more than nature needs? What do you say?

I should say that the true philosopher would despise them.

Would you not say that he is entirely concerned with the soul and not with the body? He would like, as far as he can, to get away from the body and to turn to the soul.

Quite true.

In matters of this sort philosophers, above all other men, may be observed in every sort of way to dissever the soul from the communion of the body.

Very true.

Whereas, Simmias, the rest of the world are of opinion that to him who has no sense of pleasure and no part in bodily pleasure, life is not worth having; and that he who is indifferent about them is as good as dead.

That is also true.

What again shall we say of the actual acquirement of knowledge?—is the body, if invited to share in the enquiry, a hinderer or a helper? I mean to say, have sight and hearing any truth in them? Are they not, as the poets are always telling us, inaccurate witnesses? and yet, if even they are inaccurate and indistinct, what is to be said of the other senses?—for you will allow that they are the best of them?

Certainly, he replied.

Then when does the oul attain truth?—for in attempting to consider anything in company with the body she is obviously deceived.

The Last Journey

True.

Then must not true existence be revealed to her in thought, if at all?

Yes.

And thought is best when the mind is gathered into herself and none of these things trouble her—neither sounds nor sights nor pain nor any pleasure,—when she takes leave of the body, and has as little as possible to do with it, when she has no bodily sense or desire, but is aspiring after true being?

Certainly.

And in this the philosopher dishonours the body; his soul runs away from his body and desires to be alone and by herself?

That is true.

Well, but there is another thing, Simmias: Is there or is there not an absolute justice?

Assuredly there is.

And an absolute beauty and absolute good?

Of course.

But did you ever behold any of them with your eyes?

Certainly not.

Or did you ever reach them with any other bodily sense?—and I speak not of these alone, but of absolute greatness, and health, and strength, and of the essence or true nature of everything. Has the reality of them ever been perceived by you through the bodily organs? or rather, is not the nearest approach to the knowledge of their several natures made by him who so orders his intellectual vision as to have the most exact conception of the essence of each thing which he considers?

Certainly.

And he attains to the purest knowledge of them who goes to each with the mind alone, not introducing or intruding in the act of thought sight or any other sense together with reason, but with the very light of the mind in her own clearness searches into the very truth of each ; he who has got rid, as far as he can, of eyes and ears and, so to speak, of the whole body, these being in his opinion distracting elements which when they infect the soul hinder her from acquiring truth and knowledge—who, if not he, is likely to attain to the knowledge of true being ?

What you say has a wonderful truth in it, Socrates, replied Simmias.

And when real philosophers consider all these things, will they not be led to make a reflection which they will express in words something like the following ? " Have we not found ", they will say, " a path of thought which seems to bring us and our argument to the conclusion, that while we are in the body, and while the soul is infected with the evils of the body, our desire will not be satisfied ? and our desire is of the truth. For the body is a source of endless trouble to us by reason of the mere requirement of food ; and is liable also to diseases which overtake and impede us in the search after true being : it fills us full of loves, and lusts, and fears, and fancies of all kinds, and endless foolery, and in fact, as men say, takes away from us the power of thinking at all. Whence come wars, and fightings, and factions ? whence but from the body and the lusts of the body ? Wars are occasioned by the love of money, and money has to be acquired for the sake and in the service of the body ; and by reason of all these impediments we have no time to give to philosophy ; and, last and worst of all, even if we are at leisure and betake ourselves to some speculation, the body is always breaking in upon us, causing turmoil and confusion in our enquiries, and so amazing us that we are prevented from seeing the truth. It has been proved to us by experience that if we would have pure

The Last Journey

knowledge of anything we must be quit of the body—the soul in herself must behold things in themselves; and then we shall attain the wisdom which we desire, and of which we say that we are lovers; not while we live, but after death; for if while in company with the body, the soul cannot have pure knowledge, one of two things follows—either knowledge is not to be attained at all, or, if at all, after death. For then, and not till then, the soul will be parted from the body and exist in herself alone. In this present life, I reckon that we make the nearest approach to knowledge when we have the least possible intercourse or communion with the body, and are not surfeited with the bodily nature, but keep ourselves pure until the hour when God himself is pleased to release us. And thus having got rid of the foolishness of the body we shall be pure and hold converse with the pure, and know of ourselves the clear light everywhere, which is no other than the light of truth." For the impure are not permitted to approach the pure. These are the sort of words, Simmias, which the true lovers of knowledge cannot help saying to one another and thinking. You would agree; would you not?

Undoubtedly, Socrates.

But, O my friend, if this be true, there is great reason to hope that, going whither I go, when I have come to the end of my journey, I shall attain that which has been the pursuit of my life. And therefore I go on my way rejoicing, and not I only, but every other man who believes that his mind has been made ready and that he is in a manner purified.

Certainly, replied Simmias.

And what is purification but the separation of the soul from the body, as I was saying before; the habit of the soul gathering and collecting herself into herself from all sides out of the body; the dwelling in her own place alone, as in another life, so also in this, as far as she can—the release of the soul from the chains of the body?

Very true, he said.

And this separation and release of the soul from the body is termed death?

To be sure, he said.

And the true philosophers, and they only, are ever seeking to release the soul. Is not the separation and release of the soul from the body their especial study?

That is true.

And, as I was saying at first, there would be a ridiculous contradiction in men studying to live as nearly as they can in a state of death, and yet repining when it comes upon them.

Clearly.

And the true philosophers, Simmias, are always occupied in the practice of dying, wherefore also to them least of all men is death terrible. Look at the matter thus: if they have been in every way the enemies of the body, and are wanting to be alone with the soul, when this desire of theirs is granted, how inconsistent would they be if they trembled and repined, instead of rejoicing at their departure to that place where, when they arrive, they hope to gain that which in life they desired—and this was wisdom—and at the same time to be rid of the company of their enemy. Many a man has been willing to go to the world below animated by the hope of seeing there an earthly love, or wife, or son, and conversing with them. And will he who is a true lover of wisdom, and is strongly persuaded in like manner that only in the world below he can worthily enjoy her, still repine at death? Will he not depart with joy? Surely he will, O my friend, if he be a true philosopher. For he will have a firm conviction that there, and there only, he can find wisdom in her purity. And if this be true, he would be very absurd, as I was saying, if he were afraid of death.

He would indeed, replied Simmias.

And when you see a man who is repining at the approach of death, is not his reluctance a sufficient proof that he is not a lover of wisdom, but a lover of the body, and probably at the same time a lover of either money or power, or both?

Quite so, he replied.

And is not courage, Simmias, a quality which is specially characteristic of the philosopher?

Certainly.

There is temperance again, which even by the vulgar is supposed to consist in the control and regulation of the passions, and in the sense of superiority to them— is not temperance a virtue belonging to those only who despise the body, and who pass their lives in philosophy?

Most assuredly.

For the courage and temperance of other men, if you will consider them, are really a contradiction.

How so?

Well, he said, you are aware that death is regarded by men in general as a great evil.

Very true, he said.

And do not courageous men face death because they are afraid of yet greater evils?

That is quite true.

Then all but the philosophers are courageous only from fear, and because they are afraid; and yet that a man should be courageous from fear, and because he is a coward, is surely a strange thing.

Very true.

And are not the temperate exactly in the same case? They are temperate because they are intemperate— which might seem to be a contradiction, but is nevertheless the sort of thing which happens with this foolish temperance. For there are pleasures which they are afraid of losing ; and in their desire to keep them, they abstain from some pleasures, because they are overcome by others ; and although to be conquered by pleasure is called by men intemperance, to them the conquest of pleasure consists in being conquered by pleasure. And that is what I mean by saying that, in a sense, they are made temperate through intemperance.

Such appears to be the case.

Yet the exchange of one fear or pleasure or pain for another fear or pleasure or pain, and of the greater for the less, as if they were coins, is not the exchange of virtue. O my blessed Simmias, is there not one true coin for which all things ought to be exchanged ?—and that is wisdom ; and only in exchange for this, and in company with this, is anything truly bought or sold, whether courage or temperance or justice. And is not all true virtue the companion of wisdom, no matter what fears or pleasures or other similar goods or evils may or may not attend her ? But the virtue which is made up of these goods, when they are severed from wisdom and exchanged with one another, is a shadow of virtue only, nor is there any freedom or health or truth in her ; but in the true exchange there is a purging away of all these things, and temperance, and justice, and courage, and wisdom herself are the purgation of them. The founders of the mysteries would appear to have had a real meaning, and were not talking nonsense when they intimated in a figure long ago that he who passes unsanctified and uninitiated into the world below will lie in a slough, but that he who arrives there after initiation and purification will dwell with the gods. For " many ", as they say in the mysteries, " are the thyrsus-bearers, but few are the mystics "—meaning, as I interpret the words, " the true philosophers ". In the number of whom, during my whole life, I have been seeking, according to my ability, to find a place—whether I have sought in a right way or not, and whether I have succeeded or not, I shall truly know in a little while, if God will, when I myself arrive in the other world—such is my belief. And therefore I maintain that I am right, Simmias and Cebes, in not grieving or repining at parting from you and my masters in this world, for I believe that I shall equally find good masters and friends in another world. But most men do not believe this saying ; if then I succeed in convincing you by my defence better than I did the Athenian judges, it will be well.

PLATO : *Phædo*

201 *The Kingdom of Heaven*

THE day now approaching that she was to depart this life, (which day thou well knewest, though we were not aware of it) it fell out, thyself, as I believe, by thine own secret ways so casting it, that she and I should stand alone leaning in a certain window, which looked into the garden within the house where we now lay, at Ostia by Tiber ; where being sequestered from company after the wearisomeness of a long journey, we were recruiting ourselves for a sea voyage. There conferred we hand to hand very sweetly ; and forgetting those things which are behind, we reached forth unto those things which are before : we did betwixt ourselves seek at that Present Truth (which thou art) in what manner the eternal life of the saints was to be, which eye hath not seen, nor ear heard, nor hath it entered into the heart of man. But yet we panted with the mouth of our heart after those upper streams of thy fountain, the fountain of life ; that being besprinkled with it according to our capacity, we might in some sort meditate upon so high a mystery.

And when our discourse was once come unto that point, that the highest pleasure of the carnal senses, and that in the brightest beam of material light, was, in respect of the sweetness of that life, not only not worthy of comparison, but not so much as of mention ; we cheering up ourselves with a more burning affection towards that Self-same, did by degrees course over all these corporeals, even the heaven itself, from whence both sun, and moon, and stars do shine upon this earth. Yea, we soared higher yet, by inward musing, and discoursing upon thee, and by admiring of thy works ; and last of all, we came to our own souls, which we presently went beyond, so that we advanced as high as that region of never-wasting plenty, whence thou feedest Israel for ever with the food of truth, and where life is that wisdom by which all these things are made, both which have been, and which are to come. And this wisdom is not made ; but it is at this present, as it hath ever been, and so shall it ever be : nay rather the terms to have been, and to be hereafter, are not at all in it, but to be now, for that it is eternal : for to have been, and to be about to be, is not eternal. And while we were thus discoursing and panting after it, we arrived to a little touch of it with the whole effort of our heart ; and we sighed, and even there we left behind us the first fruits of our spirits enchained unto it ; returning from these thoughts to vocal expressions of our mouth, where a word has both beginning and ending. How unlike unto thy Word, our Lord, who remains in himself for ever without becoming aged, and yet renewing all things ?

We said therefore : If to any man the tumults of flesh be silenced, if fancies of the earth, and waters, and air be silenced also : if the poles of heaven be silent also : if the very soul be silent to herself, and by not thinking upon

The Kingdom of Heaven

self surmount self : if all dreams and imaginary revelations
be silenced, every tongue, and every sign, if whatsoever is
transient be silent to any one—since if any man could
hearken unto them, all these say unto him, We created not
ourselves, but he that remains to all eternity : if then,
having uttered this, they also be then silent, (as having
raised our ear unto him that made them) and if he speak
alone ; not by them but by himself, that we may hear his
own word ; not pronounced by any tongue of flesh, nor
by the voice of the angels, nor by the sound of thunder, nor
in the dark riddle of a resemblance ; but that we may
hear him whom we love in these creatures, himself without
these (like as we two now strained up ourselves unto it,
and in swift thought arrived unto a touch of that eternal
Wisdom, which is over all) : could this exaltation of spirit
have ever continued, and all other visions of a far other
kind been quite taken away, and that this one exaltation
should ravish us, and swallow us up, and so wrap up their
beholder among these more inward joys, as that his life
might be for ever like to this very moment of understanding
which we now sighed after : were not this as much as
Enter into thy Master's joy ? But when shall that be ?
Shall it be when we shall all rise again, though all shall
not be changed ?

Such discourse we then had, and though not precisely
after this manner, and in these selfsame words ; yet, Lord,
thou knowest, that in that day when we thus talked of these
things, that this world with all its delights grew contemptible to us, even as we were speaking of it.   Then said my
mother : Son, for mine own part I have delight in nothing
in this life.   What I should here do any longer, and to
what end I am here, I know not, now that my hopes in
this world are vanished.   There was indeed one thing
for which I sometimes desired to be a little while reprieved
in this life ; namely, that I might see thee to become a

Christian Catholic before I died. My God hath done this for me more abundantly ; for that I now see thee withal having contemned all earthly happiness, to be made his servant : what then do I here any longer ?

St. Augustine

202 *The Exhortations of Father Zossima*

Young man, be not forgetful of prayer. Every time you pray, if your prayer is sincere, there will be new feeling and new meaning in it, which will give you fresh courage, and you will understand that prayer is an education. Remember too, every day, and whenever you can, repeat to yourself, " Lord, have mercy on all who appear before Thee to-day." For every hour and every moment thousands of men leave life on this earth, and their souls appear before God. And how many of them depart in solitude, unknown, sad, dejected, that no one mourns for them or even knows whether they have lived or not. And behold, from the other end of the earth perhaps, your prayer for their rest will rise up to God though you knew them not nor they you. How touching it must be to a soul standing in dread before the Lord to feel at that instant that, for him too, there is one to pray, that there is a fellow creature left on earth to love him too. And God will look on you both more graciously, for if you have had so much pity on him, how much more will He have pity Who is infinitely more loving and merciful than you. And He will forgive him for your sake.

Brothers, have no fear of men's sin. Love a man even in his sin, for that is the semblance of Divine Love and is the highest love on earth. Love all God's creation, the whole and every grain of sand in it. Love every leaf,

550

every ray of God's light. Love the animals, love the plants, love everything. If you love everything, you will perceive the divine mystery in things. Once you perceive it, you will begin to comprehend it better every day. And you will come at last to love the whole world with an all-embracing love. Love the animals : God has given them the rudiments of thought and joy untroubled. Do not trouble it, don't harass them, don't deprive them of their happiness, don't work against God's intent. Man, do not pride yourself on superiority to the animals ; they are without sin, and you, with your greatness, defile the earth by your appearance on it, and leave the traces of your foulness after you—alas, it is true of almost every one of us ! Love children especially, for they too are sinless like the angels ; they live to soften and purify our hearts and as it were to guide us. Woe to him who offends a child ! Father Anfim taught me to love children. The kind, silent man used often on our wanderings to spend the farthings given us on sweets and cakes for the children. He could not pass by a child without emotion, that's the nature of the man.

At some thoughts one stands perplexed, especially at the sight of men's sin, and wonders whether one should use force or humble love. Always decide to use humble love. If you resolve on that once for all, you may subdue the whole world. Loving humility is marvellously strong, the strongest of all things and there is nothing else like it.

Every day and every hour, every minute, walk round yourself and watch yourself, and see that your image is a seemly one. You pass by a little child, you pass by, spiteful, with ugly words, with wrathful heart ; you may not have noticed the child, but he has seen you, and your image, unseemly and ignoble, may remain in his defenceless heart. You don't know it, but you may have sown an evil seed in him and it may grow, and all because you were not careful before the child, because you did not foster in yourself a careful, actively benevolent love. Brothers, love is a teacher ; but one must know how to acquire it, for it is hard to acquire, it is dearly bought, it is won slowly by long labour. For we must love not only occasionally, for a moment, but for ever. Every one can love occasionally, even the wicked can.

My brother asked the birds to forgive him ; that sounds senseless, but it is right ; for all is like an ocean, all is flowing and blending ; a touch in one place sets up movement at the other end of the earth. It may be senseless to beg forgiveness of the birds, but birds would be happier at your side—a little happier, anyway—and children and all animals, if you yourself were nobler than you are now. It's all like an ocean, I tell you. Then you would pray to the birds too, consumed by an all-embracing love, in a sort of transport, and pray that they too will forgive you your sin. Treasure this ecstasy, however senseless it may seem to men.

My friends, pray to God for gladness. Be glad as children, as the birds of heaven. And let not the sin of men confound you in your doings. Fear not that it will wear away your work and hinder its being accomplished. Do not say, " Sin is mighty, wickedness is mighty, evil environment is mighty, and we are lonely and helpless, and evil environment is wearing us away and hindering our good work from being done." Fly from that dejection, children ! There is only one means of salvation, then take yourself and make yourself responsible for all men's sins, that is the truth, you know, friends, for as soon as you sincerely make yourself responsible for everything and for all men, you will see at once that it is really so, and that you are to blame for every one and for all things. But throwing your own indolence and impotence on others you will end by sharing the pride of Satan and murmuring against God.

Of the pride of Satan what I think is this : it is hard for us on earth to comprehend it, and therefore it is so easy to fall into error and to share it, even imagining that we are doing something grand and fine. Indeed many of the strongest feelings and movements of our nature we cannot comprehend on earth. Let not that be a stumbling-block, and think not that it may serve as a justification to you for anything. For the Eternal Judge asks of you what you can comprehend and not what you cannot. You will know that yourself hereafter, for you will behold all things truly then and will not dispute them. On earth, indeed, we are as it were astray, and if it were not for the precious image of Christ before us, we should be undone and altogether lost, as was the human race before the flood. Much on earth is hidden from us, but to make up for that we have been given a precious mystic sense of our living bond with the other world, with the higher heavenly world, and the roots of our thoughts and feelings are not here but in other worlds. That is why the philosophers say that we cannot apprehend the reality of things on earth.

God took seeds from different worlds and sowed them on this earth, and His garden grew up and everything came up that could come up, but what grows lives and is alive only through the feeling of its contact with other mysterious worlds. If that feeling grows weak or is destroyed in you, the heavenly growth will die away in you. Then you will be indifferent to life and even grow to hate it. That's what I think.

Remember particularly that you cannot be a judge of any one. For no one can judge a criminal, until he recognizes that he is just such a criminal as the man standing before him, and that he perhaps is more than all men to blame for that crime. When he understands that, he

The Knapsack

will be able to be a judge. Though that sounds absurd, it is true. If I had been righteous myself, perhaps there would have been no criminal standing before me. If you can take upon yourself the crime of the criminal your heart is judging, take it at once, suffer for him yourself, and let him go without reproach. And even if the law itself makes you his judge, act in the same spirit so far as possible, for he will go away and condemn himself more bitterly than you have done. If, after your kiss, he goes away untouched, mocking at you, do not let that be a stumbling-block to you. It shows his time has not yet come, but it will come in due course. And if it come not, no matter ; if not he, then another in his place will understand and suffer, and judge and condemn himself, and the truth will be fulfilled. Believe that, believe it without doubt ; for in that lies all the hope and faith of the saints.

Work without ceasing. If you remember in the night as you go to sleep, " I have not done what I ought to have done," rise up at once and do it. If the people around you are spiteful and callous and will not hear you, fall down before them and beg their forgiveness ; for in truth you are to blame for their not wanting to hear you. And if you cannot speak to them in their bitterness, serve them in silence and in humility, never losing hope. If all men abandon you and even drive you away by force, then when you are left alone fall on the earth and kiss it, water it with your tears and it will bring forth fruit even though no one has seen or heard you in your solitude. Believe to the end, even if all men went astray and you were left the only one faithful ; bring your offering even then and praise God in your loneliness. And if two of you are gathered together—then there is a whole world, a world of living love. Embrace each other tenderly and praise God, for if only in you two His truth has been fulfilled.

The Exhortations of Father Zossima

If you sin yourself and grieve even unto death for your sins or for your sudden sin, then rejoice for others, rejoice for the righteous man, rejoice that if you have sinned, he is righteous and has not sinned.

If the evil doing of men moves you to indignation and overwhelming distress, even to a desire for vengeance on the evil-doers, shun above all things that feeling. Go at once and seek suffering for yourself, as though you were yourself guilty of that wrong. Accept that suffering and bear it and your heart will find comfort, and you will understand that you too are guilty, for you might have been a light to the evil-doers, even as the one man sinless, and you were not a light to them. If you had been a light, you would have lightened the path for others too, and the evil-doer might perhaps have been saved by your light from his sin. And even though your light was shining, yet you see men were not saved by it, hold firm and doubt not the power of the heavenly light. Believe that if they were not saved, they will be saved hereafter. And if they are not saved hereafter, then their sons will be saved, for your light will not die even when you are dead. The righteous man departs, but his light remains. Men are always saved after the death of the deliverer. Men reject their prophets and slay them, but they love their martyrs and honour those whom they have slain. You are working for the whole, you are acting for the future. Seek no reward, for great is your reward on this earth : the spiritual joy which is only vouchsafed to the righteous man. Fear not the great nor the mighty, but be wise and ever serene. Know the measure, know the times, study that. When you are left alone, pray. Love to throw yourself on the earth and kiss it. Kiss the earth and love it with an unceasing, consuming love. Love all men, love everything. Seek that rapture and ecstasy. Water the earth with the tears of your joy and love those tears. Don't be ashamed of that ecstasy, prize it, for it is a gift of God and a great one ; it is not given to many but only to the elect.

FYODOR DOSTOEVSKY

203 *Enjoyment of the World*

YOUR enjoyment of the world is never right, till you so esteem it, that everything in it, is more your treasure than a King's exchequer full of gold and silver. And that exchequer yours also in its place and service. Can you take too much joy in your Father's works ? He is Himself in everything. Some things are little on the outside, and rough and common, but I remember the time when the dust of the streets were as precious as gold to my infant eyes, and now they are more precious to the eye of reason.

The services of things and their excellencies are spiritual : being objects not of the eye, but of the mind : and you more spiritual by how much more you esteem them. Pigs eat acorns, but neither consider the sun that gave them life, nor the influences of the heavens by which they were nourished, nor the very root of the tree from whence they came. This being the work of Angels, who in a wide and clear light see even the sea that gave them moisture : And feed upon that acorn spiritually while they know the ends for which it was created, and feast upon all these as upon a world of joys within it : while to ignorant swine that eat the shell, it is an empty husk of no taste nor delightful savour.

You never enjoy the world aright, till you see how a sand exhibiteth the wisdom and power of God : And prize in everything the service which they do you, by manifesting His glory and goodness to your Soul, far more

Enjoyment of the World

than the visible beauty on their surface, or the material services they can do your body. Wine by its moisture quencheth my thirst, whether I consider it or no : but to see it flowing from His love who gave it unto man, quencheth the thirst even of the Holy Angels. To consider it, is to drink it spiritually. To rejoice in its diffusion is to be of a public mind. And to take pleasure in all the benefits it doth to all is Heavenly, for so they do in Heaven. To do so, is to be divine and good, and to imitate our Infinite and Eternal Father.

Your enjoyment of the world is never right, till every morning you awake in Heaven ; see yourself in your Father's Palace ; and look upon the skies, the earth, and the air as Celestial Joys : having such a reverend esteem of all, as if you were among the Angels. The bride of a monarch, in her husband's chamber, hath no such causes of delight as you.

You never enjoy the world aright, till the Sea itself floweth in your veins, till you are clothed with the heavens, and crowned with the stars : and perceive yourself to be the sole heir of the whole world, and more than so, because men are in it who are every one sole heirs as well as you. Till you can sing and rejoice and delight in God, as misers do in gold, and Kings in sceptres, you never enjoy the world.

Till your spirit filleth the whole world, and the stars are your jewels ; till you are as familiar with the ways of God in all Ages as with your walk and table : till you are intimately acquainted with that shady nothing out of which the world was made : till you love men so as to desire their happiness, with a thirst equal to the zeal of your own ; till you delight in God for being good to all : you never enjoy the world. Till you more feel it than your private estate, and are more present in the hemisphere, considering the glories and the beauties there, than in your own house : Till you remember how lately you were made, and how wonderful it was when you came into it : and more rejoice in the palace of your glory, than if it had been made but to-day morning.

Yet further, you never enjoy the world aright, till you so love the beauty of enjoying it, that you are covetous and earnest to persuade others to enjoy it. And so perfectly hate the abominable corruption of men in despising it, that you had rather suffer the flames of Hell than willingly be guilty of their error. There is so much blindness and ingratitude and damned folly in it. The world is a mirror of infinite beauty, yet no man sees it. It is a Temple of Majesty, yet no man regards it. It is a region of Light and Peace, did not men disquiet it. It is the Paradise of God. It is more to man since he is fallen than it was before. It is the place of Angels and the Gate of Heaven. When Jacob waked out of his dream, he said, " *God is here, and I wist it not. How dreadful is this place ! This is none other than the House of God, and the Gate of Heaven.*"

THOMAS TRAHERNE

204 *A Life of Sensations*

I AM certain of nothing but of the holiness of the Heart's affections and the truth of Imagination—What the imagination seizes as Beauty must be truth—whether it existed before or not—for I have the same Idea of all our Passions as of Love, they are all in their sublime, creative of essential Beauty. In a Word, you may know my favourite Speculation by my first Book and the little song I sent in my last—which is a representation from the fancy of the probable mode of operating in these Matters. The Imagination may be compared to Adam's

A Life of Sensations

dream—he awoke and found it truth. I am the more zealous in this affair, because I have never yet been able to perceive how anything can be known for truth by consequitive reasoning—and yet it must be. Can it be that even the greatest Philosopher ever arrived at his goal without putting aside numerous objections. However it may be, O for a Life of Sensations rather than of Thoughts ! It is " a Vision in the form of Youth " a Shadow of reality to come—and this consideration has further convinced me for it has come as auxiliary to another favourite Speculation of mine, that we shall enjoy ourselves hereafter by having what we called happiness on Earth repeated in a finer tone and so repeated. And yet such a fate can only befall those who delight in Sensation rather than hunger as you do after Truth. Adam's dream will do here and seems to be a conviction that Imagination and its empyreal reflection is the same as human Life and its Spiritual repetition. But as I was saying—the simple imaginative Mind may have its rewards in the repetition of its own silent Working coming continually on the Spirit with a fine Suddenness—to compare great things with small—have you never by being Surprised with an old Melody—in a delicious place—by a delicious voice, felt over again your very Speculations and Surmises at the time it first operated on your Soul—do you not remember forming to yourself the singer's face more beautiful than it was possible and yet with the elevation of the Moment you did not think so—even then you were mounted on the Wings of Imagination so high— that the Prototype must be here after—that delicious face you will see. What a time ! I am continually running away from the subject—sure this cannot be exactly the case with a complex Mind—one that is imaginative and at the same time careful of its fruits—who would exist partly on Sensation partly on thought—to whom it is necessary that years should bring the philosophic Mind—such an one I consider yours and therefore it is necessary to your eternal Happiness that you not only drink this old Wine of Heaven, which I shall call the redigestion of our most ethereal Musings on Earth ; but also increase in knowledge and know all things. . . . You perhaps at one time thought there was such a thing as Worldly Happiness to be arrived at, at certain periods of time marked out—you have of necessity from your disposition been thus led away—I scarcely remember counting upon any Happiness—I look not for it if it be not in the present hour—nothing startles me beyond the Moment. The setting Sun will always set me to rights—or if a Sparrow come before my Window I take part in its existence and pick about the Gravel. The first thing that strikes me on hearing a Misfortune having befalled [sic] another is this—" Well, it cannot be helped—he will have the pleasure of trying the resources of his spirit "—and I beg now my dear Bailey that hereafter should you observe anything cold in me not to put it to the account of heartlessness but abstraction—for I assure you I sometimes feel not the influence of a Passion or affection during a whole week—and so long this sometimes continues I begin to suspect myself and the genuineness of my feelings at other times—thinking them a few barren Tragedy Tears.

JOHN KEATS

205 *The Foundation of Happiness*

AFTER experience had taught me that the things which commonly take place in ordinary life are vain and futile : when I saw that all the things which caused me fear or anxiety had nothing good or bad in them save in so far

The Foundation of Happiness

as the mind was affected by them, I determined at last to inquire whether there might be anything which might be truly good and able to communicate its goodness, and by which the mind might be affected to the exclusion of all other things : I determined, I say, to inquire whether there existed anything through the discovery and acquisition of which I might enjoy continual supreme happiness throughout eternity.

I say " I determined at last ", for at the first sight it seemed ill advised to lose what was certain in the hope of attaining what was uncertain. I could see the many advantages which accrue from honour and riches, and that I should be debarred from acquiring these things if I wished seriously to investigate a new matter; and if perchance supreme happiness was in one of these I should lose it ; if, on the other hand, it were not placed in them and I gave them the whole of my attention, then also I should be wanting in it.

I therefore turned over in my mind whether it might be possible to arrive at this new principle, or at least at the certainty of its existence, without changing the order and common plan of my life : a thing which I had often attempted in vain. For the things which most often happen in life and are esteemed by men as the highest good of all, as may be gathered from their works, can be reduced to these three headings : to wit, Riches (*divitiæ*), Fame (*honor*), and Pleasure (*libido*). With these three the mind is so engrossed that it can scarcely think of any other good.

As for pleasure, the mind is so engrossed in it that it remains in a state of quiescence as if it had attained supreme good, and this prevents it from thinking of anything else. But after that enjoyment follows sadness, which, if it does not hold the mind suspended, disturbs and dullens it. The pursuit of fame and riches also distracts the mind not a little, more especially when they are sought for their own

The Knapsack

sake, inasmuch as they are thought to be the greatest good.

By fame the mind is far more distracted, for it is supposed to be always good in itself, and as an ultimate aim to which all things must be directed. Again, there is not in these, as there is in pleasure, repentance subsequently, but the more one possesses of either of them, the more the pleasure is increased and consequently the more one is encouraged to increase them ; but, on the other hand, if at any time our hope is frustrated, then there arises in us the deepest sorrow. Fame has also this great drawback, that if we pursue it we must direct our lives in such a way as to please the fancy of men, avoiding what they dislike and seeking what is pleasing to them.

When I saw then that all these things stood in the way to prevent me from giving my attention to a search for something new, nay, that they were so opposed to it that one or the other had to be passed by, I was constrained to inquire which would be more useful to me ; for as I said, I seemed to wish to lose what was certain for what was uncertain. But after I had considered the matter for some time, I found in the first place that if I directed my attention to the new quest, abandoning the others, I should be abandoning a good uncertain in its nature, as we can easily gather from what has been said, to seek out a good uncertain not in its nature (for I was seeking a fixed good), but only uncertain in the possibility of success.

But by continuous consideration I came at last to see that if I could apply myself wholly to thought, I should then avoid a certain evil for a certain good. For I saw myself in the midst of a very great peril and obliged to seek a remedy, however uncertain, with all my energy : like a sick man seized with a deadly disease, who sees death straight before him if he does not find some remedy, is forced to seek it, however uncertain, with all his remain-

The Foundation of Happiness

ing strength, for in that is all his hope placed. But all those remedies which the vulgar follow not only avail nothing for our preservation, but even prevent it, and are often the cause of the death of those who possess them, and are always the cause of the death of those who are possessed by them.

For there are many examples of men who have suffered persecution even unto death for the sake of their riches, and also of men who, in order to amass wealth, have exposed themselves to so many perils that at last they have paid the penalty of death for their stupidity. Nor are the examples less numerous of those who have suffered in the most wretched manner to obtain or defend their honour. Finally, the examples are innumerable of those who have hastened death upon themselves by too great a desire for pleasure.

These evils seem to have arisen from the fact that the whole of happiness or unhappiness is dependent on this alone : on the quality of the object to which we are bound by love. For the sake of something which no one loves, strife never arises, there is no sorrow if it perishes, no envy if it is appropriated by some one else, nor fear, nor hatred, and, to put it all briefly, no commotions of the mind at all : for all these are consequences only of the love of those things which are perishable, such as those things of which we have just spoken.

But the love towards a thing eternal and infinite alone feeds the mind with pure joy, and it is free from all sorrow ; so it is much to be desired and to be sought out with all our might.

SPINOZA

206 *A Microcosm*

Now for my life, it is a miracle of thirty years, which to relate, were not a History, but a piece of Poetry, and would sound to common ears like a Fable. For the World, I count it not an Inn, but an Hospital ; and a place not to live, but to die in. The world that I regard is my self ; it is the Microcosm of my own frame that I cast mine eye on ; for the other, I use it but like my Globe, and turn it round sometimes for my recreation. Men that look upon my outside, perusing only my condition and Fortunes, do err in my Altitude ; for I am above Atlas his shoulders. The earth is a point not only in respect of the Heavens above us, but of that heavenly and celestial part within us ; that mass of Flesh that circumscribes me, limits not my mind : that surface that tells the Heavens it hath an end, cannot persuade me I have any : I take my circle to be above three hundred and sixty ; though the number of the Ark do measure my body, it comprehendeth not my mind : whilst I study to find how I am a Microcosm, or little World, I find my self something more than the great. There is surely a piece of Divinity in us, something that was before the Elements, and owes no homage unto the Sun. Nature tells me I am the Image of GOD, as well as Scripture : he that understands not thus much, hath not his introduction or first lesson, and is yet to begin the Alphabet of man. Let me not injure the felicity of others, if I say I am as happy as any : *Ruat cœlum, fiat voluntas Tua,* salveth all ; so that whatsoever happens, it is but what our daily prayers desire. In brief, I am content ; and what should Providence add more ? Surely this is it we call Happiness, and this do I enjoy ; with this I am happy in a dream, and as content to enjoy a happiness in a fancy, as others in a more apparent truth and realty. There is surely a nearer apprehension of any thing that delights us in our dreams, than in our waked senses : without this I were unhappy ; for my awaked judgment discontents me, ever whispering unto me, that I am from my friend ; but my friendly dreams in the night requite me, and make me think I am within his arms. I thank GOD for my happy dreams, as I do for my good rest ; for there is a satisfaction in them unto reasonable desires, and such as can be content with a fit of happiness : and surely it is not a melancholy conceit to think we are all asleep in this World, and that the conceits of this life are as mere dreams to those of the next ; as the Phantasms of the night, to the conceits of the day. There is an equal delusion in both, and the one doth but seem to be the emblem or picture of the other : we are somewhat more than our selves in our sleeps, and the slumber of the body seems to be but the waking of the soul. It is the ligation of sense, but the liberty of reason ; and our waking conceptions do not match the Fancies of our sleeps. At my Nativity my Ascendant was the watery sign of Scorpius ; I was born in the Planetary hour of Saturn, and I think I have a piece of that Leaden Planet in me. I am no way facetious, nor disposed for the mirth and galliardize of company ; yet in one dream I can compose a whole Comedy, behold the action, apprehend the jests, and laugh my self awake at the conceits thereof. Were my memory as faithful as my reason is then fruitful, I would never study but in my dreams ; and this time also would I chuse for my devotions : but our grosser memories have then so little hold of our abstracted understandings, that they forget the story, and can only relate to our awaked souls, a confused and broken tale of that that hath passed. Aristotle, who hath written a singular Tract *Of Sleep*, hath not, methinks, throughly defined it ; nor yet Galen, though he seem to have corrected it ; for those Noctambuloes and night-walkers, though in their sleep, do yet injoy the action of their senses. We must therefore say that there is something in us that is not in the jurisdiction of Morpheus; and that those abstracted and ecstatick souls do walk about in their own corps, as spirits with the bodies they assume, wherein they seem to hear, see, and feel, though indeed the Organs are destitute of sense, and their natures of those faculties that should inform them. Thus it is observed, that men sometimes, upon the hour of their departure, do speak and reason above themselves; for then the soul, beginning to be freed from the ligaments of the body, begins to reason like her self, and to discourse in a strain above mortality.

SIR THOMAS BROWNE

207 *Foreigners*

TRUE Christians are little understood by the world because they are not of the world; and hence it sometimes happens that even the better sort of men are often disconcerted and vexed by them. . . . The immortality of truth, its oneness, the impossibility of falsehood coalescing with it, what truth is, what it should lead one to do in particular cases, how it lies in the details of life—all these points are mere matters of debate in the world, and men go through long processes of argument, and pride themselves on their subtleness in defending or attacking, in making probable or improbable, ideas which are assumed without a word by those who have lived in heaven as the very ground to start from. In consequence, such men are called bad disputants, inconsecutive reasoners, strange, eccentric, or perverse thinkers, merely because they do not take for granted, nor go to prove, what others do—because they do not go about to define and determine the sights (as it were), the mountains and rivers and plains, and sun, moon, and stars, of the next world. And hence in turn they are commonly unable to enter into the ways of thought or feelings of other men, having been engrossed with God's thoughts and God's ways. Hence, perhaps, they seem abrupt in what they say and do ; nay, even make others feel constrained and uneasy in their presence. Perhaps they appear reserved too, because they take so much for granted which might be drawn out, and because they cannot bring themselves to tell all their thoughts from their sacredness, and because they are drawn off from free conversation to the thought of heaven, on which their minds rest. Nay, perchance, they appear severe, because their motives are not understood, nor their sensitive jealousy for the honour of God and their charitable concern for the good of their fellow-Christians duly appreciated. In short, to the world they seem like *foreigners*. . . . Such is the effect of divine meditations : admitting us into the next world, and withdrawing us from this ; making us children of God, but withal " strangers unto our brethren, even aliens unto our mother's children ". Yea, though the true servants of God increase in meekness and love day by day, and to those who know them will seem what they really are ; and though their good works are evident to all men, and cannot be denied, yet such is the eternal law which goes between the Church and the world—we cannot be friends of both ; and they who take their portion with the Church, will seem, except in some remarkable cases, unamiable to the world, for the " world knoweth them not ", and does not like them though it can hardly tell why ; yet (as St. John proceeds) they have this blessing, that " when He shall appear, they shall be like Him, for they shall see Him as He is ".

JOHN HENRY NEWMAN

208 *Of Vicissitude of Things*

SOLOMON saith : *There is no new thing upon the earth.* So that as Plato had an imagination that *All knowledge was but remembrance,* so Solomon giveth his sentence that *All novelty is but oblivion.* Whereby you may see that the river of Lethe runneth as well above ground as below. There is an abstruse astrologer that saith : *If it were not for two things that are constant (the one is that the fixed stars ever stand at like distance one from another and never come nearer together, nor go further asunder ; the other that the diurnal motion perpetually keepeth time), no individual would last one moment.* Certain it is that the matter is in a perpetual flux and never at a stay. The great winding-sheets that bury all things in oblivion are two : deluges and earthquakes. As for conflagrations and great droughts, they do merely dispeople and destroy. Phaëton's car went but a day. And the three-years drought in the time of Elias was but particular, and left people alive. As for the great burnings by lightnings, which are often in the West Indies, they are but narrow. But, in the other two destructions by deluge and earthquake, it is further to be noted that the remnant of people which hap to be reserved are commonly ignorant and mountainous people, that can give no account of the time past ; so that the oblivion is all one as if none had been left. If you consider well of the people of the West Indies, it is very probable that they are a newer or a younger people than the people of the old world. And it is much more likely that the destruction that hath heretofore been there was not by earthquakes (as the Egyptian priest told Solon concerning the island of Atlantis, that *it was swallowed by an earthquake*), but rather that it was desolated by a particular deluge. For earthquakes are seldom in those parts. But on the other side they have such pouring rivers as the rivers of Asia and Africa and Europe are but brooks to

Of Vicissitude of Things

them. Their Andes likewise, or mountains, are far higher than those with us, whereby it seems that the remnants of generations of men were in such a particular deluge saved. As for the observation that Machiavel hath, that the jealousy of sects doth much extinguish the memory of things—traducing Gregory the Great that he did what in him lay to extinguish all heathen antiquities—I do not find that those zeals do any great effects, nor last long ; as it appeared in the succession of Sabinian, who did revive the former antiquities.

The vicissitude or mutations in the Superior Globe are no fit matter for this present argument. It may be Plato's great year, if the world should last so long, would have some effect, not in renewing the state of like individuals (for that is the fume of those that conceive the celestial bodies have more accurate influences upon these things below than indeed they have), but in gross. Comets, out of question, have likewise power and effect over the gross and mass of things ; but they are rather gazed upon, and waited upon in their journey, than wisely observed in their effects, specially in their respective effects ; that is, what kind of comet, for magnitude, colour, version of the beams, placing in the region of heaven, or lasting, produceth what kind of effects.

There is a toy which I have heard, and I would not have it given over, but waited upon a little. They say it is observed in the Low Countries (I know not in what part) that every five and thirty years the same kind and suit of years and weathers comes about again, as great frosts, great wet, great droughts, warm winters, summers with little heat, and the like ; and they call it the *Prime*. It is a thing I do the rather mention because, computing backwards, I have found some concurrence.

But to leave these points of nature, and to come to men. The greater vicissitude of things amongst men is the vicissitude of sects and religions. For those orbs rule in men's minds most. The true religion is *built upon the rock*; the rest are tossed upon the waves of time. To speak therefore of the causes of new sects, and to give some counsel concerning them, as far as the weakness of human judgment can give stay to so great revolutions.

When the religion formerly received is rent by discords, and when the holiness of the professors of religion is decayed and full of scandal, and withal the times be stupid, ignorant, and barbarous, you may doubt the springing up of a new sect, if then also there should arise any extravagant and strange spirit to make himself author thereof. All which points held when Mahomet published his law. If a new sect have not two properties, fear it not, for it will not spread. The one is the supplanting or the opposing of authority established, for nothing is more popular than that. The other is the giving licence to pleasures and a voluptuous life. For as for speculative heresies (such as were in ancient times the Arians and now the Arminians), though they work mightily upon men's wits, yet they do not produce any great alterations in States, except it be by the help of civil occasions. There be three manner of plantations of new sects. By the power of signs and miracles, by the eloquence and wisdom of speech and persuasion, and by the sword. For martyrdoms, I reckon them amongst miracles, because they seem to exceed the strength of human nature; and I may do the like of superlative and admirable holiness of life. Surely there is no better way to stop the rising of new sects and schisms than to reform abuses, to compound the smaller differences, to proceed mildly and not with sanguinary persecutions, and rather to take off the principal authors by winning and advancing them than to enrage them by violence and bitterness.

The changes and vicissitude in wars are many, but

Of Vicissitude of Things

chiefly in three things : in the seats or stages of the war, in the weapons, and in the manner of the conduct. Wars, in ancient time, seemed more to move from east to west, for the Persians, Assyrians, Arabians, Tartars (which were the invaders) were all eastern people. It is true the Gauls were western, but we read but of two incursions of theirs : the one to Gallo-Græcia, the other to Rome. But East and West have no certain points of heaven, and no more have the wars either from the east or west any certainty of observation. But North and South are fixed, and it hath seldom or never been seen that the far southern people have invaded the northern ; but contrariwise. Whereby it is manifest that the northern tract of the world is in nature the more martial region, be it in respect of the stars of that hemisphere or of the great continents that are upon the north ; whereas the south part, for aught that is known, is almost all sea, or (which is most apparent) of the cold of the northern parts, which is that which, without aid of discipline, doth make the bodies hardest and the courages warmest.

Upon the breaking and shivering of a great State and empire you may be sure to have wars. For great empires, while they stand, do enervate and destroy the forces of the natives which they have subdued, resting upon their own protecting forces ; and then, when they fail also, all goes to ruin, and they become a prey. So was it in the decay of the Roman empire, and likewise in the empire of Almaigne, after Charles the Great, every bird taking a feather, and were not unlike to befall to Spain, if it should break. The great accessions and unions of kingdoms do likewise stir up wars ; for, when a State grows to an over-power, it is like a great flood, that will be sure to overflow. As it hath been seen in the States of Rome, Turkey, Spain, and others. Look when the world hath fewest barbarous peoples, but such as commonly will not marry or generate, except they know means to live (as it is almost everywhere at this day, except Tartary), there is no danger of inundations of people ; but, when there be great shoals of people which go on to populate without foreseeing means of life and sustentation, it is of necessity that once in an age or two they discharge a portion of their people upon other nations, which the ancient northern people were wont to do by lot, casting lots what part should stay at home and what should seek their fortunes. When a warlike State grows soft and effeminate, they may be sure of a war. For commonly such States are grown rich in the time of their degenerating, and so the prey inviteth, and their decay in valour encourageth, a war.

As for the weapons, it hardly falleth under rule and observation ; yet we see even they have returns and vicissitudes. For certain it is that ordnance was known in the city of the Oxidrakes in India, and was that which the Macedonians called thunder, and lightning, and magic. And it is well known that the use of ordnance hath been in China above two thousand years. The conditions of weapons and their improvement are, first, the fetching afar off, for that outruns the danger, as it is seen in ordnance and muskets. Secondly, the strength of the percussion, wherein likewise ordnance do exceed all arietations [1] and ancient inventions. The third is the commodious use of them, as that they may serve in all weathers, that the carriage may be light and manageable, and the like.

For the conduct of the war : at the first, men rested extremely upon number ; they did put the wars likewise upon main force and valour, pointing days for pitched fields, and so trying it out upon an even match ; and they were more ignorant in ranging and arraying their battalions. After, they grew to rest upon number rather competent

[1] Assault with a battering-ram (Lat. *aries*).

than vast; they grew to [1] advantages of place, cunning diversions, and the like; and they grew more skilful in the ordering of their battles.

In the youth of a State, arms do flourish; in the middle age of a State, learning; and then both of them together for a time; in the declining age of a State, mechanical arts and merchandise. Learning hath his infancy, when it is but beginning and almost childish; then his youth, when it is luxuriant and juvenile; then his strength of years, when it is solid and reduced; and lastly, his old age, when it waxeth dry and exhaust. But it is not good to look too long upon these turning wheels of vicissitude, lest we become giddy. As for the philology of them, that is but a circle of tales and therefore not fit for this writing.

FRANCIS BACON

209 *The Inextricable Mesh*

" SIR,—Having had to make two or three journeys at the beginning of the vacation, I have been unable to correspond with you as early as I could have wished. I was none the less urgently in need of unbosoming myself to you with regard to pangs which increase in intensity each day, and which I feel all the keener because there is no one here to whom I can confide them. What ought to make for my happiness causes me the deepest sorrow. An imperious sense of duty compels me to concentrate my thoughts upon myself, in order to spare pain to those who surround me with their affection, and who would moreover be quite incapable of understanding my perplexity. Their kindness and soothing words cut me to the quick. Oh, if they only knew what was going on in the recesses of my heart! Since my stay here I

---

[1] So in original. A word appears to have dropped out, such as *seek*, or something equivalent. The translation has *captabant*.

have acquired some important data towards the solution of the great problem which is preoccupying my mind. Several circumstances have, to begin with, made me realize the greatness of the sacrifice which God required of me, and into what an abyss the course which my conscience prescribes must plunge me. It is useless to describe them to you in detail, as, after all, considerations of this kind can be of no weight in the resolution which has to be taken. To have abandoned a path which I had selected from my childhood, and which led without danger to the pure and noble aims which I had set before myself, in order to tread another along which I could discern nothing but uncertainty and disappointment; to have disregarded the opinion which will have only blame in store for what is really an honest act on my part, would have been a small thing, if I had not at the same time been compelled to tear out part of my heart, or, to speak more accurately, to pierce another to which my own was so deeply attached. Filial love had grown in proportion as so many other affections were crushed out. Well, it is in this part of my being that duty exacts from me the most painful sacrifice. My leaving the seminary will be an inexplicable enigma to my mother; she will believe that I have killed her out of sheer caprice.

" Truly may I say that when I envisage the inextricable mesh in which God has ensnared me while my reason and freedom were asleep, while I was following with docile steps the path He had Himself traced out for me, distracting thoughts crowd themselves upon me. God knows that I was simple-minded and pure; I took nothing upon myself; I walked with free and unflagging steps in the path which He disclosed before me, and behold this path has led me to the brink of a precipice! God has betrayed me! I never doubted but that a wise and merciful Providence governed the universe and governed me in the course which I was to take. It is not, however, without considerable effort that I have been able to apply so formal a contradiction to apparent facts. I often say to myself that vulgar common sense is little capable of appreciating the providential government whether of humanity, of the universe, or of the individual. The isolated consideration of facts would scarcely tend to optimism. It requires a strong dose of optimism to credit God with this generosity in spite of experience. I hope that I shall never feel any hesitation upon this point, and that whatever may be the ills which Providence yet has in store for me I shall ever believe that it is guiding me to the highest possible good through the least possible evil.

" According to what I hear from Germany, the situation which was offered me there is still open ; [1] only I cannot enter upon it before the spring. This makes my journey thither very doubtful, and throws me back into fresh perplexities. I am also advised to go through a year of free study in Paris, during which time I should be able to reflect upon my future career, and also take my university degrees. I am very much inclined to adopt this last-named course, for though I have made up my mind to come back to the seminary and confer with you and the superiors, I should nevertheless be very reluctant to make a long stay there in my present condition of mind. It is with the utmost apprehension that I mark the near approach of the time when my inward irresolution must find expression in a most decided course of action. Hard it is to have thus to reascend the stream down which one has for so long been gently floated ! If only I could be sure of the future, and of being one day able to secure for my ideas their due place, and follow up at my ease

[1] This has reference to a post of private tutor which was at my disposal for a time.

The Knapsack

and free from all external preoccupations the work of my intellectual and moral improvement! But even could I be sure of myself, how could I be of the circumstances which force themselves so pitilessly upon us? In truth, I am driven to regret the paltry store of liberty which God has given us; we have enough to make us struggle; not enough to master destiny, just enough to insure suffering.

"Happy are the children who only sleep and dream, and who never have a thought of entering upon this struggle with God Himself! I see around me men of pure and simple mind, whom Christianity suffices to render virtuous and happy. God grant that they may never develop the miserable faculty of criticism which so imperiously demands satisfaction, and which, when once satisfied, leaves such little happiness in the soul! Would to God that it were in my power to suppress it. I would not hesitate at amputation if it were lawful and possible. Christianity satisfies all my faculties except one, which is the most exacting of them all, because it is by right judge over all the others. Would it not be a contradiction in terms to impose conviction upon the faculty which creates conviction? I am well aware that the orthodox will tell me that it is my own fault if I have fallen into this condition. I will not argue the point; no man knows whether he is worthy of love or hatred. I am quite willing, therefore, to say that it is my fault, provided those who love me promise to pity me and continue me their friendship.

"A result which now seems beyond all doubt is that I shall not revert to orthodoxy by continuing to follow the same line—I mean that of rational and critical self-examination. Up till now, I hoped that after having travelled over the circle of doubt I should come back to the starting-point. I have quite lost this hope, and a return to Catholicism no longer seems possible to me,

The Inextricable Mesh

except by a receding movement, by stopping short in the path which I have entered, by stigmatizing reason, by declaring it for once and all null and void, and by condemning it to respectful silence. Each step in my career of criticism takes me further away from the starting-point. Have I, then, lost all hope of coming back to Catholicism? That would be too bitter a thought. No, sir, I have no hopes of reverting to it by rational progress; but I have often been on the point of repudiating for once and all the guide whom at times I mistrust. What would then be the motive of my life? I cannot tell; but activity will ever find scope. You may be sure that I must have been sorely forced to have dwelt for one instant upon a thought which seems more cruel to me than death. And yet, if my conscience represented it to me as lawful, I should eagerly avail myself of it, if only out of common decency.

" I hope at all events that those who know me will admit that interested motives have not estranged me from Christianity. Have not all my material interests tempted me to find it true? The temporal considerations against which I have had to struggle would have sufficed to persuade many others; my heart has need of Christianity; the Gospel will ever be my moral law; the church has given me my education, and I love her. Could I but continue to style myself her son! I pass from her in spite of myself; I abhor the dishonest attacks levelled at her; I frankly confess that I have no complete substitute for her teaching; but I cannot disguise from myself the weak points which I believe that I have found in it and with regard to which it is impossible to effect a compromise, because we have to do with a doctrine in which all the component parts hold together and cannot be detached.

" I sometimes regret that I was not born in a land

where the bonds of orthodoxy are less tightly drawn than in Catholic countries. For, at whatever cost, I am resolved to be a Christian ; but I cannot be an orthodox Catholic. When I find such independent and bold thinkers as Herder, Kant, and Fichte, calling themselves Christians, I should like to be so too. But can I be so in the Catholic faith, which is like a bar of iron ? and you cannot reason with a bar of iron. Will not some one found amongst us a rational and critical Christianity ? I will confess to you that I believe that I have discovered in some German writers the true kind of Christianity which is adapted to us. May I live to see this Christianity assuming a form capable of fully satisfying all the requirements of our age ! May I myself co-operate in the great work ! What so grieves me is the thought that perhaps it will be needful to be a priest in order to accomplish that ; and I could not become a priest without being guilty of hypocrisy.

" Forgive me, sir, these thoughts, which must seem very reprehensible to you. You are aware that all this has not as yet any dogmatic consistence in me ; I still cling to the Church, my venerable mother ; I recite the Psalms with heartfelt accents ; I should, if I followed the bent of my inclination, pass hours at a time in church ; gentle, plain, and pure piety touches me to the very heart ; and I even have sharp relapses of devotional feeling. All this cannot coexist without contradiction with my general condition. But I have once for all made up my mind on the subject ; I have cast off the inconvenient yoke of consistency, at all events for the time. Will God condemn me for having simultaneously admitted that which my different faculties simultaneously exact, although I am unable to reconcile their contradictory demands ? Are there not periods in the history of the human mind when contradiction is necessary ? When the moral verities are under examination, doubt is unavoidable ;

and yet during this period of transition the pure and noble mind must still be moral, thanks to a contradiction. Thus it is that I am at times both Catholic and Rationalist; but holy orders I can never take, for ' once a priest, always a priest '.

" In order to keep my letter within due limits, I must bring the long story of my inward struggles to a close. I thank God, who has seen fit to put me through so severe a trial, for having brought me into contact with a mind such as yours, which is so well able to understand this trial, and to whom I can confide it without reserve."

ERNEST RENAN

210 *Love of Life*

GREATNESS of soul consists not so much in mounting and in pressing forward, as in knowing how to govern and circumscribe itself; it takes everything for great, that is enough, and demonstrates itself in preferring moderate to eminent things. There is nothing so fine and legitimate as well and duly to play the man; nor science so arduous as well and naturally to know how to live this life; and of all the infirmities we have, 'tis the most barbarous to despise our being.

Whoever has a mind to isolate his spirit, when the body is ill at ease, to preserve it from the contagion, let him by all means do it if he can : but otherwise let him on the contrary favour and assist it, and not refuse to participate of its natural pleasures with a conjugal complacency, bringing to it, if it be the wiser, moderation, lest by indiscretion they should get confounded with displeasure. Intemperance is the pest of pleasure; and temperance is not its scourge, but rather its seasoning. Euxodus, who therein established the sovereign good, and his companions, who set so high a value upon it, tasted it in its most charming sweetness, by the means of temperance, which in them was singular and exemplary.

I enjoin my soul to look upon pain and pleasure with an eye equally regulated :

Eodem enim vitio est effusio animi in lætitia quo in dolore contractio,[1]

and equally firm ; but the one gaily and the other severely, and so far as it is able, to be careful to extinguish the one as to extend the other. The judging rightly of good brings along with it the judging soundly of evil : pain has something of the inevitable in its tender beginnings, and pleasure something of the evitable in its excessive end. Plato [2] couples them together, and wills that it should be equally the office of fortitude to fight against pain, and against the immoderate and charming blandishments of pleasure : they are two fountains, from which whoever draws, when and as much as he needs, whether city, man, or beast, is very fortunate. The first is to be taken medicinally and upon necessity, and more scantily ; the other for thirst, but not to drunkenness. Pain, pleasure, love, and hatred are the first things that a child is sensible of : if, when reason comes, they apply it to themselves, that is virtue.

I have a special vocabulary of my own ; I " pass away time ", when it is ill and uneasy, but when 'tis good I do not pass it away : " I taste it over again and adhere to it " ; one must run over the ill and settle upon the good. This ordinary phrase of pastime, and passing away the time, represents the usage of those wise sort of people who think they cannot do better with their lives than to let

[1] " For from the same imperfection arises the expansion of the mind in pleasure and its contraction in sorrow."—Cicero, *Tusc. Quæs.*, iv. 31.

[2] *Laws*, i.

them run out and slide away, pass them over, and baulk
them, and, as much as they can, ignore them and shun
them as a thing of troublesome and contemptible quality :
but I know it to be another kind of thing, and find it both
valuable and commodious, even in its latest decay, wherein
I now enjoy it ; and nature has delivered it into our hands
in such and so favourable circumstances that we have only
ourselves to blame if it be troublesome to us, or escapes us
unprofitably :

Stulti vita ingrata est, trepida est, tota in futurum fertur.[1]

Nevertheless I compose myself to lose mine without regret ;
but withal as a thing that is perishable by its condition,
not that it molests or annoys me. Nor does it properly
well become any not to be displeased when they die,
excepting such as are pleased to live. There is good
husbandry in enjoying it : I enjoy it double to what others
do ; for the measure of its fruition depends upon our more
or less application to it. Chiefly that I perceive mine to
be so short in time, I desire to extend it in weight ; I will
stop the promptitude of its flight by the promptitude of
my grasp ; and by the vigour of using it compensate the
speed of its running away. In proportion as the possession
of life is more short, I must make it so much deeper and
fuller.

Others feel the pleasure of content and prosperity ; I
feel it too, as well as they, but not as it passes and slips by ;
one should study, taste, and ruminate upon it to render
condign thanks to Him who grants it to us. They enjoy
the other pleasures as they do that of sleep, without knowing it. To the end that even sleep itself should not so
stupidly escape from me, I have formerly caused myself
to be disturbed in my sleep, so that I might the better anp

[1] " The life of a fool is thankless, timorous, and wholly bent
upon the future."—Seneca, *Ep.* 15.

more sensibly relish and taste it. I ponder with myself of content; I do not skim over, but sound it; and I bend my reason, now grown perverse and peevish, to entertain it. Do I find myself in any calm composedness? is there any pleasure that tickles me? I do not suffer it to dally with my senses only; I associate my soul to it too: not there to engage itself, but therein to take delight; not there to lose itself, but to be present there; and I employ it, on its part, to view itself in this prosperous state, to weigh and appreciate its happiness and to amplify it. It reckons how much it stands indebted to God that its conscience and the intestine passions are in repose; that it has the body in its natural disposition, orderly and competently enjoying the soft and soothing functions by which He of His grace is pleased to compensate the sufferings wherewith His justice at His good pleasure chastises us. It reflects how great a benefit it is to be so protected, that which way soever it turns its eye the heavens are calm around it. No desire, no fear, no doubt, troubles the air; no difficulty, past, present, or to come, that its imagination may not pass over without offence. This consideration takes great lustre from the comparison of different conditions. So it is that I present to my thought, in a thousand aspects, those whom fortune or their own error carries away and torments. And, again, those who, more like to me, so negligently and incuriously receive their good fortune. Those are folks who spend their time indeed; they pass over the present and that which they possess, to wait on hope, and for shadows and vain images which fancy puts before them:

> Morte obita quales fama est volitare figuras,
> Aut quæ sopitos deludunt somnia sensus: [1]

[1] " Such forms as those, which after death are reputed to hove about, or dreams which delude the senses in sleep."—*Æneid*, x. 641.

Love of Life

which hasten and prolong their flight, according as they are pursued. The fruit and end of their pursuit is to pursue ; as Alexander said, that the end of his labour was to labour :

Nil actum credens, cum quid superesset agendum.[1]

For my part then, I love life and cultivate it, such as it has pleased God to bestow it upon us. I do not desire it should be without the necessity of eating and drinking ; and I should think it a not less excusable failing to wish it had been twice as long :

Sapiens divitiarum naturalium quæsitor acerrimus :[2]

nor that we should support ourselves by putting only a little of that drug into our mouths, by which Epimenides took away his appetite and kept himself alive ;[3] nor that we should stupidly beget children with our fingers or heels, but rather, with reverence be it spoken, that we might voluptuously beget them with our fingers and heels ; nor that the body should be without desire and without titillation. These are ungrateful and wicked complaints. I accept kindly, and with gratitude, what nature has done for me ; am well pleased with it, and proud of it. A man does wrong to that great and omnipotent giver to refuse, annul, or disfigure his gift : all goodness himself, he has made everything good :

Omnia quæ secundum naturam sunt, æstimatione digna sunt.[4]

MICHEL EYQUEM DE MONTAIGNE

[1] " Thinking nothing done, if anything remained to be done."
—Lucan, ii. 657.
[2] " A wise man is the keenest seeker for natural riches."—
Seneca, *Ep.* 119.
[3] Diogenes Laertius, i. 114.
[4] " All things that are according to nature are worthy of esteem."—Cicero, *De Fin.*, iii. 6.

The Knapsack

211 *The Thirty-three Happy Moments*

1^1 : It is a hot day in June when the sun hangs still in the sky and there is not a whiff of wind or air, nor a trace of clouds ; the front and back yards are hot like an oven and not a single bird dares to fly about. Perspiration flows down my whole body in little rivulets. There is the noonday meal before me, but I cannot take it for the sheer heat. I ask for a mat to spread on the ground and lie down, but the mat is wet with moisture and flies swarm about to rest on my nose and refuse to be driven away. Just at this moment when I am completely helpless, suddenly there is a rumbling of thunder and big sheets of black clouds overcast the sky and come majestically on like a great army advancing to battle. Rain-water begins to pour down from the eaves like a cataract. The perspiration stops. The clamminess of the ground is gone. All flies disappear to hide themselves and I can eat my rice. Ah, is this not happiness ?

1 : A friend, one I have not seen for ten years, suddenly arrives at sunset. I open the door to receive him, and without asking whether he came by boat or by land, and without bidding him to sit down on the bed or the couch, I go to the inner chamber and humbly ask my wife : " Have you got a gallon of wine like Su Tungp'o's wife ? " My wife gladly takes out her gold hairpin to sell it. I calculate it will last us three days. Ah, is this not happiness ?

1 : I am sitting alone in an empty room and I am just getting annoyed at a mouse at the head of my bed,

---

¹ When a Chinese draws up a set of seventeen or eighteen regulations, it is his custom (the idiom of our language) to set them down as " Articles 1, 1, 1, 1, 1, 1 ", etc.

The Thirty-three Happy Moments

and wondering what that little rustling sound signifies—what article of mine he is biting or what volume of my books he is eating up. While I am in this state of mind, and don't know what to do, I suddenly see a ferocious-looking cat, wagging its tail and staring with its wide-open eyes, as if it were looking at something. I hold my breath and wait a moment, keeping perfectly still, and suddenly with a little sound the mouse disappears like a whiff of wind. Ah, is this not happiness?

1 : I have pulled out the *hait'ang* and *chihching* [1] in front of my studio, and have just planted ten or twenty green banana trees there. Ah, is this not happiness?

1 : I am drinking with some romantic friends on a spring night and am just half intoxicated, finding it difficult to stop drinking and equally difficult to go on. An understanding boy servant at the side suddenly brings in a package of big fire-crackers, about a dozen in number, and I rise from the table and go and fire them off. The smell of sulphur assails my nostrils and enters my brain and I feel comfortable all over my body. Ah, is this not happiness?

1 : I am walking in the street and see two poor rascals engaged in a hot argument of words with their faces flushed and their eyes staring with anger as if they were mortal enemies, and yet they still pretend to be ceremonious to each other, raising their arms and bending their waists in salute, and still using the most polished language of *thou* and *thee* and *wherefore* and *is it not so?* The flow of words is interminable. Suddenly there appears a big husky fellow swinging

---

[1] *Hait'ang* is of the pyrus family, bearing fruits like crab-apples, and *chihching* blossoms in spring, with small violet flowers growing directly on the trunks and branches.

his arms and coming up to them, and with a shout tells them to disperse. Ah, is this not happiness?

1 : To hear our children recite the classics so fluently, like the sound of pouring water from a vase. Ah, is this not happiness?

1 : Having nothing to do after a meal I go to the shops and take a fancy to a little thing. After bargaining for some time, we still haggle about a small difference, but the shop-boy still refuses to sell it. Then I take out a little thing from my sleeve, which is worth about the same thing as the difference and throw it at the boy. The boy suddenly smiles and bows courteously saying, " Oh, you are too generous ! " Ah, is this not happiness?

1 : I have nothing to do after a meal and try to go through the things in some old trunks. I see there are dozens or hundreds of IOUs from people who owe my family money. Some of them are dead and some still living, but in any case there is no hope of their returning the money. Behind people's backs I put them together in a pile and make a bonfire of them, and I look up to the sky and see the last trace of smoke disappear. Ah, is this not happiness?

1 : It is a summer day. I go bareheaded and barefooted, holding a parasol to watch young people singing Soochow folk-songs while treading the water-wheel. The water comes up over the wheel in a gushing torrent like molten silver or melting snow. Ah, is this not happiness?

1 : I wake up in the morning and seem to hear someone in the house sighing and saying that last night some-one died. I immediately ask to find out who it is, and learn that it is the sharpest, most calculating fellow in town. Ah, is this not happiness?

The Thirty-three Happy Moments

1 : I get up early on a summer morning and see people sawing a large bamboo pole under a mat-shed, to be used as a water-pipe. Ah, is this not happiness?

1 : It has been raining for a whole month and I lie in bed in the morning like one drunk or ill, refusing to get up. Suddenly I hear a chorus of birds announcing a clear day. Quickly I pull aside the curtain, push open the window and see the beautiful sun shining and glistening and the forest looks like having a bath. Ah, is this not happiness?

1 : At night I seem to hear someone thinking of me in the distance. The next day I go to call on him. I enter his door and look about his room and see that this person is sitting at his desk, facing south, reading a document. He sees me, nods quietly and pulls me by the sleeve to make me sit down, saying, " Since you are here, come and look at this." And we laugh and enjoy ourselves until the shadows on the walls have disappeared. He is feeling hungry himself and slowly asks me, " Are you hungry, too ? " Ah, is this not happiness?

1 : Without any serious intention to build a house of my own, I happened, nevertheless, to start building one because a little sum had unexpectedly come my way. From that day on, every morning and every night I was told that I needed to buy timber and stone and tiles and bricks and mortar and nails. And I explored and exhausted every avenue of getting some money, all on account of this house, without, however, being able to live in it all this time, until I got sort of resigned to this state of things. One day, finally, the house is completed, the walls have been whitewashed and the floors swept clean ; the paper windows have been pasted and scrolls of paintings are hung up on the walls. All the workmen have

left, and my friends have arrived, sitting on different couches in order. Ah, is this not happiness?

1 : I am drinking on a winter's night, and suddenly note that the night has turned extremely cold. I push open the window and see that snowflakes come down the size of a palm and there are already three or four inches of snow on the ground. Ah, is this not happiness?

1 : To cut with a sharp knife a bright green water-melon on a big scarlet plate of a summer afternoon. Ah, is this not happiness?

1 : I have long wanted to become a monk, but was worried because I would not be permitted to eat meat. If, then, I could be permitted to become a monk and yet eat meat publicly, why, then I would heat a basin of hot water, and with the help of a sharp razor shave my head clean in a summer month! Ah, is this not happiness?

1 : To keep three or four spots of eczema in a private part of my body and now and then to scald or bathe it with hot water behind closed doors. Ah, is this not happiness?

1 : To find accidentally a handwritten letter of some old friend in a trunk. Ah, is this not happiness?

1 : A poor scholar comes to borrow money from me, but is shy about mentioning the topic, and so he allows the conversation to drift along on other topics. I see his uncomfortable situation, pull him aside to a place where we are alone and ask him how much he needs. Then I go inside and give him the sum and after having done this, I ask him : " Must you go immediately to settle this matter or can you stay a while and have a drink with me ? " Ah, is this not happiness?

1 : I am sitting in a small boat. There is a beautiful

The Thirty-three Happy Moments

wind in our favour, but our boat has no sails. Suddenly there appears a big lorcha, coming along as fast as the wind. I try to hook on to the lorcha in the hope of catching on to it, and unexpectedly the hook does catch. Then I throw over a rope and we are towed along and I begin to sing the lines of Tu Fu : " The green makes me feel tender toward the peaks, and the red tells me there are oranges." And we break out in joyous laughter. Ah, is this not happiness ?

I : I have been long looking for a house to share with a friend but have not been able to find a suitable one. Suddenly someone brings the news that there is a house somewhere, not too big, but with only about a dozen rooms, and that it faces a big river with beautiful green trees around. I ask this man to stay for supper, and after the supper we go over together to have a look, having no idea what the house is like. Entering the gate, I see that there is a large vacant lot about six or seven *mow*, and I say to myself, " I shall not have to worry about the supply of vegetables and melons henceforth." Ah, is this not happiness ?

I : A traveller returns home after a long journey, and he sees the old city gate and hears the women and children on both banks of the river talking his own dialect. Ah, is this not happiness ?

I : When a good piece of old porcelain is broken, you know there is no hope of repairing it. The more you turn it about and look at it, the more you are exasperated. I then hand it to the cook, asking him to use it as any old vessel, and give orders that he shall never let that broken porcelain bowl come within my sight again. Ah, is this not happiness ?

I : I am not a saint, and am therefore not without sin. In the night I did something wrong and I get up in

589

the morning and feel extremely ill at ease about it. Suddenly I remember what is taught by Buddhism, that not to cover one's sins is the same as repentance. So then I begin to tell my sin to the entire company around, whether they are strangers or my old friends. Ah, is this not happiness?

1 : To watch someone writing big characters a foot high. Ah, is this not happiness?

1 : To open the window and let a wasp out of the room. Ah, is this not happiness?

1 : A magistrate orders the beating of the drum and calls it a day. Ah, is this not happiness?

1 : To see someone's kite-line broken. Ah, is this not happiness?

1 : To see a wild prairie fire. Ah, is this not happiness?

1 : To have just finished repaying all one's debts. Ah, is this not happiness?

1 : To read the Story of Curly-Beard.[1] Ah, is this not happiness?

CHIN SHENGT'AN

212 *The Simple Way*

WHAT IS POSSIBLE

BY conserving the natural and spiritual powers it is possible to escape dissolution.

By restraining the passions and letting gentleness have sway it is possible to continue as a child.

By purging the mind of impurities it is possible to remain untainted.

By governing the people with love it is possible to remain unknown.

[1] The hero, known as " Curly-Beard," aided the escape of a pair of eloping lovers, and after giving them his home in a distant city, then disappeared.

The Simple Way

By continual use of the gates of Heaven it is possible to preserve them from rust.

By transparency on all sides it is possible to remain unrecognized.

To bring forth and preserve, to produce without possessing, to act without hope of reward, and to expand without waste, this is the supreme virtue.

DECLINING FROM STRIFE

The man who aids the King by the use of Tao forces the people into submission without resort to the use of arms. He will not regard the fruit of his actions.

Prickly briars and thorns flourish where battalions have quartered.

Bad years follow on the heels of armies in motion.

The good soldier is brave when occasion requires, but he does not risk himself for power.

Brave is he when occasion requires, but he does not oppress.

Brave is he when occasion requires, but he does not boast.

Brave is he when occasion requires, but he is not haughty.

Brave is he when occasion requires, but he is not mean.

Brave is he when occasion requires, but he does not rage.

Things become old through excess of vigour. This is called Non-Tao ; and what is Non-Tao is soon wasted !

THE VIRTUE OF CONCESSION

The wise man has no fixed opinions to call his own.

He accommodates himself to the minds of others.

I would return good for good ; I would also return good for evil.

Virtue is good.

I would meet trust with trust ; I would likewise meet suspicion with confidence.

The Knapsack

Virtue is trustful.

The wise man lives in the world with modest **restraint**, and his heart goes out in sympathy to all men.

The people give him their confidence, and he regards them all as his children.

THE GENUINE GOVERNMENT

THE righteous man may rule the nation.

The strategic man may rule the army.

But the man who refrains from active measures should be the king.

How do I know how things should be ?

I know by this :—

When the actions of the people are controlled by prohibited laws, the country becomes more and more impoverished.

When the people are allowed the free use of arms, the Government is in danger.

The more crafty and dexterous the people become, the more do artificial things come into use.

And when these cunning arts are publicly esteemed, then do rogues prosper.

Therefore the wise man says :—

I will design nothing ; and the people will shape themselves.

I will keep quiet ; and the people will find their rest.

I will not assert myself; and the people will come forth.

I will discountenance ambition ; and the people will revert to their natural simplicity.

SIMPLE VIRTUE

THE ancients who practised the Tao did not make use of it to render the people brilliant, but to make them simple and natural.

The Simple Way

The difficulty in governing the people is through overmuch policy.

He who tries to govern the kingdom by policy is only a scourge to it ; while he who governs without it is a blessing.

To know these two things is the perfect knowledge of government, and to keep them continually in view is called the virtue of simplicity.

Deep and wide is this simple virtue ; and though opposed to other methods it can bring about a perfect order.

LAOTZE

213 *Proverbs of Hell*

IN seed time learn, in harvest teach, in winter enjoy.

Drive your cart and your plough over the bones of the dead.

The road of excess leads to the palace of wisdom.

Prudence is a rich, ugly old maid courted by Incapacity.

He who desires but acts not, breeds pestilence.

The cut worm forgives the plough.

Dip him in the river who loves water.

A fool sees not the same tree that a wise man sees.

He whose face gives no light, shall never become a star.

Eternity is in love with the productions of time.

The busy bee has no time for sorrow.

The hours of folly are measur'd by the clock ; but of wisdom, no clock can measure.

All wholesome food is caught without a net or a trap.

Bring out number, weight, and measure in a year of dearth.

No bird soars too high, if he soars with his own wings.

A dead body revenges not injuries.

The Knapsack

The most sublime act is to set another before you.

If the fool would persist in his folly he would become wise.

Folly is the cloak of knavery.

Shame is Pride's cloak.

Prisons are built with stones of Law, brothels with bricks of Religion.

The pride of the peacock is the glory of God.

The lust of the goat is the bounty of God.

The wrath of the lion is the wisdom of God.

The nakedness of woman is the work of God.

Excess of sorrow laughs. Excess of joy weeps.

The roaring of lions, the howling of wolves, the raging of the stormy sea, and the destructive sword are portions of eternity too great for the eye of man.

The fox condemns the trap, not himself.

Joys impregnate. Sorrows bring forth.

Let man wear the fell of the lion, woman the fleece of the sheep.

The bird a nest, the spider a web, man friendship.

The selfish, smiling fool, and the sullen, frowning fool shall be both thought wise, that they may be a rod.

What is now proved was once only imagin'd.

The rat, the mouse, the fox, the rabbit watch the roots; the lion, the tiger, the horse, the elephant watch the fruits.

The cistern contains : the fountain overflows.

One thought fills immensity.

Always be ready to speak your mind, and a base man will avoid you.

Everything possible to be believ'd is an image of truth.

The eagle never lost so much time as when he submitted to learn of the crow.

The fox provides for himself; but God provides for the lion.

Think in the morning. Act in the noon. Eat in the evening. Sleep in the night.

Proverbs of Hell

He who has suffer'd you to impose on him, knows you.

As the plough follows words, so God rewards prayers.

The tigers of wrath are wiser than the horses of instruction.

Expect poison from the standing water.

You never know what is enough unless you know what is more than enough.

Listen to the fool's reproach ! it is a kingly title !

The eyes of fire, the nostrils of air, the mouth of water, the beard of earth.

The weak in courage is strong in cunning.

The apple tree never asks the beech how he shall grow ; nor the lion, the horse, how he shall take his prey.

The thankful receiver bears a plentiful harvest.

If others had not been foolish, we should be so.

The soul of sweet delight can never be defil'd.

When thou seest an eagle, thou seest a portion of Genius ; lift up thy head !

As the caterpillar chooses the fairest leaves to lay her eggs on, so the priest lays his curse on the fairest joys.

To create a little flower is the labour of ages.

Damn braces.   Bless relaxes.

The best wine is the oldest, the best water the newest.

Prayers plough not !   Praises reap not !

Joys laugh not !   Sorrows weep not !

The head Sublime, the heart Pathos, the genitals Beauty, the hands and feet Proportion.

As the air to a bird or the sea to a fish, so is contempt to the contemptible.

The crow wish'd everything was black, the owl that everything was white.

Exuberance is Beauty.

If the lion was advised by the fox, he would be cunning.

Improvement makes straight roads ; but the crooked roads without improvement are roads of Genius.

The Knapsack

Sooner murder an infant in its cradle than nurse unacted desires.

Where man is not, nature is barren.

Truth can never be told so as to be understood, and not be believ'd.

Enough! or Too much.

WILLIAM BLAKE

PART TEN

214 *The Last Will of Saint Louis*

THE good king took to his bed, and, well knowing he was about to quit this life for another, called to his children, and, addressing himself to his eldest son, gave them instructions, which he commanded them to consider as his last will, and the objects which they were to attend to when he should be deceased. I have heard that the good king had written out these instructions with his own hand, and that they were as follow :

" Fair son, the first advice that I shall give thee is, that with all thy heart, and above all other things, thou love God, for without this no man can be saved. Be most careful not to do any thing that may displease Him ; that is to say, avoid sin. Thou oughtest to desire to suffer any torments rather than sin mortally. Should God send thee adversity, receive it patiently, give him thanks for it, and believe that thou hast well deserved it, and that it will turn out to thine honour. Should he grant thee prosperity, be humbly grateful for it ; but take care thou do not become worse, through pride or presumption, for it behoves us not to make war against God for his gifts. Confess thyself often, and choose such a discreet and wise confessor as may have abilities to point out to thee the things necessary for thy salvation, and what things thou oughtest to shun ; and mayest thou be such a character, that thy confessor, relations, and acquaintance may boldly reprove thee for any wrong thou mayest have done, and instruct thee how thou shouldest act. Attend the service of God, and of our mother church, with heartfelt devotion, more particularly the mass, from the consecration of the holy body of our Lord, without laughing or gossiping with any one. Have always a compassionate heart for the poor, and assist and comfort them as much as thou canst.

" Keep up and maintain good manners in thy kingdom : abase and punish the bad. Preserve thyself from too great luxury ; and never lay any heavy imposts on thy people, unless through necessity forced to it, or for the defence of thy country. If thy heart feel any discontent, tell it instantly to thy confessor, or to any sober-minded person, that is not full of wicked words : thou mayest thus more easily bear it, from the consolation he may give thee. Be careful to choose such companions as are honest and loyal, and not full of vices, whether they be churchmen, monks seculars, or others.

" Avoid the society of the wicked ; and force thyself to listen to the word of God, and to retain it in thy heart. Beg continually in thy prayers for pardon, and the remission of thy sins. Love thine honour. Take care not to suffer any one to dare utter words in thy presence that may excite to sin, nor any calumny of another, whether he be present or absent ; nor any thing disrespectful of God, his holy mother, or of the saints.

" Offer thanks frequently to God for the prosperity and other good things he gives thee. Be upright, and do justice strictly to all, to the poor and to the rich. Be liberal and good to thy servants, but firm in thy orders, that they may fear and love thee as their master. If any controversy or dispute arise, inquire into it until thou comest to the truth, whether it be in thy favour or against thee. If thou possess any thing that does not belong to thee, or that may have come to thee from thy predecessors, and thou be informed for a truth that it is not thine, cause it instantly to be

The Last Will of Saint Louis

restored to its proper owner. Be particularly attentive that thy subjects live in peace and security, as well in the towns as in the country. Maintain such liberties and franchises as thy ancestors have done, and preserve them inviolate ; for by the riches and power of thy principal towns thy enemies will be afraid of affronting or attacking thee, more especially thy equals, thy barons, and such like.

" Love and honour all churchmen, and be careful not to deprive them of any gifts, revenues, or alms which thy ancestors or predecessors may have granted to them. It is reported of my grandfather Philip, that when one of his counsellors told him that the churchmen were making him lose his revenues, royalties, and even his rights of justice, and that he was surprised how he suffered it, the king replied, that he believed it was so, but that God had shewn him so much favour, and granted him such prosperity, that he had rather lose all he had, than have any dispute or contention with the servants of his holy church.

" Be to thy father and mother dutiful and respectful, and avoid angering them by thy disobedience to their just commands. Give such benefices as may become vacant to discreet persons of a pure conversation, and give them with the advice of well-advised, prudent persons. Avoid going to war with any Christian power, without mature deliberation, and if it can in anywise be prevented. If thou goest to war, respect churchmen and all who have done thee no wrong. Should contentions arise between thy vassals, put an end of them as speedily as possible.

" Attend frequently to the conduct of thy bailiffs, provosts, and others thy officers : inquire into their behaviour, in order that if there may be any amendment to be made in their manner of distributing justice, thou mayest make it. Should any disgraceful sin, such as blasphemy or heresy, be prevalent in thy kingdom, have it instantly destroyed and driven thence. Be careful that thou keep a liberal establishment, but with economy.

" I beseech thee, my child, that thou hold me, and my poor soul, in thy remembrance when I am no more, and that thou succour me by masses, prayers, intercessions, alms, and benefactions, throughout thy kingdom, and that thou allot for me a part of all the good acts thou shalt perform.

" I give thee every blessing that father ever bestowed on son, beseeching the whole Trinity of paradise, the Father, the Son, and the Holy Ghost, to preserve and guard thee from all evils, more particularly that thou die not under any deadly sin, and that we may, after this mortal life, appear together before God, to render him praise and thanksgiving, without ceasing, in his kingdom of paradise. Amen."

JOHN LORD DE JOINVILLE

215 *Sir Walter Raleigh, to his wife, the Night before he expected to be put to death at Winchester,* 1603

YOU shall now receive (my dear wife) my last words, in these my last lines. My Love I send you, that you may keep it, when I am dead, and my Counsel that you may remember it, when I am no more ; I would not by my will present you with Sorrows (Dear Bess). Let them go into the grave with me ; and be buried in the dust ; and seeing it is not the will of God, that I shall see you any more in this life, bear it patiently, and with an heart like thy self.

First I send you all my thanks, which my heart can conceive, or my words can express for your many travails and Care taken for me, which though they have not taken effect, as you wished, yet my debt to you, is not the less, but pay it I never shall, in this world.

Sir Walter Raleigh to his Wife

Secondly I beseech you, for the love you bare me living, do not hide yourself many days, after my death, but by your Travails seek to help your miserable fortunes, and the Right of your poor Child. Thy mournings cannot avail me, I am but dust.

Thirdly you shall understand, that my Land was conveyed bona fide to my Child, the writings were drawn at Midsummer twelve months ; my honest Cousin Brett can testify so much, and Dalberrie too, can remember somewhat therein. And I trust my blood will quench their Malice, that have thus cruelly murdered me, and that they will not seek also to kill thee and thine with extreme poverty.

To what friend to direct thee, I know not, for all mine have left me, in the true time of trial ; and I plainly perceive, that my death was determined from the first day.

Most sorry I am (God knows) that being thus surprised with death, I can leave you in no better estate. God is my witness, I meant you all my office of wines, or all that I could have purchased by selling it, half my stuff, and all my Jewels. But some on't for the Boy, but God hath prevented all my Resolutions, and even that great God that ruleth all in all ; but if you can live free from want, care for no more ; the rest is but vanity.

Love God, and begin betimes, to repose your self on him, and therein shall you find true and lasting Riches, and endless Comfort. For the rest when you have travailed and wearied all your thoughts, over all sorts of worldly Cogitations, you shall but sit down by sorrow in the end.

Teach your son also to love and fear God whilst he is yet young, that the fear of God may grow up with him ; and the same God will be a husband to you, and a Father to him ; a husband, and a Father, which cannot be taken from you.

The Knapsack

Baylie oweth me 200£ and Adrian Gilbert 600£. In Jersey, I have also much money owing me. Besides, the Arrearages of the Wines will pay my depts. And howsoever you do, for my soul's sake, pay all poor men.

When I am gone, no doubt you shall be sought by many; for the world thinks, that I was very rich. But take heed of the pretences of men, and their affections; for they last not but in honest, and worthy Men; and no greater misery can befall you in this life, than to become a prey, and afterwards to be despised: I speak not this (God knows) to dissuade you from marriage, for it will be best for you, both in respect of the world and of God.

As for me, I am no more yours, nor you mine, Death hath cut us asunder; and God hath divided me from the world, and you from me.

Remember your poor Child, for his Father's sake, who chose you, and loved you, in his happiest times.

Get those Letters (if it be possible) which I writ to the Lords, wherein I sued for my life. God is my witness, it was for you and yours I desired life. But it is true that I disdain myself for begging it, for know it (dear wife) that your son, is the son of a true man, and one, who in his own respect, despiseth Death, and all his misshapen and ugly shapes.

I cannot write much: God he knows, how hardly, I steal this time, while others sleep: and it is also high time, that I should separate my thoughts from the world.

Beg my dead body, which living was denied thee; and either lay it at Sherbourne (if the Land continue) or in Excester Church by my Father and Mother.

I can say no more, time and death call me away.

The everlasting, powerful, infinite and omnipotent God, that Almighty God, who is goodness itself, the true life, and true light, keep thee, and thine; have mercy on me, and teach me to forgive my persecutors and

Sir Walter Raleigh to his Wife

Accusers, and send us to meet in his glorious king-dom.

My dear wife farewell, Bless my poor Boy, Pray for me, and Let my Good god hold you both in his arms.

Written with the dying hand of sometime thy Husband, but now (alas) overthrown

Wa: Raleigh.

yours that was, But now not my own.

W: R:

216 *Nicola Sacco to his son Dante*

August 18, 1927. Charlestown State Prison

MY DEAR SON AND COMPANION :

Since the day I saw you last I had always the idea to write you this letter, but the length of my hunger strike and the thought I might not be able to explain myself, made me put it off all this time.

The other day, I ended my hunger strike and just as soon as I did that I thought of you to write to you, but I find that I did not have enough strength and I cannot finish it at one time. However, I want to get it down in any way before they take us again to the death-house, because it is my conviction that just as soon as the court refuses a new trial to us they will take us there. And between Friday and Monday, if nothing happens, they will electrocute us right after midnight, on August 22nd. Therefore, here I am, right with you with love and with open heart as ever I was yesterday.

I never thought that our inseparable life could be separated, but the thought of seven dolorous years makes it seem it did come, but then it has not changed really the unrest and the heart-beat of affection. That has remained as it was. More. I say that our ineffable affection reciprocal, is today more than any other time, of course. That is not only a great deal but it is grand because you can see the real brotherly love, not only in joy but also and more in the struggle of suffering. Remember this, Dante. We have demonstrated this, and modesty apart, we are proud of it.

Much we have suffered during this long Calvary. We protest today as we protested yesterday. We protest always for our freedom.

If I stopped hunger strike the other day, it was because there was no more sign of life in me. Because I protested with my hunger strike yesterday as today I protest for life and not for death.

I sacrificed because I wanted to come back to the embrace of your dear little sister Ines and your mother and all the beloved friends and comrades of life and not death. So, Son, today life begins to revive slow and calm, but yet without horizon and always with sadness and visions of death.

Well, my dear boy, after your mother had talked to me so much and I had dreamed of you day and night, how joyful it was to see you at last. To have talked with you like we used to in the days—in those days. Much I told you on that visit and more I wanted to say, but I saw that you will remain the same affectionate boy, faithful to your mother who loves you so much, and I did not want to hurt your sensibilities any longer, because I am sure that you will continue to be the same boy and remember what I have told you. I knew that and what here I am going to tell you will touch your sensibilities, but don't cry, Dante, because many tears have been wasted, as your mother's have been wasted for seven years, and never did any good. So, Son, instead of crying, be strong, so as to be able to comfort your mother, and when you want to

Nicola Sacco to his son Dante

distract your mother from the discouraging soulness, I will tell you what I used to do. To take her for a long walk in the quiet country, gathering wild flowers here and there, resting under the shade of trees, between the harmony of the vivid stream and the gentle tranquility of the mother-nature, and I am sure that she will enjoy this very much, as you surely would be happy for it. But remember always, Dante, in the play of happiness, don't you use all for yourself only, but down yourself just one step, at your side and help the weak ones that cry for help, help the prosecuted and the victim, because that are your better friends ; they are the comrades that fight and fall as your father and Bartolo fought and fell yesterday for the conquest of the joy of freedom for all and the poor workers. In this struggle of life you will find more love and you will be loved.

I am sure that from what your mother told me about what you said during these last terrible days when I was lying in the iniquitous death-house—that description gave me happiness because it showed you will be the beloved boy I had always dreamed.

Therefore, whatever should happen tomorrow, nobody knows, but if they should kill us, you must not forget to look at your friends and comrades with the smiling gaze of gratitude as you look at your beloved ones, because they love you as they love every one of the fallen persecuted comrades. I tell you, your father that is all the life to you, your father that loved you and saw them, and knows their noble faith (that is mine) their supreme sacrifice that they are still doing for our freedom, for I have fought with them, and they are the ones that still hold the last of our hope that today they can still save us from electrocution, it is the struggle and fight between the rich and the poor for safety and freedom, Son, which you will understand in the future of your years to come, of this unrest and struggle of life's death.

The Knapsack

Much I thought of you when I was lying in the death-house—the singing, the kind tender voices of the children from the playground, where there was all the life and the joy of liberty—just one step from the wall which contains the buried agony of three buried souls. It would remind me so often of you and your sister Ines, and I wish I could see you every moment. But I feel better that you did not come to the death-house so that you could not see the horrible picture of three lying in agony waiting to be elec-trocuted, because I do not know what effect it would have on your young age. But then, in another way if you were not so sensitive it would be very useful to you tomorrow when you could use this horrible memory to hold up to the world the shame of the country in this cruel persecu-tion and unjust death. Yes, Dante, they can crucify our bodies today as they are doing, but they cannot destroy our ideas, that will remain for the youth of the future to come.

Dante, when I said three human lives buried, I meant to say that with us there is another young man by the name of Celestino Maderios that is to be electrocuted at the same time with us. He has been twice before in that horrible death-house, that should be destroyed with the hammers of real progress—that horrible house that will shame forever the future of the citizens of Massachusetts. They should destroy that house and put up a factory or school, to teach many of the hundreds of the poor orphan boys of the world.

Dante, I say once more to love and be nearest to your mother and the beloved ones in these sad days, and I am sure that with your brave heart and kind goodness they will feel less discomfort. And you will also not forget to love me a little for I do—O, Sonny! thinking so much and so often of you.

Best fraternal greetings to all the beloved ones, love and

Nicola Sacco to his son Dante

kisses to your little Ines and mother. Most hearty affectionate embrace.

YOUR FATHER AND COMPANION

P.S. Bartolo send you the most affectionate greetings. I hope that your mother will help you to understand this letter because I could have written much better and more simple, if I was feeling good. But I am so weak.

217 *Credo*

GRANT that my heart shall not harden; that it may continue always to love all men, even as they are, wilful as children that must be led from ways of wildness, weak as the sick that must be restored to health. Grant that it may always hear the fall of the world's tears, even in the luminous warmth of moments of joy; that there may be no muddy ditch into which the golden light of the sun and the colours of its setting cannot shine.

Grant that the remoteness of the city of the sun shall not lead me to abandon the cities of the world; that if I should shut myself in a tower of ivory, it should only be to make myself a fervent worker in the field of thought and knowledge; a lot, however, which only belongs to those whose light is the light of genius. Many, too many, are those who have no eyes, or do not open them wide enough to the truths of science and philosophy; too many slaves have need of a Brutus or a Spartacus; too many crowds cry to see Christ on Calvary and on a cross that they may know that man becomes divine in sacrifice, that civilisation either advances through the thorns, or retreats.

Grant that my heart shall not take pride in its beauties and that my imagination shall not delight in deeds of heroism impossible for me; grant that my will be steeped in trivial but continual endeavours and sacrifices.

The Knapsack

Grant that my heart may become strong without becoming hard and cold, and that I may know how to reconcile the cruelty of the combatant with the tenderness of the husband, the father, the son ; grant that I may spare my neighbours vain sufferings.

Grant that the desires of the flesh shall not trouble the imagination, lest they should estrange me from that which, in the soul, is the unique Madonna, and send me in pursuit of phantoms which render the needs of the male insatiable and brutish.

Grant in carnal intimacy that the soul be not spent, and that the sin be purified by the gift of voluptuousness, which alone can withstand vice and alone can satiate the insatiable.

Grant that I may free myself from the absurd timidity and the pride which clothe me when I would be naked, and which at times make me insincere even although I love the truth more than myself.

Grant that I may free myself from excessive pity, which makes those who are nearest in spirit suffer for fear of causing suffering, or alleviate the sufferings of one who is able to impose on others with his tears and tricks of voice and expression, but who suffers less and is less worthy of pity.

Grant that I may perfect the discipline of my work and of life, so that I may husband my energy and time and means, and direct my will towards the achievement of my mission and not towards the vanity of the man of letters or the politician.

Grant that I shall not trouble, with my own discouragements, the heart of my wife, but grant that, whilst knowing how to be alone in pain, I shall know how to seek her counsel and comfort.

Grant that my beloved may be as proud of me as I am of her, and that I may be for ever tormented with discontent of myself and with anxiety to make myself stronger and less impure. Grant that my daughters and friends in thinking of me may be impelled towards the good. Grant that I may be able, in dying, to be not too discontented with my life. Grant that I may always be ready to die a death worthy of the life of a just man.

CAMILLO BERNERI

218 *A Prayer for Temporal Blessings*

OPEN thy hand O God and fill us with thy loving kindness, that the mower may fill his hand, and he that bindeth up the sheaves his bosom, and that our garners may be full of all manner of store ; and that our sheep may bring forth thousands and ten thousands in our streets : That our oxen may be strong to labour, and that there be no breaking in, or going out, that our hearts may be replenish'd with food and gladness, that there be no complaining in our streets. Give us sufficient for this life ; food and raiment, the light of thy countenance, and contented spirits ; and thy grace to seek the kingdom of heaven and the righteousness thereof in the first place, and then we are sure all these things shall be added unto us. Grant the desires and hear the prayer of thy servants for Jesus Christ his sake our Lord and only saviour. Amen.

JEREMY TAYLOR

219 *The Prayer of Socrates*

BELOVED Pan, and all ye other gods who here abide, grant me to be beautiful in the inner man, and all I have of outer things to be at peace with those within. May I count the wise man only rich. And may my store of gold be such as none but the good can bear.

PLATO : *Phædrus*

Notes and Acknowledgements

PART I

1. From *The Crowne of all Homer's Works : Batrachomyomachia or the Battaile of Frogs and Mise*. Translated according to ye Originall. By George Chapman. Published about 1624.

2. *The Whole Works of Homer : Prince of Poets* . . . appeared in 1616, but had already been published in instalments.

4. Translated from the early Anglo-Saxon text by Ezra Pound. *Cathay*, London (Elkin Mathews), 1915. By courtesy of Ezra Pound and the present publishers, Messrs. Faber & Faber.

5. *Beowulf*, XXII–XXIII. " Done into common English after the old manner," by Charles Scott Moncrieff. London, 1921. By courtesy of the publishers, Messrs. Chapman & Hall. Previously, in a struggle with the fiend Grendel, Beowulf has torn off his enemy's right arm. Grendel's mother, a monster-wife, in retaliation, carries off Æschere, a close companion of King Hrothgar. Hrothgar challenges Beowulf to avenge this deed, and this part of the poem describes the great fight that took place in the mere where the monsters lurked. Hrunting, in line 18, is the name of the sword which Unferth lends to Beowulf.

6. *La Chanson de Roland*, text of the Oxford MS., tirades 133–51. The translation by René Hague. London, 1937. By courtesy of the translator and the publishers, Messrs. Faber & Faber.

7. From Percy's *Reliques of Ancient English Poetry*, Series I, Book the Second. I have freely adapted Percy's footnotes.

PART II

8. From *The Chronicle of Geoffrey de Villehardouin, Marshall of Champagne and Romania, concerning the Conquest of Constantinople by the French and Venetians, Anno M.CC.IV.* Translated by T. Smith (London, 1829). Chaps. CXXII–CXXXII.

9. From *Memoirs of Louis IX King of France* by John Lord de Joinville, High Seneschal of Champagne. Translated by

The Knapsack

T. Johnes (1807). The action described took place in the year 1249.

10. From the same.

11. From *The Chronicles of Froissart*, translated by John Bourchier, Lord Berners. Chaps. CLXII, CLXIV and CLXVIII. I have used the modernized text of the Globe Edition (edited by G. C. Macaulay) by courtesy of the publishers, Messrs. Macmillan & Co.

12. From the same, chap. CCCC.

13. From the *Chronicle* of Mathieu de Coussy, chap. LXXI, translated by G. G. Coulton (*Life in the Middle Ages*, vol. II, pp. 121–7. Cambridge University Press, 1910). By courtesy of the translator and the publishers. The date of the event is 1453.

14. From *Recollections of Rifleman Harris*. Edited by Henry Curling. Reprinted by Peter Davies, London, 1928.

15. From *Memoirs of Sergeant Bourgogne (1812–1813)*. London (William Heinemann), 1899.

PART III

16. From *The Conspiracy of Charles, Duke of Byron*, first published in 1608. Byron's speech at the end of act III.

17. From the second part of *Tamburlaine the Great*, act III, scene 2. Tamburlaine is addressing his three sons.

18. Originally published in *Poems Lyric and Pastoral*, 1605.

20. Written at the front during the early phase of the European War of 1914–18. Capt. the Hon. Julian H. F. Grenfell, D.S.O., died of wounds on May 26, 1915. Here printed by kind permission of Lord Desborough.

21. *The Poems of Wilfred Owen*. London, 1935. By courtesy of the publishers, Messrs. Chatto & Windus.

22. From *Drum-Taps* (1865).

24. There is a tradition that this poem was written by Raleigh in the Tower the night before his execution (October, 1618).

25. From *Amoretti* . . . (1595).

29. *Antony and Cleopatra*, II, ii, 199–248.

30. From " Epipsychidion ", ll. 147–89.

35. From *The Paradise of Dainty Devices*, 1576.

42. By the prayers of Aurora, who loved him, Tithonus obtained from the gods eternal life, but not eternal youth. When he had become a shrunken old man, Aurora changed him into a grasshopper. Tennyson published this beautiful poem first in 1860, but confessed that he had written it " upward of a quarter of a century " earlier, and only disinterred it by chance.

44. From *Collected Poems of Thomas Hardy* (London, 1931), **by**

Notes and Acknowledgements

courtesy of the author's representatives and the publishers, Messrs. Macmillan & Co.

45. From *Sea-Drift* (1859).
46. From *Poems of F. Garcia Lorca*, with English translation by Stephen Spender and J. L. Gili, by courtesy of the translators and the publisher, The Dolphin, 5 Cecil Court, London. Garcia Lorca was assassinated at the outbreak of the Spanish Civil War.
47. From *Poems*, vol. II (London, 1939), by courtesy of Mrs. Frieda Lawrence and the publishers, Messrs. William Heinemann.
48. *Measure for Measure*, III, i, 5–41.
49. Henry King (1591–1669) was Bishop of Chichester and published his *Poems, Elegies, Paradoxes and Sonnets* in 1657.
51. From the same source as 44, by courtesy of the author's representatives and the publishers, Messrs. Macmillan & Co.
53. First printed in Bullen's *More Lyrics from Elizabethan Song-Books*, 1888.
55. The concluding lines of Crashaw's poem, " The Flaming Heart ".
59. Here, as in other poems by Milton, I have preserved the original spelling, because there is evidence that Milton spelt phonetically, and with deliberate variations.
60. The concluding verses of " Easter Day " from *Hymns and Spiritual Songs for the Fasts and Festivals of the Church of England*, appended to the *Psalms* of 1765.
63. The concluding verses of *Prometheus Unbound*.
66. From *Poems of Gerard Manley Hopkins* (2nd edition, Oxford, 1930), by courtesy of the poet's family and the publishers, the Oxford University Press. The sonnet has the following superscription from the Vulgate (Jer. xii. 1) ; *Justus quidem tu es, si disputem tecum : verumtamen justa loquar ad te : Quare via impiorum prosperatur ? &c.*
67. Spoken by Prospero at the conclusion of *The Tempest*.
68. *Antony and Cleopatra*, IV, xiii, 64–7.

PART IV

69. Translated by Aubrey Stewart (London, 1880).
70. William Caxton's translation of *The Golden Legend* was first published in 1483, and to the original compilation made by Jacobus de Voragine in the thirteenth century, Caxton added several lives of British saints, of which this is one, from an English source. These legends have always seemed to me to be among the greatest works of English prose, and it is difficult to understand why they are not better known. I quote from the Temple Classics edition edited by F. S. Ellis (London, 1900).
71. Same source as no. 9.

72. From *The Trial of Jeanne d'Arc*, translated from the text of the original documents with an introduction by W. P. Barrett. London (George Routledge & Sons), 1931. The extract is a record of the second session of the trial.

73. Walton's *Life of Doctor Donne* was originally prefixed to the first collection of Donne's sermons in 1640.

74. *History of the Rebellion*, book VII.

75. From the " Fragment of Autobiography " written by the first Earl of Shaftesbury and printed in W. D. Christie's *Memoirs of Shaftesbury*, 1859. Hastings was Shaftesbury's neighbour in Dorsetshire.

76. From *Memoirs of the Life of Colonel Hutchinson, Governor of Nottingham Castle and Town . . .* Written by His Widow Lucy . . . London, 1806. The Colonel was born in 1615, died 1664.

77. From *Table-Talk*, 1821.

PART V

78. B.M., Harleian 913. Printed in *Early English Lyrics* chosen by E. K. Chambers and F. Sidgwick. London (Sidgwick & Jackson), 1926.

79. B.M., Sloane 2593.

80. B.M., Royal Appendix 58.

81. B.M., Harleian 7578. Printed in Chambers and Sidgwick ; an extract from a longer poem.

82. From *English and Scottish Ballads*, edited by F. J. Child.

83. Same source as no. 81 ; Chambers and Sidgwick, no. XLI.

119. The first three verses of the second part of " A Pastoral Ballad, in Four Parts. Written 1743."

132. From act III of Coleridge's drama *Remorse*, first published 1813.

145. From *The Princess*, 1847.

148. Song from " Golden Wings ", first published in *The Defence of Guenevere and Other Poems*, 1858.

150-2. From Poems of *Gerard Manley Hopkins*, edited by Robert Bridges (2nd edition, 1930), by courtesy of the poet's family and the publishers, the Oxford University Press.

153-4. From *The Collected Poems of W. B. Yeats* (London, 1933), by courtesy of Mrs. Yeats and the publishers, Messrs. Macmillan & Co.

155. From *Collected Poems, 1909–1935* (London, 1936), by courtesy of the author and the publishers, Messrs. Faber & Faber.

PART VI

156. *Arab Bulletin*, no. 106, reprinted in *The Letters of T. E. Lawrence*, edited by David Garnet. London (Jonathan

Notes and Acknowledgements

Cape), 1938, from which source it is taken by courtesy of the publishers.

157. From *Gallipoli* (London, 1916), by courtesy of the author and the publishers, Messrs. William Heinemann.

158. From *Falklands, Jutland and the Bight*, by Commander the Hon. Barry Bingham, V.C., R.N. (London, 1919), by courtesy of the publishers, Messrs. John Murray.

159. From *In Retreat*, London (Hogarth Press), 1925.

160. From *A Roumanian Diary*, by Hans Carossa. Translated from the German by Agnes Neill Scott (London, 1929). By courtesy of the publishers, Messrs. Secker & Warburg.

161. From *Her Privates We*, by Private 19022 (Frederick Manning) (London, 1930). By courtesy of the publishers, Messrs. Peter Davies.

162. From *In Parenthesis* (London, 1937), by courtesy of the author and the publishers, Messrs. Faber & Faber.

163. From *War Birds* (London, 1927), by courtesy of the publishers, Messrs. John Hamilton.

164. From *The Spanish Tragedy*, by Jef Last. Translated from the Dutch by David Hallett. London (George Routledge & Sons), 1939.

165. From *All Our Yesterdays*, chap. XII. (London, 1930), by courtesy of the author and the publishers, Messrs. William Heinemann.

PART VII

166. B.M., Sloane 2593. Chambers and Sidgwick, no. CXLVIII.

167. From Kele's *Christmas Carolles* (about 1550) ; Chambers and Sidgwick, no. CLI.

168. From *Westminster Drollery*, 1672 ; arranged by W. H. Auden and quoted by courtesy of the publishers from *The Oxford Book of Light Verse* (The Clarendon Press, 1938).

174. From *Collected Poems, 1909–1935* (London, 1936), by courtesy of the author and the publishers, Messrs. Faber & Faber.

175. Printed by Melville at the end of his novel *Billy Budd, Foretopman* (1891), and there given out as an anonymous sailor's ballad.

176. From *The Misfortunes of Elphin*, chap. XI.

177. From *Crotchet Castle*, chap. XVI.

178. From *Folk Songs for Schools*, collected by Cecil Sharp, by courtesy of the publishers, Messrs. Novello & Co.

180. From *American Tramp and Underworld Slang*, by Godfrey Irwin.

181. From *The Oxford Book of Light Verse*, where the source is given as " songs collected by W. W. Newell ". By courtesy of the publishers.

The Knapsack

182. A standardized version of this popular ballad is given by
W. H. Auden in the *Oxford Book of Light Verse*, which I
have followed with one or two slight modifications.

191. From *Old Possum's Book of Practical Cats* (London, 1939),
by courtesy of the author and the publishers, Messrs.
Faber & Faber.

PART VIII

192. From *Journals of Gilbert White*, edited by Walter Johnson,
F.G.S. London (George Routledge & Sons), 1931.

193. From *Years of Childhood*. Translated from the Russian by
J. D. Duff. By courtesy of the publishers, the Oxford
University Press. Aksakoff was born in 1791 and died
at Moscow in 1859.

194. From *Far Away and Long Ago* (London, 1918), by courtesy
of the publishers, Messrs. J. M. Dent & Sons.

195. From *Walden, or Life in the Woods*, 1854.

196. From *Wild Wales*, 1862.

197. From *The Life and Letters of Samuel Palmer*, written and
edited by A. H. Palmer. London (Seeley & Co.), 1892.
The letter is written to his fellow-artist, John Linnell, and
is dated " December 21st, 1828 ". I have omitted the
last five paragraphs.

198. From *Swann's Way*. Translated by C. K. Scott Moncrieff.
London, 1922. By courtesy of the publishers, Messrs.
Chatto & Windus.

PART IX

199. *Lectures on the History of Philosophy*, translated from the
German by E. S. Haldane. (London, 1892.) vol. 1,
part 1.

200. *Phædo*, 64–9. Jowett's translation.

201. Translated by William Watts (1631). Bk. IX. chap. x.

202. From *The Brothers Karamazov*, translated from the Russian
by Constance Garnett. By courtesy of the publishers,
Messrs. William Heinemann.

203. *Centuries of Meditation*, edited by Bertram Dobell (London,
1908). Traherne died in 1674.

204. From a letter to Benjamin Bailey, 22 November, 1817.
From *The Letters of John Keats*, edited by Maurice Buxton
Forman (Oxford University Press, 1931).

205. From the beginning of *De Intellectus Emendatione*.

206. *Religio Medici* (1642), the second part.

207. *Parochial and Plain Sermons*, IV, 234–7 ; quoted from *A
Newman Synthesis*. London (Sheed & Ward), 1930.

209. From *Recollections of My Youth*, translated by C. B. Pitman.
London (George Routledge & Sons), 1929. Written by

Notes and Acknowledgements

Renan on the 6th of September, 1845, and addressed to his director at the St. Sulpice Seminary.

210. From bk. III, chap. XIII of the *Essays*. Cotton's translation.

211. From *The Importance of Living*, by Lin Yutang. By courtesy of the publishers, Messrs. William Heinemann.

212. From *The Simple Way*, a translation of the *Tao Tê Ching* by Walter Gorn Old. By courtesy of the publishers, Messrs. William Rider & Son (London, 1913). For a more literal translation, and an illuminating study of the *Tao Tê Ching* and its place in Chinese thought, see *The Way and its Power* by Arthur Waley (London, 1934). Tao means " a road, path, way ; and hence, the way in which one does something ; method, principle, doctrine ".

213. From *The Marriage of Heaven and Hell* (about 1790).

PART X

214. From the same source as no. 9. King Louis died in 1270.

215. From the *Life of Sir Walter Ralegh*, by Edward Edwards, vol. II (London, 1868).

216. From *The Letters of Sacco and Vanzetti*. Edited by Marion D. Frankfurter and Gardner Jackson (London, 1929). By courtesy of the publishers, Messrs. Constable & Co.

217. From *Pensieri e Battaglie* (Paris, 1938). My own translation. Berneri, an Italian professor who had sought refuge in France, went to Spain on the outbreak of the civil war in 1936 and there edited an anarchist review. He was assassinated at Barcelona on the 5th of May, 1937. He was a man of great integrity and noble ideals, as this Credo, which was found among his papers after his death, sufficiently illustrates.

218. From *A Collection of Offices*, 1658, Additionals.

219. From the conclusion of Plato's *Phædrus*.

Index of Authors

The numbers refer to the first page of each item.

The Knapsack

PAGES FOR
NOTES AND ADDITIONS